THE PROGRESSIVE PARTY IN CANADA

SOCIAL CREDIT IN ALBERTA

ITS BACKGROUND AND DEVELOPMENT

A series of studies sponsored by the Canadian Social Science Research Council, directed and edited by S. D. Clark.

⫸ T H E ⫷

Progressive Party
in Canada

BY

⫸ W. L. MORTON ⫷

UNIVERSITY OF TORONTO PRESS

Reprinted with corrections, 1967
Reprinted 1971

ISBN 0-8020-6062-5
LC 67-2778

Printed in the U.S.A.

TO

MARGARET ORDE MORTON

"The sooner we recognize that the prosperity of the farmer is the basis of the prosperity of every other industry and the legislation that is good for the farmer is good for everybody else, the sooner we will step forward to prosperous conditions."—(Letter from Dauphin district directorate of the United Farmers of Manitoba to the Dauphin *Herald*, May 4, 1922.)

"The history of Canada since Confederation—the outcome of a politico-commercial, or a commercio-political conspiracy, if consequences are any indication of motive—has been a history of heartless robbery of both the people of the Maritimes and of the Prairie Sections of Canada by the Big 'Vested' Interests—so called from the size of their owners' vests—of the politically and financially stronger Central Provinces."—(E. A. Partridge, *A War on Poverty*, Winnipeg, (1925[?]), p. 77.)

"Democracy may be simply defined as the people in action."—(Henry Wise Wood, "The People In Action," *Grain Growers' Guide*, XII, July 2, 1919, p. 7.)

Foreword

IN 1944 the Canadian Social Science Research Council, through a special grant made by the Rockefeller Foundation, undertook to sponsor a series of studies having as their primary object the investigation of the Social Credit movement in Alberta. A director was appointed by the Council and the co-operation of a number of Canadian scholars in the fields of history, economics, political science and sociology was enlisted. In deciding upon what studies should be done, as great an emphasis was placed upon the background out of which the Social Credit movement developed as upon the movement itself. This study of the Progressive party in Canada by W. L. Morton constitutes the first of the series. It is hoped that the group of studies as a whole will contribute to an understanding not only of Social Credit in Alberta but of the economic, political, and social development of western Canada generally.

Professor Morton's study focuses attention upon the strong spirit of revolt which has been so characteristic of the Western Canadian community. It is a spirit with roots deep in the past. The history of political unrest in western Canada reaches back to the Red River insurrection of 1870 and the Northwest rebellion of 1885; indeed, it might be thought to have its beginnings in the opposition to the settlement of the Red River Valley which culminated in the Seven Oaks massacre of 1816. The fact that these early struggles against outside control (by the Hudson's Bay Company or the Canadian federal state) were carried on largely by half-breeds has tended to obscure their significance. Even western Canadians have not been accustomed to think of these movements of revolt as part of the great drama of the country's development. Too often the half-breeds have been pictured as a slothful, irresponsible race of people scarcely civilized, led in 1870 and 1885 by a madman and demagogue. To place Riel's name alongside those of J. W. Dafoe, H. W. Wood, J. S. Woodsworth, and William Aberhart would be thought to disparage the memories of these

great leaders of reform. Even those people who were later
most active in keeping alive the spirit of western revolt knew
or cared little about this early champion of western rights.

This of course is not surprising. Reform movements tend
to disown those movements which come before them. They
depend in their appeal upon fostering the belief that what they
advocate is something new. They particularly wish to dispel
the notion that what they seek to do has been tried before; to
admit past failure would be to admit the possibility of failure
on their own part. Thus reform leaders seldom honour their
predecessors. When the predecessor was one who had been
so generally damned by the English-speaking Canadian public
as Louis Riel, tribute to the part he played in the movement of
western Canadian reform could hardly be expected.

Yet these half-breed uprisings were as true an expression of
the grievances, and aspirations, of the West as the agrarian
uprisings after 1900. What the West revolted against in 1816,
1870, and 1885 as in 1921 and 1935 was being taken over or
being dominated by an outside power. Until 1885 this revolt
found support within a distinctive ethnic-religious system—
the Métis nation, but, if the sense of cultural unity was later
not so strong, and never again was there a resort to arms, the
feeling of being "a separate people" nevertheless persisted.
The West sought to be left to itself; it wished to withdraw from
those alliances which placed it in a subordinate position. This
urge to separate expressed itself not only in the effort to secure
a greater measure of political autonomy but in the break of
western people from the controls of outside financial, professional, educational, social, and ecclesiastical organizations.
In 1885 Riel endeavoured to found both a new church as well
as a new state. The Progressive uprising of 1921 was closely
related to such other western movements of revolt as the organization of the One Big Union, the "People's Church," and the
wheat pools. The crusade of Social Credit against monopoly
finance, the centralization of power in the federal government
and the capitalist press, grew out of a religious movement.
Throughout, the dominant note in the social philosophy of
western people has been an unbounded confidence in themselves, a belief that their region was one with a great potential

future if the hand of the outside exploiter could only be removed. The movements to which they have thus lent support have sought not so much to make over the outside world as to withdraw from it. In that way they have been more truly movements of revolt than of reform.

However, the strong east-west pull, which so many western orators have denounced as unnatural, exerted its effects not only in limiting the development of an autonomous western economy but in placing a sharp check upon the sectionalism of the West's political movements. The East had too much to offer in the way of capital and personnel for the development of resources and in the way of business openings and positions of office for westerners seeking opportunities which their own community did not provide. The leaders of what began as radical political movements in the West tended to be particularly sensitive to the advantages of a policy of moderation. Cabinet posts, senatorships, and judgeships offered attractions, but even more these leaders came to feel that the only way they could realize their objectives was by developing in the movements they led a greater sense of responsibility for the problems of the Canadian community at large. Thus movements which began as protests against the dominance of eastern interests in the economic, political, social, and religious life of western Canada ended by becoming accommodated to the power structure of the Canadian metropolitan-federal system. They shifted from being movements of revolt to become movements of reform. In doing so, they inevitably lost the support of great masses of western people and opened the way for the rise of new movements of revolt.

Professor Morton's study presents in clear fashion the way in which the Progressive movement, strongly sectional in its early development and politically irresponsible in the sense that it sought to avoid entering into any entangling political alliances, eventually was forced to compromise its principles and accommodate itself to the parliamentary two-party system. The very success of the movement in the election battles it fought between 1919 and 1921 spelled its ultimate doom. By winning widespread support in Ontario and Manitoba as well as in the "frontier" provinces of Saskatchewan and Alberta,

the movement lost some of its militant sectionalism.   By 1926
it had become apparent that it could only retain its sectional
character and continue to remain aloof in federal politics by
becoming in effect a provincial party.   This the U.F.A. for a
time succeeded in doing and it thereby escaped the fate which
befell the rest of the Progressive movement of being absorbed
within the Liberal party.   Eventually, however, even the
leaders of the U.F.A., doctrinaire men though they were, grew
tired of playing a political role which forever denied them the
fruits of office, and out of this shift of attitudes there developed
that alliance with labour which led to the founding of the C.C.F.
political party.   Abandonment of its sectional principles resulted in the collapse of the U.F.A. in the provincial and federal
elections of 1935 and the rise of the Social Credit movement.

Professor Morton has written an important chapter of the
political history of western Canada, and his study comes
logically as the first of this series dealing with the background
and development of the Social Credit movement.   However
much the movement which grew up in Alberta in the 1930's
under the leadership of William Aberhart may have departed
from the principles of the Progressive movement, it is scarcely
possible to understand what happened in Alberta in 1935 without paying attention to this earlier western effort to bring about
the reform of Canadian economic and political institutions.
The very failure of Progressivism had much to do with the rise
of Social Credit.   The later movement grew up on ground
carefully prepared by the earlier.   Both movements were expressions of underlying forces of unrest in Western Canada.
Though there were marked differences in the way they developed, and in what they sought to achieve, there were also
marked similarities.   A change of name and of leadership did
not remove the underlying fact that in 1935 the West or at least
one part of it had risen up in revolt as it has done earlier in 1921.

S. D. CLARK

Preface

T H E theme of this book is the formation and disintegration of a third party. The great agrarian revolt of 1921 in Canada is studied in these pages as a class and sectional protest against the two-party system and the national policies associated with the traditional parties. While the principal aim has been to present a clear narrative of events, the thesis of the study is that parliamentary, or cabinet government, with its necessary auxiliary of the legislative caucus, has imposed a heavy strain on the fragile structure of the national parties in the Canadian federal state.

In the preparation of the study obligations were incurred which have proved too numerous for acknowledgment in a preface. To all those who made information available, and contributed to the completion of the study by way of criticism and comment, I am deeply indebted. I wish particularly to thank Mr. Victor Sifton for permission to read and quote from the Dafoe Papers under the conventional limitations, and Hon. T. A. Crerar for like access to his private papers, and to acknowledge my indebtedness to the Social Science Research Council of Canada, without the aid of which it would not have been possible to complete or publish the study. To that of the Council, in recognition of editorial labours and generous counsel, I join the names of Professor S. D. Clark, editor of this series, and Professor G. W. Brown, editor of the University of Toronto Press.

W. L. M.

Contents

THE PROGRESSIVE PARTY IN CANADA

CHAPTER ONE

The Background of the Progressive
Movement, 1896-1911

I n 1896 the Canadian West between Lake Superior and the Rocky Mountains was still for the most part as empty as it had been in the days of the fur trade. It is true that the Red River Valley and the Manitoba highlands of the second prairie steppe were veined by railways and chequered by the farms of some two hundred thousand settlers. Westward in the North-West Territories, however, there were only the stretches of settlement along the Canadian Pacific Railway, the scattered ranches of southern Alberta, and the sparse homesteads of the Prince Albert and Edmonton districts on the North Saskatchewan. Over wide reaches of the plains the ancient silence held. The buffalo herds had vanished; the Indian bands had been drawn into sullen concentration on the reserves. Only here and there did the red coat of a Mounted Policeman on patrol flare across the distance, the sod hut of a settler squat black on the horizon, or a lone ploughshare gleam at the furrow's end.

The empty West was testimony to the failure of the great hopes of Confederation. The political unification of the northern half of the continent, achieved in 1871, the National Policy of protection, adopted in 1879, the construction of the Canadian Pacific Railway, completed in 1885—none of these had borne the anticipated fruit of the peopling of the West[1] and the enrich-

[1]The term, "the West" is used in reference to the provinces of Manitoba, Saskatchewan, and Alberta; when British Columbia is included, the context will make the inclusion apparent. When the three provinces are specifically indicated, the term, "continental West," will be used.

3

ment of the East. The hope of 1867 that a new agricultural frontier in the hinterlands beyond the Great Lakes would quicken and expand the commerce and industry of the central provinces, making them the metropolis of a commercial empire, had been thwarted by the general depression of 1873-96. Instead of vigorous national growth, the first generation after Confederation had seen an exodus of Canadians to the United States, stirrings of secession in the Maritime Provinces and the West, and a revival of racial and religious discord following the Saskatchewan Rebellion. The new federation had still in 1896 to realize the promise of the western agricultural frontier and to achieve a thorough political integration.

In that year, however, a new era opened in Canada, one of economic growth and political consolidation. The great depression was lifting in Europe and America. New supplies of South African gold were easing the shortage of money. The London investment market was seeking such opportunities as a booming Canada would afford. The price of wheat—and this was of special significance to Canada—though not high, was becoming profitable in terms of the goods and services the grain grower purchased. Not less significant for Canada was the fact that the frontier of free land had ended in the United States, and American farmers and European immigrants were turning to the wide wheat lands and free homesteads of the Canadian West. There a new wheat frontier was being prepared, as dry farming techniques were introduced and early maturing strains of wheat developed. The West, after years of frustration, was in 1896 on the eve of a great advance.

From the western land boom of the years between 1896 and 1911 came much of the energy which animated and transformed the whole national economy. The national population increased by one-half; that of the West quadrupled. External trade more than doubled. Two new transcontinental railways were planned in hectic over-confidence and largely built. Villages became towns, and towns cities. As the wheatlands of the West broadened, the industries of the East expanded and multiplied. During the golden years of the boom a reckless optimism fired every enterprise. In terms of material achievement and mounting wealth, Canada was entering into its own.

At the same time, the political consolidation of the country was advanced. From 1867 to 1896 the Conservative party had dominated the political life of Canada and had built up a national organization from the Maritime Provinces into the West, though much remained to be done in these newer regions. In the latter year, however, the Conservatives were decisively defeated by the Liberals under Wilfrid Laurier. Fifteen years of unbroken Liberal rule followed, and in that period the Liberal party was able to complete, and indeed to perfect, its organization as a national party. In consequence, there emerged in Canada between 1896 and 1911 a full-blown two-party system.

In these years the national party system reached its fullest and most solid development. At no time had partisan loyalty been stronger,[2] party leadership more absolute, or the power of the parliamentary caucus greater than in the days of Laurier and Borden.[3] Yet the national parties remained what they had been during their formation after Confederation, federations of provincial political parties, subject to the pressures of local, racial, and religious interests.[4] The imposing national parties, each spanning the continent from coast to coast on nine provincial piers, were not as strong as they seemed. They were subject always to the loss of support by sectional groups, if their general line of policy and conduct failed to be widely acceptable in the country.

The very growth of the country accentuated the composite character of the national parties. When, for example, the growth of population in the West brought about the organization in 1905 of the two new provinces of Alberta and Saskatchewan,

[2]As a homely example: A Manitoban Liberal wrote to Laurier in 1911: "As a Liberal and father of six sons all trained to vote Liberal I do desire to let our rising generation see that we have not lost our time and votes" (Public Archives of Canada, Laurier Papers, E.E. 5, E. L. Wotton to Laurier, March 28, 1911).

[3]It is necessary to emphasize the power of the leader and the importance of the caucus in the period under discussion, as authorities on present-day Canadian politics tend rather to stress the looseness of Canadian party discipline. Cf. J. A. Corry, *Democratic Government and Politics* (Toronto, 1946), 240-1, R. M. Dawson, *The Government of Canada* (Toronto, 1947), 244-6, A. Brady, *Democracy in the Dominions* (Toronto, 1947), 103-4.

[4]For analysis of Canadian party organization see, besides the works cited in n. 3, Escott M. Reid, "The Rise of National Parties in Canada," and F. H. Underhill, "The Party System of Canada" (*Proceedings of the Canadian Political Science Association*, IV, 1932, 187-212).

the Liberal party seized upon its advantage as the government of the country to aid the growth of the Liberal party in the new provinces. It was successful in this endeavour, notably so in Saskatchewan, and that province became a bulwark of Liberalism in the West, matching the other main pillar of the party after 1896, the province of Quebec. The result was that the Liberal party had to reconcile in its bosom the social conservatism of Quebec and the agrarian radicalism of Saskatchewan. Other examples, not less striking, might be cited of how the national parties, even in the hey-day of their power, functioned less as formulators of policy than as brokers of sectional interests.

Indeed, even while the great boom was rounding out the national economy and integrating the national parties, sectional discord was developing beneath the surface of events. In the West the growing pains of a new and rapidly developing section were posing problems for the national parties, as was the rise of the Nationalist movement in Quebec.

Some of the sectional handicaps from which the West suffered were inevitable. The region was not only separated from the central provinces by the great barrier of the Canadian Shield, but was also differentiated from the other sections of Canada by a continental climate, a scant rainfall, and a monotonous terrain. Its natural resources, though great, were not diversified. The settlers of the West, therefore, were for the most part confined to the exploitation of the soil, under conditions of exceptional severity. The settlement of the West was an experiment in marginal agriculture, in which the costs, both material and human, were high, and the process of successful adaptation to new conditions slow. As a result, western Canadians were quickly sensitive to economic and political disabilities that people enjoying a greater degree of security would have accepted with comparative indifference.

The economic disabilities of the West were patent to contemporaries. As a frontier region, it was of necessity also a debtor region. The individual settler and the provincial and municipal governments borrowed heavily and by no means always wisely under the stimulus of the boom. They incurred in consequence heavy fixed charges against an uncertain and variable income. To this mid-continental region railways were a necessity, but the railways when built operated under comparatively non-competitive conditions. The concurrent growth of the grain trade and meat-packing industry created new monopolies in grain elevators and abattoirs, and made possible new exactions by middlemen. The control of banks, railways, abattoirs, and the grain trade was concentrated in Winnipeg and in the East. Commercial and national policy united to funnel the exports of the West through Winnipeg into the East in a system in which competition was diminished and the advantages of the middleman enhanced.

To such sectional disabilities, the product of national policy as well as of distance from market, local conditions, and time of settlement, which the western settler suffered as a producer of grain and livestock, were added others which he suffered as a consumer. Not only was he compelled to a great extent to buy the services of the Canadian banks, railways, and grain trade at the seller's price, but he was compelled by the protective tariff to buy the necessities of life and much of the supplies and equipment for his farm at prices which were competitive only to a degree. Had national policies afforded him countervailing advantages, the situation might have been equitable, but most of the products of western agriculture were sold at prices determined by the world market, while the bulk of his purchases were made at prices sheltered from competition by the national tariff, a tariff accepted and elaborated by both national parties.[5]

The handicaps of the West could be carried while land values were rising and the price of wheat continued favourable. When such conditions no longer obtained, the West was economically in so weak a position, for want of alternative outlets and lines of production, that its only recourse lay in political action.

[5]J. W. Dafoe gives the following account of the tariff views of Clifford Sifton, the most powerful of western Canadian Liberals and Minister of the Interior, 1896-1905: "He was no believer in the principle of *laissez-faire*. He held the view that a government, by conscious and pre-meditated acts, could change conditions, re-adjust the balance between sections and control the national prosperity. He regarded the tariff as an agency to these ends. His business judgment and his experience told him that it could injure as well as help, and that it must therefore be used with moderation and discretion. . . . He was a believer in a competitive tariff in contrast with the conception of the tariff as prohibitive. The experience of Canada for fifty years lends support to the opinion that this is the only policy which can command so diversified and general support as to deserve the title 'national' " (J. W. Dafoe, *Clifford Sifton in Relation to His Times*, Toronto, 1931, 255).

In applying political pressure to government, the farmers of the West had indeed been surprisingly successful. The Crow's Nest Pass Agreement of 1897, the Canada Grain Act of 1900, and the Manitoba railway legislation of 1901, were outstanding examples of the results of such political pressure. Yet the West laboured under political as well as economic handicaps. The retention of control of the natural resources of the West by the federal government for the purposes of land settlement and railway construction had become an established and embittered grievance. Although it is doubtful whether the West suffered any real loss thereby,[6] the effect was to increase dependence on the federal government, the policies of which were so important to its growth and prosperity. Closely akin to the struggle for transfer of control of the natural resources was the struggle for provincial status in the Territories which ended in the organization of Saskatchewan and Alberta. Both issues fostered powerfully the growth of sectional sentiment.

While developing as a distinct section acutely aware of its peculiar interests, the West became more and more conscious of its weakness in federal politics. As a sparsely populated region, its representation was a small part of the national representation in parliament. After 1896 the decennial revision of representation in the federal House of Commons lagged behind the growth of its population, and because of this the West was to be inadvertently denied the representation to which it was entitled until 1925. In the conventional representation of sections in the federal cabinet also, it had to be content with only one member, the Minister of the Interior, until 1911.

Since influence at Ottawa was exercised through the parties, western voters were forced to consider the operation of the party system with more care than voters in more favoured sections. They addressed to the parties the telling question, did they deliver the goods, did they obtain for the West what it wanted—and assumed to be in the national interest? Although the western constituencies during the years from 1896 to 1911 were remarkably faithful to the party in power, after the usage of frontier regions, western voters were to develop a growing

[6]J. A. Maxwell, *Federal Subsidies to the Provincial Governments in Canada* (Cambridge, Mass., 1937), 149.

scepticism of the benefits to be derived from their representation at Ottawa. This scepticism was deep-rooted, going back to Territorial days in Saskatchewan and Alberta, to the time when the political leaders of the Territories deliberately kept themselves separate from the activities of the national parties, the better to conduct their contest with Ottawa for greater powers and better terms.[7] The same scepticism was increased by the character of western representation at Ottawa. The representatives were men of average capacity; one indeed was the greatly talented Clifford Sifton. But Sifton's very success won him widespread distrust, and most of the others, notably Frank Oliver, who succeeded Sifton as Minister of the Interior in 1905, were men of marked party orthodoxy. The western member, in short, was a party man and subject to caucus, and therefore easily aroused the suspicion of having sacrificed the interests of his section to national policies. By the end of the period under review, the belief was growing in the West that the "national" parties were controlled in caucus by majorities drawn from central Canada, to the advantage of the sectional interests of the East.

The first real challenge to the national party structure, however, developed not out of the economic and political sectionalism of the West but out of the racial and religious particularism of Quebec. The annexation of the West had raised the question whether the western French were to enjoy the same linguistic and educational rights as the French Roman Catholics of Quebec. Such rights, granted by the Manitoba Act of 1870 and the early legislation governing the North-West Territories, were largely denied by the Manitoba School Act and other legislation of 1890, and the legislation of the Territorial Assembly after 1888. In protest against this treatment of the French Roman Catholic minority in the West, there developed the movement of Quebec *nationalisme*, a blend of ultramontane clericalism and racial sentiment. The movement found a leader and a voice when in 1899 Henri Bourassa left the Liberal party because of his opposition to the dispatch of a Canadian contingent to fight in the South African War.

[7]C. C. Lingard, *Territorial Government in Canada: The Autonomy Question in the old North-West Territories* (Toronto, 1946), 25-6.

Thereafter, until the election of 1911, Nationalist sentiment in Quebec was a threat to the unity of the Liberal party. If Laurier yielded too much to Nationalist pressure, as in the Autonomy Bills of 1905, he risked the loss of support in Ontario and the West. If he yielded too much to British imperialist sentiment, or could be made to seem to have done so, as in the Naval Bill of 1910, he risked the loss of support in Quebec. The Nationalist campaign of these years to maintain or extend in the rest of the country the linguistic and religious rights of the French Roman Catholics of Quebec, was a powerful and disturbing force in the mobile equilibrium of sectional politics.

Over all, the years from 1896 to 1911 constituted a period of great economic progress and of growth in political cohesion, as the two-party system took full form in two national parties organized from coast to coast and capable of fighting effective campaigns in every province. At the same time the peculiar circumstances of the West as a frontier area economically and politically subordinate to central Canada, and the unequal incidence of national policies on that region, were giving rise to a sharpened sectional temper. Western sectionalism had a counterpart in the Nationalist movement in Quebec, and both were growing threats to the developing political unity and to the party system of the country.

The years under review also witnessed a new development in the farmers' movement which had begun in North America in the 1870's as the agrarian reaction to the new dominance won by industrial and corporate wealth after the American Civil War and Confederation. The American organization known as the Grange entered Canada in 1872 and reached the West in 1876. In the 1880's the American Farmers' Alliance inspired the Farmers' Union of Manitoba. The next decade saw the Patrons of Industry active in co-operative enterprises and in politics, both in Ontario and the West. Political action, however, destroyed the Patrons in 1896, and their fate and that of the Populist party in the same year in the United States left among agrarian leaders an abiding prejudice against political action.

In 1901 the farmers' movement found local expression in the Grain Growers' Associations of the Canadian West. The strong position of the grain trade in dealing with the individual farmer, an advantage which local agents exploited, and the discrimination practised by the railways in favour of the grain companies, provoked united resistance among the grain growers of the Territory of Assiniboia. In November of 1901, John Miller, W. R. Motherwell, and Peter Dayman of Indian Head set their hands to the famous work of organization out of which emerged the Territorial Grain Growers' Association of Assiniboia.[8] In 1903 the Manitoba Grain Growers' Association was organized at Virden in south-western Manitoba. In 1905 a Territorial Grain Growers' Association was also organized in Alberta, but there a rival was encountered in the Alberta Society of Equity. This was a Canadian offshoot of the Societies of Equity which were springing up in the northern states of the American West. Not until 1909 and after much difficulty did the two Alberta organizations become the United Farmers of Alberta.

The primary purpose of the new organizations was to educate their members in collective action, a knowledge of their legal and political rights, and an appreciation of the dignity of their calling. The organized farmers began with a deep conviction that the root of the farmer's plight was his individualism, his isolation, and his ignorance of matters outside his narrow practical experience. They sought to arouse class-consciousness in the farmer, not because they wished to create an army for class war, but because they saw in class-consciousness the beginning of well-being and self-respect. This educational work of indoctrination and the dissemination of information was carried on in the local associations, in the annual conventions of delegates of the territorial and provincial locals and, after 1909, in the columns of the official organ of the farmers, the *Grain Growers' Guide*.

While the educational work was always and rightly regarded as fundamental to the work of the Associations, the members were men faced with practical conditions which demanded action. The grain grower was at a disadvantage as a producer and as a consumer; he sold on a buyer's, and bought on a seller's, market. To break this system of exploitation, action was taken in two ways. Producers' and consumers' co-operatives were

[8]Hopkins Moorehouse, *Deep Furrows* (Toronto, 1918), 22-6.

organized, and pressure was put on government to take over the ownership of the elevators through which the grain passed and in which it was stored. The organized farmers were groping their way towards the elimination of the middleman and the control by the farmers of the storage and sale of the annual harvest.

Of the organization and fortunes of the consumers' co-operatives and of the livestock associations there is no need to speak. But the organization of the great grain-handling co-operatives first demonstrated the strength of the farmers' movement, and made the organized farmers a force with which governments and parties had to reckon. In 1905 the stormy prophet of agrarian collective action, E. A. Partridge of Sinta-luta, proposed the organization of The Grain Growers' Grain Company Ltd. After a bitter struggle the new company was organized and admitted, though as a farmers' grain company shorn of its co-operative features, to the Winnipeg Grain Exchange in 1907. This was the origin of the United Grain Growers' Company, which later operated in Manitoba and Alberta.

Partridge picked Thomas Alexander Crerar as president of the new and greatly daring enterprise. After a boyhood on the western farm frontier, Crerar had become a farmer, a teacher, a grain buyer. Such was the young man's training for the head-ship of a major business enterprise formed and financed by farmers. He grew with the growth of the Grain Growers' Grain Company, and despite jealousies caused by his rapid rise, be-came, along with the company, a power in the West.

A farmers' grain company, however, seemed to many an inadequate solution of the problems confronting the grain grower. An agitation began for government ownership of terminal elevators and even of interior line elevators. The movement led in Manitoba, after the loss of a provincial by-election by the Conservative government to a Liberal and Grain Growers' candidate, to the purchase of a number of line elevators by the government in 1909. The experiment was badly managed and in 1912 it failed. In Saskatchewan, however, the same agitation led to the formation in 1911 of the Saskatchewan Co-operative Elevator Company. Though the organized farmers had not by these efforts won control of the marketing of the wheat crop, they had shown a remarkable capacity for collective action.

Nor was this capacity disregarded by the political parties. In the three provinces of the continental West, Manitoba, Saskatchewan, and Alberta, the wishes of the farmers' associations, as expressed in their annual conventions and by their delegations to government, soon became political imperatives. In Manitoba the Conservative government was quickly responsive to agrarian demands. The Manitoba Railway Act of 1901, the establishment of a publicly owned telephone system in 1906, the decisive action of compelling the Winnipeg Grain Exchange to accept the Grain Growers' Grain Company as a member in 1907, were all concrete examples of the care with which the provincial government had maintained agrarian interests. Nor were words lacking to underline the deeds. Premier Roblin declaimed before the Manitoba Grain Growers' Convention of 1906 in Winnipeg:

We have in this city magnificent blocks, we have great piles, as they are sometimes described, in the form of warehouses, banking institutions, and various buildings of that kind, in which hundreds if not thousands are employed, and in which large sums of money are turned over from day to day, and yet I challenge any man to prove, or even assert with any degree of authority or knowledge, that any banking institution, any wholesale house, or any departmental store, no matter how large, ever added one new dollar to the wealth of the realm; but the farmer who tills the soil and sells one bushel of wheat or grows a bullock for the market adds to the wealth of the nation. Therefore, it is to the sturdy husbandman of this country that we look for that development and that progress that we aspire to in making Manitoba one of the most important, if not the most important, Province in Canada as far as agriculture is concerned.[9]

In Saskatchewan and Alberta the governments reacted as quickly and as fully to the demands of the organized farmers, and the politicians were as assiduous as Roblin in playing to the physiocratic prejudices of the agrarian voter. In the western provinces no other course was possible, as the great majority of the electoral districts were controlled by rural voters.

[9]*Canadian Annual Review*, 1906, p. 420.

Many of the farmers' problems could be solved, however, only by action of the federal government, and here circumstances were different. While the agrarian vote might dominate politics by weight of numbers in the three continental provinces, in federal politics the West was only one section among several. The organized farmers might make representations to the federal government, but they could not hope to engage its undivided attention. None the less, it was evident that agriculture was the largest national industry, that farmers as a class had common interests, and that the majority of federal electoral districts might be controlled by the rural voters. Organization was required nationally, as in the West, to make the weight of agriculture effective on government. Although the farmers of most of the other provinces were not organized, there were two active organizations in Ontario, the Grange and the Farmers' Association, which united in 1907 as the Dominion Grange and Farmers' Association. With this body the associated farmers of the West joined in 1909 to form the Canadian Council of Agriculture. The farmers' movement thereby began to assume a national character and to develop a capacity to speak for agriculture as an organized interest.

While the farmers were being organized to bring influence to bear on government by demonstration and representation, some leaders of the movement were beginning to question whether existing modes of government and the party system could be trusted or expected to serve the farmers' purposes. The Canadian West, filling rapidly with the new immigration, was in a political ferment. There the radical democracy of the old Ontario Grits experienced a new birth on a frontier less constricted and less subject to conservative influence than that of early Ontario. From the mid-western and trans-Mississippi states came thousands of American farmers, bearing fresh memories of the Populist battles against monopoly and the money power. From Great Britain came trade unionists and Labour party men.[10] In their new environment these men found their old enemies, protection, privilege, monopoly and

[10]Cf. M. J. Coldwell, "Left Turn, Canada!" (Toronto, 1945), 1; Norman P. Lambert, "The Farmer in Politics" (*Grain Growers' Guide*, XIII (26), pp. 8 and 67): "The founders of the Grain Growers' movement . . . were mostly British radicals . . . linked up with older Canadians of rural Ontario and the Maritime Provinces. . . ."

high finance. The ideas and prejudices they brought to the West were kept alive by the rise of the Labour party in Great Britain, the development of the Progressive movement in the United States, and the agitation of the farmers' movement itself. Never was the Canadian West more part of the world, better endowed with men of capacity, more alert to the force of ideas, than in the days of the great immigration.

Particularly active in the dissemination of the advanced political ideas of the time was the *Grain Growers' Guide*. Its editor, the capable and forceful George F. Chipman, was a Nova Scotian by birth but a westerner of westerners by conviction. The *Guide* became the forum of the expression of the organized farmers' aspirations and discontents. Into it, as into a fiery melting pot, was cast the diverse stock of political ideas, panaceas, and projects of the growing, agitated West.

In the political debate in the *Guide's* columns three main features were evident: faith in democracy, hatred of corporate wealth, and distrust of the political system. Fundamental to all was the passionate belief in democracy, the conviction that the electorate was virtuous and had only to be able to make its will effective, without distortion or hindrance, for economic and social progress to follow. To it political power belonged of right: "Is not our whole system of government," queried the *Manitoba Free Press*, "built upon the principle that all political power is vested in the people at large?"[11]

The will of the people, however, as experience had often demonstrated, might be thwarted or warped by corporate wealth or privileged interests. The "new feudalism," the "new plutocracy," based on the seizure of natural resources, the monopolization of new inventions, or the grant of discriminatory legislation, dominated the political as well as the economic system.

To remedy this control of government by the money power, the reform known as "direct legislation" was proposed. Direct legislation meant the use of the initiative, or the introduction of legislation by the electorate, and the referendum, or the submission of legislation to the electorate for adoption or rejection.

[11] *Manitoba Free Press*, June 18, 1914, p. 13, editorial, "A Question of Democracy," *à propos* of an attack by Premier R. P. Roblin on direct legislation.

To these were added the recall, the power of a defined percentage of his constituents to recall, or unseat, a representative. The effect of direct legislation would have been to transfer a large part of the legislative process from representative assemblies to the electorate and to increase the power of the electorate over its representatives. It would have modified representative democracy by a considerable admixture of direct democracy. The hope of the advocates of direct legislation in the United States and Canada was that it would break the hold "bosses" and "machines," serving the "invisible government" of the "interests," were alleged to have on the government of the country.[12]   E. A. Partridge, leader in this as in the development of the Grain Growers' Grain Company and in the founding of the *Guide*, wrote in an open letter to the *Guide* in September 1909: "Among the demands [of the farmers on government] I should like to see included a demand for the introduction of the Initiative and Referendum and the Recall, with fixed dates for general elections, as much needed safeguards against the evils found in representative government when dominated by a highly organized machine designed to further the selfish interests of those who rob the people under the forms of law."[13]

The third feature of the political discussion of the times was precisely the distrust of existing institutions of government and of the party system which the advocacy of direct legislation implied.   The people was in its nature good, all power belonged to the electorate, but existing government was bad and the will of the electorate was thwarted.   Something was obviously wrong, it was argued, with the governmental system.   The evil was found to be in the party system of representative democracy. The elected representatives of the people were elected by the party organizations, which corrupted weak members of the electorate and took advantage of traditional partisanship among the voters.   Once elected the representative became the agent, not of his electors, but of the party.   The party, in its turn, was controlled by the "boss," or by the party caucus, and both by the moneyed interests which had supplied campaign funds

---

[12]See W. L. Morton, "Direct Legislation and the Origins of the Progressive Movement" (*Canadian Historical Review*, XXV, Sept., 1944), pp. 279-88.

[13]*Grain Growers' Guide*, II, Sept. 22, 1909, p. 11.

and which expected favours of government in return. The diagnosis was stated in the broadest terms by J. A. Stevenson writing in the *Guide* under the title, "The Battle for Democracy in Canada," in November 1910:

[The organized farmers] are embarking on an effort to re-establish the proper functions of representative institutions for the people of Canada and to renovate the whole system of national life. The root of the evil lies largely in our economic system. It corrupts our political system, our political system corrupts and degrades the public administration, and the corroding influence extends to the social system and business life till the disease pervades the whole community.[14]

How could the corruption of the political system be ended? By direct legislation, was one answer. Another was by the formation of a third party, a people's party or a farmers' party. If the people were to take over the whole electoral process of nomination, canvass, and election, and send to parliament, not a nominee of the parties, a professional politician or a time-serving lawyer, but one of themselves by sentiment and by occupation, surely such a person could be trusted to reflect the aspirations and carry out the will of his constituents. Along these lines the idea of a third party was disseminated among the organized farmers. Whether a third party was to be a popular, or an occupational party, was not debated during these years, nor was it realized by the farmers how vital for future political action would be the choice they made.

The *Guide* itself actively forwarded the growth of the ideas of populist democracy, direct legislation, and a third party by its editorial policy, special articles, and its correspondence columns. "The only hope of the farmers of Canada," it wrote editorially in August 1910, "is to realize that they have no more to expect from one political party than another. They must step aside and secure men to represent them who will stand out boldly in the interests of the farmers at all times."[15] Nor did its efforts go without response. A single issue in 1911 contained one letter advocating an attempt to reform both parties, one in favour of farmer candidates within the old parties and direct legislation, three in favour of a farmers' party, one urging that

[14]*Ibid.*, III, Nov. 2, 1910, p. 11.
[15]*Ibid.*, III, Aug. 10, 1910, p. 6.

candidates be pledged to support a platform, and one outlining a plan to elect independent candidates to hold the balance of power in parliament, as the Irish Home Rule party had done in Great Britain.[16] Such letters came in constantly; only occasionally did one defend the existing party system. The *Guide* was encouraged to continue its agitation. In July 1911, it wrote: "[The big interests] realize that so long as the people are willing to endorse either of the old parties that [sic] they are safe, but that if they send down to Ottawa Insurgents or Progressives then Special Privilege will not be able to plunder the people as in the past."[17] So far had the official organ of the organized farmers advanced, that it advocated, before the general election of 1911, the formation of an independent, progressive party in federal politics.

While the *Guide*, however, might agitate so far, the leaders of the farmers' organizations were more cautious. They feared a repetition of the fate of the Patrons of Industry, in which political action had resulted in the dissolution of the organization into adherents of the old parties and relatively few supporters of a third party. The agrarian leaders were prepared to approve any form of "non-partisan" political activity, such as putting pressure on the existing parties to accept the farmers' formulated demands, or nominating farmer candidates in the old parties, or introducing direct legislation which, of course, was independent of the party system, but they were not prepared to support the formation of a third, or an agrarian party. Their attitude was expressed in the constitution of the Canadian Council of Agriculture, which had as one stated purpose: "To encourage the entry of our farmers into active membership in one or other of the political associations according to individual predisposition as a means to make the political parties without distinction responsive to and representative of the demands of the people who form the bulk of the population."[18] The agitation for a third party was as yet a matter for prophets like Partridge and intellectuals like Chipman; the radical ideas of 1911 would not bear fruit until the events and the indoctrination of a decade had prepared the way for their application in 1921.

[16]*Ibid.*, III, March 15, 1911, p. 16.
[17]*Ibid.*, III, July 12, 1911, p. 5.
[18]*Ibid.*, II, Dec. 1, 1909, p. 14.

The organized farmers might not be ready for political action, but they were determined to press on government and the political parties the demands they had formulated. Of these demands, that for a lowering of the tariff became dominant between 1906 and 1910. There was still the need for further regulation of the grain trade and for increased storage capacity for grain, to avoid the harvest glut and depression of prices, in farmer-owned or government-owned elevators, and a host of current, minor demands. From 1906, however, the tariff became of ever greater importance.[19] The Tariff Commission of 1905-6 stirred anew the farmer's interest in the cost of protection to himself as a primary producer. Thereafter, as it happened, the grain growers had increasingly to seek to lower costs of production as well as costs of marketing. In 1909 the world price of wheat began a downward trend.[20] Costs of transportation and of manufactured goods rose in conjunction to wipe out that favourable margin between the price of wheat and the prices of the grain grower's needs on which the wheat boom had depended.[21] As land values ceased to rise[22] and indebtedness accumulated, the farmer listened more attentively to those who had not wearied of denouncing the protective tariff as an imposition and an iniquity.

To this view the Canadian farmer had generally been inclined since the introduction of the National Policy in 1879. The Liberal party had nurtured sentiment in favour of a low tariff, and had campaigned on a low tariff platform in 1896. After its victory in that year, however, the party had not, despite the introduction of the British preferential tariff in 1897 and one last pilgrimage to Washington for a reciprocity treaty, lived up to the expectations it had aroused. Forgotten was Laurier's declamation of 1894 in Winnipeg: "I denounce the policy of

[19]Cf. L. A. Wood, *The Farmers' Movements in Canada* (Toronto, 1924), 238-40. J. A. Hobson could write in *Canada To-day* (London, 1906),43 " . . . in Manitoba and the new provinces the tariff plays no part as a present issue." The Tariff Commission of 1905-6 may be taken as marking the beginning of the farmers' renewed interest in the tariff.

[20]D. A. MacGibbon, *The Canadian Grain Trade* (Toronto, 1932), 54.

[21]W. A. Mackintosh, *Economic Problems of the Prairie Provinces* (Toronto, 1935), 10.

[22]A. S. Morton and Chester Martin, *History of Prairie Settlement and "Dominion Lands" Policy* (Toronto, 1938), 502 and 520.

protection as bondage—yea, bondage; and I refer to bondage in the same manner in which American slavery was bondage."[23] In office the Liberals naturally and inevitably came to a tacit understanding with the powerful protected interests, and proceeded to develop and elaborate the National Policy of the Conservatives in an annual series of compromises between the sectional pressures of the Maritime Provinces, central Canada, the West, and innumerable local interests.[24]   In 1907 the astute and amiable Minister of Finance, the Hon. W. S. Fielding, brought the Canadian tariff to the form it has since retained, of a British preferential, an intermediate, and a maximum set of rates.   The tariff of that year embodied the matured fiscal policy of the Liberal party, and represented the current Liberal view that it went as far as it was possible to go in the direction of free trade while the United States maintained its hostility to reciprocity.

The revision of 1907, however, was followed by the American election of 1908, with its ambiguous pledges of tariff revision by the rival parties.   When the victorious Republicans revised the American tariff upwards in the Payne-Aldrich tariff of 1909, an agitation began in the northern United States, led by newspapers interested in Canadian pulp and newsprint, for a reduction of the rates on raw materials.   The organized farmers of Ontario and the West were encouraged by the opening of negotiations for reciprocity in March 1910, to press their demands for a lowering of the Canadian tariff.   When Laurier and Borden made pre-election tours of the West in 1910, they were beset at their train stops by the determined representatives of the Grain Growers.   With considerable bluntness, the delegates put before the leaders the trenchant views of the organized farmers on the need of a reduction of the tariff rates on the necessities of life and agricultural supplies and machinery. Borden stood firm on the traditional policy of his party, but Laurier was visibly impressed by the farmers' representations and promised a reduction of the tariff.[25]

[23]Edward Porritt, Sixty Years of Protection in Canada (Winnipeg, 1913), 316.

[24]O. J. McDiarmid, Commercial Policy in the Canadian Economy (Cambridge, Mass., 1946), chap. IX, "National Policy under Liberalism," 203-8.

[25]Wood, Farmers' Movements, 260.

The Canadian Council of Agriculture then decided to press the representations home by a great demonstration of the earnestness with which the organized farmers viewed the tariff issue.   In December of 1910 agrarian delegates from the West and Ontario, to the number of some eight hundred, descended on the Canadian capital in what was called the Siege of Ottawa. The delegates were received in state by the cabinet and heard in the Commons Chamber.   There the agrarian leaders of Canada, headed by D. W. McCuaig of the Canadian Council of Agriculture, laid the briefs of their constituents before Laurier and his cabinet.   They argued, with the blunt, harsh eloquence of their kind, the view that the protective tariff increased the operating costs of agriculture and made dear the necessities of life for everyone.   They pointed out that the tariff discriminated against the majority of the nation in favour of a privileged minority, against the outlying sections of the country in favour of central Canada.[26]   The cabinet heard them respectfully, and the Prime Minister dismissed them with his wonted grace but without further commitment.   In January 1911, however, the Minister of Finance crossed the border to resume negotiations on a reciprocity agreement with representatives of the government of the United States.

The Reciprocity Agreement of 1911 proposed the adoption by concurrent legislation of reciprocity of trade in natural products and specified manufactured commodities.   In short, it offered the primary producers of Canada free access to the American market.   The proposal, so incredible after the many refusals of such an agreement since 1866, when the Reciprocity Treaty of 1854 had been abrogated by the United States, was actually ratified by Congress.[27]

In Canada, the first reaction was that the Agreement was irresistible, and that it would prove a winning card in the hands of the Liberal party in the approaching general election.   In the Maritime Provinces memories of the Treaty of 1854 were still warm.   The West saw the Agreement as a great advance

[26]Public Archives of Manitoba, G. F. Chipman, *The Siege of Ottawa* (Winnipeg, 1911); for text, see Appendix A.

[27]For the negotiations and terms of the Agreement, see L. E. Ellis, *Reciprocity*, 1911 (Toronto, 1939).

towards freer trade. Elsewhere the first impression was that here at long last was a return to the good times of the old Treaty.

Opposition, however, soon began to gather. The Conservative party criticized the Agreement when the terms were introduced in the House, at first largely as a matter of form, then with rising conviction as the opposition in the country grew. Canada was not the Canada of 1854. Confederation and the National Policy had created an east-west system of trade which gave traffic to the railways and markets to the manufacturing industries. The opening of north-south channels, which might widen with time, threatened to injure the established interests of the railways and protected industries. In concerted revolt, signalized by the bolt from their party of eighteen Toronto Liberals led by Clifford Sifton, these interests repudiated the Liberal party, with which they had worked harmoniously since 1896, and moved to the support of the Conservatives. In the face of their opposition, Laurier advised the dissolution of parliament and went to the country in September of 1911.

The opponents of the Agreement had a powerful and sensitive body of anti-American sentiment on which to play. The memories of old troubles with the United States, of the repeated rebuffs of the many Canadian attempts to obtain reciprocity, had been aroused anew by the wound given Canadian national sentiment by the truculence of President Theodore Roosevelt in the dispute over the Alaskan boundary. To injured pride the appeal of the slogan "No truck or trade with the Yankees" was irresistible, particularly in Ontario and Manitoba. Canadian allegations of covert American imperialism were seemingly substantiated by public statements of American politicians, uttered for home consumption but eagerly reported in Canada.

The Liberal party soon found itself in difficulties before the powerful Conservative campaign, reinforced as it was by the reckless nationalism of Canadians anxious to give the Yankees a tit for many tats. In Quebec, moreover, it faced quite another set of troubles. The Naval Bill, which had established a Canadian navy, to be under Canadian control, but to be integrated with the British navy in time of war, had greatly increased the strength of the Nationalists. The degree to which it had done so had been revealed in August 1910, when the

Liberals had lost a by-election in Drummond-Arthabaska, Laurier's home territory, to a Nationalist candidate. In the general election the Nationalists campaigned with frenzied vigour against the Naval Bill, while the Conservative party refrained from nominating candidates. In Quebec, therefore, the election was a contest between Liberals and Nationalists over Canadian participation in Britain's wars, while in the rest of the country it was a contest between Liberals and Conservatives over the Reciprocity Agreement.

Nor were the Liberals able to make good in the West the losses threatened in Quebec. Control of the governments of Saskatchewan and Alberta by the Liberals gave the supporters of reciprocity an advantage in those provinces. The aggressive westerners of the new provinces were not impressed by the loyalty cry; Frederick Haultain, leader of the Conservative party in Saskatchewan remarked with dry scorn: "I am not prepared to sit at the feet of any of these Eastern Gamaliels and study loyalty."[28] And the same westerners were immune to the argument of economic nationalism. In Manitoba, however, a province a generation older than Saskatchewan and Alberta and settled first by people of British-Ontario stock, the appeal to loyalty was effective. Manitoba was bound to central Canada by ties of economic interest as well as sentiment; Winnipeg and the railway towns might well fear injury should the east-west flow of trade turn north-south. That province had also long been dominated by a Conservative administration under R. P. Roblin, which threw all its weight behind the federal party.

For the most part, the supporters of reciprocity were content to support the Liberal party. The agitation for independent political action by the farmers was too recent, the ties of party too strong, for the farmers to strike out on their own political way. The demands presented to the Laurier government in 1910 had been named "The Farmers' Platform," and approved by the conventions of the three western associations in January and February of 1911. It was intended, however, that the Platform be used for educational purposes; only the Manitoba

[28]Quoted in the *Canadian Annual Review*, 1911, p. 109; Haultain, however, opposed the Liberals in the ensuing election.

Grain Growers approved the suggestion of the *Grain Growers'
Guide* that farmers' candidates in the old parties be pledged to
support the Platform.[29] Even so, independent farmer candidates were nominated in four electoral districts, one of them,
W. J. Jackman, nominated in Strathcona, Alberta, being subject
to recall by a farmers' political association.[30] None of the
candidates was elected,[31] and the organizations themselves continued to stand fast against all attempts to commit them to the
formation of a farmers' party, or the nomination of independent
farmer candidates.

While the farmers abstained from concerted political action,
the campaign was fought out. In the result, 25 of Quebec's
seats returned Nationalist candidates, 8 of Manitoba's 10 seats
elected Conservatives, while Saskatchewan and Alberta went
solidly Liberal. The Maritime Provinces and British Columbia
were divided, but Ontario elected 74 Conservatives to 12 Liberals. Reciprocity and the Liberal party were defeated. National
pride, historic national policy, the great organized interests of
central Canada, had defeated the project which had promised
to ease the farmer's multiplying difficulties.

In the West the defeat of reciprocity was a bitter and stun-
ning blow to the organized farmers. Their anger was directed
not only towards the organized interests which had campaigned
so openly against the Agreement, but also towards central
Canada. "The West must bow to Ontario," wrote the *Guide*
after the election, "the most powerful province politically, in
Canada."[32] Nor was the bitterness merely sectional; it was
directed against the old parties also, which, the election seemed
to demonstrate, were but the tools of the organized interests, to
be used at convenience. "What is needed," the *Guide* continued, "is a radical party with the courage of its convictions."[33]
The shock of the defeat of reciprocity prepared the way for the
rise of a sectional and occupational third party. After 1911 the

[29]Report of the Proceedings of the Eighth Annual Convention of the Manitoba
Grain Growers' Association, 1911, p. 29; *Grain Growers' Guide*, III, Feb. 8, 1911, pp.
24 and 32; III, Feb. 22, 1911, p. 13.
[30]*Grain Growers' Guide*, IV, Aug. 30, 1911, pp. 4 and 23.
[31]*Ibid.*, IV, Aug. 2, 1911, pp. 4 and 5.
[32]*Ibid.*, IV, Sept. 27, 1911, p. 5, editorial, "The Election Results."
[33]*Ibid.*

western farmer was more than ever disposed to listen to such populistic doctrine as that uttered by R. C. Henders, president of the Manitoba Grain Growers' Association, before the convention of 1912:

The sovereign people have, I might say, no direct efficient control. They are sovereign *de jure* but not *de facto*, except at election time. The actual power experienced by the people consists chiefly in the periodic choice of another set of masters who make laws to suit themselves and enforce them until their term of office expires, regardless of the will of the people. We are governed by an elective aristocracy, which in its turn is largely governed by an aristocracy of wealth. Behind the government and the legislators are the corporations and trusts . . . behind the political monopolists are the industrial monopolists.[34]

Henders still found the principal remedy for these conditions in direct legislation, rather than in a third party, but even that belief marked the swelling distrust of the conventional parties.

The old parties suffered, after the election of 1911, a loss of influence and of trust throughout the West. The Conservative party, despite its success in Manitoba, became increasingly identified with the interests of central Canada, with protection and the big interests. That there was unfairness in this identification is apparent to any student of the many-sided, composite parties of the North American political tradition. The party, however, which had defeated reciprocity in 1911 had to pay in the West the price of its victory in the country at large. The Liberal party, on the other hand, could pose thereafter as the martyr of reciprocity, and the pose was to be rewarding. Yet even it incurred the odium of being the tool, though the discarded tool, of the eastern interests. The great Liberal editor of the *Manitoba Free Press*, J. W. Dafoe, wrote to a friend on the morrow of the election:

The fact is, as I have long known, Canada is now and has been for a generation, an essentially Tory country. That is to say, the right of corporations, moneyed interests, etc., to determine the policy of the country is recognized by the majority of the electors. Laurier achieved office in 1896 mainly through a series of blunders by his opponents, supplemented by their loss, in rapid succession, of able men; and upon

[34]*Ibid.*, IV, Feb. 7, 1912, p. 7.

obtaining office he held it for a long period of time by placating various powerful interests at the expense of the general public. The moment he showed signs of putting real Liberal doctrine into effect, the interests combined and crushed him. I should be very well content to see the Liberal party remain in opposition for the next fifteen or twenty years, if it will devote itself to advocating real Liberal views and building up a party which, when it again takes office, will be able to carry out a programme without regard to the desires and feelings of the privileged classes.[35]

The search for such a purged and radical Liberal party closely resembled the farmers' search for a means of political expression distinct from the traditional, composite parties. Western liberalism, if it embarked on such a search, might find it, with western agrarianism, in a sectional third party.

The defeat of reciprocity in 1911 was the first act in the agrarian revolt of Western Canada. It sharpened the distrust of the old parties which had been growing among the organized farmers. It weakened both old parties in the West. The farmers' movement was troubled as never since the days of the Patrons by an agitation for political action, an agitation the depression of 1912-15 was to invigorate.

[35]Dafoe Papers (*Winnipeg Free Press* editorial offices), Dafoe to George Iles, Sept. 27, 1911.

CHAPTER TWO

The Farmers' Movement and the Political
Parties, 1911-18

T H E agrarian revolt of the western farmers against the national
policy of central Canada and the party system developed rapidly
in strength after 1911.   Its effects were first felt, however, not
in federal but in provincial politics; the governments of Manitoba, Saskatchewan, and Alberta yielded to the farmers' pressure
before the federal parties responded to the new force in the West.

There were many reasons why the farmers' movement made
its influence felt in provincial politics, but taken together they
amounted to this, that the smaller, more homogeneous provincial
electorates exerted a more direct, effective pressure on the
provincial governments than did the complex and divided
national electorate on the federal government.   Provincial
democracy was simpler and speedier in its operation than federal;
it has been no accident, therefore, that in North America reform
movements and third parties have risen in states and provinces
before entering national politics.

The increasingly favourable attitude towards reform legislation of the western provincial governments, however, was not
entirely the result of the rise of the farmers' movement.   In
the first decade of the century a general reform movement had
also been growing in the Canadian West.   In its early stages at
least, the farmers' movement was indeed only one, though a
major, part of the general movement, a fact which often served
to veil its agrarian and sectional character.   The general reform
movement itself was at core a demand for positive state action
with respect to such matters as the prohibition of the sale of

27

alcoholic liquor, the promotion of social welfare, and the cleansing of political life. This reform sentiment was most active in the West, as a region of recent immigration and acute political grievances, in which a native conservatism had scarcely begun to develop.

In its origins the reform movement sprang from various causes, but in its demand for action by the state against certain evils it marked an epoch in the development of Canadian democracy. The great scramble for possession of the natural resources of the continent was in its last phase, the scramble in which "so long as men were making money, they cared little who made the Government,"[1] or what the government did, so long as it left them alone. "We are," remarked the *Manitoba Free Press*, commenting on the meeting of the Social Welfare Congress in Winnipeg in 1916, "at the end of the era of unchecked piratical individualism."[2]

The reform movement drew not only from the rise of a social conscience but also from the development of social purpose in the Protestant churches. Laymen were finding the doctrine and ministrations of the churches less and less satisfying.[3] They found in the farmers' organizations and the reform movement compensation for their loss of faith, an experience expressed tersely by Henry Wise Wood of Alberta, when he said in later years that "the Wheat Pool was as much a religious institution as the church." Wood was an example of the layman reformer with theological training, as was his colleague in the United Farmers of Alberta, Percival Baker of Ponoka.[4] The same type was to be found in the clergyman turned organizer and politician, men such as Rev. J. S. Woodsworth, Rev. Salem G. Bland, often a fiery preacher before the farmers' convention, Rev. R. C. Henders, himself president of the Manitoba Grain Growers, Rev. William Irvine, and Rev. R. A. Hoey.

Only in idealistic political activity could these men find outlet for their sense of mission. To them the division between secular and religious affairs was becoming meaningless. As

[1]*Manitoba Free Press*, Jan. 6, 1917, p. 13, editorial, "Partisanship."
[2]*Ibid.*, Dec. 7, 1916, p. 11, editorial, "The West In Ferment."
[3]S. D. Clark, *Church and Sect in Canada* (Toronto, 1948), 430-1.
[4]Paul F. Sharp, *The Agrarian Revolt in Western Canada* (Minneapolis, 1948), 61, n. 125.

Rev. J. S. Woodsworth wrote in "Sermons for the Unsatisfied," published in the *Guide* in 1915:

So the walls and partitions between [creed and callings] are breaking down. There are dangers: all may become secular; there are wonderful possibilities; all may become sacred. For good or for evil we are out into the new world. Exclusive religion must more and more give way to an all-inclusive religion. Religion in the future will no longer be identified with the Church and Sundays and prayer and priests, it will become the every day life of the common man—that or nothing.[5]

And the same sentiment was to be echoed in Irvine's *The Farmers In Politics:* "The line between the sacred and the secular is being rubbed out."[6]

Not only did the general reform movement mark a change in civic spirit and social aims; it also operated to weaken the spirit of partisanship in politics and to impair the functioning of the two-party system. Two particular reforms achieved in the years between 1911 and 1918 especially exemplified this tendency. One was prohibition. The issue, of some duration in Canadian politics, was very trying for the political parties, because it was certain to disrupt party lines. The advocates of temperance quite bluntly put loyalty to conscience before loyalty to either person or party.[7] For this reason the politicians sought persistently to avoid the issue by resort to local option, to plebiscites, and finally, seizing on the wide support direct legislation had obtained in the West, to the referendum. It was to the last device that the Manitoba Liberal party resorted in its platform of 1914, which included direct legislation but not the programme of the temperance organizations. The *Free Press* defended the policy in clear-cut terms:

If, in short, the Liberal party in Manitoba were to do as the temperance leaders ask, it would in the coming election poll neither the full temperance vote nor the full Liberal vote, thus reducing its present reasonably good chance of victory. On the other hand, if it retains the full Liberal strength and offers to the temperance leaders a means

[5]*Grain Growers' Guide*, July 7, 1915, p. 18, "Sermons for the Unsatisfied, IV." (Volumes of the *Guide* are not numbered, 1914-16.)

[6]William Irvine, *The Farmers in Politics* (Toronto, 1920), 53.

[7]*Manitoba Free Press*, Feb. 26, 1907, p. 1; "The time has come to put loyalty to conscience before loyalty to either person or party," wrote the Manitoba Standing Committee of Temperance and Moral Reform.

of early victory (if their estimate of the strength of their cause is correct) should it not be able to command a sufficient volume of support to ensure victory?[8]

The temperance appeal to conscience posed dangers for the party system and prepared the way for that political independence in the electorate out of which a third party was to arise.

Closely allied with the temperance movement was the agitation for the extension of the franchise to women. The alliance arose out of the belief that enfranchised women would vote to abolish, or at least to regulate, the traffic in liquor. The calculation was sound, and in the West prohibition followed hard on the admission of women to the provincial suffrage in the middle years of the period under review. The advocates of women's rights may well have calculated that the new voters would, many of them, vote independently of party ties. The calculation was natural, since reformers of all kinds were critical of the parties as being subject to corruption. It was also to be justified, for the enfranchisement of women, besides increasing the electorate, added to the "floating vote" and so weakened the party system.

It was in this growing context of the general reform movement that the organized farmers from 1911 on strove to increase the weight of agriculture in the political life of the country. In doing so, they lent their support to other reforms, such as the single tax and direct legislation. Support of direct legislation was indicative of another element which contributed to the growing political consciousness of the farmers. That was the steady wind of American reformist influence which fanned every flame with precedent, example, and slogan. Not only was there the vivid memory of Populism; not only did the *Guide* carry on its early numbers the old Jacksonian motto of "Special privileges for none, and equal rights for all"; not only was direct legislation as popular in the Canadian West during these years as in the north-western American states; there was also the contemporary American Progressive Movement, which reached its climax in the years from 1910 to 1912. Its influence was immediate and insistent on the growth of the reform movement in the Canadian West, and its precept and example, its vocabu-

[8]*Ibid.*, March 2, 1914, p. 11, editorial, "Tactics."

lary and even its name, came to characterize the ferment of
political life in the western provinces. John Kennedy, vice-
president of the Manitoba Grain Growers' Association, wrote
to the *Guide* in 1914 in support of a third party movement:
"We will call ourselves Progressives, nothing more, nothing less.
We will have no platform other than 'vote the desire of your
constituents.' "[9] Another correspondent urged the formation
of "a third or progressive party"[10] from all progressive organizations. Such a party, still another correspondent claimed,
might be "a business party for Canada," which would end
current political methods, with their corruption and sectional
domination. "In current politics," it was alleged, "the elections
were foul fights and the nominations were made by base faction
machines and fat bosses, [and] those nominees who got elected
joined their faction caucus (which was secret) and agreed to
abide by majority rule, the East thus dominating the West."[11]

It was in this political climate that the organized farmers
after the defeat of reciprocity set out to push their demands on
government more vigorously than ever. In the western provinces early success crowned their efforts. The three provincial
governments accepted most of the farmers' programme which
came within provincial jurisdiction over the years between 1911
and 1919, and soon these governments were, in all but name and
personnel, farmers' governments.

Yet, while this result might have been anticipated in the
agrarian West, it came about differently in each province, and
with results significantly different. In Manitoba, for example,
the Conservative party had been in power since 1899. Traditional Conservative voters were numerous in that province,
offshoot as it was of Ontario and formed on the British-Ontario
pattern. The party retained its hold on office by various means.
The rude political craft of its leaders, Hon. Rodmond P. Roblin
and Hon. Robert Rogers, counted for much. The government's
coolness to the temperance movement won it the valuable
support of the liquor interests. The party succeeded in organizing much of the immigrant vote, and its administration of the

[9]*Grain Growers' Guide*, March 4, 1914, p. 9.
[10]*Ibid.*, April 8, 1914, p. 10.
[11]*Ibid.*, April 15, 1914, pp. 9 and 26, letter from F. Kirkham, Saltcoats, Sask.

bilingual school system won it support among the French, Mennonites, Poles, and Ukrainians. As a zealous ally of the federal Conservative party, it was able to exploit the issue of the extension of the provincial boundaries against the Liberal party, and to reap its reward for services rendered in the federal election of 1911 in the greatly extended boundaries of 1912. The enlarged boundaries were, perhaps, a fatal gift. One of the chief sources of the government's strength was removed at a time when its liabilities were accumulating. Its political methods were of the old school, corrupt, rough, and vicious, the very methods against which the reformers and organized farmers were inveighing. The growing reform movement made the Roblin régime appear more and more anachronistic. The failure of its elevator scheme in 1912 weakened it in the eyes of the organized farmers of Manitoba.

The provincial Liberal party, during the same period, was undergoing that healthful purgation which exile from office imposes on political parties. It became a party in search of a programme and in the platforms of 1910 and 1914 adopted most of the leading proposals of the organized farmers and the reform movement. By the latter year the Manitoba Liberal party had become a vehicle of progressive reform. "The [Liberal] platform," commented the *Free Press* in 1914, "is a fine, progressive, democratic, humanistic document, significant of the new movement in politics."[12]   The party was then committed to the introduction of compulsory school attendance, temperance reform, agricultural credits, women's suffrage, direct legislation, an improved administration of justice, the improvement of the conditions of labour, a good roads system, local option on tax reform, and to seeking return of control of its natural resources to the province.[13]   The platform was a compendium of the current objects of the reform movement. In endorsing these measures the Liberal party had entered into tacit alliance with the organized farmers and the developing labour movement in Winnipeg. In consequence, advanced reformers, such as L. St. George Stubbs and F. J. Dixon, and

[12] *Manitoba Free Press*, June 20, 1914, p. 11, editorial, "Progress and Reaction."
[13] *Ibid.*, March 30, 1914, p. 11; the text of the platform of 1914 is printed in full, under the heading, "Progressive Platform of Manitoba Liberal Party."

farmers, such as John Williams and G. J. H. Malcolm, fought in the Liberal ranks or served as auxiliaries in the forward battle areas. When one of the old parties was so thoroughly progressive, there was no practical need for a third party, nor had class-consciousness among farmers or industrial workers yet reached the point of demanding an occupational party, irrespective of need.

Despite the commitment of the Liberal party to reform and its considerable reinvigoration thereby, the Roblin government survived the election of 1914. It did so, however, with a minority of five thousand of the popular vote and with the French or immigrant vote decisive in eleven of the electoral districts.[14] The end of the régime was obviously approaching, and in 1915 it was overturned by the revelation of financial irregularities in the construction of the new legislative building.

The scandal of 1915 and the passing of the Roblin Government marked the end of the crude politics of frontier days in Manitoba. The way was now open for laying the foundations of the welfare state under the impulse of the reform movement. The new Liberal government of Premier T. C. Norris proved capable of the task, and the enactment of direct legislation, women's suffrage, civil service reform, prohibition, workmen's compensation, mothers' allowance and child welfare legislation followed. By 1916 the reform movement had won control of government in Manitoba.

The great reform programme was carried out, however, by one of the traditional provincial parties, a party affiliated with the federal Liberals. Part of the legislation of the Norris government was the enactment in 1916 of compulsory school attendance and the abolition of bilingual teaching. The measure embodying these two reforms was provoked by the linguistic chaos in the province perpetuated by the bilingual system of teaching, allowed without limitation as to mother tongue by the Laurier-Greenway legislation of 1897, and by widespread abstention from school attendance in rural districts. It was passed at the very time that the federal Liberals were trying to win back the ground lost to the Nationalists in Quebec. The connection between federal and provincial parties created the

[14]Such was the analysis of the *Manitoba Free Press*, July 14, 1914, p. 11.

suspicion among supporters of the School Act of 1916 that the federal party might impose its policy on the Norris government, and caused an increase of sectional spirit in the province.

While the reform movement made the Liberal party its instrument and brought it to power in Manitoba, the same movement worked itself out in a different way in Saskatchewan. That new province inherited from Territorial days a tradition of keeping federal and local politics separate,[15] but, on its foundation, the Liberals, aided by the Liberal federal government, had formed the first administration and held control of the government thereafter against all assaults of the Conservative, or "Provincial Rights," opposition. The consequent domination of Saskatchewan by the Liberal party was the central feature of the political life of the province. The way of any opposition, whether traditional party or third party, was bound to be especially thorny in Saskatchewan.

The strength of the Saskatchewan Liberal party arose from a number of causes. The party had provided the province with a group of able administrators and politicians, notably Premier Walter Scott and Hon. J. A. Calder. Government had been efficient, progressive, and economical, and sharply aware of the environment in which it worked. The party organization was keen, tireless, and well versed in all the arts of democratic politics. The administration had, in addition, the good fortune to govern a province which was uniformly agrarian in interests and character. The urban centres of Saskatchewan were auxiliary to the agrarian economy. No one city dominated the province, and all the cities were so equally favoured in the distribution of political benefits that none had an enduring political grievance. Nor was there a class-conscious labour movement in any of the urban centres. There was no rivalry among Regina, Saskatoon, and Moose Jaw, as there was between Edmonton and Calgary in Alberta, nor between the cities and the country, as there was between Winnipeg and rural Manitoba, to disturb the even tenor of Saskatchewan politics. There was no clamour of class politics to wrench party lines or to badger government with discordant demands. In Saskatchewan the

[15]See *Winnipeg Free Press*, Dec. 26, 1946, Senator Norman P. Lambert, "The Northwest."

grain growers dominated the economy and politics of the province, and government had the comparatively simple task of accommodating administration and legislation to the requirements of the organized farmers.

Because of the dominantly agrarian character of Saskatchewan politics, the reform movement, when it entered the province, appeared among the Grain Growers. The various reforms endorsed by the annual conventions of the Saskatchewan Grain Growers' Association, such as direct legislation, prohibition, or women's suffrage, were submitted to the provincial government and usually in due course enacted.[16] The Liberal government was just as progressive as were the organized farmers of the province.

The Liberal party of Saskatchewan was, in fact, an agrarian party, and the administration was a farmers' government in everything but personnel. Even in that respect, as the power of the Grain Growers waxed, the number of farmer members in the cabinet increased. Between the administration and the Association grew up a liaison so lively and intimate that in reality the government of the province and the executive of the Association were obverse and reverse of the same coin, a coin stamped in the mint of the wheat economy. The passage from office in the Association to office in the government of men such as George Langley, C. A. Dunning, and J. A. Maharg was the outward and visible sign of the close relationship of mind and purpose. As a result, the reform movement found comparatively easy expression in Saskatchewan, and the Liberal government, unlike the Roblin administration in Manitoba, was not troubled by the new spirit in politics. Scandal did indeed

[16]Minutes of Annual Convention of Saskatchewan Grain Growers' Association, 1919, p. 4, " 'There are questions now coming before you affecting the welfare of the entire community of the province,' said Premier Martin [to the Convention]. 'It is the policy of the present government and will continue to be the policy of the present government to carry out these suggestions [of the convention].' Premier Martin said that the population of Saskatchewan is mostly rural, 72 per cent of the population being on the land. 'It is little wonder that you impress your will on the law makers of the province,' said Premier Martin in closing, 'for when you are dealing with the questions affecting the great industry you represent, you are dealing with the greatest problems before the country and you will meet with the same success which you have met in the past in making your representations to the legislators of the Province of Saskatchewan'." (These minutes are on file in head office of United Farmers of Canada, Saskatchewan Section, in Saskatoon.)

threaten the Scott government in 1916-17, but defeat was averted by a prompt and drastic house-cleaning and the replacement of the ailing Scott by the young and able W. M. Martin. The agrarian Liberal party of Saskatchewan, having survived that shock, seemed secure in power as the adequate and efficient agent of the agrarian electorate.

The political history of the neighbouring province of Alberta closely resembled that of Saskatchewan. The Liberal party had taken over the administration in 1905 and had retained control until the period under review. A tradition of keeping provincial and federal politics separate survived from territorial times. The provincial government proved itself as adaptable to the wishes of the organized farmers of Alberta as had that of Saskatchewan.

There the resemblance ended. For one thing, scandal had entered Albertan politics early. The exposure of loose dealing in the letting of contracts for the construction of the Alberta and Great Waterways Railway, a provincial undertaking, nearly defeated the government and did cause a split in the Liberal party. The immediate damage was repaired by the brilliant Hon. A. L. Sifton, who became premier and consolidated the Liberal hold on power. The rift in the party ranks, however, permanently weakened the party in Alberta, and early founded in that province a cynical distrust of politicians that made the electorate receptive of new movements.[17]

In the second place, the province of Alberta was in physical resources and population different from Saskatchewan. To wheatlands Alberta added range lands, irrigated land, and vast coal deposits. Its economic development was more varied, even in frontier days, than was that of the monolithic wheat economy of Saskatchewan. A diversity of interests, comparatively speaking, characterized the electorate of Alberta, and the organized farmers could not speak for everyone, as in Saskatchewan. The cattlemen, the sugar-beet growers, the coal

[17]L. G. Thomas, "The Liberal Party in Alberta, Dec., 1905-1921" (*Canadian Historical Review*, XXVIII, Dec. 1947, p. 420): "The Alberta Great Waterways scandal is perhaps the most important event in the political history of Alberta. It broke the Liberal party in the province and although the party retained power in the province for eleven years the break went unmended and only the strong personality of Sifton held the fragments together."

miners, had from time to time their various views to urge on government and the parties. Nor had the Albertan government avoided the rise of interurban rivalry as had that of Saskatchewan. The disappointment of Calgary's hopes of preferment in the matter of the site of the capital and of the university, and the lavish endowment of Edmonton with these and other favours, created a rivalry which coloured Albertan politics and helped to make Calgary a centre of political dissent.

Alberta, then, was different from Saskatchewan and was even more different from Manitoba, but the differences mentioned do not wholly account for the maverick characteristics the province was already beginning to develop. Two further factors remain to be considered if the high-strung, volatile character of Alberta is to be understood.[18]

Alberta was the frontier of frontiers, the outermost limit of arable land on the continent. Between 1911 and 1916 it was still absorbing the last great wave of immigration in the history of North American settlement. The story begun at Jamestown and Quebec was ending along the foothills of the Rockies and across the great plateaux of the Peace. The characteristic frontier malaise of debt, dislocation, and restlessness was active in the province. All these factors were aggravated by physical factors. Alberta was the last frontier by virtue of distance from the original centres of settlement. Distance meant increased freight charges, an intensified sense of being at the mercy of remote metropolitan powers, the bankers of Montreal, the grain buyers of Winnipeg, the politicians of Ottawa. These were the conditions of an exaggerated sectionalism. And to sharpen tempers already touchy, there were added the agricultural hazards of drought in the south and of frost in the north of the province.

The intensification of the strains of a pioneer economy and a frontier community was not offset by solidity of political and social traditions. Alberta's population was made up almost equally of three groups: native Canadians, British immigrants, and American immigrants. The result was that the British-Ontario political tradition did not establish itself easily or

[18]I am deterred from ascribing the tension of Albertan life to altitude by consideration of the Swiss, a notably phlegmatic people.

firmly in Alberta. In Manitoba it was dominant, in Saskatchewan it had been maintained, though modified by the agrarianism of that province. Alberta, however, was to shape its own political traditions and to make its own parties. Its social and political life was hybrid in character, and possessed all the organic possibilities of a sport, by reason of the lack of a dominant native tradition and from the vigour of the two main immigrant groups, British and American.

The history of the farmers' movement in Alberta bears out the view that Alberta's difference arose in some considerable measure from the weakness of old Canadian elements in its life. The rise of the Society of Equity in Alberta and the difficulty with which union with the native organization of the Grain Growers was brought about illustrates the lack of strong native traditions in the province. The Society of Equity, had it continued, would have maintained an American organization on Canadian soil and full connection with Societies across the border. The Grain Growers, had they absorbed the Society, would have brought the organized farmers into the general pattern of the organized farmers' movement of the West. The union was a compromise, the United Farmers of Alberta, which was always conscious of a difference between itself and the Grain Growers of Saskatchewan and Manitoba.

The rise of the immigrants to power is illustrated by the election of Henry Wise Wood to the vice-presidency of the United Farmers of Alberta in 1915 and to the presidency in 1916.[19] Wood was an example of the potent force non-Canadian leaders were in making the farmers' movement in Alberta distinctive. American-born, a native of Missouri, Wood was forty-five years of age when he came to Alberta in 1905, at the peak of the land rush into the Canadian West. He had been educated for the ministry of the Campbellites at Christian College, Canton, Missouri.[20] He had remained a "Seeker" after graduation, but had become a farmer, a calling he had pursued in various states of the trans-Mississippi West. In the 1880's he had participated in the formation of the Farmers'

[19]For biographical details and an estimate of Wood's character, see Sharp, *Agrarian Revolt*, 191-6.

[20]Now Culver-Stockton University, Canton, Mo.

Alliance and of the Populist party. From the defeat of the Populists and the wreck of the Alliance he had formed a conviction that farmers' organizations should not enter politics. This experience, much brooding thought on religious and social problems, and much desultory reading, including some Marxist literature,[21] was the intellectual capital of the tall, loose-jointed, weather-beaten man, bearing some suggestion of Lincoln in manner and mien, who took up land at Carstairs, Alberta. He farmed there with indifferent success, by all accounts; he joined the Society of Equity in 1906 and the United Farmers in 1909; in 1911 he became a British subject. In no way, however, was he to come into prominence in affairs, save for passing notice of his eloquence at a Liberal party convention in 1911, until his election to the vice-presidency of the U.F.A. in 1915. He brought to that office not only the accidental quality of a personality of great force, but a large body of experience in agrarian organization and politics and a body of ideas distilled from that experience. Few Canadian farm leaders, however they might match Wood's personal qualities, could hope to match his experience.

Though Wood was in many ways a unique example, an increasing number of other immigrants assumed roles of leadership in the U.F.A. As there was no prejudice one way or another, this reliance upon immigrants for leadership was the result of free competition of talent and personality. By 1918 the composition of the Executive and Board of Directors of the U.F.A. was as follows: American-born, eight; Canadian, five; British, five; New Zealand-born, one.[22] On the whole, if judgment may be based on the record of elected leaders, the British and American immigrants were more capable, more influenced by current ideas and more inclined to political and economic dissent. It is plain that in these years, Alberta was not only subject to more intense sectional feeling than its eastern neigh-

[21]The superficial resemblance between Wood's "groups" and the "soviets" of the Russian Revolution, rather than Wood's knowledge of Marxism, lay behind Col. J. A. Currie's description of him as "an American radical, steeped in the doctrines of Karl Marx." Wood had some acquaintance with Marxist thought, considerable for his day and circumstances, but it does not seem to have been extensive and it certainly was not sympathetic.

[22]United Farmers of Alberta Annual Report, 1918.

bours but was developing a more radical spirit than the leaders
of the organized farmers had yet invoked.

While the organized farmers were successfully pressing
agrarian measures, such as agricultural credits, and the leading
proposals of the general reform movement, on the provincial
governments of the West in the years after 1911, their pressure
on the federal government had slackened. The vanquishers of
reciprocity were not likely to accept any considerable portion of
the "Farmers' Platform" of 1910, though they did wisely make
a concession to western grievances by lowering the duty on
agricultural implements in 1914. The Grain Act of 1912 and
the abortive proposal that the federal government should
purchase terminal elevators were the limit of significant Conservative consideration of the desires of the western farmers.
The organised farmers retained their prejudice towards reciprocity, the Agreement of 1911 being still on the statute book of the
United States. Because of this lack of sympathy between the
administration and the farmers' associations, there was little for
the latter to do but wait until in the course of time the life of
parliament ran out and the government had to go to the electorate. In the normal course it would not have to do so until 1916,
and would almost certainly not do so before 1915.

The outbreak of war in Europe and Canadian participation
in it still further decreased the farmers' interest in federal
politics. The war raised other issues. Many farmers were
frankly isolationist and accepted Canadian participation re-
luctantly.[23] Only when they came to see it as a struggle to
decide "whether Democracy or Autocracy" should triumph,
"whether the smaller nations should be free," did support of
the war accord with their principles.[24] The war also pulled the
Canadian economy out of the slump which had begun in 1913
and had become severe by 1914. By 1915, a war boom was
under way which was also a wheat boom and a land boom of the
same kind as that of 1896-1911.[25] The Canadian West entered
a second period of forced growth, which quieted its sectional

[23]*Grain Growers' Guide*, Aug. 5, 1914, p. 6; also Feb. 19, 1913, p. 8.
[24]*Ibid.*, Aug. 12, p. 5.
[25]Wheat acreage mounted from 9,335,400 acres in 1914 to 16,125,451 in 1918
(*Canada Year Book*, 1915, p. 170, and 1919, p. 187).

grievances momentarily but which, in the long run, was to aggravate them intensely.

For these reasons, the remoteness of the next general election and preoccupation with the war and the war boom, the organized farmers refrained from much activity between 1911 and 1915. On the other hand, the *Grain Growers' Guide* kept alive the discussion of the most effective means of making the weight of agriculture felt in politics. Its editorial campaign for the election of farmer representatives, begun in 1911, was continued and provoked much favourable response in the form of letters to the editor.[26] The *Guide* in 1915 increased its agitation, as the election neared, and came out for the election of independent, free trade members. "Week by week," it wrote, "the feeling is growing that the only way the West can secure a square deal in federal legislation is by sending down to Parliament men free from obligations to either of the old political parties," men who would be free to vote for the tariff policy desired by the West.[27] The *Guide's* agitation was not without effect; in 1915 R. C. Henders, president of the Manitoba Grain Growers, was nominated as an "independent, free trade" candidate in Macdonald and Rev. Thomas Beveridge as an "independent progressive" candidate in Souris.[28]

An equally active interest in political action by the farmers was revealed in the annual convention of the Manitoba Grain Growers in January of 1916. The formation of an agrarian third party by the Association was, not for the first time, urged by a number of delegates. The proposition had indeed been adumbrated when the president, R. C. Henders, delivered the following passage in his address:

Our great source of weakness, and the one which I sincerely hope we will give our best endeavours to overcome during the year 1916 is this: That farmers as a class have not in the past, and do not even now readily develop the spirit of class consciousness. . . . All other classes, as a result of their combination, and because of the fact that they place class interests above political preferment, are able to wield influence in the halls of our legislatures. We pass resolutions, divide

---

[26]See *Grain Growers' Guide*, April 22, 1914, p. 26; June 3, 1914, p. 8; June 10, 1914, pp. 8 and 14; Dec. 16, 1914, p. 27; Oct. 6, 1915, p. 8; June 6, 1917, pp. 22 and 25, etc.
[27]*Ibid.*, May 12, 1915, p. 5, editorial, "Elect Free Traders."
[28]*Ibid.*, May 26, 1915, p. 5; May 26, 1915, p. 9.

our influence along party political lines and so weaken our case politically that in the great game of party politics we play little or no part. The banker, the manufacturer, the railway interests, when they have personal interests to serve know no politics. With them, business is their politics. Until we learn that lesson—further, until we go home and practise that lesson—we need not hope or expect to succeed in bringing to rural life that consideration which it merits.[29]

The proposal was defeated, especially by the efforts of the executive, which feared the Association would be destroyed by political action as farmers' organizations had been in the past. It was evident from the debate, however, that opponents of the proposal were not opposed to independent political action by the farmers of Manitoba, but to committing the Association itself to political action.[30] The Association contained Liberals, Conservatives, and third-party men. An attempt to make the Association the political organization of a third party would have cost it the support of those members who remained devoted to their traditional parties.

The debate in the Convention was discussed by the *Guide*:

Year by year the demand for a third party, or independent party or something similar, grows stronger in the West. It comes up for discussion at the Annual Conventions and in the local associations. An error, however, is being made in attempting to convert the farmers' associations into political organizations. It would be most undesirable even if it were possible to turn the farmers' organizations into political parties. These organizations have all their work to do in education, organization and commerce, and it would be a very dangerous matter to force them into the political field. In fact, such a proposition cannot be considered seriously. But nevertheless political action is necessary and can be carried on without interference with or danger to the organizations.

The biggest question in the West today is that of Free Trade and we believe the organization of a Free Trade League would provide the opportunity for political action whenever it was necessary or wise.[31]

It would seem that the debate had forced a clarification of the meaning of political action by the organized farmers. It was becoming clear that they might do one of three things:

[29] *Ibid.*, Jan. 12, 1916, pp. 7 and 31.
[30] *Ibid.*, p. 32, article, "Free Trade Party Proposed."
[31] *Ibid.*, Jan. 19, 1916, p. 5, editorial, "Independent Political Action."

secure the nomination of candidates pledged to a farmers' platform within the old parties, nominate farmers' candidates to
form the nucleus of a third party, or carry their organizations
into politics to constitute an occupational party.   It was the
last which had been voted down by the convention of 1916 in
Manitoba, and the second which the *Guide* had advocated.

For the remainder of 1916, the *Guide* pushed vigorously its
programme of a Free Trade League, which might become a free
trade party.   Adherence to the League was proposed to the
United Farmers of Alberta by Chipman himself, and, on the
motion of Henry Wise Wood, was unanimously approved.   At
the same time a motion calling for the formation of a third party
by the organization was defeated.[32]   The Saskatchewan Grain
Growers in convention also approved the League.[33]   The general
editorial comment of the *Guide* reveals that the purpose of the
League was to demonstrate the strength of low tariff sentiment
in the West, and, if necessary, to provide the basis for independent political action.   Reviewing "Liberal Tariff Policy" in
August, it remarked: "Unless the Liberals can be depended
upon to reduce the tariff very considerably there is no advantage
in returning them to power.   More and more it becomes evident
that the West should declare a Western policy in Western
interests and send to Ottawa members who will support that
policy regardless of the two old political parties."[34]   Pleas by
Liberal politicians for the support of the Grain Growers, such
as that made by Hon. C. A. Dunning, "I believe that from the
West . . . it is possible to develop such a force for true Liberalism
as will affect the whole of the party, and so render reform easy,"
were met with outbursts from the *Guide*, such as, "The time has
come when the Western representatives should represent
Western people and Western views and cut off connections with
the privilege-ridden, party blind, office-hunting Grit and Tory
parties that make their headquarters at Ottawa."[35]

Not only in its editorial columns but also in its special

[32]*Ibid.*, Jan. 26, 1916, p. 5, editorial, "The Alberta Convention."

[33]*Ibid.*, March, 1916, p. 6, editorial, "Free Trade League," July 26, 1916, pp. 7
and 12, article by Roderick McKenzie, "The Failure of Protection."

[34]*Ibid.*, Aug. 2, 1916, p. 5.

[35]*Ibid.*, Aug. 30, 1916, p. 5; editorial, "Western Men Should Explain." Dunning's
statement is quoted in part in the *Canadian Annual Review*, 1916, p. 722.

articles, the *Guide* rang the changes on the need for a third party.   It had two correspondents of outstanding capacity and conviction in Edward Porritt and J. A. Stevenson.   Porritt was known for his free trade views and his belief in the corrupting influence of protection from his *Sixty Years of Protection in Canada* and his *New Feudalism*, books advertised and distributed by the *Guide's* book department.   In September 1915, he wrote: "It would now seem that a new party, opposed to both the Liberals and the Conservatives, or to a coalition of these parties, must come into existence and assert itself continuously and vigorously if the end of the war is to be the beginning of a less dismal era in Canadian politics."[36]   Stevenson, for his part, urged the creation of an independent third party on the model of the British Labour Party, arguing that the agrarian radicalism of the West could not remain in alliance with the eastern wing of the Liberal party, fearful as it was of tariff reform and devoted to the special pre-occupations of Quebec.   "The logical result [of the conservatism of the eastern Liberals]," he wrote in mid-1916, "is that a separate western party with its own radical wing ought to be constituted at the earliest possible moment."[37]

The *Guide* and other advocates of independent political action were suddenly encouraged by a demonstration in North Dakota of the successful use of the tactics they were urging on the organized farmers of the Canadian West.   In North Dakota the farmers' movement had been represented since 1900 by the Societies of Equity.   In 1915-16 a movement for political action, the Non-Partisan League, sprang up and was organized with extraordinary efficiency by A. C. Townley.[38]   In 1916 the League won the governorship and legislature of the state by the simple process of capturing the nominating conventions of the old parties and nominating candidates of the League.   The *Guide* hailed the victory of the League as a shining example of what the farmers of the West ought to attempt.   "So long as the farmers of Canada or any other country are willing to vote blindly for either one of the old political parties, just so long

[36]*Grain Growers' Guide*, Sept. 15, 1915, pp. 8 and 18.
[37]*Ibid.*, July 12, 1916, p. 8, article, "Future of Western Democracy."
[38]See T. Saloutos, "The Rise of the Non-Partisan League in North Dakota" (*Agricultural History*, XX, Jan., 1946, pp. 43-61).

will they remain a nonentity in shaping the legislation of the country."[39] Roderick McKenzie, a founder of the Manitoba Grain Growers, went down to North Dakota and reported in the *Guide* what he had learned. "Cannot," he asked, "a number of progressive farmers in our prairie provinces get together, settle on a platform . . . and advocate the measures of reform which the West demands at the approaching general election?" In outlining the steps to be taken in such a campaign McKenzie revealed that he had grasped the key of the League's success when he pointed out that the campaigners, above all, would have "to influence the nomination of candidates."[40] The Non-Partisan League's victory in North Dakota thus quickened the agitation for political action by the farmers of the Canadian West.

The endorsation of the Free Trade League by the farmers' organizations, the *Guide's* campaign, and the example of the Non-Partisan League moved the farmers' national organization, the Canadian Council of Agriculture, to prepare the ground for political action by the farmers, or for the endorsation of their demands by one or other of the political parties, by issuing in December 1916, the Farmers' Platform. This document was a revision and extension of the Farmers' Platform of 1910. The main plank was an emphatic and reasoned demand for the reduction of the tariff. The Platform called for the immediate reduction of the British preferential tariff to one-half the general rates and free trade with Great Britain in five years, reciprocity with the United States, the placing of agricultural implements and supplies on the free list, the reduction of the tariff on all necessities of life and the immediate extension of all tariff concessions to Great Britain. To provide for any loss of revenue through these changes, the platform proposed a direct tax on unimproved land values, and sharply graduated income, corporation, and inheritance taxes. Other necessary reforms were the nationalization of all railways, telegraph, and express companies, the future alienation of natural resources under short-

[39]*Grain Growers' Guide*, Sept. 6, 1916, p. 5, editorial, "Farmers Capture Government."

[40]*Ibid.*, p. 18. The League had captured the nominating primaries and named League candidates without respect to party affiliations.

term leases only, direct legislation, the publication of political campaign funds, the abolition of the patronage system, complete provincial control of the liquor trade, and the admission of women with the provincial franchise to the federal franchise. This strong platform was published with a commentary, the greater part of which was devoted to an attack on the protective tariff.[41]

In preparing and publishing the platform, the Council was not attempting, of course, to launch a third party. It was attempting to carry out what it considered its proper task of defining the purposes of the organized farmers, as they were expressed by the local associations and the annual conventions. The Platform was published as an authoritative statement of the political programme of the organized farmers, in the hope it might influence the policy of government and the platforms of the parties. The procedure kept the non-partisanship of the Council intact, while it did make it possible for the electors in rural electoral districts to put pressure on party delegates or candidates to commit themselves to the support of the Platform, or even to nominate independent candidates.

The latter use was indeed made of it, in seven federal electoral districts in the West. The candidates in these districts, two of whom were Henders and Beveridge, already mentioned, were independent of the old parties, were farmers, and were pledged to support the Farmers' Platform in the general election and in parliament.[42] Whether more might not have been nominated must remain uncertain, for two events occurred in 1917 to upset the strategy of the Council of Agriculture and of the *Guide*. One was the entry into Saskatchewan and Alberta of the Non-Partisan League—Manitoba was not touched; the other was the formation of the Union Government.

The Non-Partisan League spread into Saskatchewan immediately after its political victory in North Dakota in 1916. Its ideas and methods were carried from below the border by American Canadians who had ties on both sides of the line. The sharp class-consciousness of the League, and its advocacy

---

[41]*The Farmers' Platform* (Winnipeg, 1916).   For text, see Appendix B.

[42]They were: J. A. Maharg, Maple Creek; R. C. Henders, Macdonald; J. S. Wood, Portage la Prairie; Thomas Beveridge, Souris; P. Broadfoot, Neepawa; W. J. Ford, Nelson; R. McKenzie, Brandon (*Grain Growers' Guide*, Oct. 10, 1917, p. 11.

of public ownership of essential agricultural services, such as elevators, and of the agricultural processing industries, such as flour mills, recommended it to many farmers. Its system of canvassing for new members through the agency of organizers furnished with automobiles—a novelty on western roads—and paid a percentage of a high membership fee, insured its rapid spread. In the southwest of the province, around Swift Current, where a dry spell was beginning, the organizers of the League were quickly successful. Many of the new members were also members of the Grain Growers' Association. Pressure was at once put on the executive of the Association, and an attempt was made in the convention of 1917 to take the older and stronger Association into politics on the model of the League.[43] The attempt was thwarted by the executive, so skilfully as to leave the impression that the League had never been a serious threat to the Association, nor to the Liberal party.

The impression was further strengthened by the results of the League's own participation in the provincial election of 1917. Caught with its organization incomplete and lacking the support of the Grain Growers, the League succeeded in nominating only eight candidates. Of these seven were defeated, four of them losing their deposits. The eighth, D. J. Sykes of Swift Current, was elected by acclamation, having been nominated by both the Liberal and Conservative organizations, and being, therefore, pre-eminently non-partisan. The Saskatchewan League, rent by quarrels after the election, was never to recover from the rout of 1917. The power of the Grain Growers was greater than ever, and their former choice of co-operation over public ownership, as in the creation of the Saskatchewan Co-operative Elevators Company, was strikingly affirmed in the face of the League's programme of public ownership.[44] The League, none the less, had greatly increased agrarian class-consciousness, and had given the idea of agrarian political action a decided stimulus; thereafter the Grain Growers had to reckon with a more radical alternative to which members dissatisfied with the progress of the Association might turn.

The activities of the League in Saskatchewan during the

[43]Minutes of Annual Convention of Saskatchewan Grain Growers' Association, 1917, pp. 58-9.

[44]Toronto *Globe*, April 18, 1917, p. 7, special correspondence by N. P. Lambert.

fall of 1916 caught the attention of H. W. Johnson of Alderson, Alberta, who carried the gospel back to the western province.[45] A Non-Partisan League of Alberta, independent of those of North Dakota and Saskatchewan, was organized in December, and its first convention was held in February 1917.[46] The Albertan League at once gained the support of the *Nutcracker*, a witty, radical weekly published in Calgary by William Irvine. The *Nutcracker* later became, as the *Alberta Non-Partisan*, the official organ of the League.

The same rapid success in gaining members followed the organization of the League in Alberta as in Saskatchewan. Again, however, the new organization was caught with its preparations incomplete by a provincial election called on short notice for June 1917. Only four candidates were nominated. Of these two were elected, James Weir of Nanton and Mrs. Louise C. McKinney of Claresholm, the latter the first woman to be elected to a British legislature. The Albertan League did not, unlike that of Saskatchewan, go to pieces after the hurly-burly of an election for which it was unready. The central executive remained strong and active, and was not disrupted by the post-election quarrels which had destroyed the League in Saskatchewan. The work of organization continued, with no less noteworthy an organizer in the southern part of the province than J. S. Woodsworth. In consequence of the continued activity of the League, the pressure which it was putting on the United Farmers of Alberta to support political action by the farmers as a class, also continued.

The Albertan League, however, did not confine its political efforts to provincial politics, but nominated four candidates in the federal election of 1917. They were agrarian candidates, and in that wartime election asserted the need of conscripting wealth as well as men. This unorthodox stand led to the imputation that they were pacifists, and all four were defeated.[47] Their participation in the election, none the less, meant that, with the seven independent farmer candidates previously

[45]*Alberta Non-Partisan*, Nov. 11, 1918, p. 6.
[46]*Ibid.*, March 29, 1918, pp. 10-11.
[47]For a full account of the Non-Partisan League in Canada, see Sharp, *Agrarian Revolt*, chaps. v and vi.

mentioned, there were eleven agrarian nominees in the field, that number being one-quarter of the forty-three seats in western Canada.

The incipient political revolt of the western agrarians was not allowed to develop further and run its course. The election of 1917 was not an ordinary election; it was a wartime contest, and the government which called it was the Union Government formed in October 1917. The new government was a coalition of the Conservative party and that section of the Liberal party which had supported the passage of the Military Service Act in July 1917. In December the government went to the country with its policy of conscription for military service and a programme from which the tariff was conspicuously absent. The western agrarians found that their major political concern was to be overwhelmed in the passion and hysteria of a wartime election.

The events which led to the conscription election of 1917 are not part of this narrative. It will be sufficient to note the manner in which the conscription issue of 1917 disrupted the national Liberal party and freed the agrarian western wing from the alliance with the conservative Liberals of Quebec. Since 1911 Laurier and the Liberal leadership had been endeavouring to undercut the Nationalist movement in Quebec. The controversy over Regulation 17, an administrative order of the Department of Education in Ontario, which required the use of English as the language of instruction in the French districts of that province, offered an opportunity. In 1916 Ernest Lapointe, a Quebec Liberal, had moved a resolution in the House of Commons asking the federal government to intervene on behalf of the French in Ontario.[48] On the vote, the Liberal party had split, nine western Liberals and some from Ontario voting with the government and against the resolution.[49]

The vote on the Lapointe Resolution was significant in revealing how the stresses of war, which had inflamed the dispute over Regulation 17, were impairing relations between the two races, and, in particular, were threatening to disrupt the Liberal party. In differences over national policy in war the Liberals

[48]Can. H. of C. Debates, 1916, IV, 3676.
[49]Ibid., 3825-3826.

of the West might find cause for doing what some at least had had in mind since the defeat of reciprocity. The reaction of the *Manitoba Free Press*, the editor of which had been in Ottawa urging western Liberals to oppose the Resolution, was indicative of the rising temper of western, and Ontario, Liberals:

Whatever may be the political consequences of this blunder to liberalism in Canada at large, Western Liberalism will not suffer for it if it adheres to the independence which its representatives have displayed at Ottawa this week. These developments at the capital must tend to strengthen the feeling which has been growing steadily for years that Western Liberals need not look to the East, at present, for effective and progressive leadership. The time is ripe for Western Liberals to decide that they will rely upon themselves—and thus do their own thinking, formulate their own policies and provide their own leaders. Canadian public life will thus be given what it sorely needs—a group of convinced radicals who will be far more interested in the furthering of their programme than in office-holding and will be indifferent to the time-servers and opportunists to whom the enjoyment of office is the be-all and end-all of political existence. "To your tents, O Israel."[50]

It was just such a break in Liberal ranks as this which took place the next year in 1917.[51] When Laurier had declined Prime Minister Borden's proposal of May 1917 to form a coalition of the Liberal and Conservative parties to prosecute the war to its end, the latter, convinced of the necessity of compulsory military service if reinforcements were to be obtained for the Canadian forces in Europe, introduced the Military Service Bill. In the vote on the measure, the Liberal party split. Nine out of fourteen western Liberals voted for it, three were absent, and two voted against it.[52] Ten Ontario Liberals voted for the Bill, and only four English-speaking Liberals from west of the Ottawa, all of whom sat for predominantly French-Canadian districts,

[50]*Manitoba Free Press*, May 13, 1916, p. 17, editorial, "Consequences."

[51]Dafoe Papers, Dafoe to Augustus Bridle, June 14, 1921: "I was," wrote Dafoe, "behind the scenes in most of the negotiations and spent most of the summer of 1917 in Ottawa. . . . The first stage was a struggle in the Parliamentary party between Laurier and his immediate following who were determined to poll the entire opposition strength against conscription, and those members who were determined that under the conditions it was time to abstain from party warfare."

[52]*Can. H. of C. Debates*, 1917, III, 3085.

voted with the opposition. Conscription, like the Lapointe Resolution, had split the Liberal party along the line of the Ottawa river.[53] The conservative Quebec wing, with its inheritance of contractual privilege derived from the Capitulations and the Quebec Act and its sense of limited civic obligation born of its position as a minority in Confederation and the Empire, stood in opposition to the agrarian and radical wing of Ontario and the West, with its democratic assumption of the right of the majority to prevail.

Laurier, however, with consummate skill had made the vote an open one. He hoped still to re-unite the party for the forthcoming election. A united party might well have brought him to power, for the Conservative administration had many counts against it. To many Liberals, however, an election fought on party lines presented grave dangers, the enforcement of the Military Service Act by a party government graver dangers still. A struggle therefore began within the Liberal party, the Laurier and anti-conscriptionist Liberals seeking to hold the party together, the conscriptionist Liberals endeavouring to win a sufficient number of supporters away from Laurier to constitute with the Conservative party a Union Government on terms of equality.

In the contest the hopes of the conscriptionist Liberals came to centre on the West. The Liberals of the Maritime Provinces were divided, the party organization of British Columbia was strongly pro-Laurier; in Ontario the Laurier Liberals succeeded in creating chaos in the party.[54] In the western provinces lay the chief hope of a decisive accession of strength to the conscriptionist forces in Canada. The West had been moving towards independence of the old parties since the defeat of reciprocity, which had in particular injured the prospects of the federal Conservatives in that section. Nor had the provincial

[53]*Manitoba Free Press*, July 7, 1917, p. 9, editorial, "The Vote." See also the analysis of the vote in the *Canadian Annual Review*, 1917, p. 345.

[54]Dafoe Papers, N. W. Rowell to Dafoe, July 21, 1917. See Arthur R. Ford's "Some Notes on the Formation of the Union Government in 1917" (*Canadian Historical Review*, XIX, 1938, pp. 360-1), for the manner in which the Hon. Charles Murphy conveyed the sentiments of the pro-Laurier delegates to members of the subsequent Winnipeg Convention. A copy of the stenographic extracts of speeches made in the Ontario meeting is in the Crerar Papers (see bibliographical essay).

Conservative parties identified themselves with the general reform movement which was sweeping the West. The responsiveness of the provincial Liberal parties to the reform movement had, on the other hand, the effect of increasing the differences between the democratic and agrarian Liberalism of the West and the conservative Liberalism of Quebec and the Maritime Provinces. The struggle over Regulation 17 and the passage of the Manitoba School Act of 1916, issues arising from the right of a democratic majority to impose uniformity, had served to widen the differences to a positive breach. In 1917 conscription, another exercise of majority rule, completed the cleavage. The West by tradition and conviction was disposed to favour conscription and to break the ties of party.

The changing political sentiment of many western Liberals may be traced in the editorial columns of the *Manitoba Free Press*. From being an organ of the Liberal party in 1911 it had evolved into an advocate of non-partisan union government in 1917. At first, though shaken in its allegiance by the defeat of reciprocity, the *Free Press* had denounced the talk of forming a third party in the West.[55] It had supported the reform movement warmly, but had contended that the people of the West, "decisively democratic and progressive," had found themselves adequately served by the Liberal parties of the provinces.[56]

The war, however, had suggested the need of a non-party government to ensure the most effective use of the nation's resources. The Lapointe Resolution completed the evolution towards non-partisanship. Both the paper publicly and its editor privately began to urge the formation of a western, progressive Liberal party which would no longer be controlled by Quebec and which would be independent and radical. For the remainder of 1916 the theme of an independent western Liberal party was elaborated by the *Free Press*. In July it saw the prospect of a fusion of western Conservatives dissatisfied with "Toryism" and of leaderless Liberals "in a great movement that promised to send a body of representatives to Ottawa at the next election which would be numerous enough to give the West,

[55] *Manitoba Free Press*, Feb. 25, 1913, p. 14, editorial note.
[56] *Ibid.*, April 22, 1913, p. 4, editorial, "The Strength of Progressive Sentiment in the West."

at last, the power in Parliament it should wield".[57]   The
American West, it was noted in November, had elected Wilson
over Hughes.   In Canada, East and West as sections were
deeply divided, largely by differences with respect to taxation
and markets; "a compromise on relatively moderate terms
might yet [have been] practicable; but the time for such an
adjustment [was] growing short."[58]

With sectional tension mounting and the war going badly
overseas, the old party affiliations were losing their significance.
The *Free Press* began to reason them away.   The party system,
it argued, was only effective in normal times if based upon "a
reasonable mass of honest non-partisan opinion," in which case
it served "to clarify issues and policies, to fix responsibility for
public measures and to save the country from benevolent but
futile abstractions."   War, however, called for a united effort
by a united nation.[59]   In the increasing intensity of that conflict,
party labels, for the *Free Press*, were being burned away, and
in this it spoke for a growing body of opinion in the West.

The evolution of the paper towards non-partisanship was
completed when Borden committed his government to compulsory military service and invited the Liberal party to enter a
coalition government in May 1917.   "The first effect of Sir
Robert's stroke," commented the *Free Press*, "has been to
destroy for the time being the Liberal party as a national
institution. . . ."[60]   The victory of the Saskatchewan Liberal
party in June provoked the sweeping observation that the
Conservative party was extinct in the West, and that the
Liberal party was breaking up under the stress of war.

The Canadian West is overwhelmingly for the vigorous prosecution
of the war.   It is equally pronounced in its support of national and
fiscal policies which, to the occupants of the ministerial benches at
Ottawa, represent the extreme of heterodoxy.   It has no confidence
in the present Dominion Government as a whole or in any member of
it as an individual.   It admits of no allegiance, either, to the leaders
of the other side of Parliament House.   The Canadian West is in the
mood to break away from past affiliations and traditions and in-

[57]*Ibid.*, July 15, 1916, p. 13, editorial, "Western Liberals."
[58]*Ibid.*, Dec. 26, 1916, p. 7, editorial, "East and West."
[59]*Ibid.*, Jan. 6, 1917, p. 13, editorial, "Partisanship."
[60]*Ibid.*, June 12, 1917, p. 9, editorial, "The Situation at Ottawa."

augurate a new political era of sturdy support for [an] advanced and radical programme. The break-up of parties has given the West its opportunity; and there is no doubt but that it will take advantage of it."[61]

While there was much in this passage that was personal and wishful, there was also much that was discerning and prophetic. The West was moving towards the position at which the *Free Press* had already arrived.

Both the prematureness of the assertion that the national Liberal party had been destroyed in the West and the basic truth of the description of the growing political independence of the western electorate, were revealed by the convention of western Liberals held in Winnipeg in August 1917, and by the convention's aftermath. A "call" for the convention had been sent out from Ottawa in July by a group of western Liberal members of parliament. Their purpose was to obtain from western Liberals an authoritative declaration of support for conscription, and the organization of a western Liberal party which would repudiate Laurier's leadership and enter a coalition to enforce military service. The Laurier Liberals, however, were strong in the party organizations of Alberta and British Columbia, and in those provinces and, to a lesser degree, in Saskatchewan, they elected enough delegates to make impossible a forthright repudiation of Laurier and an unmistakable endorsement of conscription. In consequence of the evenly balanced struggle of the Laurier and Unionist factions in the convention, the major resolutions were verbose and ambiguous. On publication they created the impression that Laurier's leadership had been confirmed and union government and conscription rejected. As Dafoe, one of the principal organizers of the convention, was to write:

The Western Liberal Convention of 1917 was a bomb which went off in the hands of its makers. It was decided upon at Ottawa by a group of conscription Liberals; the intention was to bring into existence a Western Liberal group free from Laurier's control who would be prepared to consider coalition with Borden on its merits but the Liberal machine in the West went out and captured the delegates with the

[61]*Ibid.*, June 28, 1917, p. 9, editorial, "The Saskatchewan Victory."

result that the Convention was strongly pro-Laurier. Active Liberal
Unionists like Calder, Arthur Sifton, Crerar, Norris, Pitblado, etc.,
in place of splitting the Convention up the middle, which was the
policy I strongly but vainly urged, compromised their position and
were nearly lost in consequence.[62]

The defeat of the western Liberal Unionists in the Winnipeg
Convention did not, however, end their efforts to win western
Liberalism away from Laurier. They had failed to capture the
federal organization in the West, but they might yet achieve
their purpose by detaching the provincial party from the
federal, as the leadership of the three provincial parties was
almost wholly Unionist. "The Free Press," wrote Dafoe,
"turned all its guns on the Convention as not representing
Western Liberalism, and, as the sequel showed, it was quite
within the mark in saying so. The entire strength of Western
Liberalism, with exceptions hardly worth mentioning, went
solidly into the Union Government when the coalition government was consummated."[63] The reversal of the verdict of the
convention was brought about by the work of Hon. A. B. Hudson
of Manitoba, Hon. J. A. Calder of Saskatchewan, and Premier
A. L. Sifton of Alberta in swinging the provincial organizations
to the support of Union Government. It was also aided by the
passage of the War Time Elections Act, which struck a heavy
blow at the federal Liberals by disfranchising enemy aliens
naturalized since 1902, most of whom, particularly in Saskatchewan and Alberta had been won for the party by the Liberal
organizations. At the same time the western Unionists appealed
to the growing non-partisanship of western farmers by the
inclusion of T. A. Crerar and Henry Wise Wood in the negotiations for the formation of a Union Government.

How important the attempt to obtain the support of the
organized farmers was thought is revealed by a wire from
Clifford Sifton to Dafoe in August 1917. Sifton was in Ottawa
taking part in the effort to find a non-party leader to replace
Borden as prime minister, many Liberal Unionists and the
organized farmers being strongly opposed to Borden as head of

[62]Dafoe Papers, Dafoe to Augustus Bridle, June 14, 1921.
[63]*Ibid.*

the Union Government.   Of the attempts Sifton said:

If it fails absolutely nothing in sight except to let present people go to country as they are.   It means defeat and national disaster. We appeal to patriotism of Wood and Crerar.   Their presence absolutely necessary.   Carvell, Turriff and two or three other Liberals will be in if it goes through.   Would be a purely war government and no one would compromise political opinion.   We would much like their assurance that we can depend on them if our arrangements succeed.   Main difficulty is to get Conservative[s] to agree but project in hand will be greatly strengthened if they will come in. Idea is for Crerar to take Interior and Wood Agriculture.[64]

This plea for the support of the two farmer leaders, men not hitherto prominent in politics, and whose weight in public life arose solely from their position in the farmers' movement, revealed how thoroughly the need of appealing to the new political independence of the farmers had been grasped and how thoroughly the old limits of party had been transcended.   The old parties had been proved inadequate and it was necessary to go where power was actually concentrated.

Crerar had long been a figure of power among the organized farmers, and Wood had emerged as such in the past two years. In politics Crerar was a Liberal and an agrarian, but a national, not a sectional Liberal, an economic, not a class agrarian.   In his economic thinking he was a *laissez-faire* free trader, holding the creed of the old school of Sir Richard Cartwright and the Liberal party before 1896.[65]   Crerar had formed intimate political ties with the Norris Liberals of Manitoba and with Dafoe of the *Free Press*, and their influence confirmed and perhaps refined his agrarian but broadly national liberalism. In 1917 he was representative, as few, if any, others could claim to be, of both western Liberalism and the western organized farmers.   Wood, on the other hand, was as yet an unknown quantity in politics, and his personal aversion to participation in politics was not appreciated; he was summoned solely as an agrarian leader.

[64]*Ibid.*, Clifford Sifton to Dafoe, Aug. 12, 1917 (deciphered telegram).

[65]*Ibid.*, Dafoe to Clifford Sifton, Nov. 10, 1920: "The fact of the matter is, Crerar is nothing more or less than a Liberal of the type with which you and I were familiar prior to 1896."

Both answered Borden's request to come to Ottawa, and gave their support to the Union Government to be formed under Borden's leadership. Crerar accepted the portfolio of agriculture in the new ministry, but Wood declined, if indeed he was offered, a seat in the cabinet, characteristically preferring leadership in the farmers' movement to political office.[66] In this way the support of the western agrarian movement was put behind the Union Government. That support in part explained the progressive features of the government's programme such as reform of the civil service.[67] From that programme, however, any allusion to the tariff was omitted, and the West, which had done so much to make the Union Government possible, gave its support without demanding a concession on the subject of its closest concern.

Some confusion was indeed created in the farmers' movement by the action of Crerar and Wood. The *Guide* and the advocates of independent political action viewed the emphasis placed on conscription by the Union Government with dismay. The Non-Partisan League was joined by the farmers' associations of the West and Ontario in the demand that, if there were to be conscription of men, there should also be conscription of wealth.[68] They feared the effect of conscription on the supply of farm labour, and were increasingly alarmed by the prospect that the "win-the-war" campaign would drown out the demand for fiscal reform. The *Guide* warned its readers repeatedly of the danger of "fusion" candidates of the old parties eliminating or defeating farmers' candidates, and pointed out the folly of electing candidates on the "win-the-war" ticket for a five-year term when the war would be over in one or two years.[69]

As candidates of the government were nominated across the West, the farmer candidates already in the field were moved to protest collectively that they were supporters of union, that is to say, non-partisan, government, and were committed to conscription, provided it was conscription, not only of men, but

[66]Dafoe, *Sifton*, 425; Ford, "Notes on the Formation of the Union Government," 363.

[67]Toronto *Globe*, Oct. 19, 1917, p. 1.

[68]*Grain Growers' Guide*, X, Jan. 23, 1917, p. 11; X, Feb. 6, 1917, p. 5.

[69]*Ibid.*, X, Sept. 26, 1917, p. 5, editorial, "West's in Danger"; X, Oct. 3, 1917, p. 5, editorial, "The Fusion Movement."

also of wealth, by means of income and excess profits taxes and "national control of every industry affected by war conditions." If such measures of conscripting wealth were adopted, they, for their part, would forgo their demand for the immediate reduction of the tariff.[70] It was charged that the "win-the-war" propaganda was a device employed to shield the big interests of finance and industry from attack. The *Guide* shared this suspicion; the East was taking care of its interests, let the West look after its own, was the view it frankly expressed.[71] The *Free Press*, on the other hand, rebuked the farmer candidates for their attitude, alleging that their fears were groundless, since Borden had consulted the leaders of the organized farmers. Crerar's presence in the cabinet, it declared, was sufficient assurance that the Union Government would not lose sight of the need of reform.[72]

The incipient agrarian political revolt of 1917 was struggling against hopeless odds, and, as the campaign developed in passionate excitement over conscription, was pushed aside. Only five farmer candidates were elected, and they as supporters of the Union Government.[73] The tariff was not generally discussed and the Union Government was not forced to make any commitment on the issue. The western agrarian bloc, which the *Guide* and many among the organized farmers had hoped for, had been headed off. War hysteria and the fundamental nationalism of the West had disrupted the orderly evolution of the farmers' movement.

In the country at large the Union Government was victorious. It had encountered marked resistance to conscription of farm labour, but had overcome it by granting generous exemptions. Otherwise, except in Quebec, the war spirit and ruthless organization overrode the not inconsiderable opposition offered by the Laurier Liberals. The extent of the government's

[70]*Ibid.*, X, Oct. 10, 1917, pp. 11 and 59, article, "Stand of the Farmers' Candidates."

[71]*Ibid.*, X, Oct. 3, 1917, p. 5.

[72]*Manitoba Free Press*, Oct. 5, 1917, p. 11, editorial, "Candidates on the Farmers' Platform."

[73]The successful candidates were: T. A. Crerar, Marquette; R. C. Henders, Macdonald; A. Knox, Prince Albert; J. A. Maharg, Maple Creek; J. F. Reid, Mackenzie. All were leading Grain Growers.

victory was a majority of seventy-one in a House of two hundred and thirty-five. Sixty-two of Quebec's sixty-five seats had gone to the Liberals, a victory which eliminated the Nationalists from federal politics. The Maritime Provinces gave nineteen seats to the government and ten to the Liberals. Ontario, out of eighty-two seats, returned seventy-four Unionists, offsetting Quebec. British Columbia went solidly Unionist. In the continental West, forty-one out of forty-three were Unionist.[74] In a very real sense, since a change of thirty-six seats would have wiped out the Unionist majority, the West might claim to have made the Union Government, and at the cost of sinking its sectional interests.[75]

Thus the war blew up the old party structure of Canada, already groaning under the stresses which the particularism of Quebec and the agrarian sectionalism of the West had imposed upon it. In the explosion went that alliance of Quebec and western Liberalism, of conservative "nationalism" and agrarian radicalism, which had increasingly characterized the Liberal party. What the defeat of reciprocity had done to the Conservative party in the West, the election of 1917 did to the Liberal. At the same time the reform movement and the beginnings of the farmers' revolt against the party system, despite the hope of western Liberals that they might influence the policy of the Union Government, were ridden down by a surge of national sentiment. The western provinces were of federal creation; their basic social and political pattern had been shaped by old Canadian colonization. The West, despite its sectional grievances, was fundamentally nationalist and had accepted Dafoe's dictum that "Canada was in the war as a principal,"[76] as a nation, not as a colony.

Yet the submergence of the political hopes of the organized farmers and of the advocates of independent political action was

[74]*Canadian Annual Review*, 1917, pp. 641-2.

[75]Toronto *Globe*, Dec. 12, 1917, p. 1, "To the West must go the credit of having decided the fate of the Union Government . . ."; P.A.C., Murphy Papers, Political, 1917-19, Frank Oliver to Charles Murphy, Oct. 6, 1918: "It is the West that makes the Union Government. . . ."

[76]*Manitoba Free Press*, Aug. 22, 1917, p. 9, editorial, "An Explanation," in which is printed the text, containing the phrase quoted, of the win-the-war resolution drafted by Dafoe in preparation for the Winnipeg convention.

also a deliverance. The Union Government was, unintentionally, a powerful demonstration of non-partisanship. The electorate of the West came out of the election of 1917 purged of old party loyalties. It had undergone a political emancipation, and thereafter the old traditional ties of party were to remain permanently weak across the West. The effect on the old parties in the West was disastrous. Their federal organizations were destroyed: The Conservative party lost its identity as a federal party. Its three provincial organizations in the West were not used in the election, as the stronger Liberal organizations were called on to fight the Unionist battle. Thereafter the Conservative organizations rusted unused and practically untended from 1917 to 1930, especially in Saskatchewan and Alberta. Within the Liberal party there was civil war, and the factions smarted with bitter animosity. At the same time, the provincial Liberals, in fighting the federal organization of the Laurier Liberals, had not bound themselves to the Union Government. Federal and provincial political organizations were separated, in effect, in both parties, as had been the practice in the Territories. In short, Union Government had created the conditions for the rise of an independent political movement.

After the election of 1917 domestic politics were submerged, as the supreme effort of the war absorbed all the national energy. The cost of war, the mounting inflation, the inroads of rust and drought in the West, the unsettled question of the tariff, these were things which could be borne in silence, until victory released the pressures they were creating. With the release of these pressures there began the disintegration of the government elected in 1917.

CHAPTER THREE

The Beginnings of Political Action,
1919-20

I T I S not surprising that the years 1919 and 1920 saw the disintegration of the Union Government. Indeed, only the length of its life is surprising; this prolongation had much to do with the farmers' movement breaking out of the conventional bounds of the party system. The Union Government had been the child of military necessity. Its formal baptism as a government of national consolidation and bi-partisan reform had been taken seriously by only a few of its more earnest sponsors and not at all by the congregation, the Canadian electorate. With the ending of the war, the government began to decay, and there were few to mourn it. The attempts to prolong its life as a government of reconstruction won little support, and by midsummer of 1919 its future was doubtful. The great question in Canadian politics was whether a return could be made to the two-party system, or whether the breaking of traditional bonds in 1917 would leave a body of independent voters who would seek expression in a new party.

It was made certain in the session of parliament in 1919 that the western farmers had returned to the discontents of 1911-17, discontents inflamed by drought, inflation, and a decade of indoctrination by the farmers' organizations. Western Unionist members of parliament were informed by their constituents that the needs of the West must again be taken into account in the national councils. The members, who had led the organized farmers to the support of Union Government in 1917, had in 1919 either to win impressive concessions from the government,

61

especially in the reduction of the tariff, or face the accusation that they had betrayed, under the enervating influence of Ottawa and the caucus, the interests of their constituents and their section.

The West had put aside its particular views in 1917, but with no intention that they should be forgotten or not brought up for review at the earliest possible moment. The drive for the reduction of the tariff missed no more than a single stride because of the crisis of 1917. In the late summer of 1918 the Canadian Council of Agriculture resumed the campaign, the last action in which had been the publication of the Farmers' Platform in December 1916. In this they were matched by the Canadian Manufacturers' Association and its auxiliary, the Canadian Reconstruction Association, which were organizing the defences of the tariff. On August 21, when the tide of war had definitely turned in Europe, the Council decided to revise the Platform, and appointed a committee, consisting of W. J. Healy of the *Free Press* and its own newly appointed secretary, N. P. Lambert, to bring it up to date.[1] The revised, or rather, transformed Platform was adopted by the Council on November 29.[2]

The new Farmers' Platform, which was soon to be given the ringing title of "The New National Policy," was in fact a comprehensive programme, which, put into effect, would have reshaped the development of the Canadian economy. It was a flat challenge to the "National Policy" in force since 1879, of using the powers of government to foster Canadian manufacturing at the expense of agriculture and the consumer. As one of its drafters wrote, "it was a New National Policy for Canada in contrast with the old National Policy of 1879."[3] The core of the new Platform, as of that of 1916, was the demand for immediate reciprocity in natural products with the United States, the extension of the British preference to fifty per cent of current rates, and the introduction of free trade with Britain within five years, a programme which proposed a complete reversal of the policy of 1879.[4]

[1]P.A.M., Minutes of the Canadian Council of Agriculture, Aug. 21, 1918, p. 18.
[2]*Ibid.*, Nov. 29, 1918, p. 29.
[3]N. P. Lambert, "Reaching Across Canada" (*Ontario Agricultural College Review*, XXXIII, March, 1920, p. 318).
[4]For text of Platform, see Appendix C in this volume.

In approving the new Platform for submission to its constituent organizations, the Council came face to face with a
question of political method, which had already troubled the
farmers' movement. What was to be done with the Platform?
Was it merely to be pressed on the old parties for adoption, or
was it to be used as a rallying point for a new, third party?
The Council was apparently divided on the question, though it
would seem that the original intention of the majority was simply
to repeat the demonstration made by the publication of the
Platform of 1916. "There was little or no expectation," wrote
N. P. Lambert, "that on the strength of [the Platform] a demand for direct political action would be made by the different
farmers' associations at their annual conventions. . . . The
draft of the Farmers' Platform was issued to develop an intelligent, well-informed electorate, not to create a party machine."[5]
When, however, it was resolved to submit the Platform to the
member organizations for approval, the question was raised
whether the formation of a separate political party should be
recommended as the means of implementing the Platform.
The issue was left open, the Council resolving "that this Council
recommends to the provincial associations that they take action
in whatever manner they deem advisable to secure the nomination and election of candidates at the next federal election
who will support and endorse the platform adopted by this
Council."[6] The way was left open to the pledging of candidates
of any political affiliation to the Platform, or to the formation
of an agrarian party. That it was the former procedure the
Council of Agriculture favoured was revealed when in April
1919, it took note of the adoption of the Platform by the provincial associations, and urged that care be taken to appeal to
the electorate at large as well as to the organized farmers.[7]

It is to be noted that the Platform dealt with federal matters
exclusively, and that the Council was thinking of political
action in the federal field only, in November 1918.

The revised Platform was adopted at once by the annual
conventions of the four great provincial associations. The

[5]N. P. Lambert, "From Platform to Party" (*Grain Growers' Guide*, XII, Dec. 10,
1919, p. 8).
[6]P.A.M., Minutes of the Canadian Council of Agriculture, Nov. 29, 1918, p. 29.
[7]*Ibid.*, April 1, 1919, pp. 43-4.

United Farmers of Ontario accepted it, adding two advanced amendments, on December 23, 1918,[8] the Grain Growers of Manitoba on January 10,[9] the United Farmers of Alberta on January 17,[10] and the Saskatchewan Grain Growers on February 18, 1919.[11] In all the associations it was decided that the locals in any federal constituency might organize a political group to nominate and elect a candidate who would accept the Farmers' Platform. The farmers' candidate might be a sitting member, or a candidate of one of the old parties. The test of his acceptability was to be his readiness to be "pledged" to the Platform, that is, to do his utmost to have its terms carried out or to resign his seat in parliament. In the work of political organization, the locals and their political associations were to receive the assistance of the central office of the provincial associations.

The resolution passed by the U.F.A. convention was characteristic, except in its explicit reference to independent action:

Whereas our organization has reached a state of development in freedom from partisanship, in mobilization of thought and numerical strength that political action not only becomes possible, but is now necessary to our continued progress; and whereas the nature of this organization, and the very ground work of its development, demands that it should continue to be independent of any class or party, and free from any sectional influence to the end that purely democratic and independent political action shall be promoted.

Now, therefore, be it resolved: (1) We urge the Locals in the various Federal districts to take immediate steps looking to the organization of district units for the purpose of holding at least one convention each year in each of such Districts; (2) the central U.F.A. office shall, upon request of 10 per cent of the Locals in any District, render whatever assistance it can in calling and arranging for such Convention; (3) the primary purpose of such Convention shall be to discuss ways and means of taking independent political action and selecting an independent candidate; (4) each Convention shall be responsible for its actions in putting a candidate in the field, in financing

[8]*Grain Growers' Guide*, XII, Jan. 8, 1919, p. 5, editorial, "Ontario Farmers' Convention."

[9]*Ibid.*, XII, Jan. 15, 1919, pp. 25 and 29.

[10]*Ibid.*, XII, Jan. 29, 1919, p. 33.

[11]*Ibid.*, XII, Feb. 26, 1919, pp. 36-7.

and electing such candidate, but nothing in this Resolution shall prevent any officer of the Provincial organization giving what assistance he can when called upon.[12]

The effect of this procedure was to refer the question of political action to the locals of each federal constituency. Throughout the summer of 1919 the locals of every federal electoral district in Saskatchewan and Alberta, and some in Manitoba, organized district political associations; no candidates were nominated, but ways and means of strengthening the organization and of raising funds were discussed. A "Liberty Drive" was organized, as the sale of war bonds had been, for raising campaign funds in the electoral districts, and great success was reported. What the results would have been had an election been called in the summer of 1919, can only be conjectured. Presumably a considerable number of farmer candidates would have been elected, some as independents, some as members of one or other of the old parties, especially of the Liberal party in the West. How such members would have conducted themselves in parliament can only be surmised. Cabinet government, with its imposition on the majority party of the need of maintaining the executive, would have prohibited the formation of a "farm bloc," such as was shortly to appear in Washington. Some farmer members would, in all probability, have continued in the futility of independence, and the rest have come to terms with the party system.

It is apparent that neither the Council nor the associations contemplated the organization of a distinct, third party at the beginning of 1919. On the other hand, it is hard to believe that the whole procedure was designed simply to enlighten the public and provide a model platform for farmers' candidates; not even the organized farmers possessed such visionary idealism. When it is considered that the Conservative party could not, with its history of devoted attachment to the National Policy, accept the tariff proposals of the Platform, it is pertinent to ask whether the hope of many of the designers of the Platform might not have been to convert a Liberal party which would soon be attempting reunion after the breach of 1917, and which would be in search of a platform. A tariff plank modelled on that in

[12]*U.F.A. Annual Report*, 1919, pp. 52-3.

the Farmers' Platform would go far to restore the fortunes of the party in the West and in much of rural Ontario. The number of professed Liberals in the Council of Agriculture and on the executives of the associations went far to justify the widely held belief that such was the main purpose of the Platform.

Insofar as this was the strategy of the Council of Agriculture, it was from the beginning threatened by a sudden spread and intensification of the movement for political action by the farmers. By 1919 such a movement no longer attracted only a few individuals in scattered electoral districts. The ending of the political lull of 1918 with the Armistice, the increasing inflation, the drainage of labour to the cities, the prevalence of drought in the south-western areas of the West, had strengthened greatly the demand for independent political action. Only the winning of two provincial by-elections by farmers' candidates in Ontario showed on the surface of politics how the current was beginning to run. Beneath the surface, however, the political movement had acquired an unanticipated drive. Careful observers were aware of the fact. J. W. Dafoe wrote on July 21, 1919: "My own information, which I think is pretty accurate, is that regardless of what the Liberals do at Ottawa [in reorganizing] there will be a farmers' movement in Western Canada, which neither Crerar nor anybody else can control."[13] The possibility was already apparent that the farmers, committed to bring their weight to bear in nominations, would sweep on beyond the intentions of their leaders and elect independent candidates. Such a spirit among the farmers would jeopardize any finely poised plan for bringing Liberals and agrarian radicals together in a low tariff party. "I note that the *Grain Growers' Guide* in its current issue is whooping it up for independent action," continued Dafoe on July 24, 1919. "There is a certain amount of hypocrisy about this for some of the most influential leaders among the Grain Growers—Crerar, Langley, Dunning notably—hope to make a deal with the Liberals; but the fact is they have started something they cannot control."[14]

[13]Dafoe Papers, Dafoe to Clifford Sifton, July 21, 1919.
[14]*Ibid.*, Dafoe to Clifford Sifton, July 24, 1919.

While Dafoe's reading of the situation was correct, the hope that the Liberal party might seek the support of the organized farmers continued for some time longer. Events in parliament meanwhile had further advanced the developing political movement. The demand from the West for a reduction of the tariff had been raised as soon as parliament had assembled. J. A. Maharg, member for Maple Creek, had been one of the independent farmer candidates of 1917 nominated before the Union Government was formed. He had been elected as a supporter of that administration. In addition, Maharg was president of the Saskatchewan Grain Growers' Association and of the Saskatchewan Co-operative Elevators Company. No representative of western agrarianism in the House had better credentials. In the debate on the Address from the Throne, Maharg read the Farmers' Platform into Hansard, and declared that the West demanded a significant reduction of the tariff and the maintenance of a fixed price for wheat. "I wish to say in conclusion," he stated, "that Western Canada is watching this Government very closely. It is also watching this House, and individual members of this House very closely, and unless something is done—I want to be very clear and emphatic in this statement—to attempt to remedy conditions in so far as the West is concerned, you will at least have a number of by-elections on your hands before this House meets again next session."[15]

Notice had thus been served that the demands of the West were no longer to be kept silent. Behind Maharg's blunt warning was the pressure on the western Unionist members from their constituents. So great was this pressure that a separate caucus of western Unionists was formed to attempt to find ways and means of meeting the wishes of their constituents while remaining supporters of the government. Early in April thirty western Unionists met, among them four cabinet ministers, T. A. Crerar, J. A. Calder, Unionist Liberal from Saskatchewan, Martin Burrell, Unionist Conservative from British Columbia, and Arthur Meighen, Unionist Conservative from Manitoba. The caucus revealed a marked determination to obtain a reduction of duties on farm implements, other articles of farm use, and on the necessities of life generally. No dif-

[15]*Can. H. of C. Debates*, 1919, I, p. 540.

ference between Conservative and Liberal Unionists was apparent; western indifference to party ties was developing fast. After the caucus an unnamed Conservative Unionist was reported in the Toronto *Globe* as saying: "I was a Conservative before I was born, and this forming of Union Government has practically given me the first opportunity of seeing national questions in an impartial way. I believe the same influence is at work all over Canada, and that from now on politicians will have to face an independent electorate."[16]   A little later the same sentiment was expressed in the House of Commons by W. D. Cowan, Conservative Unionist member for Regina: "We have had, for the first time, I fancy, in the history of Parliament, a western caucus and in that we have been united. Old time Liberals united with old time Conservatives on the one point that they should try to get substantial reductions in the tariff, because the tariff, as it exists to-day, and as it has existed for a number of years, has borne with undue weight on the people of the western provinces."[17]   A western, bi-partisan caucus was, of course, a novel and potent example for the West to consider of sectional, non-partisan pressure exerted from outside the confines of a government party caucus.

The western Unionist caucus did induce the government, it would appear, to propose in the budget the abolition of the five per cent increase in the British preferential duties and the seven and one-half per cent increase in the general rates, which had been imposed in 1915 as a measure of war taxation,[18] the reduction to apply to agricultural implements and certain of the necessities of life. It was further proposed, as an offset to the refusal to make further reductions, to lower freight rates on manufactured goods moving from eastern to western Canada. In face of the belief of the Minister of Finance, Sir Thomas White, that 1919 was a "war year" and that heavy taxation was necessary to meet the costs of demobilization and reconstruction, the proposals were a fair, if not a generous, compromise between the demands of the West and the needs of government.

They were not, however, so regarded by the West or by a

[16]Toronto *Globe*, April 9, 1919, p. 1.
[17]*Can. H. of C. Debates*, 1919, IV, p. 3475.
[18]*Canada Statutes*, 5 Geo. V, chap. 3.

number of the western supporters of the government. These western members found an example and a leader when on June 6 Crerar resigned from the cabinet on the ground that the proposed reductions in the tariff were inadequate.

When it came to a consideration of what the fiscal policy of the country should be [he said in the House when explaining his action], I found myself in sharp issue with the Government, and holding the views that I did, and representing in the Cabinet, in a measure, the opinion of the farmers of Canada . . . and knowing the opinion of the farmers of Western Canada . . . there was, I felt, only one course for me to follow . . . and that was to tender my resignation to the Prime Minister, which I did.[19]

Crerar's resignation was a major demonstration of the growing force of the western demand for a reduction of the tariff; the strength of this force was further emphasized when on June 18 twelve western Unionists voted for the amendment to the budget of A. R. McMaster, Liberal free trader from Brome, an amendment calling for extensive reductions in the tariff rates.[20] In the division on the budget itself, Crerar and eight western Unionists voted against the government.[21]

While this group had condemned the concessions on the tariff as insufficient, the remainder of the western Unionists were content to accept them as adequate in the circumstances, and voted with the government. In doing so, some defended their action on the ground that they were national representatives, and not the delegates of their constituents, or of the organized farmers. Such was the defence put forward by R. C. Henders, member for Macdonald and president of the Manitoba Grain Growers. Henders, like Maharg, had been an independent farmers' candidate as early as 1915. His fate at the hands of the Grain Growers was indicative of their temper at the time

[19]*Can. H. of C. Debates*, 1919, IV, p. 3329. The *Free Press* (June 7, 1919, p. 9), predicted of Crerar's resignation that it would lead to the emergence "sooner or later of a Western progressive party under its own leadership."

[20]*Ibid.*, p. 3678.

[21]*Ibid.*, p. 3679. The bolters were W. A. Buchanan, J. A. Campbell, M. Clark, T. A. Crerar, F. L. Davis, J. F. Johnston, T. MacNutt, J. F. Reid, L. Thomson and W. H. White. That their action was unprecedented in Canadian history was revealed by an examination made for the writer by Mr. C. Sumner, B.A., of the budget and related divisions from 1879 to 1919.

and typical of that of the western Unionists who supported the budget of 1919. Henders' resignation as president of the Manitoba Grain Growers' Association was demanded of him by the executive of that body. The action was reported at the next annual convention in the curt sentence: "We therefore repudiated his stand, accepted his resignation, and re-affirmed our confidence in the principles of the Farmers' Platform."[22] Western representatives were to be held by every means available to the terms of the Platform. Such was the treatment accorded the man whose impassioned denunciations of the privileged interests in 1912 have already been quoted. The mood of the western farmers had become as uncompromising as the Covenanting ancestors of Colonel J. A. Currie of Simcoe whom the gallant member had invoked in defending the National Policy in the debate on the Address.[23]

The nine bolters on the budget had taken issue with the government on the tariff only. They could scarcely cross the floor of the House even on the tariff, because the parliamentary Liberal party, made up largely since 1917 of representatives of seats east of the Ottawa river, had few low tariff members to bid them welcome. Indeed, on May 9, D. D. McKenzie, member for Cape Breton North and House leader of the party, had expressed himself with considerable frankness on the tariff. "I am not," he said, "a very high protectionist . . . but I cannot help knowing that protection has done much for certain industries in this country."[24] For the member from industrialized Sydney to take such an attitude was understandable, but there was no point in western Unionists breaking with the government on the tariff in order to sit under his leadership. Accordingly, although continuing to give the government independent support on matters other than the tariff, the nine western Unionists moved to the "cross benches," from which only the capture of the Liberal party by the low-tariff agrarians might have removed them. In fact, their action was to prove the beginning of the parliamentary Progressive party.

While the farmers' movement in western Canada was making

[22]*Canadian Annual Review*, 1920, p. 741.
[23]*Can. H. of C. Debates*, 1919, I, p. 566.
[24]*Ibid.*, III, p. 2254.

its weight felt in federal politics, startling developments were occurring in Ontario. There the organized farmers were actually electing representatives to the provincial legislature and were making ready to enter candidates in the forthcoming provincial election. The United Farmers of Ontario had been organized in 1913-14 out of the Dominion Grange and Farmers' Association and the local Farmers' Institutes. It had grown rapidly and had acquired the same representative character in Ontario agriculture as had the farmers' organizations in the West, with which it was affiliated in the Canadian Council of Agriculture. The U.F.O. had also been moved by the same determination as the western associations to have the Farmers' Platform put into effect in federal politics, and had been the first of the associations to adopt the Platform. That measure, however, had not been sufficient to satisfy the determination of the U.F.O. convention of 1919 to take political action. It went on to approve a provincial platform which had been drawn up by E. C. Drury, Manning Doherty, and W. C. Good,[25] all of whom were new leaders in the political movement in Ontario. The platform called for economy in government, the abolition of party patronage, the limitation of government intervention in business coupled with government aid to co-operative enterprise, equal educational opportunities for rural and urban children, good local roads rather than main highways, forest conservation, cheaper electric power, prohibition, direct legislation, and proportional representation.[26] The adoption of the platform was the signal for the local clubs of the U.F.O. to begin the work of political organization over a large part of the province. The U.F.O. had deliberately given its approval to the farmers' entering politics in Ontario.

In doing so, it was really sanctioning a movement which had already begun. In October of 1918 the farmers' clubs of Manitoulin had organized for political action and had elected Beniah Bowman as a farmers' representative to the provincial legislature in a by-election held in that electoral district, in face of strong opposition by representatives of the Conservative govern-

[25]Statement by W. C. Good.
[26]*Farmers' Sun*, Aug. 13, 1919, p. 1; for text of the Platform, see M. H. Staples, *The Challenge of Agriculture* (Toronto, 1921), 147-50.

ment of Premier Sir William Hearst. Thereafter the farmers' political movement in Ontario flamed up, dominating the annual convention of 1919, and leading to the election of J. W. Widdifield, the farmers' candidate, in the by-election held in North Ontario in February 1919. It was apparent that the organized farmers' candidates would be a major element in the general election, which could not be long delayed, as none had been held in Ontario since 1914.

The sudden, fiery zeal with which the U.F.O. acclaimed the New National Policy and entered provincial politics sprang from three main causes, the tariff, rural depopulation, and conscription. Many Ontario farmers and agrarian leaders, particularly E. C. Drury, for many years Master of the Dominion Grange and a Liberal candidate in 1911, had become convinced since 1906, along with their western fellow farmers, that the tariff was a costly injustice inflicted on agriculture. Drury himself had written of the Siege of Ottawa that "the western men [had come] with several purely western questions [but] . . . the eastern men had come on one question only—the tariff."[27] The defeat of reciprocity had been as severe a blow to such men as to the western farmers, and they played their part in shaping the Farmers' Platforms of 1916 and 1919.

Not all Ontario agriculturists were advocates of tariff reduction. All, however, were affected by rural depopulation. The growth of industry in Canada, the growth of the West itself, leading to the development of the transport and commercial centres of both East and West, had caused urban population to gain rapidly on rural after 1900. The acceleration of industrialization caused by the war had quickened the process. Wartime wages had pulled labour off the farms into the cities in both East and West. Complaints of the drain appeared in the correspondence columns of the *Guide*.[28] President R. C. Henders deplored the phenomenon before the Manitoba Grain Growers' convention in 1918.[29] In Ontario, where industry exerted its greatest pull, rural depopulation was most pronounced and most resented. The provincial platform of the U.F.O. placed

[27]Toronto *Globe*, Jan. 4, 1911, p. 1.
[28]*Grain Growers' Guide*, XI, Jan. 9, 1918, p. 11.
[29]*Ibid.*, XI, Jan. 16, 1918, pp. 8, 24, and 25.

it first among the reasons for the farmers' entering politics, and the *Farmers' Sun*, official organ of the U.F.O., concurred in the emphasis.[30]

The loss of rural population was attributed by the farmers to the tariff, which favoured industry at the expense of agriculture. The short working-day and high wages of the city, which protected industry and extravagant governments sanctioned, enhanced the attractiveness of the city over the country. These conditions were maintained by legislatures in which farmers had ceased, it was alleged, to be represented in proportion to their numbers. The remedy for protective tariffs and rural depopulation was therefore to elect farmers to the legislatures who would see to it that farmers' views were taken into account in legislation and administration.

The third cause of the Ontario farmers' irruption into politics, conscription, which many observers thought the prime and main cause,[31] touched the same springs of resentment. The Union Government had been compelled in the election of 1917, in order to make sure of victory, particularly in the rural districts of Ontario, to grant generous exemptions of farm labour from military service. In April 1918, the military situation compelled the government to cancel the exemptions. The action was widely protested by the farmers' organizations and by the Canadian Council of Agriculture.[32] The government, however, stood firm. The U.F.O. thereupon organized a mass delegation of farmers to protest the cancellation by a descent on Ottawa. The *Comptoir Co-Opératif* of Quebec did the same, and there were a few delegates from the West and the Maritime Provinces. The delegation, to the number of some hundreds, was rebuffed by the government and derided by a section of the press.[33]

The effect of the repulse was to crystallize the slowly forming conviction of the organized farmers of Ontario and to a lesser degree of the West, that the farmer would not receive fair treatment from government until he had replaced the lawyers and professional men, who made up the bulk of the country's

[30] *Farmers' Sun*, April 3, 1919, p. 1.
[31] Staples, *Challenge of Agriculture*, 145.
[32] *Grain Growers' Guide*, XI, July 10, 1918, p. 4.
[33] See the infamous "The Sons of the Soil" by H. F. Gadsby in *Toronto Saturday Night*, June 1, 1918, p. 4.

representation in the legislatures,[34] by independent farmers elected by farmers to represent farmers. Such was the burden of the speeches made at a farmers' convention in Massey Hall, Toronto, on June 7.[35] The by-election in Manitoulin in October 1918, had been the first opportunity to express the new conviction, and eagerly had it been seized. In the North Ontario by-election the new viewpoint was forcibly stated by the farmers' local political association when it resolved:

That hitherto the Agricultural interest has not been fairly or sufficiently represented in legislation; and by reason thereof grave errors in legislation have been made, to the grave detriment not only of the farming community, but also, through the farming community, of the whole nation; that in order that the farmers may be properly represented, it is necessary for them to enter the political field; that their representatives in Parliament be non-partisan, and should deal with every question which may arise upon its merits and from the standpoint of the farmer, showing how it will affect the country as a whole.[36]

The organized farmers of North Ontario in their resolution were defining a new aspect of the farmers' movement in politics. The intent of the Council of Agriculture in putting out the Farmers' Platform had been to forward a programme by any reasonable means, by having it adopted in whole or part by a political party, by having it advocated in the electoral districts and parliament by independent candidates and members, or, it might be, even by having it taken up by a new, third party. The U.F.O. locals of North Ontario, however, were advocating a new and distinct principle, that of occupational representation. In consequence there was to emerge from the hitherto inchoate promptings of the advocates of agrarian political action a clean-cut conflict between the proponents of occupational representation and those of a third party, radical in spirit but composite in its elements.

[34]C. W. Peterson, *Wake Up, Canada* (Toronto, 1919), 34-5, gave the relative numbers in the ten legislatures of Canada, in lawyers, 222, other professions, 163, business, 329, working men, 5, farmers, 161. Only 18.3 per cent of the members were farmers, whereas the rural population was over half that of the country. Peterson's estimate was noted at the time.

[35]Staples, *Challenge of Agriculture*, 145.

[36]*Canadian Annual Review*, 1919, p. 384.

It was no doubt a perception of this conflict which led Drury to say at Fenelon Falls in June of 1919: "The Grain Growers of the West and the United Farmers of Ontario form the nucleus of a new party which is going to sweep the two old parties into a single organization, which they really are, a new party that will stand for wisdom, justice and honesty in public affairs; a party untainted by campaign funds contributed by selfish interests, and that will cleanse the whole public life of Canada. . . . We intend to hoe our own row."[37]

The objection to Drury's concept of a new and purified party was that it assumed the continuance of the party system. Many of the organized farmers had come to hold the party system itself to be a positive evil, and wished to replace it by the representation of interests co-operating in government. The farmers' clubs of Manitoulin, in expressing their "Political Views," in effect answered Drury: "In place of partyism we would substitute a fair and equitable representation of all the interests of the country, meeting in Parliament, not to struggle against each other as though the government of our country were a game but to unite in promoting the general welfare of the community."[38] Two ideals were in conflict in the statements of Drury and the Manitoulin Clubs, and the point at issue was whether the farmers' movement in politics was to lead to the formation of agrarian groups in parliament or to the rise of a new "People's Party" in the country.

The entry of the Ontario farmers into politics not only forced into the open the question of what sort of political movement was to be developed, but altered significantly the prospects and spirit of the farmers' movement in the West. Hitherto that movement had been strongly sectional in character. It had been a protest against eastern exploitation of the West. Many of the leaders and members were aware that it was a protest also against the exploitation of one class, or interest, by other classes or interests, but the concentration of industry and urban labour in the East had made the sectional exploitation more apparent. The political uprising of the Ontario farmers served to diminish the sectional aspects of the movement and to bring out its class

[37]Toronto *Globe*, June 27, 1919, p. 7.
[38]*Farmers' Sun*, Sept. 10, 1919, p. 11.

character. The conflict ceased to be so much one of East and West as one of agriculture and industry. The *Grain Growers' Guide* had been truculently western in tone in its early years. In 1917, however, it noted that the rise of the U.F.O. had given Ontario the central position in the farmers' movement, and that the change from a sectional to a national character was clear gain for the movement. The early political victories of the Ontario farmers still further altered its tone, and raised hopes of achievements of a scope quite impossible for the farmers of the West.[39]

The possibilities of a national farmers' movement were also noted by a shrewd contemporary observer, Sir John Willison, one-time Liberal journalist and biographer of Laurier. With Sifton he had opposed the Autonomy Bills and reciprocity and was in 1919 president of the Canadian Reconstruction Association, by means of which the Canadian Manufacturers' Association was fighting the farmers' attack on the tariff. In February 1919, Willison wrote to Premier Hearst urging him to make the tariff an issue in the forthcoming election in Ontario:

> In connection with an argument I made this morning may I point out that if the United Farmers can dominate Ontario the programme of the Western Grain Growers will prevail in Canada. That would mean low tariff, prostration of industries, much unemployment, exodus of Canadians to American industrial centres, summary stoppage of the establishment of American factories in Canada and a great check to industrial and national development. I do not suggest that the tariff is perfect. I think it should be greatly revised as soon as normal conditions are restored although I am not clear that the revision should be downward. The programme of the Grain Growers is industrially and nationally impossible. In Saskatchewan and to a lesser degree in Alberta and Manitoba the Liberal Governments make the tariff the chief issue in Provincial politics. How long can you keep the issue out of Ontario politics since hostility to the tariff is the chief bond of union among the organized farmers[?][40]

---

[39]The editorial policy of the *Grain Growers' Guide* was sectional in tone down to 1917. It changed as soon as the U.F.O. began to stir, noting in that year that Ontario held the central position in the farmers' movement and declaring that the Westerners had always admitted it, knowing that without Ontario the movement would remain merely sectional; X, April 11, 1917, p. 5; editorial, "Organization in Ontario."

[40]P.A.C., Willison Papers, Willison to Hearst, Feb. 19, 1919.

Willison's argument somewhat exaggerated the importance of the tariff in the farmers' political movement, but he rightly perceived the possibility of a national low-tariff party arising out of that movement. What agrarian leaders like Drury, Crerar, Langley, and Dunning hoped for, Willison rightly feared. A force which might prove to be the retribution for the defeat of reciprocity was stirring among the organized farmers.

Before the agrarian Liberals would throw themselves into an independent movement, however, the policy of the old Liberal party towards the New National Policy would have to be decided. The party remained divided by the great breach of 1917. In that cleavage it had lost its western wing and its contingent from Ontario. Among the faithful there was little sentiment for low tariff, and much social conservatism. Eastern Liberalism, in consequence, controlled the party. If it were to be reconstituted as a national, composite party, the return of thousands of Liberals who had voted for the Union Government would have to be made possible, and such concessions made on tariff policy as would win back the agrarian vote of Ontario and the West. To attempt these things, however, would be to risk the danger of inflaming the bitterness which existed between Laurier and Unionist Liberals, particularly among the leaders, and to make concessions sufficient to win the West might be to alienate support in the East. A protectionist speech by Hon. G. P. Graham provoked a warning by Hon. Frank Oliver that such utterances would kill the party in the West.[41] There were rumours that the Quebec Liberals were divided by a contest for leadership between Ernest Lapointe, who represented the *rouge*, or radical tradition in Quebec Liberalism, and the conservative Sir Lomer Gouin and Rodolphe Lemieux, a contest which might result in the two latter supporting the Union Government.[42] Only by great adroitness could the Liberal party close the breach of 1917, hold its supporters in the East, and make the tariff concessions which would head off an agrarian third party in Ontario and the West.

The party was providentially permitted to address itself to this complex task by the death of Laurier in January 1919.

[41]P.A.C., Murphy Papers, Political, 1908-1919, Oliver to Murphy, Jan. 27, 1919.
[42]Dafoe Papers, Dafoe to Clifford Sifton, July 21, 1919.

The loss of the venerated leader was merciful, in that it gave at once a great memory to which to appeal, and occasion to call a national convention to elect a new leader and draft a platform. On May 8, 1919, the house leader, D. D. McKenzie, issued a call to the party to meet in convention in August. The preparations were proceeding when the nine western Unionists bolted in June, and while the farmers' political movement in Ontario waxed stronger during the summer. The work of organization was carried on by Laurier Liberals under the chairmanship of Hon. Charles Murphy, and there is no reason to doubt that the correspondent of the Montreal *Gazette* was correct in reporting of the convention when assembled that "it [was] a Laurier convention and [would] be easily stampeded against any one who [had] shown at any time defection from the late leader. . . . The light [might] be in the window but penance [would] have to be done [by Unionist Liberals] on returning to the fold."[43] In the reconstituted party the Laurier faithful were to dominate, and this augured ill for plans to restore the party's fortunes in the West.

It is, on the other hand, to be noted that the organizers of the convention had appealed directly to the organized farmers. The Canadian Council of Agriculture and the provincial associations had been invited to send representatives to the convention. The Council, however, declined the invitation, and contented itself with submitting to the organizers a lengthy memorandum in which the Farmers' Platform was expounded.[44] Crerar himself was under pressure from Murphy and Andrew Haydon to attend the convention, but declined.[45] Whatever their hopes of a re-invigorated Liberal party, the agrarian leaders, aware of the temper of their followers, were obliged to refrain from anything which would seem to identify them with one of the old parties.

The fate of the Liberal Unionist members of parliament, as distinct from ordinary party members, had meanwhile been decided. After the secession of western Unionists on the McMaster amendment to the budget and on the budget vote, a

---

[43]Montreal *Gazette*, Aug. 4, 1919, p. 1.
[44]*Grain Growers' Guide*, XII, Aug. 13, 1919, p. 7.
[45]Andrew Haydon, the late Senator Haydon, was to be Liberal organizer in 1921.

Unionist caucus had been held on June 26. Crerar and Dr. Michael Clark, Liberal Unionist and doctrinaire free trader from Red Deer, were reported to be the only notable absentees. At the caucus Prime Minister Borden urged that the coalition be continued, and it was so decided.[46] The Liberal Unionists, in agreeing to continue in the Union Government as a coalition, were in effect asserting that it was possible to be at once Liberal and Unionist. But the election of a Laurier Liberal to the leadership of the Ontario party was a repudiation of Hon. N. W. Rowell, chief Liberal Unionist from Ontario. The organization and domination of the national convention by Laurier Liberals made this act of repudiation general. The Liberal Unionists were left a parliamentary rump without support in the country, or a political future as Liberals, an unhappy and unjust fate for many able and honourable men.

The cleavage between Laurier and Unionist Liberals was of much less significance in the largely Unionist West. In Saskatchewan and Alberta the Liberals made a strong effort to bring about unity in the western delegation in order that a low tariff plank might be obtained in the platform. The "call" issued by the Albertan Liberals stressed the need of western unity if the protectionist forces in the party were to be defeated.[47] The Liberal leaders of Saskatchewan, including Premier Martin, emphasized that the tariff would be the main issue in the next election and advanced the claim that support of the Liberal party, which had suffered defeat in the cause of reciprocity in 1911, was the only hope of ensuring a reduction of the tariff.[48] The provincial Liberal convention in Regina actually endorsed in principle the tariff plank of the Farmers' Platform.[49]

In Manitoba, on the other hand, the Norris Government, which had supported the Union Government as a unit in the election of 1917, did not attempt to influence the election of delegates to the convention. Norris declined to attend the meeting of the party organization, giving the Winnipeg strike of June and July 1919, as the reason for his absence. He

[46]Montreal *Gazette*, June 27, 1919, p. 1; Toronto *Globe*, July 19, 1919, p. 6.
[47]Montreal *Gazette*, June 2, 1919, p. 10.
[48]Toronto *Globe*, July 9, 1919, p. 7, report of Martin's speech at the Liberal convention in Saskatoon.
[49]Regina *Leader*, July 12, 1919, p. 4.

declared that his government would wait to see the outcome of the convention before giving its support to the reorganized party.[50] As a result, Norris' own credentials were challenged at the convention,[51] and the Manitoba delegation was given to understand that independence would not be tolerated. Despite the attitude of the organizers of the convention, the western Liberals in attendance continued, by one means or another, to make it clear that their adherence to the party was conditional upon the framing of a platform and the election of a leader such as would enable them to contain the farmers' movement.

In the drafting of the tariff plank of the platform the western delegates had their way, and the plank moved by the Hon. George Langley of Saskatchewan and accepted by the convention was in substance the tariff plank of the Farmers' Platform; to Sir John Willison it was "largely identical"[52] with the tariff section of the Platform. The Liberal plank, however, proved unsatisfactory to critical western agrarians, whether Liberal or independent, because it contained no repudiation of protection as a principle. And Langley's resolution had been accepted with such manifest reluctance by the representatives of the protectionist interests and by the Quebec delegation as to leave little doubt of the sentiments of a powerful segment of the convention and to put the good faith of the party immediately in doubt. The western Liberals had won a barren victory.

Nor did the record and personality of the new leader dispel the doubts engendered by the cold acceptance of the tariff plank. Three qualities were desirable in the new leader. He should be an English Canadian, to balance the long leadership of the late French chieftain. He should be acceptable to Quebec as one worthy to wear "the mantle of Laurier," that is, he ought in 1917 to have opposed conscription and Union Government. He should also be able to win back the western support lost in 1917 All these qualities were available to the convention, but all three were united in none of the five candidates for the leadership, Hon. W. S. Fielding, Hon. G. P. Graham, Hon. W. L. Mackenzie King, Hon. W. M. Martin and Hon. D. D. McKenzie.

[50]Toronto *Globe*, Aug. 4, 1919, p. 2.
[51]Montreal *Gazette*, Aug. 6, 1919, p. 1.
[52]P.A.C., Willison Papers, Willison to Hearst, Aug. 7, 1919.

The support of the solid Quebec delegation, however, was the key to victory, and this support was given to King. On the fifth ballot he was elected over Fielding, of reciprocity fame,[53] by a vote of four hundred and seventy-six to four hundred and thirty-eight. The *Globe* reported that the voting had gone as follows: "The bulk of Mr. King's vote came from Quebec, where his support was solidified. He also carried a scattering Ontario vote, and a following of the 'Old Guard' from Alberta and the Maritimes. Saskatchewan almost solidly, Ontario and British Columbia in large part, and the Maritime Provinces and Manitoba and Alberta partially gave Mr. Fielding his vote."[54]

The new leader was a Laurier Liberal and an English Canadian from Ontario. He had, however, no connection with the West, where he was comparatively unknown. So lacking was he in appeal to the West that his election seemed to an unfriendly observer an effort to redress the effect of the tariff plank: "a western policy and an eastern leader, or, to be more definite, a prairie policy and a Quebec leader," was the comment of the reporter of the *Gazette*.[55] Only by an explicit and prompt endorsation of the tariff plank could King have warmed the hearts of western voters. This he studiously refrained from doing in his speech of acceptance; indeed, in a phrase with which he was to be taunted in after years, he referred to the platform as a whole no more than as "a chart" on which a course might be plotted for the party.[56] King had treated as a matter of general guidance what the western delegates had meant to be specific instruction.

The effect of the Liberal convention in damping the hopes of the West for reduction of the tariff was to remove one of the

[53]Montreal *Gazette*, Aug. 9, 1919, p. 1. The significance of Fielding's defeat to the agrarian Liberals is suggested by the following passage: "As for the Liberals he [Crerar] thinks there is a chance that as a result of the Liberal convention to be held early next month, the Dominion-wide Liberal party may be revived under the leadership of W. S. Fielding with an advanced radical programme. He thinks Fielding is the only man in sight who can lead a re-united Liberal party." (Dafoe Papers, Dafoe to Clifford Sifton, July 21, 1919).

[54]Toronto *Globe*, Aug. 8, 1919, p. 2.

[55]Montreal *Gazette*, Aug. 8, 1919, p. 1.

[56]*The National Liberal Convention: The Story of the Convention and the Report of the Proceedings* (Ottawa, 1919), pp. 199-200.

last remaining barriers to independent political action by the organized farmers. The fond hopes of the agrarian Liberals that they might impose their fiscal policy on the reconstituted party were dashed, and the farmers were proceeding to repudiate the old parties and the party system.

How completely the Liberal convention had failed to attract the support of the western agrarians was revealed by the Assiniboia by-election of September 1919. The Grain Growers had organized in the district to nominate a candidate on the Farmers' Platform and had chosen O. R. Gould as their candidate. No supporter of the Union Government was put forward, and Gould might have won by acclamation had not Hon. W. R. Motherwell, a founder of the Territorial Grain Growers' Association, but also a pugnacious and orthodox Liberal, charged into the arena with more vigour than discretion. It would seem to have been entirely his own decision to contest the election, for, if the Liberals had not already decided to treat the embattled farmers as being merely Liberals in a hurry, they were to do so after the election.[57] Motherwell was defeated by a majority of over five thousand votes, and the farmers returned their first member to parliament. Motherwell's intervention in the election had awkward consequences for the federal Liberals and those of Saskatchewan. It seemed to commit them to opposition to the farmers' movement and was one of the factors which were to force the Saskatchewan government to sever its ties with the federal Liberals, since to have supported Motherwell in his quixotic campaign "would have been a plain invitation to the Grain Growers political party to invade the provincial field of politics."[58]

In agrarian Saskatchewan, Gould's victory was surprising only in the size of his majority. The election in November of a farmers' candidate, T. W. Caldwell, president of the newly organized United Farmers of New Brunswick, by an even greater majority of five thousand, five hundred and ninety-six, was, however, unexpected. Caldwell was returned for Victoria-Carleton in the St. John valley, where the electorate with the

[57]That the Liberals declined to enter a candidate and that they approved Motherwell's entry were both asserted at the time: *Grain Growers' Guide*, XII, Oct. 15, 1919, p. 5; *Manitoba Free Press*, Oct. 30, 1919, p. 13, article, "The Assiniboia Result."
[58]*Manitoba Free Press*, Oct. 30, 1919, p. 13, article "The Assiniboia Result."

immemorial conservatism of the Maritime Provinces had voted Liberal and Conservative time out of mind. Nor did the fact that three cabinet ministers, including Arthur Meighen, had campaigned on behalf of the government and denounced "class politics," diminish the surprising character of Caldwell's victory.[59] The abstention of the Liberals from participation, however, went far to explain the farmers' triumph, as a similar abstention in Glengarry-Stormont in Ontario did to explain the election of J. W. Kennedy, a farmer candidate, over a government candidate. The farmers in their startling irruption into politics in 1919 were spared the trials of three-cornered contests. When a farmer candidate fought an election outside his home district, he might indeed have a hard contest, as did R. H. Halbert, of Dufferin County, in the North Ontario by-election of December 9, which added one more to the string of farmers' victories

While the farmers were winning these startling victories in federal politics, the vigorous campaign of the organized farmers of Ontario had come to fruition in the provincial election. In rather more than one-half the provincial electoral districts, the U.F.O. locals had formed political associations and nominated farmers' candidates. The central executive of the U.F.O., hampered by lack of funds, took little part beyond extending its blessing and giving what aid it could when called upon by the political associations. The farmers fought the election constituency by constituency in a soldier's battle.

As the U.F.O. candidates were nominated, an interesting pattern began to emerge. On September 26, the *Globe* noted that of the fifty-six seats not contested by the U.F.O., forty-six were held by Conservatives and had been traditionally Conservative. Of the fifty-five in which U.F.O. candidates had been nominated, most were traditionally Liberal.[60] The later eight or nine U.F.O. nominations were not to alter this pattern significantly, and the coincidence between the areas of U.F.O. activity and those of the old Grit party was marked. It made evident the basic pattern of the electoral support received by farmers' candidates. That support was drawn from three sources. The first was discontented rural Liberals, disillusioned

[59]*Grain Growers' Guide*, XII, Nov. 5, 1919, p. 5.
[60]Toronto *Globe*, Sept. 26, 1919, p. 6.

by the weakness of the provincial Liberals and suspicious of French and clerical influence in the federal party. The second was frustrated rural Conservatives, weary of voting Conservative to no purpose in traditionally Liberal seats. The third was doctrinaire agrarians, who had repudiated the party system and were working for direct representation by farmers of agrarian interests.

The second group, the Conservative agrarian, was of great interest and importance in the farmers' political movement. Although both Liberal and Conservative party strategists were prone, though for different reasons, to diagnose the movement as one of exaggerated low tariff Liberalism, the fact is that the votes of former Conservatives were not less important to the success of the farmers' movement in politics, than the votes of former Liberals. Even if the Conservative voters were less numerous, they may well have been the margin which gave victory to the farmers' candidates. In Ontario the importance of the Conservative agrarian vote was noted at the time. The *Manitoba Free Press* declared in July that the U.F.O. candidates were supported by many Conservatives who had opposed conscription in 1917, and who followed the U.F.O. in 1919 rather than return to their former party.[61] It later quoted J. J. Morrison, secretary of the U.F.O. and a prickly, warm-hearted old agrarian, soon to emerge as leader of the doctrinaires, as saying that two-thirds of the U.F.O. candidates were former Conservatives.[62] Assuredly many of them were. One of these, H. C. Nixon,[63] made during the campaign a succinct statement of his position: "Although the Nixons have been Conservatives of U.E. Loyalist stock for generations, I have always held myself independent. I voted for a Liberal on Reciprocity and on temperance, and certainly believe that organized farmers must continue independent if they would exert the greatest influence for good in the government of the country."[64]

[61] *Manitoba Free Press*, July 20, 1919, p. 13.

[62] *Ibid.*, Oct. 6, 1919, p. 11.

[63] U.F.O. and Liberal-Progressive member of the Ontario legislature for Brant, 1919-44; provincial secretary, 1919-23; provincial secretary in Liberal government, 1934-43; Liberal leader and premier, 1943-4.

[64] *Farmers' Sun*, July 30, 1919, p. 9.

The election campaign was confused by the many three-cornered contests and by an accompanying referendum on prohibition. When the results were in, the U.F.O. had won forty-three seats, the Liberals twenty-eight, the Conservatives twenty-six, Labour twelve, and independents two.[65] The U.F.O., fighting local contests with scarcely any central direction, had emerged from the campaign with the largest group of members-elect. A sympathetic observer wrote that the organized farmers had at most hoped to hold a balance of power, with only thirty-one seats counted sure, and that they were both surprised and embarrassed by their success.[66] The farmers had sought legislative independence and were faced with administrative responsibility.

It was not long in doubt that the lieutenant-governor would call on the leader of the U.F.O. members-elect to form an administration. The members-elect had therefore to choose a leader and decide whether they would assume the responsibility of carrying on the government. They did not approach these problems as an organized political party. Locally elected, they were responsible only to their constituents. Many were opposed to party government and critical of the conventions by which it worked in the parliamentary system, the primacy of the leader, the discipline of caucus, the rigour of the party line. Some were acquainted with a new idea suddenly published among the organized farmers at this time, the idea of an executive proportionately representative of all groups in the legislature and holding office until dismissed by a vote of want of confidence, which William Irvine had been advocating in the *Alberta Non-Partisan*. W. C. Good, on the morrow of the election, urged the adoption of the principle by the new government in a letter to the *Globe*,[67] and both he and Irvine attempted to persuade the meeting of the members-elect to undertake to form an administration on the

[65]*Ibid.*, Oct. 22, 1919, p. 1; the figures are substantiated by the *Parliamentary Guide*, 1920.

[66]J. W. Ward, "The U.F.O. Landslide in Ontario" (*Grain Growers' Guide*, XII, Oct. 29, 1919, p. 38).

[67]Toronto *Globe*, Oct. 23, 1919, p. 6; Good advocated the election of ministers by the legislature, the ministers to be individually responsible for the work of their departments, the whole to constitute what he termed "the municipal system . . . that system by which all our large businesses and organizations are carried on."

new model.   They failed to have their novel proposal accepted,[68] and the U.F.O. members-elect made no effort to alter the working of cabinet government in Ontario. Nor did they choose an unconventional leader.   When negotiations with Sir Adam Beck, the able but uncompromising head of the Ontario Hydro Commission, broke down, J. J. Morrison, chief of the doctrinaire agrarians, declined the leadership.   The meeting then turned to E. C. Drury, and gave the leadership to a man who believed that the farmers' movement might be the beginning of a new radical party, and who was opposed to its creating a new occupational group.[69] "May we not hope," asked the new leader, "that before long this movement, which has had its birth in our particular class, may expand and broaden till it shall become, not merely a Farmers' Party, but, in a very real sense, a People's Party?"[70]   Drury reached an understanding with the Labour members-elect and began his administration without a majority in the legislature.   The hurried attempt to apply occupational representation to parliamentary government had been only a breeze on the surface of events, but it had clearly revealed the beginning of a split between those who hoped for a third party and those who believed in occupational representation.

The doctrine of occupational representation, however, though present in Ontario, was not to achieve its full definition or to attract its greatest public notice in that province.   It was in the provincial by-election in Cochrane, Alberta, that Henry Wise Wood was to give the new principle of representation clear definition and instant notoriety under the name of "group government."

That the Cochrane by-election should have produced a clarification of this aspect of the farmers' political movement was the result of the unique personality of Wood, and of the

[68]Staples, in his *Challenge of Agriculture*, pages 150-1, gives an account of the discussion at the meeting of the members-elect, but says nothing with respect to the leadership.   Group government was first discussed, then a refusal to form a government, and finally a working alliance with Labour was agreed upon.

[69]Statement of W. C. Good; the decision was not announced until October 29 (*Canadian Annual Review*, 1919, p. 667). See also the extensive account in W. R. Plewman, *Adam Beck and the Ontario Hydro* (Toronto, 1947), 237-8.

[70]*Canadian Annual Review*, 1923, p. 571; the quotation is from Drury's statement on accepting office, Oct. 29, 1919.

influence of the Non-Partisan League in Alberta. The U.F.A. had authorized its locals, as had the other associations, to organize for political action in the federal electoral districts. Like the other western associations, it had not authorized the locals to organize for political action in provincial politics. The U.F.A. had, in short, accepted the strategy of the Council of Agriculture of pressing the Farmers' Platform on the parties and government in what was to be a political demonstration rather than the systematic creation of a third party. In this strategy not much thought was given to provincial politics, though in April 1919 the Council, observing the action of the U.F.O. in entering Ontario politics, had given its approval to the other associations doing likewise.[71]

The decision of the U.F.A. to sanction political action by its locals stimulated the Non-Partisan League to renewed activity. The Albertan League had survived its defeats of 1917. From its foundation it had exerted pressure on the U.F.A. membership and locals to induce that organization to take political action. Wood and other U.F.A. leaders had opposed the pressure of the League with success until the publication of the Farmers' Platform. The League did not consider itself a rival of the U.F.A., and its leaders professed to be interested only in the success of independent political action, even at the cost of its own absorption.[72] It would seem probable that the League, faced with difficulty in maintaining its organization, hoped, after the decision of the U.F.A. to support political action in federal politics, to induce the more powerful organization to accept its programme.

That programme included participation in provincial as well as federal politics. When the executives of the two organizations set up a joint committee to prepare a plan of co-operation in March 1919, little difficulty was found in deciding upon co-operation, or in drafting mutually acceptable articles of agreement. The articles were substantially the political

[71]Such is L. A. Wood's statement in *Farmers' Movements*, page 330, which was probably the contemporary understanding of the Council's action; the resolution in question, however, is not explicit (P.A.M., Minutes of the Canadian Council of Agriculture, April 1, 1919, pp. 43-4).

[72]H. Higginbotham, "Political Action in Alberta" (*Grain Growers' Guide*, XII, April 16, 1919, pp. 7 and 48).

programme of the League; business administration in government, political action in provincial as well as federal politics, the financing of the political movement by its own members, a central office to supervise the activities of the electoral district associations, the acceptance of the *Alberta Non-Partisan* as the official organ of the movement, and the observance of the principle that political platforms should be passed clause by clause at conventions and not as a whole.[73]   These articles were submitted to the federal electoral district conventions of the U.F.A. political associations, beginning with that at MacLeod, and eventually all were ratified by the subsequent conventions in the federal districts where conventions had not been held earlier.   The result was that the U.F.A. was committed, subject to ratification by the convention of 1920, to political action in provincial politics.

The executives of the League and the U.F.A. had meantime established a central political association with O. L. MacPherson of the U.F.A. as chairman.   The work of co-ordinating the political activities of the League and the U.F.A. was then completed, and with that the Non-Partisan League disbanded. Its leaders and the *Non-Partisan* declared that, with the organized farmers of the province committed to political action, the essential work of the League was completed.   Certainly the League had added impetus and conviction to the entry of the U.F.A. into politics, and had infused that organization with its own doctrine and spirit.

The League had permeated the U.F.A. but it had not won a complete victory.   The federal district conventions had witnessed not only the acceptance of the League's programme by the U.F.A. political movement, but also a contest between Henry Wise Wood and the advocates of the League in which the latter were defeated.   The contest was over, not the substance of the programme of political action, but the method of taking action.   The League had fostered a sharp, agrarian class-consciousness, but it had aimed at the creation of a political party open to all farmers and also to all members of other economic interests who might accept the platform of the League. The result would have been the creation of a third party.

[73] *Alberta Non-Partisan*, June 5, 1919, pp. 8 and 14.

The proposal came squarely up against Wood's fear, derived from his experience of the defeat of the Populists in the United States in the 1890's, that the creation of a third party by the organized farmers would lead to the defeat of that party and the destruction of the farmers' organizations. The decision of the farmers' associations to take political action in federal politics and the pressure of the League to have the U.F.A. set about the creation of a third party presented Wood with a dilemma. He was aware that the farmers could not be kept from political action of some kind; but he was convinced that political action as a third party would be disastrous to the farmers' movement. How to escape this dilemma was the problem he sought to solve in 1919. The solution he proposed was that the U.F.A. should enter politics, not to create a third party, but as an organized economic interest or "group." Only in this way, he persuaded himself, could the greatest of the evils of the party system, control from the top by professional politicians and caucus, be avoided.[74]

All democratic organization [as opposed to the "autocratic" organization of political parties] begins at the bottom and works upward [he wrote of the decision of the U.F.A. to enter politics], so we had to begin at the bottom. Now beginning at the bottom, democratically speaking, means beginning with the individuals and organizing them into local units. The U.F.A. had already done this work in the development of the local U.F.A. units. There was no necessity that we should organize other local units purely for political purposes. So we began to build our political organization on the local U.F.A. units. Out of these we propose to build our next higher units, adaptable to the service of political purposes, which would be the district units.

Solidarity . . . must be maintained. . . . For this reason I would strongly advise that the U.F.A. local be the only door through which admission can be had to our political organizations.[75]

By the application of the principle that only members of the U.F.A., and bona fide farmers, could become members of the

[74]An excerpt from a record of an interview with Wood in 1940 by Mr. L. D. Nesbitt, is quoted by permission. "When I could not keep the organization out of politics," said Wood, "I conceived the idea of going in as an organization instead of as a party. I conceived that group government might succeed."

[75]Henry Wise Wood, "Political Action in Alberta" (Grain Growers' Guide, XII, May 7, 1919, pp. 7 and 42).

U.F.A. political movement, Wood sought to ensure that the
U.F.A. would remain an economic organization in politics and
not develop into a political party.   In a long-drawn struggle,
little noted at the time, he succeeded, despite eloquent opposition by James Weir, Mrs. L. C. McKinney, and William Irvine
of the League, in persuading all the U.F.A. district associations
to adopt his principle.[76]   By the end of the summer of 1919 the
U.F.A., therefore, was committed to political action, both
federally and provincially, as an organized economic interest.

Such was the preparation, as it turned out, of the U.F.A. for
contesting the provincial by-election in Cochrane with the
Liberal government of Alberta.   The decision to contest the
election was taken locally by farmers excited by the entry of
the U.F.A. into politics and irritated by the professional non-
chalance with which the Liberal party machine moved into the
district.   The district U.F.A. locals nominated Alex. Moore, a
farmer, to oppose the Liberal candidate, E. V. Thompson.   The
Conservative party decided not to nominate, but gave the
farmers their blessing, and left it a straight fight between the
Liberals and the U.F.A.[77]   The U.F.A. Central Political Association came to the assistance of Moore, and Wood himself entered
the campaign, the first of the U.F.A. political movement.

Wood took the occasion to expound, not only his convictions
with respect to the need of preserving a closed economic organization, but also the deeper social philosophy on which it rested.
This he did in a speech delivered at Crossfield in the electoral
district of Cochrane; a speech of which no complete copy or
record seems to exist.   Wood began the Crossfield speech by
expounding his belief that the course of human history had been
characterized by the conflict of two antagonistic principles,
competition and co-operation.   This exordium was admirably
summarized in a report of the speech in the *Calgary Herald:*
"A synopsis of Mr. Wood's thesis was briefly that there have
been two contending principles at work in the world since the
dawn of history—competition and co-operation, that competition is the life of autocracy and destructive in its tendencies,

[76]*Alberta Non-Partisan*, June 5, 1919, pp. 8 and 14.
[77]Calgary *Morning Albertan*, Oct. 10, 1919, p. 1; report of Moore's reading a letter
from R. B. Bennett approving his candidature and the farmers' movement in politics.

and co-operation is the life of democracy and constructive in character. One principle, he held, works against the other, each tending constantly to a higher plane through reaction upon the other."[78]

The dialectic of the intensifying clash of organized interests, the competitive interests of autocracy, the co-operative interests of democracy, was, in Wood's view, to find its reconciliation in an established "equilibrium of interests."[79] The organized strength of each, founded on the mobilization of every member, would prevent the exploitation of any interest and of any individual. Wood himself phrased it as follows:

We go down there [to Edmonton] as farmers, we ask something we are not entitled to. The other classes are just as thoroughly organized as we, and they will resist any unjust demands, and that resistance of each other will eventually bring them to a common level, on which these great class differences will be settled, and they will never be settled in any other way. . . .

Now, I know we are just as selfish, as individuals, as any other class, and I know that if we were organized as a class we would be inclined to do unjust things, and we are just as bad as any other people and they are just as bad as we are. But when every class is organized, and we come together and find these things will be a resisting force when another class tries to do something wrong, and it is only through the law of resistance that these things will be properly carried out.[80]

From the rough phrases emerges the completed pattern of Wood's thinking on political action. The U.F.A. embodied the farmers of Alberta in a democratic and co-operative association founded on the active participation of every member in the locals. As such, it was a repudiation of the principle of competition which had up to that time dominated economic life, and

[78] *Calgary Herald*, Oct. 22, 1919, p. 1.

[79] L. A. Wood's excellent phrase, *Farmers' Movements*, 338.

[80] *Calgary Herald*, Oct. 22, 1919, p. 1. That there were significant external sources of Wood's idea of group government the writer doubts. The *Farm and Ranch Review* (XVII, May 20, 1921, p. 7), declares that Wood derived the idea from Walter F. Cooling's *Differential Political Economy*, a work the writer has been unable to discover. Cooling did write *Public Policy* (Chicago, n.d., received in Library of Congress, June 7, 1916), in which the idea is clearly expressed. Mr. J. T. Hull assures the writer that Wood had read and possessed an exact knowledge of M. P. Follett's *The New State* (Boston, 1918), which might have been influential if read before the idea was formulated.

the principle of autocracy which had dominated politics. The U.F.A. was committed by the democratic decision of its members to political action. It was not, however, to enter politics as a political party; to have done so, would have been to succumb to the "competition" and "autocracy," the party strife and caucus rule, of the traditional party system. It was to enter politics as an economic organization. In the permanent ties of a common economic interest were to be found that stable base which would prevent political action ending in disaster for political movement and association, as it had done for so many farmers' organizations in the past.

In the Crossfield speech Wood also elaborated the effect political action by an organized economic interest would have on representative government. It would, he said explicitly, legitimize the lobby, and make it the avowed and public basis of government.

Mr. Wood went on to describe what lobbying meant [ran the *Herald's* report] saying it was the obtaining of legislation by hired experts sent to influence parliaments and legislatures by special interests. "When we get all classes thoroughly organized," he said, "and with proper representation through proportional representation, which I understand we are to have soon, then each class will send its representatives to the legislatures and parliaments according to its numerical strength, and the representatives will go as our lobbyists, not hired, but belonging to us body and soul, and go there to settle class differences."[81]

The traditional parties would have no place in a political society of organized economic interests, and no place in a legislature in which such interests were represented. Moreover, the representation of the organized interests in the legislature would lead inevitably to their representation in the cabinet, as Irvine and Good were at the very time proposing to the U.F.O. members-elect in Ontario.

Wood, and those who thought with him, had advanced far beyond the simple political demonstration planned by the Council of Agriculture in the autumn of 1918. They were attempting to graft a programme of guild socialism on the farmers' movement and a programme of group representation

[81] *Calgary Herald*, Oct. 22, 1919, p. 1.

on the political movement. Such ideas were widely current at the time; thinkers like Wood, publicists like Irvine, students like Good, sought their practical application to the fast developing agrarian revolt.

It was the Crossfield speech in the Cochrane by-election which first drew general public attention to the new trend in the farmers' political movement. James Weir, the Non-Partisan League member of the Alberta legislature for Nanton and a sturdy opponent of Wood's policy of the "closed door," denounced the doctrine of the Crossfield speech as "Sovietism." Wood's political opponents in the campaign accused him of attempting to destroy the British system of responsible government, as indeed he was, but not for the reasons his critics implied. To this charge Wood replied good-naturedly, "that the British Empire had never been destroyed by so few people before,"[82] and went on to point to the results of the Ontario election: "In old Ontario a few days ago the farmers did what we are trying to do and the Yanks had nothing to do with it."[83] Protest was general and startled across the country as reports of the speech appeared in the press. Even the *Manitoba Free Press*, detached from its moorings to traditional Liberalism and veering towards cautious support of the farmers' political movement, was shocked by the Crossfield speech. It declared that the new doctrine would establish "the Soviet system" in Canada. To make members lobbyists rather than representatives would be the very antithesis of democratic government. "It [was] the doctrine of class war," and its effect would be to make the representatives of the people the delegates of a class and turn responsible government into "class war."[84]

Nor was the alarm caused by the doctrine of "group government," as it was promptly dubbed, altogether unjustified. Wood's theory of occupational representation was revolutionary in concept, if not in method. It accepted the fact of economic conflict and proposed to institutionalize it. It would have altered in its political application the working of representative

[82]*Western Independent*, Oct. 29, 1919, p. 12; successor to *Alberta Non-Partisan*.

[83]*Morning Albertan*, Oct. 24, 1919, p. 1.

[84]*Manitoba Free Press*, Nov. 5, 1919, p. 13, editorial, "The Farmers and Provincial Politics."

and responsible government. It would surely have abolished, as unnecessary, the traditional party system. "Group government" had immediate and practical effects as well as long-range implications. By attacking the party system and by refusing to recognize any distinction between federal and provincial politics, the advocates of "group government" threatened to upset the political designs of such agrarian leaders and sympathizers as Drury, Crerar, Dafoe, and Lambert. The strategy of these leaders was to guide the farmers' revolt against the old parties in such a way as to force, in federal politics only, a realignment of the existing two-party system in terms of such issues as the tariff. With the Cochrane by-election there had opened right across the farmers' political movement that division, already observed in Ontario, between those who thought to use the farmers' insurgence in politics to form a new radical and low-tariff political party, and those who thought to introduce into provincial legislatures and federal parliament representation of the corporate interests of agriculture.

Whatever direction or form it might take, however, political action by the organized farmers was assured when the winter of 1919-20 began. The Canadian Council of Agriculture accordingly decided in November, after canvassing the situation province by province, to call a conference to provide some central guidance for the political movement. The resolution ran:

Whereas, the new national policy advocated in the platform of the Canadian Council of Agriculture is based upon the broad national economic interests of Canada without respect to any particular class or occupation;

And, whereas, political organization has been promoted within the provincial bounds of Alberta, Saskatchewan, Manitoba and Ontario;

And, whereas, conditions now demand the better co-ordination of the political effort organized thus far for the purpose of electing supporters of the national policy to the Dominion parliament;

Be it resolved, that the executive of the Canadian Council of Agriculture be instructed to invite representatives from the provinces named herein, to a conference for the consideration of these matters.[85]

That the expectation was that a new federal party would emerge from the rapidly developing events was made clear a

[85]*Grain Growers' Guide*, XII, Nov. 19, 1919, pp. 5 and 46; P.A.M., Minutes of Canadian Council of Agriculture, Nov. 12, 1919, p. 75.

month later by the secretary of the Council, N. P. Lambert, who wrote in the *Guide:* "It was decided [in the November meeting], if possible, to co-ordinate the various schemes in each of the provinces into a federal organization. Accordingly, . . . a conference will be held in Winnipeg, under the auspices of the Council of Agriculture, for the purpose of creating what actually promises to be a new national party."[86]

The Winnipeg conference duly met under the chairmanship of Henry Wise Wood. The attempt to form a federal organization at once precipitated a struggle between the advocates of occupational representation, of whom Wood was chief, and the advocates of a new party led by Crerar. While the decision was made to provide central direction to independent political action by the farmers, Crerar and his followers could not obtain anything like a party organization, or a national leader, for the movement. On the other hand, the followers of Wood had to accept a clause in the resolution declaring the intention of the assembled representatives to elect as many supporters of the Farmers' Platform as possible, which invited "the support and assistance of all citizens who believe in the principles of this [the Farmers'] Platform."[87] The farmers' movement as a whole was thus committed to independent political action with the conflict between the advocates of a new party and those of group government still unresolved.

[86]*Grain Growers' Guide,* XII, Dec. 10, 1919, p. 8.
[87]*Canadian Annual Review,* 1920, p. 110; *Western Independent,* Jan. 14, 1920, p. 8.

CHAPTER FOUR

The Progressive Movement and the
General Election, 1920-21

By THE beginning of 1920 the organized farmers were committed
to independent political action. The fact was signalized by
the formation of a definite and permanent agrarian group in
the parliamentary session of that year. Led by Crerar, the
group consisted of eleven members; four were farmers' representatives elected to support Union Government in 1917, four
farmers' representatives elected to oppose that government in
1919, and three western Unionists.[1] The group met in caucus
at the opening of the session on February 26 and formally
constituted themselves the "National Progressive Party." The
name "Progressive" was a natural choice, the term having been
loosely used by the advocates of political action for a decade.
The adjective "national" reflected the new ambition sprung
from the expansion of the farmers' movement into the East and
the determination to fight the old parties on their own ground.
The group was scarcely to be considered a party such as the
old parties, for it lacked both a national leader and a distinct
political organization. None the less, its existence and activities
in parliament meant that the farmers' political movement from
the spring of 1920 had a national focus and an earnest of what
the farmers in politics might achieve.

[1]The members were: T. W. Caldwell, Victoria-Carleton; Dr. Michael Clark,
Red Deer; Hon. T. A. Crerar, Marquette; O. R. Gould, Assiniboia; R. H. Halbert,
North Ontario; J. F. Johnston, Last Mountain; J. W. Kennedy, Glengarry-Stormont;
Thomas MacNutt, Saltcoats; J. A. Maharg, Maple Creek; J. F. Reid, Mackenzie;
Levi Thomson, Qu'Appelle.

While the Progressive party was coming into being in federal politics, the movement for political action in the provinces continued. In Alberta, Wood triumphed in the annual convention over the advocates of a distinct political movement. The convention accepted his principle of political action by the farmers' economic organization, and dissolved the Central Political Association set up in July 1919.[2] In Manitoba, the old Manitoba Grain Growers' Association was transformed into the United Farmers of Manitoba, the title indicating the increased militancy of the members. The change of title was accompanied by an attempt to commit the association to political action. The resolution was resisted by those who argued that the remedies for the farmers' ills lay in federal politics. After a debate of seven hours' duration, the issue was compromised. It was agreed that provincial political action should be left to the initiative of the locals of the provincial electoral districts. If, however, a majority of the districts should decide for political action, the executive of the U.F.M. was to call a convention of accredited delegates to draw up a provincial platform.[3]

The same demand for political action was voiced in the convention of the Saskatchewan Grain Growers. The introduction of the subject into the deliberations had been preceded in that staunchly Liberal province by the election of a farmers' candidate, W. H. Harvey, for Kindersley in December 1919. Encouraged by this victory and stimulated by the organization of the federal district associations, one of which had won Assiniboia, the advocates of provincial political action for the first time sought to press their views upon the convention of the Saskatchewan Grain Growers. They obtained only the passage of a resolution appointing a committee to draft a provincial political platform for submission to the locals.[4] Even this resolution was rescinded before the convention ended, and the upshot was that the matter was referred to the locals for an opinion. Few of the locals responded.[5]

[2]*Annual Report of the U.F.A.*, 1920, p. 50.
[3]*Grain Growers' Guide*, XII, Jan. 14, 1920, p. 5; *U.F.M. Handbook*, 1920, p. 67.
[4]Minutes of Annual Convention of the Saskatchewan Grain Growers' Association, 1920, pp. 86 and 114-19.
[5]*Ibid.*, 1921, p. 32.

The Liberal government of Saskatchewan might still claim, after the defeat of the advocates of political action in the Grain Growers' convention, to represent the agrarian interests of the province. Yet the pressure for political action, both federal and provincial, was such as to make it impolitic for the Saskatchewan Liberals to resume co-operation with the reorganized federal party. The mere suspicion that the federal and provincial parties were friendly had to be met by Premier Martin in a speech delivered at Preeceville on May 5, 1920. He expressly dissociated the "Martin Government" from the federal Liberals, setting forth the view that the association of federal and provincial parties had been harmful in the past. "I have therefore decided," he declared, "that as long as I remain a member of the Government I will devote my time and my best endeavours to the affairs of the Province. I will not be responsible for the organization nor [sic] for the policies of any Federal political party."[6] The farmers' movement, even when it did not result in independent political action, was by 1920 strong enough to prevent the re-integration of the federal and provincial organizations of the national parties, an effect almost as harmful to the party system.

In Manitoba, however, even separation from the federal party, an excellent legislative record, and the presence of one farmer in the cabinet and of nine among its supporters, did not save the Norris Government from attack by the organized farmers when in June 1920, it dissolved the legislature and went to the country. There was, it is true, no concerted attempt by the farmers to defeat the administration; it was too popular for that. The belief that only farmers could properly represent farmers had, none the less, taken hold, and farmers' candidates were nominated in 26 electoral districts out of 55.[7] The contests were local soldiers' battles, fought without central direction or assistance. Attempts, in some instances successful, of opponents of the School Act of 1916, and of members of the Conservative party, to gain nomination as farmers' candidates led to a confusion of political lines. Not only was the intervention of

[6]*Canadian Annual Review*, 1920, p. 755; *Regina Daily Post*, May 6, 1920, quoted in Minutes of Annual Convention of S.G.G.A., 1921, p. 65.

[7]Wood, *Farmers' Movements*, 342.

the Manitoban farmers in the campaign unco-ordinated; it also lacked the drive which resentment of the conscription of farmers' sons had imparted to the political action of the U.F.O. in 1919.

Yet the results of that intervention were startling enough. Twelve farmers' representatives were elected, eight as United Farmers pure and simple, four as covert opponents of the School Act as well. The Norris Government had only twenty-one supporters returned, less than a majority of the legislature; Labour, Conservatives and independents accounted for the remainder.[8] The farmers, by their unco-ordinated efforts, had deprived the government of a majority; if they had been organized, they would have overwhelmed it.

The reorganization of the Liberal party, the commitment of the organized farmers to independent political action, and the loss of six out of eight by-elections in 1919 also compelled reconsideration by the Union Government and its supporters of the decision of June 26, 1919, to continue as a Union Government. Forces were at work among its supporters, too, seeking to bring about a reorganization of the basis of the administration. Conservative Unionists had not anticipated the submergence of their party in a coalition. There was a keen awareness that the unionist character of the administration was wearing thin, and that in fact the Conservative party was being held responsible by public opinion for the record of the government. The increasing weight of the Conservatives in the coalition justified the public in its opinion, and suggested strongly the advisability of a return to party lines. At the same time the diminishing number and influence of the Liberal Unionists made them less and less valuable as colleagues. As a group of thirty votes, they could not be dispensed with, yet their position after the Liberal convention was such that they had no choice but absorption into the Conservative party or political extinction.

To more partisan Conservatives, therefore, the time seemed to be ripe for a return to party lines and a renewal of the Conservative party organization. A move in this direction was made, at the instigation, it would seem, of Hon. Robert Rogers, a notorious partisan and Minister of Public Works in the

[8]*Parliamentary Guide*, 1921, p. 459.

Borden Government until 1917. The Conservative organizations of Manitoba and Ontario in December 1919, and February 1920 respectively, in effect repudiated Borden's leadership,
and the coalition.[9] The revolt was undoubtedly inspired by
the practical consideration that the Union Government had no
electoral organization behind it. As Hon. Arthur Meighen,
Minister of the Interior, commented in a speech delivered in
February 1920:

> The Government of Canada for two years and four months has
> been carried on without party organization, indeed without the
> existence behind it of any definite party at all. The natural conse-
> quences have followed; those of our people who supported the Govern-
> ment and raised it to power, most of them at least, have felt disposed
> not to be unfair. That was the best that could be looked for. No
> one felt called upon to champion or defend. There has been nothing
> in the nature of party fidelity and support on the part either of the
> public or the press, such as every preceding administration has enjoyed.
>
> On the other hand, an opposition organized on party lines, with
> clearly defined press support, has never ceased to attack with all the
> old means of warfare. Besides, another party entity has appeared in
> the political arena, and breathes out threatenings and slaughter
> against us. It entices many of our friends by attacking our foes, and
> its program now seems to be to assail our opponents with words, and
> ourselves with both words and votes.[10]

The electoral position of the Liberal Unionists was even
more perilous; fusion with the Conservative party would destroy
the western Unionists completely.[11] The Union Government
thus hung in mid-air, sustained by no electoral organization,
and isolated from the electorate. There was no possibility of
its creating an organization of its own, and in the face of an
approaching general election there was no choice before it but
to fall back on the Conservative party organization.

---

[9] *Canadian Annual Review*, 1919, pp. 395-6 and 738.

[10] Toronto *Globe*, Feb. 19, 1920, pp. 1 and 3.

[11] Montreal *Gazette*, June 21, 1920, p. 13; also *Can. H. of C. Debates*, 1921, I, p. 483.
The supporters of Union Government met in one caucus; had they also created a
common political organization, the result would have been "fusion"; had they kept
both caucuses and organization distinct, the result would have been "coalition."
F. L. Davis deplored the failure to adopt a consistent policy, Montreal *Gazette*,
June 21, 1920, p. 13. See also J. A. Currie, in *Can. H. of C. Debates*, 1919, I, p. 566.

The increasingly Conservative character of the administration was confirmed by the budget of 1920. Sir Henry Drayton, Minister of Finance in succession to Sir Thomas White, defined the fiscal policy of the government as one of providing for "a thorough revision of the tariff" after inquiry by a royal commission into its operation, in order to provide adequate revenue, stabilize legitimate industries, develop the natural resources of the country, promote trade within the Empire, "prevent the abuse of the tariff for the exploitation of the consumer," and safeguard Canadian interests in the struggle for commercial and industrial supremacy.[12]   The budget itself made no significant concessions to the demands for reductions in the tariff rates.   This fact, coupled with Drayton's statement of policy, was interpreted as committing the government to a policy of moderate protection.   The budget was accordingly a clear test of opinion on the tariff; protectionists would have to support, low tariff men would have to oppose, its passage.   The Liberal amendment was defeated by a majority of only twenty-six, six Liberal Unionists voting for it.[13]   The government was accordingly committed to the defence of the National Policy, the traditional policy of the Conservative party; with it it carried twenty-eight Liberal Unionists, two of the bolters having joined Crerar.   A line had finally been drawn between the supporters of protection and those of low tariff policies, and at the same time the uncertainty as to the character and future of the Union Government was ended.

The air having been cleared, a caucus of Unionists was held on July 1, in which it was decided to form a permanent "National Liberal and Conservative Party," for which a platform was published and for which a new leader was to be chosen.   Hon. N. W. Rowell's announcement of his intention to retire at the same time emphasized the degree to which the foundation of the new party was in fact a revival of the old Conservative party.[14] The Conservative press hailed the decision with great satisfaction.

[12]*Can. H. of C. Debates*, 1920, III, p. 2491.
[13]*Ibid.*, pp. 3077-8.
[14]Toronto *Globe*, July 2, 1920, p. 1.

A National Party with a National Policy [wrote the *Gazette*], that is sufficiently comprehensive to embrace all Canadians of Liberal mind and broad views, who believe in orderly progress, in the value of conciliatory measures, and have firm faith that the future holds in hand a gift of greatness for the Dominion if its people wisely shape its policy.   The Platform of the National Policy is one on which all men of moderation can stand.   It is not a class creed that is offered, nor a sectional policy. . . .   It does adhere to fiscal protection . . . but there is a happy medium in fiscal policy, as well as in other things.[15]

The new party, in short, was welcomed as a party committed to protection; as such, it stood sharply opposed to the organized farmers' political movement.   It seemed in midsummer of 1920 as though Canadian political formations might divide along the line of protection and low tariff, the logical outcome of the long-delayed repercussions of 1911.

The reorganized party promptly secured for itself a new leader.   Borden, worn out by the strain of the war prime ministership, resigned his office after consultation with party members, and advised the governor-general to call on Hon. Arthur Meighen to form a new administration.   Meighen, though a western member who had thundered in 1910 against the "ramparts of gold"[16] behind which the protectionist friends of the Laurier administration sheltered, was a Conservative of Conservatives.   His elevation to the leadership confirmed the character of the party, and brought to the cause of protection a militant champion, whose bitter eloquence and fighting spirit were matched with the needs of a failing government and a desperate cause.

There was need of such qualities in the leader of the protectionist party, for in midsummer of 1920 the farmers' movement was extending into all nine provinces of Canada, carrying the doctrines of agrarian organization and political action into every rural electoral district.   The United Farmers of New Brunswick had been organized as early as 1918, and by March of 1920 were strong enough to be admitted to the Council of Agriculture.[17]   A United Farmers' organization had begun in

[15]Montreal *Gazette*, July 3, 1920, p. 12.
[16]*Can. H. of C. Debates*, 1910-11, I, p. 1917.
[17]Wood, *Farmers' Movements*, 302.

British Columbia in 1917 but its growth had been checked by the existence of Farmers' Institutes supported by the provincial government.[18]   In 1920 the United Farmers of Nova Scotia was formed and the work of organization began in Prince Edward Island in the same year.[19]   The *Fermiers-Unis* of Quebec had sprung up in 1919, in part as a reaction to the rebuff of the anti-conscription delegation of 1918, but the movement had been distracted by competitive associations and political rivalries.[20] Even when allowance was made for the obstacles to organization and the imitative nature of the movement in British Columbia and the provinces east of the Ottawa, the outlook was alarming for the defenders of protection.   The farmers of Canada united in political action might indeed be expected to be capable of reversing the National Policy.

There could be little doubt that, in the provinces where the farmers' movement spread, the new organizations were the result, rather than the cause, of political action.[21]   In the two provinces where the United Farmers were strongest, New Brunswick and Nova Scotia, they plunged at once into politics. In Nova Scotia a provincial platform was prepared, and, though no concerted action was taken, several farmers' candidates were nominated locally for the election of July 1920.   Seven out of fifteen candidates were returned.[22]   Although Labour also elected five out of eleven candidates, the Liberal government of Nova Scotia did not suffer the fate of the Norris Government of Manitóba, that of being reduced to impotence.   In October 1920, however, the United Farmers of New Brunswick were to elect ten members and hold a virtual balance of power.[23]   The organized farmers of Quebec, Prince Edward Island, and British Columbia, on the other hand, did not achieve sufficient strength to risk political action in 1920.

[18]*Ibid.*, p. 307; P.A.M., Minutes of Canadian Council of Agriculture, Nov. 12, 1919, p. 72.

[19]Wood, *Farmers' Movements*, p. 303; *Grain Growers' Guide*, XII, May 5, 1920, pp. 10 and 14; *Canadian Annual Review*, 1920, p. 131.

[20]Wood, *Farmers' Movements*, 304-5.

[21]Wood attributes the rise of the farmers' movement in the Maritime Provinces to rural depression and depopulation (*Farmers' Movements*, p. 301).

[22]*Grain Growers' Guide*, XII, Aug. 4, 1920, p. 5.

[23]*Ibid.*, XIII, Oct. 27, 1920, p. 5.

While the spread of the united farmers was alarming to the defenders of protection and the party system, the results of the by-elections of the summer and fall of 1920 were reassuring after the farmers' victories in 1919. A farmer-labour candidate carried Timiskaming against the government; Fernand Rinfret carried St. James, Montreal, for the Liberals against a Labour candidate; the Liberals also gained Kamouraska by acclamation. The government, however, won Saint John City and County against the Liberals and Colchester against the farmers, both being in the Maritime Provinces. Later in the year it was to carry Yale in British Columbia against a farmers' candidate supported by the Liberals. The farmers, for their part, carried only East Elgin in Ontario, in spite of the embarrassment of having two candidates. The government might well feel that the farmers' insurgence had lost its initial impetus, and that a bold counter-attack would be rewarding.

The new Prime Minister began such an attack in the autumn of 1920, in speeches delivered in Quebec and in New Brunswick. These speeches served notice that the drift which characterized the Union Government had ended. A new administration had replaced it, an administration with character. Meighen defined that character. His government was one committed to the National Policy, to maintenance of a moderate protective tariff, and to resistance to the agrarian demand for "the old Cartwright policy that the [Liberal] government of 1896 found they could not put into effect without ruining the country."[24] It was a national government, neither class nor sectional. "We are asked to believe," he said, "not in so many words, but in fact, that we should have class domination instead of a true democracy, with a government of all classes and for all classes,"[25] as his government was. Meighen denounced the farmers' political movement as promoting not only free trade but also class rule, and as addicted "to Socialistic, Bolshevistic and Soviet nonsense,"[26] to "freak governments and heterogeneous parliaments and experimental policies of state."[27] The farmers were even

[24]Montreal *Gazette*, Aug. 25, 1920, pp. 1 and 6; also Sept. 22, 1920, pp. 1 and 10.
[25]*Ibid.*, Aug. 25, 1920, pp. 1 and 6.
[26]*Ibid.*
[27]*Ibid.*, Aug. 12, 1920, pp. 1 and 9.

declared to be in alliance with "the Winnipeg and Vancouver seditionists"[28] who had promoted the general strikes in those cities in 1919. The government of Prime Minister Meighen was taking up position as defender of traditional policies and established classes in blunt opposition to the marshalling forces of the farmers' political movement.

None of these speeches, however, was delivered in the continental West, just as none of the by-elections of 1920 had been held there. When the Prime Minister spoke in the West in October, his words, while they evoked the plaudits of the faithful in the cities, found no response among the farmers. They were not prepared to listen to a defence of the tariff as a necessity for the industrial development of Canada, or to be moved by reproaches that the farmers' movement was dividing the country along class lines.[29]

A very different approach by W. L. Mackenzie King provoked no warmer response. The tenor of his speeches made during a tour of the West in September had been that no vital difference existed between the Liberals and the organized farmers. In this the Liberal leader misjudged the temper of the agrarian movement. It was a revolt, not only against the tariff, but also against the party system, of which Mr. King was a distinguished proponent and an eloquent defender. J. W. Dafoe commented:

Mr. King was very discreet in his references to the political movements in the West which are outside the old party lines. He devoted his attack exclusively against the Government which, of course, was popular with Western audiences, and he gave his blessing, so to speak, to the Farmers' Party and to the Labor movement, and deplored that they were not co-operating with the Liberals in a common assault against the administration. He may have had hopes that some kind of official alliance could be entered into by which there could be a division of constituencies in Western Canada, but, if so, he will by now have abandoned them if he has the faculty so necessary to a successful political career of seeing things as they are and refusing to follow phantoms. There is not the slightest chance for any alliance of this nature.[30]

[28]*Ibid.*, Sept. 23, 1920, p. 11.
[29]*Canadian Annual Review*, 1920, p. 415.
[30]Dafoe Papers, Dafoe to Clifford Sifton, Nov. 10, 1920.

The farmers were indeed too far committed to political action to yield to the attacks of Meighen or the blandishments of King. The political movement was fully launched and only the approaching general election would determine its extent and force. The fact was formally recognized by the Canadian Council of Agriculture when in December 1920, it accepted the Progressive parliamentary group as the representatives of the farmers' political movement, and recommended Crerar to the provincial associations as the national leader of the Progressive movement. "Resolved," ran the motion, "that the Council of Agriculture recognizes the third parliamentary group in the House of Commons as the present parliamentary exponents of the New National Policy, and gives its full endorsation to their action in choosing as their leader the Hon. T. A. Crerar, and commends him as national leader to all provincial organizations."[31] The associations accepted the recommendations in the annual conventions of 1921.

The creation of the Progressive party was complete. It had been forced from below by the spontaneous action of the rank and file of the members of the organized farmers in Ontario, Alberta, Manitoba, and indeed throughout the movement. Resentment of the victory of the eastern wing of the Liberal party in the convention of 1919 and the growing unpopularity of the Union Government and of its successor the Meighen administration, had contributed to the demand for independent political action. The action of the agrarian leaders in the Council of Agriculture and in the associations in responding to the pressure from below had been slow and hesitant. They had in the majority preferred to try to influence the policies of the existing parties rather than to embark on political action. The failure of the old parties to frame platforms and find leaders acceptable to the aroused farmers had forced their hand. By the end of 1920 the agrarian leaders were committed to leading in the attack on the tariff and the party system forces which they had been unable to control.

While the farmers' political movement had resulted in the creation of a third party, it had not, however, achieved internal harmony at the beginning of 1921. The new leader, in accepting

[31]*Grain Growers' Guide*, XIII, Dec. 15, 1920, p. 3.

the leadership of the Progressive party, had declared: "A man's duty lies largely to the people who elect him, but in a larger, and I venture to say a more complete sense, his duty lies to the whole people of Canada."[32] Crerar, that is, conceived the new party as a national and composite one, the parliamentary members of which would be national representatives and not the delegates of a class. Yet Wood had already promulgated his doctrine of occupational representation, and it had not only found powerful exponents, such as J. J. Morrison of Ontario, but, interpreted to mean that only farmers could adequately represent farmers, had pervaded the whole Progressive movement. This conflict between the proponents of a new political party, which might absorb the left wing of the Liberals and drive the right into the Conservative party, and the advocates of occupational representation, which if established would destroy the old party system, remained unresolved as the Progressive party prepared for the approaching general election.

The two groups within the Progressive movement may, for convenience, be called the Manitoban and Albertan. It was among the Manitoban Progressives, led by Crerar, that the grand strategy of forcing a realignment of political parties on the tariff was most in favour. They had the support of the *Grain Growers' Guide* and its handful of able writers, G. F. Chipman, W. J. Healy, J. W. Ward, and J. T. Hull, and contributors such as N. P. Lambert and J. A. Stevenson. They also had the independent but powerful support of the *Manitoba Free Press*; its editor was indeed to define the purpose of Manitoba Progressivism. "The basis of [such a party as the Manitoba Progressives desired]," the *Free Press* declared editorially, "is already made. It is the common acceptance of an economic policy which makes the encouragement of the basic industries of Canada—agricultural, mining, forestry, fishing—the first charge upon the interest and sympathy of the State."[33]

In Alberta, on the other hand, the concept of group government had received its fullest development. The Albertan Progressives did not think in terms of economic interests advanced by party conflict. They were the advocates, not of party

[32] *Manitoba Free Press*, Dec. 16, 1920, p. 15, editorial, "Sound Doctrine."
[33] *Ibid.*, Nov. 10, 1922, p. 15, editorial, "At the Crossroads."

conflict, but of group co-operation, each economic interest to be represented by an occupational delegation in legislatures freed of the conventions of the party system, such as government and opposition parties. The effect would be a profound alteration, not only of representative government, but also of the economic structure of the country. The economic group of the Albertan Progressives would cut across sectional lines. Being public and legitimatized lobbyists, the members of such a group would act as producers' delegates, concerned with the distribution of governmental favours among their constituents. No longer would the dominant interest of central Canada, by means of a territorial parliament and the party caucus, be able to exploit the hinterlands by the device of free trade within the national boundaries combined with protection against external competition. Group would offset group, and each would look after its own without regard to sectionalism. The Albertans were accordingly comparatively indifferent to the tariff issue, but bitterly hostile to the party system. They did not approve, and would not lend themselves to, the Manitoban grand strategy. As a result, they were difficult colleagues, and their novel doctrines gave support to the embarrassing charge that the Progressive party was a "class" organization.

The division over political strategy was not the only cause of disharmony in the Progressive movement at the beginning of 1921. An issue of economic policy had arisen to divide the farmers; that was the question of whether government control of the selling of wheat was to be continued. In 1917 a Board of Grain Supervisors had been appointed to buy the national wheat crop at a price fixed annually and to act as selling agent for the whole crop. The purpose had been to control the soaring price of wheat in the interests of the war effort of Canada and its allies. The crop of 1918 had been similarly handled. The prospect of the free market being resumed in 1919, with a possible fall in prices, touched off a lively struggle in the farmers' associations. It was a conflict of principle, for the New National Policy, in calling for an end of the protective tariff, assumed the operation of a free market economy. On the other hand a fall in the price of wheat would be a disaster to the financially over-extended western farmers, and the temptation to demand a continuation of price-fixing was strong. The Manitoba Grain Growers had followed their leaders in affirming their belief in a low tariff and the ending of price-fixing for wheat; the U.F.A. followed Wood to the extent of refraining from asking for a fixed price. The Saskatchewan Grain Growers, however, stung by a declaration of the Canadian Manufacturers' Association in favour of retaining the wartime increases in the tariff, and more deeply interested in wheat than the farmers of Manitoba and Alberta, strongly demanded a continuance of a fixed price and government sale. In so doing they undoubtedly expressed the wishes of most western farmers.

The government had responded by creating the Canadian Wheat Board to dispose of the 1919 crop, for which the farmers had been guaranteed a minimum price, but in 1920, the act creating the Board was not renewed. The wheat growers, who had seen the price of wheat controlled in the interest of the consumer, were now inclined to ask that it be controlled in the interest of the producer. Moreover, they had seen in the operations of the Wheat Board a demonstration of the advantages of a central selling agency. The demand arose, therefore, for its re-establishment. To this demand, which was to assume a frantic character with the fall in the price of wheat in the summer of 1921, the leaders of the Progressive movement had to pay heed, however much they might be in favour of a return to the free market, as many, including Crerar, were, and however aware they might be of the constitutional difficulties created by the lapse of the war powers of the federal government. The effect was to widen the cleavage within the Progressive movement.[34]

Immediately, however, the struggle for the Wheat Board had the effect of renewing the impetus of the farmers' political movement, which had slackened somewhat by 1920. As the summer of 1921 passed, and it became apparent that there would be no Wheat Board for the crop of that year, the western farmers turned to political action with startling vehemence. Ten years of frustration and indoctrination suddenly came to a head.

[34]H. S. Patton, *Grain Growers' Co-operation in Western Canada* (Cambridge, Mass., 1928), 200-9.

The signs of this renewed vigour were evident in the spring of 1921. In Saskatchewan the Liberal government mended its fences and anxiously watched the trend of events. The question of committing the Grain Growers' Association to entry into provincial politics had been raised again in the annual convention. After a stormy two-day debate, the matter was again referred to the locals for further consideration and disposition at the next convention. What forces were at work was revealed by the charge that the Conservatives were behind the attempt to force provincial political action and by the attack on the Martin Government's administration of the School Act. "The School Question," it was declared, "goes down to the bottom of politics in this country."[35] The Non-Partisan League had reappeared, "for the purpose of forcing provincial action," said one observer, "[in a province] where the government is so strong in the councils of the Grain Growers that it can probably prevent political action."[36]

Premier Martin met the situation astutely. Before the provincial Liberal convention on May 14, he reaffirmed the separation of provincial and federal politics announced in his Preeceville speech a year earlier, and declared that it was "the desire of the Government that the public business of Saskatchewan should be dealt with on its merits and not confused or affected by issues which affect the whole of Canada and questions which are of Federal jurisdiction." On May 23, J. A. Maharg, president of the Grain Growers' Association, was made Minister of Agriculture. In spite of these measures and the rejection of provincial action by the Grain Growers, a convention of independents, many of whom had already been nominated as candidates for election to the provincial legislature, was held in Saskatoon on May 31.[37] So threatening did the situation seem that the Premier called an election for June, a measure frankly designed to scotch the farmers' entry into provincial politics. The Martin Government was returned, but so serious was the danger that a month's further delay might have meant defeat.

[35]Minutes of Meeting of Directors of S.G.G.A., July 28, 1920, pp. 11-12; Minutes of Annual Convention of S.G.G.A., 1921, pp. 95-100; for brief account, see *Canadian Annual Review*, 1921, p. 780.

[36]Dafoe Papers, Dafoe to Clifford Sifton, Jan. 26, 1921.

[37]*Canadian Annual Review*, 1921, p. 811.

As it was, twelve independents, or Progressives, were elected Grave as the portent was for the Liberals in the province the party had dominated since 1905, it was even more so for the Conservatives. Only three Conservatives had run, of whom two were elected. The historic Conservative vote of Saskatchewan, loyally cast in election after election, had either not been cast in 1921, or had been given to Progressive candidates.

If, however, in Saskatchewan the Liberals were badly shaken but managed to survive the agrarian uprising, in Alberta both old parties were routed. On June 27, a federal by-election was held in the electoral district of Medicine Hat. This by-election was to prove the classic piece of the farmers' movement in politics. The seat had been made vacant by the death of the sitting member, Rt. Hon. A. L. Sifton. A popular and respected native son and one-time member of the provincial legislature, Colonel Nelson Spencer, was nominated as the Conservative candidate. The Liberals refrained from entering the contest. The U.F.A., which had been organized for political action in the district since 1919, nominated a local farmer, Robert Gardiner. The nomination was carried out by election of the candidate from among ten nominees in a closed convention of U.F.A. delegates. Gardiner in his speech of acceptance pledged himself to the principles of group government and, what had become an accepted practice by that time in the Progressive party, placed his signed recall in the hands of a committee of the convention.[38]

The campaign that followed was marked by the frenzied zeal of U.F.A. electioneering, which attracted national attention and concern. Behind the frenzy lay four years of complete or partial crop failure, uncertainty with respect to the price of wheat, and the sense of crusade arising from the farmers' entry into politics. Wood worked actively in the district, and did much to direct the storm of the farmers' campaign. Assurance of victory was increased by the co-operation of organized labour in the city of Medicine Hat. Gardiner won the seat by an unparalleled majority of nine thousand seven hundred and sixty-five votes. It was a shattering defeat for the government, and beside it the Conservative victory in York-Sunbury, New

[38]*Grain Growers' Guide*, XIV, April 6, 1921, pp. 5 and 9.

Brunswick, and the Liberal victory in Yamaska, Quebec, were of little significance. So great was the emphasis of the Medicine Hat victory, that the West seemed to have repudiated the Meighen Government.

The West was indeed in open revolt against traditional policies and parties. In July the Liberal government of Premier Charles A. Stewart called an election. The Alberta government, like that of Saskatchewan, had been friendly to the farmers' movement. The Premier himself was a farmer, liked and respected by the organized farmers. If the cabinet was dominated by professional politicians, it was not because the Premier had not been pressed to take farmers into his administration. He had indeed made an effort to persuade some agrarian leaders to join him, among them probably Wood, but none had been willing. The placing of farmers' candidates in the field was done not as a means of defeating the Stewart Government but as a means of putting an end to party politics and introducing a group of farmers into the legislature. As in Ontario, the farmers sought, not power, but representation, and were to be embarrassed by the quite unexpected magnitude of their victory.[39] As an observer wrote after the election, "it [was] an open secret in Alberta that the Farmers did not really wish to secure enough seats to have to take upon themselves the responsibility of forming a government."[40] The campaign itself was distinguished in two respects, by the revolutionary zeal of the farmers' electioneering, and by the complete absorption of the Conservative party and vote by the U.F.A. Even the recent house leader of that party, George Hoadley, ran as a U.F.A. candidate as the only way "to beat the Grits." As had happened in Saskatchewan, the long Liberal dominance of Alberta drove the Conservatives into the U.F.A. political movement, but there the result was to deliver control of the province into the hands of the U.F.A. The farmers captured thirty-eight out of sixty-one seats, and Herbert Greenfield, vice-president of the U.F.A., became, on the nomination of Henry Wise Wood, Premier of Alberta.

[39]For the substance of this passage the author is indebted to the Hon. J. E. Brownlee, Premier of Alberta, 1925-34. Cf. *Grain Growers' Guide*, XIV, May 18, 1920, p. 20.

[40]Lillie Young McKenney, "Alberta's New Farmer Government" (*Manitoba Free Press*, Aug. 6, 1921, p. 25).

The federal and provincial victories of the U.F.A. precipitated the long-awaited general election. No parliamentary
government, defeated as the Meighen Government had been in
Medicine Hat, could remain in office advisedly. There was
serious reason to delay the election in that redistribution of
federal seats according to the census of 1921 had not been carried
out. In that redistribution the West would have more seats
and the rest of the country proportionately fewer. In the
fierce sectional temper of the West, it was a grave matter to
deny it full representation. Prime Minister Meighen, however,
decided that the repudiation of his administration was too
emphatic to admit of delay in going to the country.

The decision was made public in a speech delivered on
September 1 in London, Ontario. The announcement was also
the opening of the Conservative campaign. The place was
admirably chosen, the setting appropriate. London, with its
trust companies and its industries, was not unfitted to serve as
symbol of the natural and acquired wealth of Ontario. Yet it
was situated in the heart of the rural districts which in 1919 had
returned farmers in political revolt to the Ontario legislature.
If these districts were to return farmer members to parliament,
the western agrarian attack on the National Policy, from which
London and urban Ontario had drawn so much, would be carried
far towards victory. The farmers' movement in politics must
be stopped in Ontario, if it were to be stopped at all.

In this strategic city Meighen chose to begin the campaign
which could hardly end except in defeat, but which, courageously
fought, might bring victory on the morrow of defeat. Before
an audience of 3,000, packed in the Grand Opera House, the
Prime Minister shook off the weight of his government's unpopularity, and passed to the attack. His cause was the
National Policy, the policy of a moderate tariff and of national
development. The fiscal policy of Canada must, he said, be a
national and an independent policy. It must not, and the
words rang in the galleries, be made subordinate to that of the
United States, on which no reliance could be placed:

Surely if we have learned anything from the days of the sixties to
the days of the twenties, we have learned that, situated as we are on
this continent, the young beside the old, the small beside the big, the
scattered beside the colossal, the Canadian beside the American, we

must guard the industrial structure and integrity of our country, and there is only one way to do it.

It can be done by a tariff system and it cannot be done without a tariff system—a tariff system made by the Canadian people for the Canadian people, made on a clear, sound and impregnable principle, and that system must not rest on the insecure foundation of arrangements with the United States. The language I use is the language of Macdonald, but it is also the language of Blake. It interprets the conduct of the leaders of both parties throughout almost the whole of our history, it expresses the considered judgment of the vast body of our people on every appeal from Confederation to this hour. I believe it is the overwhelming sentiment of Canadians today.

He went on to say that in safeguarding the policy of economic nationalism, sanctioned by history and embedded in sentiment, his administration was challenged. "But where does the challenge come from? There is a challenge from the official opposition under Mr. Mackenzie King. They challenge, I know, with muffled drums, and uncertain chorus, and no one knows what is their song or where they are going or what they intend to do." But their platform contained a low tariff plank; let Mr. King say what it meant.

Not there, however, was the danger:

The real challenge comes from another quarter. A new party has arisen in this country. It took its birth in Western Canada. There it flourished and there it has its stronghold still. By adroit organization, by special periodicals, and propaganda, by class appeal, misinformation has been scattered, prejudice has been embedded, and the harvest is a political party whose set purpose is to reverse the fiscal policy of this country. It has grown to full maturity; it has demonstrated great strength. It has carried several contests in rural ridings, and recently in Alberta it registered a triumph by almost ten thousand majority. That is something new upon a tariff issue. They followed that up by sweeping from power the Government of that province. These are facts we cannot ignore, and the manly thing to do is to accept their significance and get up and face them. The breath of life of that party is free trade. . . .

They have brought themselves to believe that the tariff is an instrument of oppression, the godfather of privilege, the foe of the common people.[41]

So did Meighen, seeing that Ontario was the battleground

[41]Montreal *Gazette*, Sept. 2, 1921, pp. 1 and 9.

on which the farmers must be stopped, come out as the fighting champion of protection. He made a direct set at the Progressives as free traders and proponents of class politics, and dismissed the Liberals as vague wanderers in a political abyss. On these lines the Conservative campaign was to be fought, disastrously, for "in ten years the bogey of 1911 had ceased to be terrible."[42] Meighen in effect had accepted the truncation of the Conservative party, and made it a party of principle, the party of protection. No principle, however flexible, could be squared with the diversities of Canadian geography and economic interests. In the National Policy, interpreted merely as a policy of protection, was no integrating formula of victory.

Meighen's attack, however, had struck squarely at the tender spot of the Progressive party. Had the party been captured by Albertan Progressivism, it would not have been concerned with the charge of being a class party, but it would have had to accept the limited vote a party based on occupational representation could hope to obtain in its first appeal to the electorate. The Manitoban variety of Progressivism still prevailed, however, and the leaders, hoping to appeal to urban as well as rural voters, were sensitive to the charge of "class." In his opening speech of October 5, at Brandon, Manitoba, Crerar was concerned to deny that the movement was a class movement, and by doing so went on the defensive. On the defensive in this matter the Progressive leaders thereafter remained. The defection of Dr. Michael Clark, who, having been refused the Progressive nomination in his old seat of Red Deer, came out in opposition to the Progressives and accepted the Liberal nomination in Yorkton, seemed to confirm the class character of the movement. Clark justified his withdrawal from the Progressives on the ground that he had discovered that they had become a class party. There could be no doubt that in Alberta they had become something very different from what "Red Michael," a Gladstonian Liberal, had intended. The vocal doctor's mutiny was somewhat offset by Hon. George Langley's open support of the Progressives in October,[43] but the

[42]*Canadian Forum*, II, Dec, 1921, pp. 453-4, editorial, "The General Election of 1921."

[43]*Manitoba Free Press*, Sept. 28, 1921, p. 13. Wood, of course, thought group government would end "class legislation." The class aspects of his idea had only to do with organization and not with policy.

charge, made by one who had been a member of the Progressive parliamentary group that the party was a class party, though well enough understood in the West, was used to damage the Progressives in the East.

So also was the charge that they were free traders—the "free wreckers" of Meighen's London speech. Crerar was driven to declare that while the tariff was a leading issue, it was not "the only issue." "The supreme issue today," he said, "is whether our government is to be free or fettered, and whether legislation in the future shall be for the few or for the many."[44] What was challenged by the farmers was not the tariff, but the principle of protection. "I stand opposed to the principle of protection," he said at Brandon, "and I trust I ever shall. Our policy rests on this consideration; that the wealth of Canada can be best developed or added to by developing the natural resources of the country."[45] What was envisaged in the farmer's programme was not the immediate introduction of free trade, but the gradual reduction of the tariff, and the increase of direct taxation to make good the loss of revenue. "We recognize," Crerar declared in his election manifesto, "that changes must be brought about in a manner that will give a fair opportunity to Canadian industries, now enjoying protection, to adjust themselves to them."[46] This stand Crerar reiterated in Ontario. At Brampton he declared that Meighen's emphasis on the tariff misrepresented the programme of the Progressives, "because he thinks he can—as has been done in the past—stampede the people, particularly the people of Ontario, on this question of the tariff." The temporary character of the tariff policy of 1879 had been lost sight of, and the tariff was now "a system of exploitation." Yet the Progressive aim was not the abolition of the tariff, but the gradual elimination of the protective element in it.[47]

Similarly Wood, speaking at the nomination of G. G. Coote in MacLeod, declared that the issue was not the tariff. "The

[44]*Grain Growers' Guide*, XIV, Oct. 19, 1921, pp. 7 and 19; text of Crerar's manifesto.
[45]*Ibid.*, XIV, Oct. 12, 1921, p. 22.
[46]*Ibid.*, XIV, Oct. 19, 1921, pp. 7 and 19.
[47]Toronto *Globe*, Oct. 18, 1921, p. 1.

issue is between the political party system and the system we have built up."[48]   Here the accents are those of Woodite Progressivism, but on this point Woodites and Crerarites were in accord for tactical reasons.   They passed together to the attack in denouncing the old party system by which the "big interests" were able to corrupt the electorate and govern the country. Crerar criticized the Conservative party for the way it secured its campaign funds, and challenged both parties to make public, as Progressive candidates were doing, the sources of their funds. As an example of the way in which private corporations exerted an undue influence through campaign subscriptions, he pointed to the uncertainty of the future of the National Railways, and declared that a plot was afoot to turn them over to private interests.[49]   He detected a similar tenderness towards "big business" in the delay granted the Riordon pulp and paper company in the matter of corporation taxes.   The Royal Commission of Inquiry into alleged malpractices of the United Grain Growers Company he curtly dismissed as an attempt by the government to discredit him personally.   In the populist charge that the old parties were the venal agents of the "big interests," both Albertan and Manitoban Progressives found a basis of agreement and an answer to the accusation that they were a "class" party.

The denial of the class character of the Progressive party, however, was not accompanied by a well-planned attempt to win the labour vote, and this failure betrayed the essential agrarianism of the Progressives.   Local co-operation there was, as in the Medicine Hat by-election, and in the Calgarys during the general election.   These instances, however, were exceptional.   Inflation had strained farmer-labour relations; differences of outlook with respect to working hours—the eight-hour day moved the farmer to sardonic amusement—and daylight-saving, widened the breach.   In Ontario, the attraction of rural population into the cities continued to arouse resentment among the farmers.   In the West the Winnipeg strike of 1919, the leadership of which had been condemned by the *Grain Growers' Guide* for preaching openly "the doctrines of Bolshe-

[48]*Grain Growers' Guide*, XIV, Oct. 5, 1921, p. 27.
[49]*Ibid.*, XIV, Oct. 12, 1921, p. 34.

vism, confiscation and rule by force,"[50] had not been forgotten.

Increasingly also the more radical features of the Farmers' Platform, such as taxation of unearned land values and nationalization of coal mines, which might have appealed to the socialistic elements of labour, were ignored by Progressive speakers. On the tariff issue, there was a deep cleavage between the farmers and certain elements of organized labour; the Canadian Manufacturers' Association was able to quote Tom Moore and D. M. Draper of the Canadian Trades and Labor Congress, and J. T. Roster of the Trades and Labor Council of Montreal, as critics and opponents of the farmers' proposed fiscal changes.[51] In Ontario, especially in Hamilton, labour was protectionist, and this constituted one reason for the failure of the U.F.O. to repeat in the federal elections their successes of 1919.[52] Thus the protests of the Progressives against the charge of class, though well-founded with respect to the leaders, were not borne out by the sentiments and acts of many of the followers. Where there was not outright opposition among the farmers to co-operation, it was largely left to labour to come into the movement or stay out as it wished.

Such class isolationism in turn revealed an extraordinary feature of the campaign fought by the Progressives. The movement was directed against the old party system, and in particular against the control by the party organization of the district nominating conventions. Hence no interference with the autonomy of each electoral district, even by the acknowledged leaders of the movement, would be tolerated. The only attempt at organization was to call a convention. This convention then nominated whom the delegates saw fit. Thereafter the election of the candidate was the sole responsibility of his supporters, who subscribed funds, conducted the canvass, and voluntarily carried out the work of the local campaigns. The provincial organization could do little, save supply speakers when requested. National organization there was none, beyond the Canadian Council of Agriculture, which did little more than

[50] *Ibid.*, XII, May 21, 1919, p. 5, editorial, "The Sympathetic Strike," a moderate comment.

[51] *Farmers' Advocate*, LVI, Oct. 12, 1921, p. 1153.

[52] *Canadian Forum*, II, Dec., 1921, p. 454, editorial, "The General Election of 1921."

issue some election literature. Nor was there really a national leader, for Crerar, strictly speaking, was House leader and no more. There was, in addition, no national organizer and no central party fund. The absence of the usual organization of a party campaign in a general election was deliberate and planned. Nothing else would have been tolerated. In such circumstances, no general strategy was possible. Only the speaking tour of Crerar created the appearance of a national campaign. For good or ill, the Progressives failed to transcend their agrarian origins, and won the seats they carried as an agrarian party.

The character of the Progressive campaign was determined by the fact that the independence of voter and candidate was the essence of the Progressive movement. This independence was called "constituency autonomy." The meaning of the term was that candidates should be nominated and supported, not by a party organization, but solely by the electors of their electoral division. "The genius of the Farmers' Movement," wrote the *Farmers' Sun*, "is its freedom from central control."[53] It was a reaction against the practice of the old parties of influencing nominations, "importing" candidates, of sending workers and funds into a district, and generally making the election, not a local effort, but part of the strategy and general operation of the party organization. The Progressives, partly in that parochial spirit Goldwin Smith had thought so strong among Canadian electors, partly as a means of ensuring the election of farmers' candidates, flatly repudiated any such intervention, even by their own organization and leaders. In one instance, a political association refused to entertain the name of a candidate suggested to it by Crerar himself, but in convention nominated him notwithstanding. "Our constitution," Roderick McKenzie had declared, "does not contemplate that in these electoral districts the choice should be made by a party to represent a party, but by the electors to represent the electors. . . . The purport of the movement inaugurated by the farmers is that whenever the time comes to make a choice of representatives to parliament, the electors get together to make their selection."[54]

[53] *Farmers' Sun*, Nov. 14, 1922, p. 6.
[54] *Grain Growers' Guide*, XI, March 5, 1919, p. 26.

Guided by this concept, the farmers had organized their own political conventions, which for the most part were "closed" to all but members of the organizations, and nominated their candidates with a zealous and extraordinary freedom from such prior arrangements as usually characterized political conventions. They next proceeded, following a practice inaugurated by the Non-Partisan League, to raise their own funds locally by subscription, or by a two-dollar levy on supporters of the Farmers' Platform. All electioneering was done by local volunteers, and the election was carried out with the district beholden to no one. These methods were the foundation of the new independence of party ties the Progressives felt, and it was achieved by the deliberate attempt to elect a representation which would not be made up of party-picked lawyers and professional politicians under obligation to the suppliers of party funds.

The representative, being thus freed of party ties, was at the same time placed under obligation to his constituents. He belonged to them in the first place, by every tie of neighbourhood and common endeavour. The effects of Ottawa, Toronto, Winnipeg, or Edmonton, however, on the homespun virtues and clear-cut views of members were notorious. How was the new model representative to be saved from the seducing wiles of politicians, the delights of Winnipeg, the enervating air of Ottawa? To this flaw in representative government, that the representative ceases to be representative while serving, the Progressives had given much thought. They had approved many of the devices which the American Progressives had instituted south of the border. One such was the recall. Several Canadian Progressive candidates were required to deposit a signed "recall," a formal resignation, in the hands of a committee of the nominating convention. The practice had first come to public notice in the Assiniboia by-election of 1919, and the Progressive victor, O. R. Gould, had been challenged on the point in the next session of the House. Gould's admission that he had signed a recall had provoked a motion to have the practice made illegal by the Dominion Franchise Bill then before the House, which had failed of adoption.[55]   Much concern

[55]*Can. H. of C. Debates*, 1920, II, p. 1185; III, pp. 2027, 2030, and 2037.

had been expressed in parliament and the press over the unorthodox procedure, but to little effect. Many, if not most, of the western Progressives elected in 1921 were subject to recall.

The recall was a weapon for use in emergency only; for ordinary times the instruction of representatives was a more effective procedure. The Progressives were peculiarly jealous of their representatives, demanding the maintenance of close and full communications between them and constituencies by mail, press, and the spoken word. To the general terms of the Farmers' Platform were often added local platforms, which were held to be binding on the representative. J. J. Morrison had aptly expressed this Progressive attitude when, after repeating his favourite definition of democracy as "the consensus of opinion of the majority of the people crystallized into law," he had gone on to ask: "How can the consensus of the majority of the people be followed when a man is elected and does not see his electors for four years? Democratic government is impossible without contact. It is necessary to find out the will of the people."[56] Woe to the Progressive member who should neglect to mend his fences! On current issues and on matters not foreseen by drafters of platforms, the representative might receive direction from his constituency political association, from locals or, particularly in the case of the U.F.A., from the annual conventions of the organization, the U.F.A. considering members to be representatives of the organization as well as of their constituents. From 1922 on, for example, the U.F.A. federal representatives were given directives by the annual conventions, as occasion required, and always considered themselves to be bound not by the terms of the Farmers' Platform, but by the Declaration of Principles adopted by the U.F.A. in 1921. The Declaration in part read: "Our organization is continuously in authority and while through it we formulate declarations of principles, or a so-called platform, these are at all times subject to change by the organization."[57] This was to raise the question of the relative authority of the convention and the constituency association over the representative. Meantime its effect was to make the U.F.A. member a decidedly inde-

[56] *Farmers' Sun*, July 31, 1919, p. 3.
[57] *Annual Report of the U.F.A.*, 1921, p. 39.

pendent and difficult colleague in an attempt to form a parliamentary party.

With such new methods did the Progressives fight the campaign, and while they and the Conservatives attacked one another on the tariff and agrarian issues, the Liberals held "a midway position."[58] "To support the Government of today is to endorse reaction; to experiment with class in matters of government is to invite the unknown," declared King at Toronto. "The Liberal party with its traditions and aspirations offers a means of escape from both extremes, neither of which is in the national interest."[59] It was not a position to be despised, though its possibilities were somewhat underestimated at the time.

The Liberals began with sixty-odd seats from Quebec secure. At least half those of the Maritime Provinces could be added. The French seats of Ontario could be counted on. Some seats in British Columbia were safe. The problem for the Liberal strategists was therefore to win some Liberal representation in the areas where the Progressives were at their weakest. How could this be done? By opposing Progressive candidates, and taking the very doubtful risks of battle, or by looking to post-electoral coalition? The problem had been approached cautiously by King in his western tour of 1920. In general, the line then decided on was followed: to avoid opposition, to fight no Progressive candidate deliberately unless local circumstances so required, to point to the agrarian record of the party, and to leave the way open for accommodation. A very real effort was made by King and Andrew Haydon, Liberal organizer, on the one hand, and Crerar, Drury, Morrison, and Wood, on the other, to avoid three-cornered contests, but their efforts were defeated by local agrarian sentiment or ambition and, in some instances perhaps, by Conservative tactics. The Progressives, in the view affected by the Liberal strategists, were merely Liberals in a hurry. An election pamphlet stated the matter succinctly: "Liberals and Farmers should unite . . . there never

---

[58]O. D. Skelton, "The Canadian Election" (*New Republic*, XXVIII, Nov. 23, 1921, p. 368); *Canadian Forum*, II, Dec., 1921, pp. 453-4, editorial, "The General Election of 1921."

[59]Montreal *Gazette*, Sept. 21, 1921, p. 11.

was a Farmers' Party while the Liberals were in power."[60]

Another feature of Liberal strategy was to avoid a commitment on tariff policy. King, as noted above, had by no means crossed the *t*'s and dotted the *i*'s of the tariff plank of the platform of 1919. Some of his eastern followers more or less openly repudiated it, as did F. F. Pardee before the Reform Club of Montreal. French Liberals made no bones of their intention that there should be no great changes in the tariff, and appealed to the electors in those terms. "Why throw stones at us on the tariff?" asked P. J. A. Cardin, Liberal candidate in Richelieu. "Why should people fear the return of the Liberals to power as far as the tariff is concerned? . . . The Liberal party protects, and will continue to protect, the legitimate aspirations of financiers, manufacturers, merchants, and also looks after the interest of the mass of the people, and wants a tariff by which Canada can develop and all citizens be happy to live in their country."[61] And at an elaborately staged banquet for King in Montreal, Gouin, Lemieux and Premier Taschereau rang the changes on the need of maintaining the "Laurier tariff," and subtly implied what would be the consequences of any departure from this policy.[62]

King himself spoke with varying degrees of emphasis, and ranged widely. He made a low-tariff pronouncement in West Toronto in which he declared: "It is for the principle of a tariff of revenue that the Liberal party has stood in by-gone years; it is for that principle that the Liberal party stands today, and it is for the principle of a tariff for revenue that the Liberal party will continue to stand, if returned to power in the present conflict."[63] At Summerside he reiterated the reference in his speech accepting the leadership to the platform and the tariff plank of 1919 as "a chart."[64] At Melville he denied that he had ever deviated from the principle of a tariff for revenue.[65] The climax was reached in his declaration at Brantford in favour of

[60]P.A.C., Pamphlet No. 5081, "Group Government Compared with Responsible Government" (published by Liberal National Committee).

[61]Montreal *Gazette*, Sept. 21, 1921, p. 8.

[62]*Ibid.*, Sept. 25, 1921, p. 8.

[63]Toronto *Globe*, Sept. 21, 1921, p. 1.

[64]*Canadian Annual Review*, 1921, p. 460.

[65]*Ibid.*, p. 462.

a revenue tariff which would protect industries, farmers, and people of all classes, except the wealthy, and their monopolies, mergers, trusts, and combines.[66] In all this King was advocating, with appropriate local stresses, a revenue tariff with incidental protection.[67] The assiduous search for a policy to fit all the angularities of the diverse sections and interests of Canada laid King open to Meighen's classic gibe at his interpretation of the platform of 1919 as being: "Protection on apples in British Columbia, Free Trade in the Prairie Provinces and rural parts of Ontario, Protection in industrial centres in Ontario, Conscription in Quebec and Humbug in the Maritimes."[68] This had the Meighen sting, but while it was unjust to King, it was by no means an unfair version of the diverse views expressed by his local followers.

A more positive feature of King's campaign was his attack on the government's use of orders-in-council as unconstitutional and on the government itself as being without a mandate since the end of the war. He denounced government by order-in-council and the prolonging of the life of parliament after the confidence of the electorate had clearly been lost. "The only difference," he asserted, "between Mr. Meighen and Lenine [sic] and Trotsky is that the latter use physical violence to retain power while Mr. Meighen uses legislative violence."[69] The line of attack seemed to have little effect in the campaign, which was dominated by the tariff and class issues, but it was an interesting forecast of the new leader's devotion to that popular democracy, the democracy of the mandate and the plebiscite, which had made its appearance in the Liberal party under Laurier. Here was a leader who was a democrat rather than a liberal, whose constitutionalism was in effect, as in 1926, to reduce the constitution to the results of the latest election. It was to be one of the curiosities of Canadian politics that King's French followers were seldom to note where this democratic logic

---

[66]*Ibid.*, p. 463.

[67]Skelton, "The Canadian Election," 368.

[68]*Canadian Annual Review*, 1921, p. 454. The passage occurred in a speech delivered in Montreal on November 14, which is reported in the *Gazette*, but not verbatim.

[69]*Ibid.*, p. 460.

led in a country in which the French were a permanent minority.[70]

The Liberal strategy, however, if not clear-cut or heroic,
was realistic. There was a search for an integrating formula of
victory which would create a national majority and orientate
the sections and racial communities of Canada along some
agreed line of policy. In 1921, resentments were to prove too
hot and divisions too deep for such a formula to be found, but
the Liberals were seeking the foundations of a traditional
composite party in a way the uncompromising stand and desperate fortunes of Meighen forbade, and the agrarian origins of
the Progressives precluded. The Liberals, for all their short-
comings, were on the eve of another era of political predominance.

The campaign as a whole was fought with vigour by three
"young" leaders, any one of whom, as the cards fell, might
dominate his country for a generation, Meighen, King, and
Crerar. Meighen passed from London to the west coast and
back into the Maritime Provinces, avoiding Quebec except for
Montreal, attacking, attacking, attacking. Crerar toured the
continental West, Ontario, and the Maritime Provinces, and
spoke in plain, blunt fashion; he was frequently embarrassed by
the unruly and unrestrained agrarianism of his followers, and
hampered by the fact that he was not so much contending for
office as conducting a grand manœuvre to bring about a realignment of political forces. King, in swinging across the country,
displayed that verbal voluminousness, that unflagging zeal for
political drudgery, which was in time to weary and beat down
all opponents. The three young men, however, exercised their
arts of persuasion in vain. The electorate, seemingly charmed
by none, had made up its mind and waited grimly for the polls
to open.

One decisive event, none the less, had occurred. From the
first, the continental West had been conceded to the Progressives,
as Quebec was on the whole conceded to the Liberals. The
Maritime Provinces and British Columbia were held to be fair
fighting ground. Ontario was therefore the province where the

[70]Cf. A. R. M. Lower, *Colony to Nation* (Toronto, 1946), 531-2.

decision was to be sought, if any were to be found in the chaos of the day. As was said in the Montreal *Gazette:* "It is in this province [Ontario] that the future of the Progressive party will be decided."[71] It was generally thought the Ontario Progressives would carry many seats. It was plainly necessary that they should, if the party were to dominate the situation at Ottawa. The possibility of their doing so accounted for the Liberal strategy, which was to avoid three-cornered contests as far as possible, while criticizing sharply the class characteristics of the Progressive movement, and to keep in touch with Crerar and Drury with a view to a post-electoral coalition.

The Liberals followed this policy up to about three weeks before polling day. Then King suddenly started denouncing coalition as a possibility, alleging that Canada had had enough of coalitions. Liberal candidates appeared in constituencies hitherto left to the Progressives. In Crerar's seat of Marquette, for example, L. St. George Stubbs replaced a Liberal candidate who had accepted the nomination, but failed to campaign. The Martin Government began to support any Liberal candidate who seemed likely to win, such as W. R. Motherwell in Regina. Nomination day, November 22, saw nineteen three-cornered contests in the West and forty-two in Ontario, no account being taken of independents, or of multi-cornered contests in which representatives of the three major parties took part. What had happened? Undoubtedly the loosening of party discipline, and its repudiation by the Progressives on the principle of "constituency autonomy," had made it all but impossible for the leaders to prevent the local organizations putting up candidates when they chose. There was also some evidence that, at the time mentioned, the moneyed interests despaired of Meighen's fate, and threw their weight to the Liberals, as a party which had demonstrated that it was safe enough and not likely to truckle to the agrarians, if it but carried enough seats to make independence possible. The change was signalized by a much noted meeting of Senators J. A. Calder and W. B. Ross in Montreal, the former, of course, a Saskatchewan Liberal, the

[71]Montreal *Gazette*, Nov. 23, 1921, p. 1. The *Gazette* estimated that the Progressives would have to carry 35 of the 70 Ontario seats they were contesting if they were to be a serious political factor.

latter a Conservative.   Thereafter, both Liberals and Conservatives "ganged up" in Saskatchewan and Ontario to "drift the Progressives."[72]   Such tactics threatened the Progressive hopes of repeating the victory of 1919 in Ontario and of electing 75 candidates, to hold the balance of power in a House in which neither old party would have a majority.

The significance of the threat to Progressive hopes in Ontario was revealed by the results of the election.   In the country at large the outcome was at once startling and indecisive.   All Canada was split into three parts, a Liberal East, a Progressive West and a divided Ontario.   The Conservative party suffered an unparalleled, though by no means an unexpected, defeat. Fifty members of that party were returned to parliament, from the native strongholds of Conservatism in industrial Ontario and from those Orange and Loyalist seats east of Toronto which had been Conservative from Confederation and before.   Other Conservative members were *rari nantes in gurgite vasto*, save in ever conservative Vancouver Island and the lower St. John valley.   The Conservatives had suffered not so much a defeat of the National Policy, even as interpreted by Meighen in his London speech, as a defeat of a party which had won power in 1911 and 1917 in extraordinary circumstances, and which had incurred the odium attaching at once to coalitions and to wartime administrations.

The Liberals had won, for their part, one hundred and seventeen seats, all but twenty-seven of them east of the Ottawa. The conservative parts of Canada had reasserted their hold on the party, revealing it once more as at base the party of minorities and marginal areas, the conservative bulwark of the racialism of Quebec, and of the steady ways of the Maritime Provinces. The Liberals, in the circumstances, had also done well in Ontario, and had kept their footing in British Columbia.   Such outlying seats might prove to be stepping stones to the reconstruction of a national party.   In the continental West, however, only three seats were won, all of them urban, and one of those was held by the independent Liberal, A. B. Hudson.   The Liberals were victors in the election, but were short of a bare

[72]Dafoe Papers, Dafoe to Clifford Sifton, Dec. 7, 1921; Sifton to Dafoe, Dec. 8, 1921.

majority of the House by one seat; in the continental West, they, like the Conservatives, had been repudiated.

The Progressives, who had thus carried the West out of the traditional parties, knew at once the sweet thrill of victory and the bitter taste of defeat. For a new party they had done astonishingly well, and had caused what was felt to be a revolution in Canadian politics. The election of sixty-five members was an impressive record of the forces of discontent, which had welled up since 1911 and brimmed over in the Progressive movement. Yet they had failed to carry as many seats as they had hoped in Ontario, and that failure gave the Liberals the possibility of independence in parliament, and denied the Progressives a decisive balance of power. Ontario, like Canada, had divided three ways, and so dashed the wild hopes aroused by the victory of 1919 that that province, the principal beneficiary of the National Policy and Confederation, would repudiate protection. In that province, indeed, not only the Conservatives and the Liberals, but even a few Progressives, were protectionists of one shade or another.

The last-minute attack of the Liberals had taken the edge off the Progressive victory in the full flush and ardour of the farmers' revolt. Other reasons than election manoeuvres, of course, may be alleged to account for the comparative failure of the Progressives. The resentment at the cancellation of exemption from military service was largely forgotten, and in any event told against the administration but not against the Liberals. One observer had early noted that the U.F.O. in 1919 had not won "the village vote."[73] They had failed to win it in 1921 also.[74] To this result Morrison's relentless urging of the necessity of preserving the agrarian character of the U.F.O. political movement had contributed. Crerar himself estimated that while the Progressives in the West had obtained about eighty per cent of the village and town vote, in Ontario they had failed to win more than ten per cent.[75] Probably also the Drury Government's failure to meet the expectations of economy it had

[73]P.A.C., Murphy Papers, Political, 1908-19, W. H. McGuire to Murphy, Dec. 12, 1919.
[74]Toronto Globe, Dec. 9, 1921, p. 1.
[75]Crerar Papers, Crerar to Arthur Hawkes, Jan. 17, 1922.

aroused, and its opposition to the extension of electric radial railway lines contributed to the decline in the Progressive vote.[76] The campaign of the old parties and their press against the western "free traders," the "class agitators," and "the Americans" could not have been without its effect. Whatever the causes, certain it was that the sudden hopes of 1919 were as suddenly dashed in 1921.

The Progressives, moreover, carried but a single seat east of the Ottawa. The agrarian stirrings of 1920 in the Maritime Provinces had proved misleading. The co-operative enterprises, the political organization, and the press of the United Farmers of the Maritime Provinces had failed to develop strength. Only five Progressives, moreover, came from British Columbia, and they too, like certain of the Ontario members-elect, had their local interests to defend. The party, therefore, could not claim to be a national party, or even to represent the agricultural interests of all Canada. The twenty-four Ontario members-elect, those of British Columbia, and the lone Caldwell from New Brunswick, served but to mask the real character of the Progressive party, an agrarian and sectional bloc from the continental West, the representation of the monolithic wheat economy.

The future, it was clear, might well belong to W. L. Mackenzie King, if he could somehow find a foothold, or better, in the West and, subduing the now dominant protectionist elements in his following, revive the old Laurier alliance of Quebec and the marginal elements of Canada in a national party representative of all sections, communities, and creeds. To this he addressed his efforts when summoned to assume the prime ministership.

[76]Toronto *Globe*, Dec. 9, 1921, p. 1.

The Political Failure of the Progressives,

1 9 2 1 - 2 2

O N T H E morrow of the election an attempt was made to form a government to consist of Liberals and Progressives. The prime minister expectant, W. L. Mackenzie King, approached the Progressive leaders of Liberal persuasion, Crerar and Drury. Andrew Haydon, national organizer of the Liberal party, visited Winnipeg on December 13, and conveyed to Crerar assurances of the policy and personnel of the new administration. J. W. Dafoe, a consultant in the ensuing negotiations, wrote to Clifford Sifton at the time: "There were a number of conferences last week between Mr. Haydon on one side and Mr. Crerar and his friends on the other, and a number of telegrams passed between Mr. Haydon and Mr. King and Mr. Lapointe in the East."[1] Haydon's presence in the Royal Alexandra Hotel had been disclosed by a telegraph operator to the press,[2] but in spite of the consequent embarrassment, the negotiations proceeded. Crerar was advised by a circle of friends, of whom Dafoe was one, and A. B. Hudson, K.C., independent Liberal member-elect for South Winnipeg, another. Meantime King himself was in touch with Drury in Toronto.

Both Crerar and Drury were impressed by the terms offered. Dafoe had wired Sifton on December 14: "Parties here seem impressed by assurances policy and membership, imply re-

[1]Dafoe Papers, Dafoe to Clifford Sifton, Dec. 19, 1921.

[2]The statement is based on the account of an informed observer; Haydon's presence in Winnipeg was noted in the *Montreal Daily Star*, Dec. 14, 1921, p. 1.

jection Montreal bunch."[3]   Both, however, were wary of the reaction of their own followers and of that of King's new and uncertain friends in Montreal.

Crerar [wrote Dafoe of a meeting held on December 17] read a long telegram from Drury, the latest of a series he had had from him.   I should say from reading this telegram that Mr. Drury bit at first at the proposition to go into the Dominion Government but the more he considered the question the more dubious he became.   In his telegram on Saturday (the latest) he said he did not think it would be wise for the Progressives to go into the Government unless means were taken to preserve the identity of the party and written guarantees were given of the acceptance by the Liberals of the basic principles of the Progréssive platform.   He also said he did not think he could possibly take a portfolio himself upon any terms.   This statement of views by Drury exactly corresponded with the opinion the meeting [of Crerar and his advisers] had reached by itself.   This was practically unanimous in the view that co-operation would only be possible on the basis of a formal coalition which would be a protection for Mr. Crerar against his own people.[4]

This stand having been taken, Hudson, who was present at the meeting, left next day, December 18, for Ottawa to "inform King [of the] arrangements; [the] only possible basis [to be] coalition with written guarantees."[5]   Crerar, for his part, was bound to consult his followers.   Accordingly, they were called to meet at Saskatoon on December 20.   If the convention approved the stand taken in Winnipeg, Crerar would then go to Ottawa to negotiate directly with King.[6]

The Saskatoon convention was attended by thirty-two out of thirty-nine western members; the absentees, it is illuminating to note, were too "hard up" to attend.[7]   The meeting lasted eight hours, an indication of the seriousness with which the issues were debated.   It was a private conference, to which the press was not admitted, and no statement of proceedings or decisions was published.   Four accounts of what took place were made public at the time and subsequently.   Taken to-

[3]Dafoe Papers, Clifford Sifton to Dafoe, Dec. 14, 1921.
[4]Ibid., Clifford Sifton to Dafoe, Dec. 19, 1921.
[5]Ibid., Dafoe to Clifford Sifton, Dec. 18, 1921.
[6]Ibid.
[7]Crerar Papers, Crerar to T. W. Caldwell, Jan. 6, 1922.

gether, they make up a probable general account of the course of the discussion and of the decisions reached.

The first was a contemporary report by a special correspondent of the Montreal *Gazette*, put together, it is to be assumed, from conversations with the members-elect. "This much is positively known," it ran, "that the Progressive leader presented to the gathering a certain proposition which had been made to him on behalf of the Liberal leader, and the acceptance of which would create an alliance between the two parties, or between such of them as followed their leader the whole distance. Included in the arrangement would be the acceptance by Mr. Crerar of a portfolio—probably any one he might choose, except finance."[8] The correspondent then went on to surmise that pledges had been required by the Progressives.

The next public statement of the outcome of the Saskatoon meeting was that made by Crerar himself on January 11, 1922, to the annual convention of the United Farmers of Manitoba in Winnipeg. The Progressive leader in his address first repudiated the charge that the Progressive movement was a class movement. He then read the text of a resolution adopted by the Saskatoon convention:

That this meeting of western supporters of the National Progressive party, having taken under consideration the existing political situation in Canada and the course the Progressive party should follow, is of opinion that the gravity and importance of our many national problems call for a strong government;

That the first consideration of the Progressive party will be to support the legislation the country needs, both in the economic and the administrative sense, and in the larger sense of promoting and developing the spirit of Canadian national unity, and we will extend to the Hon. Mr. King's government all reasonable co-operation and support in any efforts it may make to enact into legislation those economic and administrative reforms which have been advocated by the National Progressive party, while at the same time maintaining the complete identity and organization of the Progressive party. (Sgd.) T. H. McConica, *Chairman.* (Sgd.) R. M. Johnson, *Secretary.*[9]

This resolution embodied only a conditional offer of support, and made no reference to the entrance of Progressive leaders

[8]Montreal *Gazette*, Dec. 21, 1921, p. 1.
[9]*Manitoba Free Press*, Jan. 12, 1922, p. 3.

into the Liberal administration. None the less, it was apparently intended to terminate disclosures to the public, with Prime Minister King's statement at Newmarket on January 19, in which he explained his stand during the negotiations. On January 17, however, the Canadian Press had sent out a report of a speech made by Robert Gardiner, member-elect for Medicine Hat, to delegates from that electoral district to the U.F.A. convention in Calgary. In his remarks, Gardiner reported Crerar as having explained to the Saskatoon meeting that the Liberal party consisted of two wings, "one Progressive and the other autocratic."

"The position," he [Crerar] said, "was that the reactionary wing of the Liberal party would take control of the Liberals unless the Progressive Liberals got assistance from the Progressive farmer members. It was up to the farmer members to see that the reactionaries did not secure control."

Mr. Crerar, therefore, proposed that a coalition arrangement should be effected between the Progressive Liberals and the farmers, and a resolution was offered embodying the arrangement, but attention was called to the fact that the Alberta delegate (Mr. Gardiner) had not expressed his opinion.

"Being thus challenged," said Mr. Gardiner, "I took the floor of the convention and explained our position as clearly as I could. I said the Alberta members wanted absolute independence on the question of forming a coalition with any other party and they would serve the constituency they represented and that I felt I could not serve the best interests of Medicine Hat by lining myself up with one of the old political parties. I explained how we believed in the group system of organization. There was no question in my mind, but that Mr. Crerar was there for the purpose of forming a coalition with the Progressives of the Liberal party."[10]

The report then continued to the effect that Gardiner voted for a resolution committing the Progressives to support progressive legislation, which was evidently the resolution made public by Crerar at the U.F.M. convention. He was further reported, however, to have opposed one committing the members-elect to giving "tacit approval of any Progressive representative" (and to have said that the words, "and especially

[10]*Winnipeg Tribune*, Jan. 17, 1922, p. 5; the Montreal *Gazette* carried the report in less detail, Jan. 17, 1922, p. 1.

Mr. Crerar," were in the first draft) who might enter the King Government on his own responsibility. This resolution was said to have been carried by a large majority. Gardiner then went on, so the report concluded, to warn his audience that the farmers would have to watch their representatives. He declared that he himself would not blindly follow any leader, and expressed the hope that the Progressives would become the official opposition.

The report was misleading, if it were read to imply that Gardiner was the only Alberta member present. It did, however, reveal that there was opposition in the convention to Crerar's proposals, whatever their precise nature, and that it came from the U.F.A. members, the protagonists of constituency autonomy and group government in their most uncompromising forms. Its most significant revelation, which was not publicly contradicted, was that another resolution than that which Crerar had made public had been adopted, a resolution which approved the entrance of individual Progressive leaders into the Liberal cabinet.

The next public statement of what happened at the Saskatoon convention was made in 1924 as a result of the open split in the Progressive group which occurred in the session of that year. Milton Campbell, Progressive member for Mackenzie and a member of the newly seceded "Ginger Group," wrote in *The Progressive*, organ of the farmers' movement in Saskatchewan:

In order to understand this situation [following the secession of 1924] better, I may state shortly after the election, the Progressive members-elect of the three prairie provinces were summoned to a conference at Saskatoon by Mr. Crerar. After secrecy had been impressed on the gathering, the leader unfolded a plan whereby four or five Progressive members were to be given seats in a Liberal cabinet in return for the merging of the two parties, or the formation of a coalition. . . . A minority vigorously opposed the proposed coalition, and these are largely the same members who have continued the fight for more independent action throughout the three sessions of this parliament, and a number of whom have recently seen fit to sever their connection with the party organization. The proposal did not materialize, for the reason that, at a later conference with the Ontario members, Mr. Crerar failed to secure their support.[11]

[11]*The Progressive*, July 10, 1924, p. 5.

Campbell's statement, like Gardiner's, was one made by a member of the dissident minority. It was, however, fair in tone, and its statements of fact were not contradicted, except on the point of the character of the proposed co-operation of Liberals and Progressives, which was indeed the point of misunderstanding and controversy throughout the negotiations and subsequently. It did, at the same time, illustrate how the cleavage in Progressive ranks was present from the first, and added the information that four or five cabinet posts had been offered, no doubt tentatively, to the Progressives.

A reply was at once made to Campbell's statement by R. M. Johnson, who had been Progressive member for Moose Jaw until unseated on a technicality, and secretary of the Saskatoon meeting:

The writer [he declared] acted as secretary at the Saskatoon conference and is still in possession of the minutes, and has a distinct recollection of the proceedings, not only there, but in Toronto where he accompanied Messrs Crerar, Forke and Speakman, to meet the eastern members, also at Ottawa, to which the delegation immediately proceeded.

Certain proposals had been submitted by the prime minister, whereby western representatives might be had in the cabinet, with the probability of securing a larger measure of Progressive legislation than was otherwise likely. . . . There never was, at any of these conferences, the slightest suggestion of any affiliation of the Liberal and Progressive parties. Opinion was quite pronounced against it; but, in Saskatoon, without a single dissentient, the meeting was in favor of such co-operation as would secure to the west the legislation it desired, and at the same time preserve the identity of the Progressive group. It was clearly understood that any one entering the government must do so as an individual only.[12]

Johnson's letter was couched in general and cautious terms and was written in defence of the Progressives who were disposed to co-operate with the Liberals on terms. It makes it clear, however, that there was, beyond the resolution made public by Crerar, an understanding, if not a resolution as asserted by Gardiner, that Progressive leaders might as individuals enter the cabinet, presumably without being repudiated by the body of members-elect.

[12]*Ibid.*, July 31, 1924, p. 5.

From these various statements, it is apparent that King's original offer, or suggestion, was a generous one, which would have given the provinces of the continental West at least one member each in the cabinet, and satisfactory undertakings as to policy.[13] On this basis, Crerar and his lieutenants were authorized by the Saskatoon conference to negotiate further, the U.F.A. members, or some of them, dissenting. Coupled with the authorization, however, was the emphatic stipulation that the co-operation of Liberals and Progressives should take the form, not of fusion, but of a coalition in which the identity of the Progressive group would be preserved.[14]

On this understanding Crerar, accompanied by Alfred Speakman, member-elect for Red Deer, and R. M. Johnson, began the journey east. In Winnipeg, on December 21, the three men conferred briefly with Henry Wise Wood, George Langley, J. A. Maharg, and other leaders of the farmers' movement. There Robert Forke, member-elect for Brandon, joined the delegation, which then proceeded to Toronto.[15]

In Ontario, the report of the proposed alliance provoked a wave of opposition among the following of the U.F.O. The electoral contests had been bitter, and the class-consciousness of the farmers was hardening under J. J. Morrison's leadership. The support of former Conservatives had provided a very large part of the Progressive vote. Moreover, the U.F.O., like the U.F.A., had faced the same issue earlier in provincial politics, and had decided, not against the co-operation of groups, but against coalition with the old parties, or with any party. The opposition to participation in the new federal administration had found expression in a resolution of the U.F.O. convention on December 14: "That it is in the interests of Canada that the

[13]This is alluded to in the Montreal *Gazette*, Dec. 23, 1921, pp. 1 and 7, where in an "authoritative" report of the Saskatoon convention it was alleged that Crerar had described King's offer as a promise to lower the tariff substantially and to give the Progressives four seats in the cabinet. The number is probable enough, as four would have meant one each for the three western provinces and one for Drury.

[14]The point here is that in a coalition the Progressives would have retained their own caucus and their own organizations in the electoral districts. Union Government had been a fusion with a single caucus and, as it happened, no organization. See the penetrating comments of F. L. Davis, Unionist member for Neepawa (referred to in n. 11, chap. IV, *Can. H. of C. Debates*, 1921, I, p. 483).

[15]*Canadian Annual Review*, 1921, pp. 520-1.

National Progressive party should remain intact, and devote itself, earnestly, in the next Parliament to effecting by legislation the recommendations upon which it was elected."[16]   It was no doubt this temper, so "earnestly" expressed, which had turned Drury from his first impulse to accept King's proposals.   The temper was kept on edge by the unrelenting opposition of the *Farmers' Sun* to an alliance of Liberals and Progressives.   The *Sun* stood fast in its advocacy of the farmer members remaining in the role of an agrarian representation.   "They," it wrote of the U.F.O. members-elect, "are not in the House simply to oppose or to retard legislation, but rather to safeguard the interests of the rural people.   They can influence legislation and yet not be responsible for carrying on the government'"[17]

Of the brief conference of leaders in Winnipeg, or of that of the Ontario members-elect in Toronto, no illuminating public account appears to exist.   It is to be assumed, however, that Wood and Morrison, if they did not strenuously resist the proposed co-operation, at least maintained a dogged silence which did not mean consent.   On the other hand, neither meeting imposed a check on the journey of the delegation to Ottawa, nor, it would seem, did either effect a change in the instructions it had received from the Saskatoon convention. R. M. Johnson wrote in 1924 that "the whole thing was again discussed at Toronto and the proposal laid before the members there.   Any suggestion of amalgamation or affiliation with the Liberal party would not be tolerated, but any honourable means for securing Progressive legislation should be used.   Miss Macphail will probably remember the writer, speaking as a Western man, stating this to be the stand of the Saskatchewan Progressives."[18]   The passage may imply that the Toronto conference accepted the stand approved at Saskatoon.   Such a reading is doubtful, however, in view of the reiterated hostility of the U.F.O. and the *Farmers' Sun* to coalition.   It is especially so in view of Clifford Sifton's report to Dafoe that the Ontario Progressives were opposed to coalition, but that Crerar seemed to have thought he might have persuaded them to support a

[16]*Ibid.*, 520.
[17]*Farmers' Sun*, Dec. 24, 1921, p. 6.
[18]*The Progressive*, July 31, 1924, p. 5.

coalition, if favourable terms had been made with King.[19]   This report was written of a conversation with Crerar after the negotiations had broken down.   Clearly, uncertain as was the support of the western Progressives for coalition, the support of the Progressives of Ontario was even more doubtful.   The last stage of the journey, from Toronto to Ottawa, must therefore have been made with hopes of success severely diminished.

The delegation reached the capital on December 24, and Crerar at once called on King.   It was soon evident that there had been misunderstanding from the first, or that King had altered, or been forced to alter, the terms of his offer, or that the conditions Crerar had brought from his supporters were such as King was unable or unwilling to accept.   It is possible, indeed, that all three of these things had affected the result. Available evidence does not afford a detailed or positive explanation of the sudden termination of the negotiations, but does admit of a reasonable conjecture as to why in general the discussion came to an abrupt end.

It may, in the first place, be taken as established that the original offer was sufficiently generous to provoke a favourable response from the majority of the Progressive members-elect.[20] The doubt as to the genuineness of the offer, expressed by Dafoe, who did "not think that Mr. King [had] any real appreciation of the reasons for the strength of the Progressive Movement," and that he merely sought to capture Crerar and Drury,[21] a doubt Sifton shared,[22] reveals a factor in the situation, though there would seem to be little question of the sincerity with which the offer had been made.   What does emerge is that, whereas King envisaged that acceptance of his offer would lead to a fusion of Liberals and Progressives, the Progressives for their part declined to consider anything but a coalition which would preserve the organization and identity of their group. King was to say at Newmarket on January 19, 1922: "Over and over again I have said that the Progressive Party is a sort of advanced Liberal group.   I decided I would be true to what I

[19]Dafoe Papers, Clifford Sifton to Dafoe, Dec. 30, 1921.

[20]But cf. Dafoe, *Sifton*, 485: ". . . the absorption by a Liberal government of one or two Farmer leaders.   These were the only terms offered."

[21]Dafoe Papers, Dafoe to Clifford Sifton, Dec. 19, 1921.

[22]*Ibid.*, Clifford Sifton to Dafoe, Dec. 14, 1921; Dafoe, *Sifton*, 484-5.

said in that regard, and I made known to the Progressive leaders that I was prepared to take into my cabinet representatives of the Progressive Party on the one condition that they come into a Liberal Cabinet. I was not prepared for coalition or compromise. I was prepared to take a broad interpretation of the word Liberal."[23]

On this understanding, King's proposal was one leading to the fusion of Liberals and Progressives. In the debate on the Address in reply to the Speech from the Throne he was to repeat his declaration:

The fact which confronted me [the Prime Minister said] when I was forming the Government was the circumstances I have just mentioned, that in three of the provinces, the representation was almost exclusively Progressive representation. To my mind there can be nothing more unfortunate for the Dominion than that any part of it should have cause to feel that it is not to have its voice in the councils of the country. I feel that the whole purpose of Confederation itself would be menaced if any great body of opinion, any considerable section of this Dominion of Canada, should have reason to think that it was without due representation in the shaping of national policies, and in the carrying on of our public affairs. I was anxious, therefore, that so far as the Government which I was endeavouring to form was concerned, Western Canada should never be able to say that the Liberal party adopted other than a generous attitude towards those who opposed some of its followers. So, Mr. Speaker, I made it known to gentlemen who, I believed, were representative of Progressive thought and opinion that I was prepared to consider taking into the government members of the Progressive party who enjoyed its confidence; but I made it quite plain that I would only consider that representation on the basis of its coming into a Liberal administration.[24]

King had sought, then, to create a composite Liberal party, which would have been representative of all sections of the country in the established Canadian tradition, and which would have imposed on the Progressives the rule of the legislative caucus from which they had revolted. Whether Haydon had made this as clear in Winnipeg, as King had made it in Ottawa, may be doubted, but obviously there never was a hope of

[23]*Canadian Annual Review*, 1922, p. 216.
[24]*Can. H. of C. Debates*, 1922, I, p. 48.

persuading all, or possibly even a majority of, the Progressives to accept such a proposal. Somewhere in the course of the negotiations misunderstanding had developed, or other factors had intervened. Crerar, in his reply to King, alleged misunderstanding:

My Hon. friend the Prime Minister [he said], I think was animated by a sincere desire to do what was in the best interests of the country, but when he states that he made it quite clear in any proposals or suggestions he made, that this ministry was only to be a Liberal ministry, I must say I did not so understand it. When these proposals were *first* made they were discussed or suggested on the basis of policy and on the basis of the personnel of the government, and that, to my mind, was the essential thing.[25]

These statements reveal a major inconsistency of purpose in the two leaders. The Progressive leader, indeed, stood in the role of a man who had missed his cue. As R. M. Johnson was to write later: "At Ottawa, for the first time, was revealed the fact that something more than mere co-operation was expected; so all negotiations were called off, and the western men went home."[26] Clearly there had been a fundamental and genuine misunderstanding on both sides as to the nature of the co-operation that could, or would, be undertaken.

There is also reason to believe that Crerar found on arrival in Ottawa that King had changed, or been forced to change, the terms of his offer. The proposed personnel of the government had been considerably altered.[27] What had happened is indicated by reports in the press. It has already been noted that in the last weeks of the election campaign there were many rumours of a shift of the Montreal "interests" from the support of the Conservatives to that of the Liberals. The rumours were not without substance. The interests had put their trust in the Liberal leaders of Montreal and upper Quebec, Sir Lomer Gouin, Sir Rodolphe Lemieux, and Premier A. Taschereau, as the guardians of the tariff and the protagonists of the private ownership of railways. These men were outspoken champions of the Laurier tariff, and favourable to the disposal of the

[25]*Ibid.*, p. 51; the italics are the writer's.
[26]*The Progressive*, July 31, 1924, p. 5.
[27]Dafoe Papers, Clifford Sifton to Dafoe, Dec. 30, 1921.

National Railways to private interests. After the election, however, King had associated with himself in the work of cabinet-making, not Gouin or Lemieux, but Lapointe, a Liberal in the *rouge* tradition from lower Quebec, and *persona grata* to the Progressives of Liberal sympathies. That King and Lapointe had proceeded to negotiate with Crerar and Drury was known from December 14, when Haydon's presence in Winnipeg was noted in the *Montreal Daily Star*.

As a result, there was vehement protest from the press of Montreal. King and Lapointe were put under heavy pressure to break off the negotiations or to reduce their offer, with the threat, indeed, if they did not, of having "solid" Quebec split. The character of the pressure may be gathered from the hysterical outburst of the *Montreal Daily Star*, which on December 24, the day the Progressive delegation reached Ottawa, ran an editorial in a box with liberal blackface under the heading, "Will Quebec Be Betrayed By Treachery?" Quebec, it was declared, had given its all—its sixty-five—to the Liberals, and now union with the men it had fought was proposed. "An anti-Quebec drive" was in progress. What Quebec member was deserting his province? "Is there a traitor in the Quebec guard?" If there were, he would never be re-elected in any riding of Quebec.[28] Such pressure, coming from the press and, it may be assumed, from the party and through private channels, could not be ignored. The pressure reached full intensity when on December 23 Sir Lomer Gouin came up to Ottawa from Montreal. It is not necessary to accept J. K. Munro's statement, in *Maclean's Magazine*, that "the election was Montreal made and Montreal controlled,"[29] or that "Mr. King proposed; Sir Lomer Gouin disposed,"[30] to believe that this visit was not without its effect. So much smoke no doubt indicated the source of the fire which shrivelled King's original offer to the Progressives.

To the weight of Montreal was added that of Saskatchewan. Not only were the "interests" anxious to have Gouin in the

[28] *Montreal Daily Star*, Dec. 24, 1921, p. 1.

[29] J. K. Munro, "O, Demos, Where Is thy Sting?" (*Maclean's Magazine*, XXXV, Jan. 1, 1922, p. 14).

[30] J. K. Munro, "Made in Montreal" (*Maclean's Magazine*, XXXV, Feb. 1, 1922, p. 14).

cabinet as a guarantee that no rash fiscal policy would be adopted; Premier Martin and the Liberal faithful of the West also were anxious that the claims to cabinet rank of W. R. Motherwell, lone western Liberal representative, should not be set aside in favour of a Progressive.[31]

Such representations could not be ignored, and beyond doubt contributed to the break-down of the negotiations. It is also to be noted that the conditions drafted by the Progressives, coalition, not fusion, and the preservation of the identity of the party, were in themselves not acceptable to King. Such terms he was deterred from accepting by his public declarations against coalition, though he might have been prepared to discuss them in private. Further, the declared stand of Crerar and the Progressives required that the Montreal interests and protectionist Liberals be scantily, if at all, represented in the cabinet. The Progressives had discussed written guarantees as to policy, terms which A. B. Hudson had been authorized to lay before King. On this point there was speculation, such as the special correspondence published by the *Gazette* on December 24, to the effect that Crerar's terms were the return of the natural resources of the West, an attempt to revive the reciprocity agreement of 1911, the continuance of the Canadian National Railways as a publicly owned system, a tariff for revenue, and five cabinet seats.[32] But the prime minister-elect of a government, in a by no means desperate situation between antagonistic forces which balanced one another, would hardly have felt obliged to give written and explicit guarantees as to policy.

It should be noted that any successful conclusion of the negotiations would have resulted in a loss of supporters by both leaders, of Albertan Progressives by Crerar as well as protectionist Liberals by King. Both therefore had to calculate their losses in considering any proposal and strive to hold them to a minimum. The opposition of the Albertan Progressives, however, was not a decisive factor, being at worst a calculated loss. Neither was the pressure of the Montreal interests decisive.

[31]Montreal *Gazette*, Dec. 26, 1921, p. 1, a report in which it is alleged that Crerar demanded the elimination of Gouin, Motherwell, and Oliver.
[32]*Ibid.*, Dec. 24, 1921, p. 1.

True it was that the possible effect of that pressure in the province at large, the only sure bastion of the Liberal party, made it formidable. To Quebec, a Liberal-Progressive coalition would have been curiously reminiscent of the Union Government of 1917. The protectionist sentiments of Montreal and the social conservatism of Quebec might, under duress, have found even the Conservative party congenial. There was, however, a fundamental weakness in the position of Gouin and his following; they could not afford to drive King into the arms of the Progressives, to have him form with them a Liberal-Progressive government. In the final analysis, then, it was the new Prime Minister's determination to lead a composite, national party, representative of all sections and meeting in one caucus, which was the rock on which the negotiations came to wreck.

Whatever the influences, the calculations, and the errors which had contributed to the failure of the attempt to bring Liberals and Progressives together, one stark fact emerged, that Canada would have, not a strong government drawn from all sections, but a weak one with a questionable title to be termed national. Once it was decided that the new administration would be, not Liberal-Progressive, but Liberal, the cabinet was completed. It was a cabinet in which Quebec had no less than five members, among them the arch-reactionary, in western eyes, Sir Lomer Gouin, as Minister of Justice. Only the venerable Fielding, Lapointe, and the Prime Minister himself, gave it some grace of liberalism. For the rest, it was made up of Laurier Liberals and party lieges, to constitute a cabinet which was more representative than distinguished. The representation of the West was somewhat awkwardly secured. The presence of the solitary Saskatchewan Liberal, W. R. Motherwell, a famous agrarian who had been returned from the urban seat of Regina, brought Saskatchewan's name to the roll. After some wanderings in the political void of Alberta, Hon. Charles A. Stewart, Liberal premier of that province until July 1921, found a seat in the Quebec riding of Argenteuil. Manitoba was to remain without representation in the cabinet until 1923, when E. J. MacMurray became Solicitor-General. By these shifts did Prime Minister King achieve that national representation he had sought in his negotiations with the Progressives. The effect, however, was rather to emphasize the fact that the continental West had seceded from the classic party structure.

The announcement of the personnel of the cabinet was received with satisfaction in Montreal. The agrarian advance, which had seemed about to carry the farmers into the very seats of power, had been stayed. Fielding, the moulder of the Laurier-Fielding tariff, and Gouin could be trusted to see that no profane agrarian hand was laid on the ark of the National Policy. The needle of power, after wild flickerings, had steadied where commercial toryism thought it should, over the purlieus of St. James Street.

Among the organized farmers, too, there was manifest relief that coalition had failed. From the *Farmers' Sun* came an editorial, carrying the heading, "No Alliance"; it expressed satisfaction with the outcome, and declared that while the Progressives should support the government in progressive measures, they should not in any event enter the government.[33] The executive of the Saskatchewan Grain Growers' Association issued a statement opposing coalition and declaring that the Progressives should maintain their independence.[34] These were but public expressions of the opinion of individual Progressives, and reflected the fact that at the bottom of the Progressive movement lay a profound distrust of the old parties.

There is no doubt in my mind [wrote Dafoe] that under no circumstances could Crerar have taken the whole strength of the Progressive movement with him if he had gone into the government, even though he had had his due proportion of colleagues and there had been provision made for preserving the identity of the Progressives. Correspondence which I am in receipt of from farmers out in the country makes it clear to me that they regard the whole movement as one of the old fashioned manœuvres by which they were to be buncoed in the interests of the big corporations.[35]

On the other hand, those Progressives and their sympathizers who had desired some kind of effective co-operation between

[33]*Farmers' Sun*, Dec. 26, 1921, p. 1.
[34]*Manitoba Free Press*, Jan. 13, 1922, p. 13.
[35]Dafoe Papers, Dafoe to Clifford Sifton, Dec. 31, 1921.

Liberals and Progressives in the administration were disappointed, but hoped that time might remove the obstacles encountered at the first attempt; the outcome of the negotiations they ascribed to mismanagement.[36] The *Manitoba Free Press*, however, could comment as follows on Crerar's speech to the U.F.M. on January 11, 1922: "The Progressive party by reason of the circumstances controlling its creation and development, is not at the moment capable of advancing beyond the position defined by the Saskatoon resolution; and perhaps it is just as well that Mr. King's own domestic embarrassments precluded him from making an offer to the Progressives which it would have been difficult for them either to accept or reject."[37] Perhaps also, it surmised, the experience of a session would diminish the parochialism and allay the suspicions of the Progressives; perhaps some break in the political game would give King greater freedom of action. "The future of both the Progressive and Liberal parties must now wait upon events. If the Liberal government by its policies and administration commands the support and approval of the Progressives, the basis for a later merger will be laid, perhaps at the first session of the new House; whereas if it becomes evident that Progressive and Liberal ideas in legislation have to wait until the Progressives are themselves strong enough to give effect to them a great field of usefulness will open up before the new party."[38] The hopes of the Manitoban Progressives, in other words, had suffered a check, but time might operate to produce that progressive Liberal party which was their aim.

The failure of the December negotiations, however, important as it was, decided only one thing, that the Progressives were not to be represented in the cabinet. They would still stand in some relationship to the government, and what that was to be was left undecided by the break-down of the attempt at co-operation in the cabinet. The Progressives might support, oppose, or alternately support and oppose, the legislative programme and administrative acts of the government. They were to choose the last course, as indeed had been indicated by the Saskatoon resolution.

[36]Dafoe, *Sifton*, 485; Dafoe Papers, Clifford Sifton to Dafoe, Dec. 30, 1921.
[37]*Manitoba Free Press*, Jan. 13, 1922, p. 13.
[38]*Ibid.*, Jan. 4, 1922, p. 13, editorial, "Waiting Upon Events."

This was the natural course for the Progressives to follow, in the light of the history and character of the movement. There was, however, a report in the press at the close of the negotiations, which alleged that, though no Progressive was to be included in the cabinet, an understanding as to Progressive support in the House had been reached by King and Crerar. Such an understanding was inherently probable. King and Crerar were seeking the same thing, the constitution of a new party national in scope and reforming in temper, a progress ive Liberal or a liberal Progressive party. A common aim would make for mutual understanding, and an understanding would have great attractions for both. To King it would mean a measure of independence of his conservative followers, and some assurance of his being able to carry a legislative programme with at least some liberal features. To Crerar, believing as he did that the Progressive platform could only be realized by the normal parliamentary method of the acceptance by a disciplined majority of responsibility for maintaining an administration in power, it offered a chance to enact some parts of that platform. It might in addition lead to eventual co-operation in government.

The report that an understanding had been reached between King and Crerar was published in the *Winnipeg Tribune* on December 26, 1921, the Monday following Crerar's meeting with King on Saturday, December 24. Crerar and his companions spent Saturday night and Sunday in Ottawa, where, of course, they would be the quarry of reporters, and where they would discuss the collapse of the negotiations and the future course of the Progressives. The special correspondence published in the *Tribune* was occupied with just those matters.

The report began by asserting that the negotiations for the inclusion of leading Progressives in the cabinet had been broken up by Sir Lomer Gouin and Hon. Raoul Dandurand on Friday, December 23, and by Premier Martin and W. R. Motherwell. Despite this, however, an understanding had been reached by King and Crerar as to co-operation in the House. The understanding was that the Progressives were not to become the opposition, but should sit on the Speaker's left, to the left of the Conservatives, who would be the official opposition. In that position, the Progressives were to give the government their support on matters, such as railway policy, in which King might lose some of his following from Quebec. The report continued:

Upon the highest authority it can be said that his [Crerar's] remarks were in substance as follows: "There can be no doubt that there are certain conditions in Quebec, arising out of which King has had to capitulate in a measure to Gouin and his supporters at least for the time being. Those conditions are indicated in some degree by an article in the *Montreal Star*. If you saw it, you saw it was cleverly done."

"The Progressives," Mr. Crerar continued, "must form their own caucus and, so long as Mr. King pursued Progressive policies must give him support, that Mr. King must be able to feel that so long as 10 or 20 or 30 of the Quebec members may not agree with him as to policy to be pursued on certain subjects, railways for instance, he will be able to count on the Progressives to the extent that he could say to himself, 'Well gentlemen, you can go your own way in this matter,' feeling assured of Progressive support to carry him through."

The report then continued to quote Crerar to the effect that it would be necessary for the Progressives to have whips, a caucus and party solidarity and discipline, if they were to be prepared and able to give such support when it was needed. The "Quebec Betrayed" article from the *Star* was appended.[39]

What was the source of this direct and explicit report? No other major paper carried a similar story, which indicated that the Progressive leader and his companions granted no interview to the press, as was to be expected. The report, moreover, does not purport to be an interview. It is a report, in part professedly verbatim, of certain remarks alleged to have been made by Crerar. If they were not made in an interview, they were made, if at all, in confidence to the reporter or in private to Forke, Johnson, and Speakman. The *Tribune* was not a paper to publish a fabrication, and a fabrication would have invited prompt exposure. No public notice was taken of it, not even by Meighen, who was to use the report of Gardiner's speech at Calgary in the debate on the Address. Nor could the article have been a violation of confidence, for Crerar would not even in confidence have discussed with the press the details of a

[39]*Winnipeg Tribune*, Dec. 26, 1921, pp. 1 and 2.

private conversation with King, or have been so emphatic about the need for party discipline. It must then have been based on information obtained by eavesdropping, and as such would be substantially authentic. Though the paper did not quote Crerar directly to the effect that an understanding had been reached with King, in view of what preceded and what followed, the report bears the hallmark of authenticity. Between the progressive Liberals and the liberal Progressives there was a large measure of tacit agreement, scarcely requiring definition, and especially on railway policy. Co-operation to achieve common ends could only be assured if the Progressives would accept the usual parliamentary discipline. About this Crerar as leader was naturally and properly concerned.

Any understanding there may have been, tacit or explicit, was at most an understanding between the leaders. The public course the Progressives would pursue in the House remained to be decided by the members. The decision would be almost as significant for the future of the group as the failure of the proposal for co-operation in the cabinet had been, because without some support from the Progressives the life of the government would be precarious, and might be short. The fact was that the Progressive members were the second largest group in the House of Commons. While no Canadian precedent since Confederation governed the circumstances, it was clearly in accord with parliamentary usage that the second largest group should become the official opposition and alternative government. The group, however, at its first meeting on the opening of parliament, decided at once and without difficulty not to become the opposition, but to yield that position to the Conservatives under Meighen. In so deciding, the Progressives, it must be said, "feared their fate too much," and betrayed that disposition of third parties to shun responsibility on which George Langley had commented long before.[40]

The fear of responsibility had some justification. The Progressive group, though composed of very fair parliamentary material, was not an alternative government. The members were almost all farmers and the majority was without parliamentary experience. Of the sixty-five, fifty-two were active

[40]*Grain Growers' Guide*, III, Sept. 21, 1910, p. 6.

farmers, and one a retired farmer.   Nine of the remaining twelve followed occupations auxiliary to farming, one was a clergyman, one a school teacher, and one a lawyer.   In no respect, except the absence of legal training, was the group inferior to any other sixty-five members of the House.   Of the whole representation, however, only eight had previous parliamentary experience, and of these one was Crerar himself and one T. H. McConica, member for Battleford, who had been member and president of the Senate of Ohio between 1892 and 1895.[41]   Their lack of parliamentary experience was a serious handicap to the group and a constant anxiety to its leaders.

The decision not to become the official opposition, however, had deeper origins than lack of parliamentary skill.   Two motives, by no means separate or distinct, had governed the Progressive uprising.   One, represented by the Manitoban Progressives, was the desire to recapture the historic Liberal party of rural democracy and low tariff from the protectionist elements of Quebec and Ontario, and to reinvigorate it with the democratic force of the West.[42]   The hope for the success of that policy had rested on two premises: that the Quebec Liberal bloc would split into the old factions of *bleus* and *rouges*,[43] and that the West could be brought into the Liberal party.   The failure of the King-Crerar negotiations marked the disappointment of that hope, and made it necessary at least to wait upon more favourable times.   To commit the Progressive group, however, to opposition while coalition with the Liberals was still in view would be to render the hope all but impossible.

The other motive was to destroy the system of party government itself.   The general insistence on constituency autonomy pointed in this direction.   In the group government doctrines of Wood a complete scheme of occupational representation and non-party government had been adumbrated.   The first effect

[41]All details are from the *Parliamentary Guide*, 1922.

[42]Dafoe Papers, Dafoe to Clifford Sifton, Nov. 10, 1920: "Assuming that Mr. Crerar succeeds in entering the next Parliament with a following of seventy-five members, which is not at all beyond the possibilities, I am satisfied that a fusion of the Liberals and the Farmers for the purpose of carrying on a Government will be quite practicable, provided the tariff is made along the lines I have indicated."

[43]*Ibid.*, Dafoe to Clifford Sifton, July 21, 1919: "There is, I am told, a contest going on in the French Liberal party between Lapointe who represents the Rouge tradition and Lemieux who is pretty tender to 'the interests'."

of the new system would have been to destroy the control of the political party by caucus, and so to have ended the domination of politics by the "interests." In describing the Progressive revolt Milton Campbell, member for Mackenzie, was to write:

For twenty years or more, the organized farmers have striven manfully to break the centrally controlled political machinery, machinery through which they found it very difficult to express their views and to secure representation in parliament. To this end, they carried on an educational propaganda for many years, but the difficulty in securing necessary reforms through their economic organizations at last drove them into the political field. There, they created their own political machinery, and financed their own candidates. Thus it was confidently hoped that all members elected under such a plan would realize their primary responsibility to their constituents instead of, as formerly, to a party organization, which, in turn was controlled by certain interests which had liberally subscribed to its campaign funds.[44]

The Albertan Progressive concept, however, went far beyond the establishment of the independence of members. The elected members of each economic interest were to constitute a group in the legislature, which would be composed entirely of such groups. In a legislature so constituted, the traditional organization of government and opposition parties would be impossible, with the passing of party government there would be an end of the domination of the legislature by the cabinet and of the cabinet by the prime minister, which, in the eyes of Albertan Progressives, were simply additional aspects of that party "autocracy" of which the caucus was the most serious evil. Instead of such a party cabinet there would be a composite cabinet, made up through the proportional representation of the groups in the legislature, which was to hold office until deliberately dismissed by a vote of want of confidence in the legislature. The new conception of cabinet government had been described by William Irvine in *The Farmers in Politics:*

A group government, as I conceive it, implies that each group would be represented in the Cabinet. No group of any strength would be able to shirk responsibility, as, under the two-party system, is done by the opposition. The group government might be repre-

[44]*The Progressive*, July 10, 1924, p. 5, editorial, "The Progressive Split."

sented by a circle. The Cabinet or Executive, which will be as representative of the assembly as the assembly is of the people as a whole, will be the center of the circle. Just as the center of the circle is equidistant from any point in its circumference, so would responsibility be placed equally upon every group within the circle of parliament. Thus the British principle of responsible government would not be impaired, but safeguarded and extended.[45]

By such devices the Albertans hoped to put an end to the mock warfare of government and opposition and to institute stable, "non-political" government. Influenced by such views, the Albertan Progressives could not but join the Manitobans in the decision not to become the official opposition. They had been elected, not to support or oppose government, but to represent their constituents.

The Progressives, therefore, seated themselves on the left of the Speaker and of the Conservatives. They were thus in line with the official opposition and opposite the seats of the government and its supporters. In that position they sought to make it visible that they were, as Crerar declared, "an independent party, standing for the principles [they believed in] and prepared to further those principles by every honest and legitimate means within [their] power."[46] As such, the Progressives were free to support the government when they approved its measures, or to oppose it when they did not. Free in this way, it was their first duty and prime concern to hold a watching brief for their constituents and the Farmers' Platform, regardless, the Albertan Progressives would have said, of the consequences to the working of party government. It was a brave experiment, inspired by political naiveté, and marked by a curious over-emphasis on the importance of legislation and an ill-advised indifference to the importance of administration.

By this act the Progressives took up, more or less deliberately, the position of the balancing group in the House. There had been much talk of "holding the balance of power" at Ottawa, in the columns of the *Guide* and throughout the West, and now it seemed that the position had been attained. It was one which appealed to the sore temper of the agrarian and

[45]Irvine, *Farmers in Politics*, 238.
[46]*Can. H. of C. Debates*, 1922, I, p. 51.

sectional West; in this position the West, long dominated, could by a mechanical advantage force its will on central Canada. Had the Progressives represented wrongs as ancient as Ireland's, and had they produced a Parnell, they might have played "the Parnellite role,"[47] and re-acted something like the Home Rule drama of the 1880's. The new political weight of the West would in such circumstances have been promptly acknowledged. As it was, there was no Parnell, and the Progressives did not hold a decisive balance, though at any time death, illness, or by-elections might place the government at their discretion. It was easy to believe, however, that such a means of influence might be a better method of achieving their aims than the presence of their leaders in the administration.

Whatever they might do, hold the balance of power, support the Liberals in progressive legislation, or seek in some way to play an effective and consistent role in parliamentary deliber- ations, some parliamentary organization was necessary. The Progressives, under Crerar's leadership, as one of the few members of the group with parliamentary experience, at once began the practice of meeting in caucus. A chief whip was appointed, J. F. Johnston of Last Mountain, and one whip of each provincial group—Robert Forke of Manitoba, Andrew Knox of Saskatchewan, Alfred Speakman of Alberta, and R. H. Halbert of Ontario.[48] They thus assumed the usual organization of the old parties. The principle of constituency autonomy, however, the strong leaven of independence in the whole group, and the concept of group government held by the U.F.A. members, precluded their accepting easily the principle of party unanimity once agreement had been reached by ma- jority vote or assent in caucus. Without such discipline, dis- tasteful as it might be, the Progressives could not hope to force their programme on the Liberals, much less to exercise a balance of power.

Even if they had been a unified group, instead of the restive and unreliable band they were, the position was one of great peril to themselves and of possible advantage to the government.

[47]Crerar Papers, Dr. T. A. Patrick to Crerar, June 6, 1919.

[48]W. Paterson, "The Progressive Political Movement, 1921-30" (unpublished M.A. thesis of University of Toronto, 1940), 50.

Prime Minister King could in fact count on Progressive support for the most part since, however much the Progressives might dislike the composition of the Liberal party, they perforce disliked the proclaimed policy of the Conservatives more. In the happy position once enjoyed by Charles II, King knew the Progressives would not lightly defeat him to make Meighen prime minister. Only the Albertan Progressives could regard the two old parties as indifferently steeped in iniquity. This it was which made the first King ministry possible, namely, the sympathy and support of the crypto-Liberals in the Progressive group. Such a division within the group, however, meant that it was really incapable of holding an impartial balance. Only a solid group, equally oblivious of the fates of the two old parties, could have played the game of the balance of power. Such solidity the Progressives did not possess when the Fourteenth Parliament opened, and were never to achieve.

The course of the first session need not be narrated in detail; only the debates which chiefly revealed the difficulties and weaknesses of the Progressives will be examined. The Progressives, it is first to be noted, by declining the role of official opposition, had incurred handicaps imposed by the rules of the House, as the first days of the session were to reveal. The rules had been evolved under the two-party system, and made the existence and functioning of a third party difficult. Notable in this respect was the rule prohibiting an amendment to an amendment on the motion to go into Committee on Ways and Means.[49] The effect as long as the rule held was to make the Progressives unable to define their stand on fiscal policy in the debate on the budget. They were faced with the alternative of accepting the government's motion and with it its tariff proposals, or the opposition's amendment. The consequence of the situation was, in the debate on the budget in 1922, to split the Progressives and to expose the difficulties of holding the balance of power.

Many illustrations of the difficulties faced by the Progressives were to be afforded by the debates on fiscal policy, the group's major interest. The tariff policy of the new administration was to be dominated by the long experience of Fielding. As Fielding

[49]*Can. H. of C. Debates*, 1922, III, pp. 2473-4.

of reciprocity fame, he was to the westerners some offset to Gouin and the dreaded influence of Montreal. But Fielding was also the man who had presided over the reconciliation of the Liberal party with the National Policy, and who had brought to perfection the tariff which was its sure foundation, and he it was who now made it possible for many protectionist Liberals to remain within the party of their hereditary allegiance. After the lesson of 1911, and the ending of the standing offer of reciprocity by the United States with the passage of the Fordney-McCumber tariff in 1922, there was to be no opportunity for the veteran Maritimer to repeat his famous tack of 1911. Stability was to be the motto of his latter-day budgets; the fiscal vessel was laid on a steady course. He might, like other Ministers of Finance before him, privately sound out official opinion in Washington; he might even break out the flag of reciprocity again in the standing offer of 1923; but so long as American agriculture demanded and obtained protection, reciprocity could not be a serious factor in Canadian fiscal policy. To these considerations must be added the composition of the Liberal party in the House, shorn of its western wing and with over half its members from Quebec; the weight of Montreal in the administration; above all, the need of revenue to carry the war debt and meet the deficits of the Canadian National Railways. No Minister of Finance in such a time could risk any radical change of fiscal policy.

In these circumstances, the Progressives were not likely to find it easy to bring themselves to support the government in the budget division. On tariff policy they were almost as sharply severed from the Liberals as from the Conservatives, except for the Albertan Progressives, who were sometimes inclined to agree with the Labour members in dismissing the tariff as at most a symptom of more fundamental economic ills. The clear-cut adherence of the Conservative party to protection, however, meant that Manitoban Progressives had to settle for a stable tariff, one, that is, without increases, rather than defeat the government and risk a Conservative victory in the ensuing election. Accordingly, the government could count on support from at least part of the Progressive group, and the effect of its doing so was to divide further the Manitoban from the Albertan Progressives.

At the same time, the government could not forget the wrecked Liberal party of the West, manned only by a skeleton crew of cabinet ministers. To repair this wreck, some downward revision of the tariff, as well as other concessions, were necessary. In 1923 the loss of two by-elections in the East was to emphasize the need of gaining strength in the West. These concessions, though they had to be made in time, could on the whole be postponed until the eve of the election, by which time the eastern supporters of the government might be convinced of the substantial reliability of the Liberal party in tariff matters.

By such considerations was fiscal policy and the course of the debates to be influenced during the ensuing sessions. The budget of 1922 lowered the tariff on many items, but all reductions were minute, in the opinion of the Progressives. Fielding announced the reductions as the redemption of the pledge contained in his amendment to the budget of 1921, which he declared was binding on the government rather than the tariff plank of 1919.[50] The Conservative opposition moved an amendment, which challenged a comparison of the budget with the plank of 1919. Crerar then moved a sub-amendment, which was the same in substance as the Conservative amendment, but added a repudiation of the principle of protection. It was at once challenged on the point of order. The Speaker ruled it out of order, and, despite an able plea by Crerar that the rule prohibiting a sub-amendment to the motion to go into Committee on Ways and Means was founded on an error of a pre-Confederation Speaker, the ruling was upheld by a Liberal and Conservative majority of the House.[51] Thus Progressive criticism of the budget was stifled.

The mere drafting of the sub-amendment, moreover, had produced the first of those dissensions between Manitoban and Albertan Progressives which were to rend the group. Crerar had to be emphatic in caucus to enforce unity.[52] Even so, there

[50]*Ibid.*, 1921, III, p. 3155.
[51]*Ibid.*, 1922, III, pp. 2521-3.
[52]Dafoe Papers, Dafoe to Sifton, June 8, 1922.

were dissentients. On the vote on the Conservative amendment, two Progressives and the two Labour members voted with the Conservatives.[53] On the vote on the main motion, two Progressives voted with the government, and thirty-nine against, the motion being carried 119 to 101.[54] The episode revealed how the group might be split by the operation of the rules of the House, and the use of disruptive motions by the old parties.

In the fluid circumstances prevailing, however, division within the ranks was a danger which menaced the old parties, too, as the fate of the government's proposals for dealing with the Crow's Nest Pass railway rates was to illustrate. The statutory limitations on rates on grain and specified commodities moving east over the Canadian Pacific line, and specified commodities moving west, had been suspended in 1918 by order-in-council under the War Measures Act. In 1919, by an amendment to the Railway Act, the rates in question had been placed under the jurisdiction of the Board of Railway Commissioners for a term of three years. In 1922 the term was about to expire, and the rates under the Agreement would come into force again. The railways opposed the restoration of the pre-1918 rates, and the government proposed to refer the matter to a select committee. The proposal was at once attacked from two sides, by the Conservatives who wished the rates to remain under the control of the Railway Commission, and by the Progressives who wished the statutory rates to come into force again. Then the progressive wing of the Liberal party rallied to the defence of the resumption of the statutory limitations in a revolt which might have upset the government. The rebels were Liberals from western Ontario, the Maritime Provinces, and lower Quebec, about one-half the party in number, who were reported to have become restive under Gouin's seeming control of policy, and to have been provoked by his flatly protectionist speech in the budget debate and his opposition to the McMaster resolution to prohibit cabinet ministers from holding directorships.[55] The threat to party

[53]Can. H. of C. Debates, 1922, III, corrected list, p. 2972.
[54]Ibid., p. 2914.
[55]Dafoe Papers, Dafoe to Clifford Sifton, July 11, 1922.

unity was averted by the intervention of the Prime Minister, who disciplined the Liberal caucus, and committed it to a proposal to restore the Crow's Nest Pass rates on grain and flour. The proposal was acceptable to the Progressives. All Liberal members but one voted with the Progressives to defeat the Conservative amendment to leave the rates under the Railway Commission. The Prime Minister then introduced a bill to restore the rates on grain and flour, which was in due course enacted.[56]

The restoration of the Crow's Nest rates was the most notable legislative achievement of the Progressive group. It had been accomplished, however, not by the tactics of the balance of power, but by a determined group asserting a sectional interest, in doing which they were fortunate enough to profit by a division in the government's following. Such divisions are very rare in Canadian politics, and the Progressives were not to benefit by another.

Legislation which similarly evoked a sectional unity among western Progressives, in which their colleagues from Ontario joined, was that which provided for the re-establishment of the Wheat Board, upon the three western provinces passing concurrent legislation; it was a government measure, however, which received assured Progressive support, and so caused no division in Liberal or Progressive ranks. It is significant because it added to the already mutual suspicion of Crerar and the Albertan Progressives. The demand for the continuation of the Wheat Board had grown with the collapse of the price of wheat which followed its termination in 1920. The deepening distress of the western farmers had made the demand irresistible. Crerar, however, had not joined in the demand, but publicly declared himself to favour, as a permanent policy, the co-operative marketing of grain. To justify his stand, he pointed to the fact that the Farmers' Platform contained no plank calling for the continuation of the Wheat Board.[57] When the matter came up in the House, he insisted that the extent of the federal government's powers be ascertained, and, when that was settled, he proposed that a Board be set up to market the

[56]*Can. H. of C. Debates*, 1922, IV, pp. 3588-97.
[57]*Canadian Annual Review*, 1921, p. 479, letter to E. A. Partridge, Nov. 14, 1921.

crop of 1922 and the government's plan given a fair trial.[58]   It was a consistent, cautious, and defensible stand, but it brought reproaches from farmers who regarded the United Grain Growers Ltd., of which Crerar was still president, as merely another private grain company, and its lukewarmness aroused the indignation of followers who were under instructions from their constituents to obtain the restoration of the Wheat Board.

On the budget, then, the Progressives were baffled, but they had accomplished notable things in the restoration of the Crow's Nest rates on grain and flour and, as it seemed at the time, in the re-establishment of the Wheat Board.[59]   The internal division inherent in the composition of the group had, however, been revealed.   The joint action of Liberals and Progressives on the Crow's Nest rates, moreover, had begun the drift of a number of Manitoban Progressives towards the Liberals.   This drift was accentuated by the disharmony within the group, and was signalized at the end of the year by the return of two Ontario Progressives, J. A. Binette of Prescott and W. J. Hammell of Muskoka, to the Liberal party.[60]

It was not, however, surprising that a new group, sprung from a movement of political insurgence, should have encountered dangers and developed dissensions.   Time and deliberate measures of precaution might act as offsets to these difficulties.   Crerar's policy was to try to perfect parliamentary discipline in the group and let experience do its sobering work.

Less practical, but theoretically better designed to create conditions under which the third party could prosper, was William Irvine's suggestion, made in the debate on the Address, that the convention be adopted that an administration should not resign except on an explicit vote of want of confidence.[61] The idea, however, was too novel to win a favourable hearing, and Irvine did not introduce a motion to that effect until the following session.

[58]*Can. H. of C. Debates.* 1922, I, p. 780; *ibid.*, III, p. 2922.

[59]The refusal of the legislature of Manitoba to pass the required concurrent legislation, as had been done in Saskatchewan and Alberta, brought to nothing the federal legislation of 1922 for a Wheat Board.

[60]*Canadian Annual Review*, 1922, p. 232.

[61]*Can. H. of C. Debates*, 1922, I, p. 217.

Equally significant for the future of Progressive candidates at the polls, and timely because of the great disparities between the popular votes won and the candidates elected by the various parties in 1921, was W. C. Good's renewal of a resolution moved in the previous parliament in favour of the alternative vote and proportional representation.[62] Despite an able and scholarly presentation by the mover and much favourable comment, including that of the Prime Minister, the debate was adjourned and not resumed.

The session of 1922, all told, was one in which the Progressives learned the difficulties of being an independent third party under parliamentary government conducted according to rules developed for the two-party system. It had been made plain that the balance of power could be held only by a tightly organized group, undistracted by sympathies with any particular party or the desire to keep any particular administration in office. The Progressive party in 1922 was not such a group.

The session had seen begun, however, that precipitation of the Progressives into their two component groups, the Manitoban, or Crerarite, Progressives who wished to liberalize the Liberal party, and the Albertan, or Woodite, Progressives who sought to establish group government by occupational representation. How this precipitation had proceeded was to be revealed by the resignation of Crerar as Progressive leader in November 1922.

That act, decisive for the future of Manitoban Progressivism as it proved to be, was preceded by a second attempt at reaching a basis for administrative co-operation with the Liberal government. At the end of the session, in late July and early August, the press was full of rumours of a *rapprochement* between Liberals and Progressives. The root of this new endeavour to find a more satisfactory basis for the administration was friction within the Liberal party itself, revealed by the episode of the Crow's Nest rates legislation. This had prompted an outburst by Senator L. O. David, as reported in the Montreal *Gazette*, in which the Senator suggested a union of protectionist Liberals

[62]*Ibid.*, II, pp. 1633 *et seq.*

with the Conservatives.[63] On this the *Manitoba Free Press* commented:

It has long been a prediction of close observers of Canadian politics that once the interests which govern Canada find that their system of ruling by appearing to divide has definitely broken down they will unite all their forces in one solid phalanx and proceed to hold the citadel against all comers. They have not yet finally determined that the good old game is up. The air still resounds with plaintive appeals that the electors in the sacred name of the Constitution and Responsible Government shall return to their party allegiance and re-decorate themselves with the tags they have discarded. A growing disbelief that these appeals will be fruitless is evidenced by the *Gazette* and the venerable Senator. The reforming and progressive elements can no longer be buncoed; and, therefore, the time has come for all staunch defenders of standpatism to get together and trounce these disturbers of the peace. This in effect is what the *Gazette* and the Senator say. It may be taken for granted that they speak for powerful forces capable of acting swiftly and decisively when their interests are at stake. It may be that we are at the next stage of the evolution of Canadian politics.[64]

The *Free Press* further remarked the existence of two distinct wings in the Liberal party, the Liberals of the right wing "being nothing more or less than Conservatives."[65] On July 11, Dafoe reported to Clifford Sifton that the talk of Progressive members returning from Ottawa ran on the theme of the rift in the Liberal party. The possibilities were said to be that Gouin, J. A. Robb, and G. P. Graham might resign, and A. B. Hudson be taken into the cabinet as Minister of Justice. Were that to happen, the Progressives would probably support the government, though without representation in the cabinet. The only opponents of such an understanding were a few members from Ontario and half a dozen from Alberta.[66]

At the end of the session Progressive members in the West were canvassed by their provincial whips for their opinion on the advisability of arriving at an understanding with the

[63]Montreal *Gazette*, June 19, 1922, p. 6.
[64]*Manitoba Free Press*, June 20, 1922, p. 13; editorial, "The Re-alignment of Parties."
[65]*Ibid.*, June 19, 1922, p. 15, editorial, "Tendencies at Ottawa."
[66]Dafoe Papers, Dafoe to Clifford Sifton, July 11, 1922.

Liberals. Milton Campbell was to write in 1924: "Further negotiations [to those of December, 1921] between the Progressive leader and the Liberals were evidently carried on during 1922, and during the summer the provincial Progressive whips were called into conference by the leader. These whips later called their provincial members together to discuss a working agreement with the Liberals."[67] The definite nature of the procedure outlined implies that the whips were given a definite proposition by Crerar to put before the members, and such a proposition could only have been made after consultation with Liberals of standing, presumably, of course, the leaders of the progressive Liberals, such as Lapointe and possibly Fielding.

Nothing came of the canvass, as many Progressives were opposed to a working alliance with the Liberals, or dubious of its merits. Nor did the threatened rift in the Liberal party materialize. This second failure to bring into being a national party of reform, however, contributed decisively to Crerar's weariness of public life. He accordingly laid his resignation before a conference of Progressive members and leaders of the organized farmers held in Winnipeg on November 10, 1922. It was presented in the form of a letter to T. W. Caldwell, chairman of the conference. In his letter, Crerar stated that he was resigning from the leadership in order to devote himself to his duties as president of the United Grain Growers, which in the difficult times prevailing required his whole attention. He then went on to make it clear that, in any circumstances, he would have remained as leader only if a clear-cut decision had been made, and affirmed that the party was not an agrarian class party.

My retention of the leadership of the Progressive party [he wrote] would depend upon a clear understanding and statement of the Progressives' program, not on questions of policy, . . . but on questions of organization and upon the vital question of whether the Progressive movement in our politics shall descend into a class movement or not.

The greatest obstacle the Progressive movement had to combat

[67]*The Progressive*, July 10, 1924, p. 5; see also the *Grain Growers' Guide*, XV, Nov. 22, 1922, p. 4, a report of the Progressive conference, at which Crerar and J. F. Johnston alluded to the discussions with respect to coalition in the summer of 1922.

in the last federal election was the fear in the hearts of thousands of electors in Canada who were in general sympathy with its policies, that it would become purely a class movement. The attitude of Mr. Wood in Alberta, and of Mr. Morrison in Ontario—and I do not here question the sincerity of either—I am bound to say gave grounds for this fear. Mr. Morrison's attitude is perfectly clear. He says the farmers have never been represented in our legislatures as they should have been, and he says to the farmers of the constituencies where they are strong enough to have a chance of doing it, "Elect your own man as a farmer, and keep him independent in the House to voice your interests."

In Alberta Mr. Wood advocates a new theory which, he says, if applied, will revolutionize and correct all the abuses that have hitherto existed in the mechanism of governments. It is that the evils in our political system have grown from the so-called "party system," and that we shall never be right until we introduce a new order of things. This he proposes to do by having members of parliament or legislatures elected upon the occupational basis. That is, the different occupations in the country will elect their quota of members and to these will be confided the task of organizing and carrying on the administration and functions of government, and of composing their differences to the point where they can agree on some line of public policy and some form of administration.

This view is further amplified in a recently published statement by a U.F.A. constituency executive officer in Alberta, in which it was seriously laid down that their federal member of parliament should be guided and directed in his work by the U.F.A. locals in his constituency. . . . [This] betrays a complete misunderstanding of the duties and responsibilities of a member. . . . [In this argument you] would have 235 members, each guided and directed by his constituents, some of whom were thousands of miles away, attempting to seriously carry on the work of government.[68]

The principle of the control of members by their constituents he declared to be unworkable, and affirmed the belief that members of parliament should represent all classes and all electors. The evils of the party system, he remarked in reply to Wood's views, lay not in the organization of the parties but in the corrupt use of patronage for the ends of party. This evil had, however, been scotched already, and was on the way

[68]*Grain Growers' Guide*, XV, Nov. 15, 1922, pp. 3, 4, 23, and 24.

to being ended. For the future, the Progressive party should bring its policy up to date. This would be accomplished by the adoption of a programme supporting the development of Canadian nationhood in the British Commonwealth and the League of Nations; the reduction of tariff rates to make the tariff a revenue tariff; the promotion of means of lowering the costs of production as well as of raising prices; the practice of economy in public finance; a fair trial for public ownership of the national railways; the introduction of the inspection of banks; and proportional representation and the alternative vote. In parliament, the party should co-operate with the government in the enactment of liberal measures. As for other forms of co-operation, Crerar declared: "Any fusion with any party in the House had never been considered."[69] In the future there should be no blind adherence to any party or group, and a clear recognition that "the balance of power game" would destroy the Progressives.

By this frank and challenging statement the divided nature of the Progressive group was brought out into the open. Henry Wise Wood replied in the press at once, and with equal bluntness. He had, he was reported as saying, no objection to the co-operation of group with group, but attempts at fusion should have been denounced sooner. Co-operation had always been possible, but co-operation did not require that Progressives should accept cabinet posts.

Mr. Crerar [he said] misses the point at issue between himself and those who differ with him. . . . The question is not whether others than farmers shall form the movement, but whether the movement shall be widened by the process of organizing a Federal party on the old lines, controlled and financed from headquarters. . . . Local autonomy is the guiding principle in farmer organization today, and it is for the preservation of that principle which safeguards the movement against "fusion" or a form of "co-operation" which means not co-operation, but ultimate union, that those who join issue with Mr. Crerar are contending at this time.

Nor was the conflict of opinion academic or superficial. "Between him [Crerar]," concluded Wood, "and those who believe

---

[69] The distinction between fusion and coalition is to be noted again.

in democratically organized citizenship taking political action as such, there is an irreconcilable conflict of opinion."[70]

Thus the lines were clearly drawn between those who wished to make the Progressive movement a democratic party of reform, purged of the evils of party patronage and "professional" politics, and those who denied that the traditional party system admitted of reform and sought to replace it by the representation of occupational groups. Both sides had much in common, the representation of agrarian interests, the cleansing of political life, a dislike and distrust of the "interests." Both feared the consequences of a split in the movement. The conflict, however, was fundamental. The Crerarites were reformers only; the Woodites, though constitutionalists in profession and practice, were in concept revolutionaries. Group government in full flower would have been anarcho-syndicalism.

Because the two wings still had much in common and because the Manitoban Progressives, pragmatic and easy-going men in general, greatly outnumbered the Albertans, the conference in Winnipeg ignored the fundamental nature of the division. Crerar's resignation was followed by the strongly intimated reluctance of the Canadian Council of Agriculture, which foreshadowed its withdrawal of support the following spring, to continue to act as the central organization of the Progressive party. These changes might have been expected to precipitate a clear-cut division, which would have driven the Manitoban Progressives over to the Liberal party and left the Albertans an independent group. The conference, however, proceeded to discuss organization, and then to elect Robert Forke leader, after a number of "favourite son" nominees had withdrawn their names.[71] The Manitoban ascendancy in the party was to continue.

Forke was a bluff, amiable Scots Canadian of transparent honesty and transcendent modesty, who after a long career in municipal politics had been elected Progressive member for Brandon in 1921. The kindly "laird of Pipestone" had been

---

[70] *Farmers' Sun*, Nov. 14, 1922, p. 1; see also *Grain Growers' Guide*, XV, Nov. 15, 1922, p. 25.

[71] Forke was reported to have been elected over J. T. Shaw of Calgary. Shaw later declared that he had withdrawn his name before the ballot had been taken.

one of the members of Crerar's delegation to Ottawa in December 1921. He made his mark in the debate on the Address, and, with R. A. Hoey, had been favoured by Crerar to succeed him in the leadership.[72] Forke, like Crerar, was a western agrarian Liberal who hoped to redeem the federal Liberal party but who thought continued Progressive independence a necessary means to that end. His election, then, made little change in the situation except perhaps to improve somewhat the prospects of unity in the party, by the substitution of his light hands on the reins for the sometimes brusque grasp of Crerar.

Whether the Albertan Progressives accepted the continuance of Manitoban leadership without opposition or reservation, the reports do not reveal. That the change was not likely to produce harmony in the party had been revealed by the division which had arisen during the attempt to provide an organization for the federal political movement.

If there were to be such an organization at all, it was necessary to supply the soon to be vacated place of the Canadian Council of Agriculture, which was preparing to withdraw its support. To that end, the following resolution was passed unanimously: "That it is desirable in the national interest that an organization should be created for the furthering of Progressive principles throughout Canada, and that for this purpose a committee of one member from each province be appointed to draft recommendations and submit the same to this conference."[73] The committee was appointed and reported:

That, in the opinion of the elected representatives of the Progressive party, the Progressive movement is big enough to include men and women of common ideals from all walks of life, and that steps should be taken whereby practical expression can be given to those ideals.

That, while it is not desirable to interfere with existing methods whereby this has been wholly or in part accomplished in the various provinces,

And whereas the Canadian Council of Agriculture has ceased to function as the co-ordinating agency of the political activities of the different Progressive organizations;

[72]Dafoe Papers, Dafoe to Clifford Sifton, Nov. 2, 1922.
[73]*Farmers' Sun*, Nov. 14, 1922, p. 1; *Grain Growers' Guide*, XV, Nov. 22, 1922, p. 4.

We realize the necessity of some Federal co-ordinating agency, and would recommend that immediate steps be taken to hold a conference of the different Provincial Progressive organizations, for the purpose of creating such an agency and that a committee be appointed from this meeting to confer with the provincial bodies.[74]

Gingerly and awkwardly as it was phrased, the proposed resolution failed to bridge the gap between those who wished to broaden the movement into a national party, and those who were proponents of constituency autonomy and group government. A counter-resolution was submitted in writing, signed by R. Gardiner, J. T. Shaw, H. E. Spencer, A. Speakman, W. T. Lucas, D. M. Kennedy, G. G. Coote and L. H. Jeliff, all U.F.A. members except Shaw, the independent from Calgary. In it they protested that "We, realizing that political organization is a matter primarily and entirely for constituency organizations, withhold our assent to this resolution."[75] Agnes Macphail handed in the supporting statement: "Believing as I do in constituency control of political organization and initiative, I withhold my assent to this resolution."[76] True to their principles, these members had ensured that no jealous constituents could say that they had sacrificed the control of the member by his electors to the central office of a national organization.

The dissent by Albertan Progressives was met generously by adding as an amendment to the Committee's proposed resolution, the following clause: "That after discussing the matter of a national Progressive organization, we agree to lay the matter before our constituency executives, or any organization that is proper to the Province concerned, for their decision."[77] The resolution was then adopted unanimously, and Robert Forke, T. H. McConica, R. H. Halbert, and T. W. Caldwell were named to the committee; no Albertan was a member. With that the attempt to begin the formation of a national organization was left, and though it was to be renewed in the future, no such organization was ever created to take the place of the Canadian Council of Agriculture.

[74] *Farmers' Sun*, Nov. 14, 1922, pp. 1 and 5.
[75] *Ibid.*
[76] *Ibid.*
[77] *Ibid.*

Subsequent developments were to make it evident that the failure of this attempt to form a federal political organization for the Progressive movement had doomed the party to disintegration. In so far as they contributed to the failure by their adherence to their principles of constituency autonomy and occupational representation, the Albertan Progressives were responsible for the break-up of the Progressive party. For while they rested securely on their own electoral organization of the U.F.A., the other Progressives were left in mid-air without the support of constituency organizations, except for such as their constituents might care to maintain without benefit of the doctrine of group organization. In this fashion, the Progressive political movement was left to fall between the two stools of party and economic group organization.

At the end of 1922, the Progressives had undergone outwardly only a change of leader. But an internal cleavage had developed in the movement, which had caused, and was to cause, differences over policy, tactics, and organization. These differences already threatened to destroy it as an independent third party. At the same time, the Manitoban Progressives had failed to develop, in the party as a whole, or among themselves, that discipline of organization and clearness of purpose which alone could accomplish their purpose of forcing a realignment of parties, with themselves as the nucleus of a popular party of reform. The Albertan Progressives, by their rigid insistence on constituency autonomy and occupational representation, the former fatal to the legislative caucus on which cabinet government rested, the latter contrary to the principle of general and territorial representation, were attempting to introduce into Canadian political practice procedures incompatible with its traditions and functioning. Each of the two wings of the party, pursuing conflicting aims, had failed to advance its own ends, and had thwarted and irritated the other. The disintegration of the movement was well begun.

The Disintegration of the Federal Progressive Party, 1923-25

T H E parliamentary session of 1922 and its aftermath had seen the issues determining the character and future of the Progressive party drawn and in substance decided. The Progressive representation had failed to become either a genuine national party or a definite occupational group. The three succeeding sessions of 1923, 1924, and 1925 were to see the ebbing of the Progressive movement and the break-up far advanced of the federal representation into two groups, a liberal group of the Manitoban persuasion and a doctrinaire group of the Albertan school.

Though mutual suspicions served to increase the division,[1] the root of the differences exposed in 1922 was plain. The Manitoban Progressives, while seeking to diminish electoral corruption and eliminate political patronage and graft in the spirit of the reform movement, believed that to realize the Progressive programme a parliamentary and national party, capable of acting as a unit in the House and in elections, was a necessity. The Albertan Progressives, for their part, believed that to adopt the forms and practices of party organization would be to impair that firm control of the representative by his constituents which their electoral methods had established, and to become once more a composite party "autocratically" controlled from the top down, not democratically directed from the bottom up. This was the pure doctrine of Wood, in reality

[1]Dafoe Papers, Dafoe to Clifford Sifton, May 6, 1922: "Crerar is suspect in the matter of the Wheat Board."

168

American "grass-roots" democracy as compared with Canadian parliamentary democracy. "To turn," he wrote, "from organized political action [by occupational groups] in which the people move systematically, from the bottom up, is to turn from democracy. To turn to the political party, which is to be guided by an executive committee—guided from the top down—is to turn back to individualism and political autocracy."[2] So believing, the Albertan Progressives could not but be uneasy members of the parliamentary representation of the movement, and the three sessions were to furnish occasions on which the fundamental cleavage between the two wings was evident. The conference of November 10, 1922, in fact, had altered nothing except in the replacement of Crerar by Forke. The two opposing views of the nature and future of the parliamentary representation remained unchanged on both sides.

The Manitoban view was expounded at length in the editorial columns of the *Manitoba Free Press* on November 10, 1922. The Progressive movement, it declared, was at the crossroads. It remained a movement still, having neither widened into a party nor contracted into a "caste" group. It might become an occupational group, but that would prove a way of lingering death. It ought to become a party, a party which, however, need not be fiercely partisan or corrupt. "But," it went on, "the legitimate equipment of a party they [the Progressives] will require if they are ever to amount to anything—some organization, some discipline, some machinery, some sense of obligation to one another, and enough money to carry their gospel to the gentiles." The basis for such a party lay to hand, an economic policy designed to encourage the basic industries of the country. "The only test," the editorial affirmed, "for association with the Progressive party should be acceptance of this belief. A bootblack who subscribes to this doctrine ought to be just as much a member of the party as the largest farmer in Canada." Caste sentiment would have to be eliminated from the movement, as the votes of the towns and villages would be needed. The "fierce proscriptive spirit" should be exorcized from the minds of Progressives; had it been done

[2]H. W. Wood, "Shall We Go Forward Or Turn Back?" (*The U.F.A.*, Sept. 1, 1922, p. 1).

before, they might have gained the support of half a dozen leading parliamentarians such as A. R. McMaster. As a party, they would have to seek office. "Some of the Progressives," the editorial continued, "appear to have an idea that they can exercise power without assuming responsibility. In the long run the two things cannot be divorced. If they have clearly defined national policies they will find they can only give effect to them by obtaining power." If the movement were to give rise to a party, would the result be a continuing third party? It might be. A party was but a means to an end, and the country was bigger than any party. The Progressives, on the other hand, might absorb the liberal elements in the Liberal party, or the Liberal party the Progressives; it would little matter which, in the event.[3]

These views, cogently expressed as they were, had not prevailed in the conference. The Albertan members had successfully defended the principle of constituency autonomy. The official organ of the organized farmers of Alberta, *The U.F.A.*, therefore approved the outcome of the conference, and noted with satisfaction that two groups within the Progressive representation had in effect been recognized, the U.F.A. being one.

The whole controversy [it went on to remark] turns upon the differences between the Alberta plan of democratic organization on the one hand, and the political party system on the other. The Albertan members recognize that they are in fact elected for legislative purposes only. They could not logically assent to the creation, by themselves as elected members, of any form of centralized committee to assume control of the political activities of the electorate. This control cannot be democratically exercised unless it is vested entirely in the organized citizens themselves.[4]

The elected member, in short, was in this view the delegate of his constituents. His business was to advance the legislation they desired, untrammelled by caucus. Neither he nor a party organization was to spend time and energy in working for his re-election; nomination and election being the exclusive business

[3]*Manitoba Free Press*, Nov. 10, 1922, p. 15, editorial, "At the Cross Roads." This was published, no doubt for effect, the day the conference met. The prose is the prose of Dafoe, but the sentiments are Crerar's as well.

[4]*The U.F.A.*, Nov. 15, 1922, p. 3.

of the voters. Out of such members neither a parliamentary nor a national party could be built, and this, in the Albertan view, was clear gain and an immense reform of political methods.

While the Albertans had successfully avoided the merging of their group in a national party, the Manitoban Progressives, for their part, had retained the leadership of the parliamentary representation of the movement by the election of Forke, who was Crerar's choice.[5] Forke at once made it clear that the character of the party's leadership had not changed. Speaking at Souris on November 14, he said: "We must carry our ideals and principles to a logical conclusion, and, if ever called, must not be afraid to take up the reins of Government. . . . I believe the Progressive movement wider in extent than is generally acknowledged. It has a platform broad enough for all classes to stand on."[6] And, indeed, while Crerar remained a member of the House, there could be little doubt where the actual leadership lay. The approaches of Prime Minister King were, until 1925, made to Crerar and not to Forke.[7]

So far as any change had been made in policy, and King's approaches and the ultimate outcome were to show how inconclusive it was, it lay in the acceptance by the conference of Crerar's and J. F. Johnston's assurances that fusion with the Liberals had never been intended, and its pronouncement that the Progressive party remained "unalterably opposed" to any fusion with the Liberals.[8] This reflected at once the distrust of the Albertan, and of many Manitoban, members of dealings with the old parties, and also the conclusion of the leaders of the Manitoban Progressives that the time for administrative co-operation has passed. The party had no choice thereafter but to continue as an independent group in the House, and to wait upon events.

As the character of the leadership was unchanged, so also were the difficulties of the group. Not even all the Manitoban Progressives were convinced that the purpose of the movement

[5]Dafoe Papers, Dafoe to Clifford Sifton, Nov. 2, 1922.
[6]Quoted in Paterson, "The Progressive Political Movement," 69, no reference given.
[7]Dafoe Papers, Dafoe to Clifford Sifton, March 12, 1923; Dafoe to J.A.S., Jan. 26, 1924.
[8]*Grain Growers' Guide*, XV, Nov. 22, 1922, p. 4.

was the creation of a new, reform party, willing to assume office. In them also, and in their constituents, the spirit of independency was strong. At the annual convention of the U.F.M. in January 1923, Forke, Hoey, and Crerar sought to win approval of their policy of "broadening out." "The Progressives," declared Hoey, "had by their rejection of fusion accepted responsibility for spreading their ideals in other parts of the Dominion." Forke pointed out that the movement sought not only a better economic policy for the country, but also better conditions in politics. The desire for a purification of political life had the effect, when the organization of a Progressive party was proposed, of arousing the fear the old abuses might return. Broadening out, however, was a necessity, since a policy of holding the balance of power was impracticable. A national majority would have to be gained, if Progressive objectives were to be realized. Broadening out, Forke asserted, would not destroy the control of their representatives by the U.F.M. locals. Crerar, in his turn, urged that Progressive local associations, political only and not occupational, should be created. Such associations would supply the necessary organization and be thoroughly democratic. The real abuse of the old party system was not the organizations, but "the patronage system, secret campaign funds and private payment of election expenses."[9]

The convention, however, rejected these counsels, and passed two political resolutions. The first declared that a principal cause of the Progressive movement was "the manifest evils of political partyism" and repudiated the thought of the amalgamation of the Progressives with any political party. The second endorsed the mode of political action in use, and affirmed the opposition of the convention to any change in the relationship "between the constituencies and the members of parliament."[10] The jealous independency and obstinate idealism, thus asserted in the teeth of the three Manitoban leaders, was to keep flashing out from the movement during its entire course. In the next session, for example, T. W. Bird, member for Nelson, was to throw out in the course of debate the decla-

[9]*Ibid.*, XVI, Jan. 17, 1923, pp. 16, 19, and 20.
[10]*Ibid.*, p. 7.

ration: "The Progressive party has no ambition for power and a statement of its policy does not look forward to any assumption of power."[11] Well might the leaders think that they had undertaken to make bricks without straw. The same convention of the U.F.M. was to reveal a more insidious danger, in that it gave far more time to the discussion of co-operative marketing than of political action. The swing from political to economic action had begun.

The change, however, was only one among others which were taking place in the political situation. As one shrewd and informed observer saw it, the Progressive party was not making headway, nor was it likely to do so. To A. B. Hudson, the results of the Quebec provincial elections of 1923 were a check to the Liberals who followed Gouin, and marked the end of the Quebec bloc, though the *bleus* might not make gains while Meighen remained Conservative leader. In Ontario, the predominance of Quebec in the government had aroused the Orangemen, which precluded the hope that the provincial Liberals might recover in that province. The Ontario Progressives, for their part, would lose heavily and might disappear. In British Columbia, Liberal prospects were poor. As a result, the provinces of the continental West were the critical area. The division between Liberals and Progressives, in these circumstances, might well bring disaster to the liberal cause. "It becomes more clear every day that the failure of our proposed alliance was a tragedy."[12] Thus the outcome of the election of 1925, except for the Liberal *débâcle* in the eastern Maritime Provinces, was coming into sight two years before it occurred, and Dafoe could write in the same vein as Hudson to a distinguished correspondent overseas, adding, however, that even in the event of a falling off of support of the Liberal party the Progressives might hold the balance of power.[13]

In the critical area dominated by the western Progressives, yet another change took place in the spring of 1923. The withdrawal of the Canadian Council of Agriculture from support of the movement, of which the conference of November had been

[11]*Can. H. of C. Debates*, 1923, III, p. 2793.
[12]Dafoe Papers, A. B. Hudson to Dafoe, Feb. 27, 1923.
[13]*Ibid.*, Dafoe to Alfred Zimmern, Feb. 27, 1923.

advised, was carried out. The future course of the Council with respect to political action had been discussed at the meeting of August 1922. President H. W. Wood had first been heard on the relation of the Council to political action. "He pointed out that there were two ideas, the Group idea and the Party idea, and that Farmers' organizations in the past had met calamity when they had adopted the Party idea in politics." Crerar then expounded his belief in the necessity of creating a national political organization for the Progressives. Thereupon Langley asked Crerar to define his intentions, and Crerar in reply read certain conclusions reached by a caucus of Progressive members in Ottawa at the end of the session. These proposed the separation of the Progressive political movement from the Council. Discussion then ended. No action had been taken at the time, and all that was revealed was that both Wood and Crerar desired the withdrawal of the Council, the former in order to take it out of politics, the latter to push forward the creation of a national organization of the Progressives.[14]

The actual withdrawal took place in March 1923. On the motion of George Bevington and Colin H. Burnell, the Council ended its leadership of the farmers' political movement, and left it to the provincial organizations.[15] Its one further act with reference to political action was to revise the Farmers' Platform, and submit the revision to the provincial organizations. This was an up-to-date version of the Platform, substantially like the old one, except that the planks calling for taxation for unimproved land values and direct legislation had been dropped, and public ownership of utilities had been substituted for the nationalization of coal mines.[16]

The reasons for the withdrawal were probably twofold. It is true that Wood, in his rivalry with Crerar, had come to dominate the Council, and that he wished to effect the withdrawal.[17] In May 1923, he published an article explaining that the Council had withdrawn, not from its legitimate political

---

[14]P.A.M., Minutes of Canadian Council of Agriculture, Aug. 1, 1922, p. 158.
[15]Ibid., March 28, 1923, pp. 178-9.
[16]Grain Growers' Guide, XVI, Dec. 5, 1923, p. 45.
[17]Sharp, Agrarian Revolt, 210-11.

activities, but from political action as such, because certain elements in the farmers' movement had wished to continue to use it as a co-ordinating agency for the Progressive political movement. To have done this, he declared, would have been to expose the Council to the fate which had overtaken all farm organizations in the United States that had taken political action. Thereafter the Council would leave political action to the provincial organizations.[18] The argument was incomplete, but the implication was that one of these organizations, the U.F.A., was taking political action as a group and the others might follow its example. The Council, however, which had no membership of its own, could only be a political directory which might draw the U.F.A. into a party organization.

The withdrawal was thus a victory for the group idea, and as such an incident in the struggle between Manitoban and Albertan Progressives over the character of the political organization of the farmers' movement. There was also, however, another and substantial reason, which was not made public, for the withdrawal. Not only were the farmers' organizations suffering from a calamitous loss of members and revenue, but the farmers' commercial companies, the United Grain Growers and the Saskatchewan Co-operative Elevators, were also feeling the effects of the agricultural depression. They could not continue to run the risk of alienating the support of Liberal or Conservative members by supporting political action by the organized farmers. Accordingly, as the Secretary of the Council[19] wrote in confidence to an American inquirer a year later: "The point was eventually reached where it became necessary for the Council either to re-organize without the commercial companies, or cease to take part in politics. This, I think, is the real reason for the resolution adopted by the Council in March, 1923."[20]

From the spring of 1923, therefore, the Progressive political movement was left without central direction, except for such as might be given by a new national committee, or could be given

[18]*The U.F.A.*, May 15, 1923, p. 1. Wood said: "If the Council has at any time controlled or financed any party or group in the House, I didn't know about it."

[19]John Ward, successor to N. P. Lambert as secretary of the Canadian Council of Agriculture.

[20]P.A.M., Files of Canadian Council of Agriculture, J [ohn] W [ard] to Wm. Wirth, Editor, *Missouri Farmer*, June 21, 1924.

by the parliamentary leader and caucus. The opening of the session, none the less, saw the group reassembled as in 1922, except for the change in leadership, the substitution of E. N. Hopkins for R. M. Johnson, who had been unseated for technical irregularities in his election, and the defection of Binette and Hammell. Forke, in the debate on the Address, declared that no alteration of purpose had occurred in the party: "We still retain the same position we have held all along. We are neither opposing nor supporting the government; we are here to give expression to and to advance the ideas and principles we hold to be in the best interests of Canada and to see them, if possible, carried into effect in the form of legislation."[21] And a by no means sympathetic political commentator noted that he seemed determined to keep the Progressives balanced between the government and the opposition.[22]

The organization of the previous session was retained with a caucus, provincial caucuses, a whip, who was still J. F. Johnston, provincial whips, and the exercise of party discipline in voting, speaking, and assignment to committees, but such organization was only in a measure successful, as the session of 1922 had revealed, and as future sessions were to demonstrate. The genius of the Progressive political movement in both its wings, as already noted, was the independence of the individual member. "The Progressive Movement," wrote Crerar, "particularly in Western Canada, was built largely on the individual Member of Parliament, that is, he was to be free from the old party machinery and to follow his own judgment."[23] The reins of party, by all accepted standards of the old parties, had to be lightly held. "No one," Grant Dexter, an intimate observer, noted, "pretended that a vote in caucus bound the group as a whole."[24] That this was a matter of principle rather than of practice the following analysis of Progressive voting suggests: during 1922 (fifteen divisions), with government four, with opposition one, against both eight, mixed vote two; during 1923 (thirty-five divisions), with government two, with opposition

[21]*Can. H. of C. Debates*, 1923, I, p. 35.
[22]*Canadian Forum*, III, Feb., 1923, p. 133.
[23]Crerar Papers, Crerar to H. B. Mitchell, June 10, 1922.
[24]Grant Dexter, "Will the Prairies Go Solid Again?" *Maclean's Magazine*, XXXVIII, Oct. 15, 1925, p. 75.

six, against both twenty-two, mixed vote five. That is, in only seven out of fifty divisions, was the group divided.[25]

So much freedom had not been heard of in the days of the old parties. It was exercised by the Progressives on divisions which were not routine but controversial, when unity would have counted most, and the spirit which made it possible operated to keep discipline at all times light and tentative. The relaxing of the bonds of caucus was a major contribution of the Progressive movement to Canadian political life. "The old days when a government could bring down a measure, and push it through whether their supporters in the House liked it or not have pretty well disappeared," Crerar had observed during the first session,[26] and the observation remained true as long as Progressive influences lingered in the House of Commons.

Light as were the bonds of the Progressive caucus, Albertan members found them irksome. Their objections, moreover, were fundamental. In the first place, they complained, the parliamentary party system stifled criticism by threat of dissolution, and silenced the expression of economic needs by splitting the vote of economic interests. "In Canada," Henry Spencer asserted, "the economic needs of the various provinces differ considerably. The situation is such that each of the provinces might be represented in both of the parties, and yet, when votes are registered, members from the same province be opposed, owing to the fact that votes are cast for Party reasons and not for economic ones."[27] The unconscious sectionalism of this passage was, of course, revealing. In the second place, the parliamentary party system was competitive and not co-operative. "The Party System," Spencer's indictment continued, "exists in a continual struggle for power and not for legislation."[28] In this view there was genuine idealism, naïve though it might seem to the hardened parliamentarian. "I would like," said Agnes Macphail in an interview, "to see in all our Parliaments a group representing agriculture as such, but not having power under our two party system. Where one party must

[25]Spencer Files, quoted by permission of Mr. H. E. Spencer from a table displaying Progressive voting in these terms, 1922-35.

[26]Crerar Papers, Crerar to G. F. Chipman, March 18, 1922.

[27]Spencer Files, 1924; H. E. Spencer, "Parliament and the Party System."

[28]*Ibid.*

take the power, all others combine against them.   And power is very dangerous—it preys on the weaknesses of humanity. Under a co-operative group government, we would have to share the power as well as the responsibility.   In such a government the only criticism would be honest, from conviction."[29] Members holding such views, and working out a social philosophy for a co-operative society governed by co-operative methods, could not be at ease amid the conflict of organized parties.

For this reason, the session of 1923 saw a renewal of the attempts made in 1922 to alter parliamentary and electoral conditions in ways which would make possible the realization of the Albertan Progressive ideals of government.   Early in the session William Irvine, close ally of the Albertan Progressives, introduced the motion: "That, in the opinion of this House, a defeat of a government measure should not be considered a sufficient reason for the resignation of the government, unless followed by a vote of lack of confidence."[30]   In support of the motion he argued that "Parliament [had] lost its old supremacy [and was] dominated by the cabinet through the party caucus."[31]   "This practice of cabinet control by threat of election," he continued, "has a tendency to confuse the issues," the issue of the measure before the House with the issue of the life of the administration and of parliament.[32]   The proposal was one designed, therefore, to restore the supremacy of parliament and the independence of individual members. The motion was supported by J. T. Shaw, who had already declared that his amendment to the Address need not in his opinion be considered to express want of confidence in the government.[33]   T. W. Bird touched the core of the matter, however, when he pointed out that "the really important aspect of this discussion [was] its bearing upon the third party in the House,"[34] and went on to claim that more consideration should be given to the right of the Progressives to express themselves

[29] *The U.F.A.*, Oct. 1, 1923, p. 6, interview with Miss Agnes Macphail, M.P.
[30] *Can. H. of C. Debates*, 1923, I, p. 208.
[31] *Ibid.*
[32] *Ibid.*, p. 209.
[33] *Ibid.*, p. 72.
[34] *Ibid.*, p. 226.

under the rules of the House, a stand in which he was supported by Forke.[35]

On the other side, members of the old parties who took part in the debate opposed the motion with sharp criticism. The Prime Minister in particular defended caucus "as the means whereby a government [could] ascertain through its following what the views and opinions of the public, as represented by the various constituencies, [might] be. It [was] not a means of over-riding parliament."[36] To him the practice of dissolution, following on the defeat of an administration in the House was a safeguard of democracy. "The whole effort manifest in the evolution of parliament," he declared, "[had] been to bring the ministry to the point where, if for any reason whatever it cease[d] to hold the confidence of parliament, it [would] be obliged to go to the people."[37] That this doctrine produced the results complained of, the grinding of parliament between upper and nether millstones of cabinet and electorate, the Prime Minister was prevented by his instinctive Gritism from perceiving. His supporters from both sides of the House agreed with him in effect, and saw in the motion either a superfluous restatement of established convention, or a pernicious innovation. Like Charles A. Stewart, they were stout in their support of caucus. "Under responsible government we [should] always have to have a caucus," contended Stewart. Otherwise members of the governmental party would be free to differ from the proposals of their leaders, and to bring about the defeat of the government. If disagreement there must be, the place for it was in caucus, and once a majority had spoken in caucus, disagreement was ended. Only so, he asserted, could stability of government be maintained.[38]

The motion, thus opposed by the conventional arguments, received no encouragement from members of the old parties, and the attempt of the Progressives to win greater freedom of expression for individual members and sectional groups—to

---

[35]*Ibid.*, p. 232.

[36]*Ibid.*, p. 219.

[37]*Ibid.*, p. 221; this speech, and Irvine's are quoted extensively in *Constitutional Issues in Canada, 1900-1931*, compiled by R. M. Dawson (Toronto, 1933), pp. 135-45.

[38]*Can. H. of C. Debates*, 1923, I, pp. 238-9.

escape from the sovereignty of caucus—was voted down one hundred and three to fifty-two. The Progressives, except J. F. Johnston, voted for, and the rest of the House against, the motion.[39] Few in the debate noted the vital distinction between a government resigning, and a government advising dissolution, on suffering defeat in the House. Most talked in terms of a government resigning, and assumed it would advise dissolution.

No more fortunate was W. C. Good's motion to provide for an experiment in proportional representation in the next federal election. This motion of the previous session had led to the appointment of a select committee, which had reported in favour of the alternative vote in single-member constituencies, to which the House had agreed, and had commended proportional representation. In supporting his motion, Good added little to his argument of the year before and the debate was not illuminating. A number of members, both Liberal and Conservative, expressed the fear that a general adoption of proportional representation would lead to the multiplication of groups. The Prime Minister opposed this view, but it was no doubt effective in bringing about the defeat of the motion in an open vote of ninety to ninety-two, the Progressives and some Liberals supporting the motion.[40] The failure was not serious, but the elimination of the alternative vote from the Redistribution Bill of 1924 was to be, because the measure might have enabled a few Ontario Progressives to win three-cornered contests. Its defeat, therefore, contributed in some degree to the diminution of Progressive strength in the election of 1925. The old parties, with a sound instinct, had remained true to the knock-out system of single-member constituencies which made for their survival.

In the same vein as the motions of Irvine and Good, the Progressives repeated Crerar's effort to have the rules of the House altered so as to permit an amendment to the amendment of the motion to go into the Committees of Supply, or Ways and Means.[41] The debate was marked by the same reluctance, save for intervention in support of the Progressives by

[39]*Ibid.*, pp. 243-4.
[40]*Ibid.*, pp. 389-434.
[41]*Ibid.*, II, p. 1299.

McMaster, on the part of the old parties to liberalize the conventions of parliament so as to allow the free operation of a third party. They voted down the Progressive motion, and the reform had to await further demonstration that the old order of the two-party system was not soon to be restored.[42]

Meantime the Progressives, despite the embarrassment of rules and conventions designed for the two-party system, were making their weight felt by the use of the unusual procedure of moving an amendment to the Address. This was done on February 5 by R. A. Hoey and T. W. Caldwell, no doubt as a result of a decision taken in caucus to meet the difficulty of making their views known on fiscal policy.[43] The amendment expressed the opinion that, in view of prevailing distress, "substantial reductions of the burden of customs taxation should be made with a view to the accomplishing of two purposes of the highest importance; (1) diminishing the very high cost of production which presses so severely on the primary producers of the country at this time; (2) reducing the cost of living to the great masses of the common people, many of whom are being forced out of the country by prevailing economic conditions."[44]

The comment of the *Manitoba Free Press* revealed the intention, and perhaps the public effect, of the motion when it said: "The Progressive party, by moving the Hoey amendment and by supporting it by speeches and vote, are at one and the same time keeping alive the low tariff movement and revealing the Liberal apostasy in office to policies professed in opposition. They are establishing in the eyes of the country the fact that the government and the opposition are with respect to fiscal policy, merely wings of the same party."[45] Beyond doubt, the amendment did much after the events of November to unify the group at the outset of the new session, and to define its character in the public mind.

Unfortunately, the effect of the motion was marred, and the vulnerability of the group to the disruptive tactics of the old parties once more made evident, by an amendment to the

[42]*Ibid.*, p. 1307. The change was obtained in the Parliament elected in 1926; see A. Beauchesne, *Rules and Forms of the House of Commons of Canada*, 3rd edition (Toronto, 1943), p. 129; Standing Order 49, March 22, 1927.

[43]*Can. H. of G. Debates*, 1923, I, p. 167, speech of T. H. McConica.

[44]*Ibid.*, p. 65.

[45]*Manitoba Free Press*, Feb. 10, 1923, p. 11.

amendment moved by J. T. Shaw, member for Calgary West. The capable but erratic Shaw had been considered a Progressive, but he had behaved in unruly fashion at the Winnipeg conference of November 1922, and now proclaimed his complete independence. His sub-amendment called for every effort being made to practise economy in public expenditures.[46]   In thus seeking to convert the Hoey amendment into a double-barrelled criticism of the government, Shaw was probably acting, as suggested by L. H. Martell, Liberal member for Hants, in conjunction with the Conservative opposition.[47]

The government, thus doubly challenged, declared through Fielding that it regarded both amendment and sub-amendment as tests of confidence.[48]   It thus placed itself in the position where it might be defeated and be forced to dissolve parliament, if Progressives and Conservatives voted solidly for the sub-amendment.   When the vote was taken on the sub-amendment, the Progressives split,[49] those who voted with the Liberals stating frankly that they were not prepared to risk the defeat of the government for the sake of the unity of the group or the principle of economy.[50]   On the Hoey amendment, they were re-united, Progressive and Labour members voting solidly for the motion, which was defeated by the combined Liberal and Conservative forces, one hundred and forty to fifty-four.   This vote was signalized by A. R. McMaster, the free-trade Liberal from Brome, parting company with his party colleagues to vote for the Progressive amendment.[51]

Despite the union of Liberals and Conservatives on the amendment, however, the debate on the Address had been marked by a change of tactics on the part of the Conservatives. In 1922 they had harried the Progressives, denouncing them as auxiliaries of the government.   In 1923 all was, on the contrary, cordiality and good-fellowship, a response, it might be, to Forke's declaration of the independence of the third party, or to new-kindled hopes of its speedy disintegration.   A very

[46]*Can. H. of C. Debates*, 1923, I, p. 72.
[47]*Ibid.*, p. 105.
[48]*Ibid.*, p. 99.
[49]*Ibid.*, p. 177.
[50]*Ibid.*, p. 169.
[51]*Ibid.*, pp. 178-9.

definite result of the new affability of the Conservatives was their yielding to the Progressives their right, as the official opposition, to move the amendment to the motion to go into Committee on Ways and Means.[52] The Progressives were to have a chance to make their views on fiscal policy formally known.

Fielding brought down on May 11 what was to prove to be his last budget.[53] It confirmed the suggestion in the Speech from the Throne that no changes were to be expected, and justified the action of the Progressives in moving the Hoey amendment. The Minister of Finance developed the argument that the reductions of 1922 had fulfilled the Liberal commitments of his motion of 1921, which, he had claimed, expressed Liberal tariff policy rather than the plank of 1919. The Laurier-Fielding tariff had been restored by those reductions, and the time had come to assure business that the tariff would be stable. "Speaking broadly," said the old statesman, "it is possible to give the country a reasonable assurance of stability of tariff. . . ." The tariff, however, was not only to be stable; it was also to be moderate. "The tariff as it will be when the changes proposed today come into effect will be a moderate tariff and probably as low as the country can afford." Moderation was, indeed, the condition which alone could give stability. The policy of a moderate tariff was itself conditioned by a standing offer of reciprocity of trade with the United States.[54] Thus the ancient Maritimer, with debonair, old-world deftness, offset the concession to industry of a stable tariff by holding out the prospect of reciprocity with the United States, long desired by the continental West and the Maritime Provinces. It was to balance a fact with a hope, a deed with a delusion; apart from that, Liberal tariff policy had come to rest dead centre between the protectionist followers of Meighen and the agrarian low-tariff men.

It was, therefore, a budget against which Conservatives and Progressives could combine, though for opposing reasons. Nor did the Progressives fumble the opportunity which the courtesy of the Conservatives had opened to them. Forke's speech, in

[52]*Ibid.*, III, p. 2711.
[53]*Ibid.*, p. 2640.
[54]*Ibid.*, pp. 2648-99.

moving the Progressive amendment, was moderate in tone, as all that kindly gentleman's utterances were, but the amendment itself was an incisive and massive indictment of Liberal policy. The budget, it alleged, was a repudiation of the platform of 1919; it rested on the principle of protection; and it continued indirect and oppressive taxation at a time when the primary producers and the consumers of the country required relief. The amendment proposed, therefore, "an immediate and substantial reduction of the tariff, particularly on the necessaries of life and the implements of production," an increase in the British preference, reciprocity with the United States, the consequent loss of revenue to be offset by an increase of taxation on unearned incomes and on luxuries.[55] Here at last was the New National Policy, brought out in fighting trim on the floor of the House. At no time after December 1921, was the Progressive party more united, better knit, or more purposeful; and as a group it pressed home the attack on the low-tariff flank.

Meantime on the other flank the protectionist phalanx had been wheeling to the assault. To the Conservatives the concept of a moderate and stable tariff was, of course, acceptable. "I have stood all my life," said their leader, "for a policy of moderate protection in this country. Under the conditions of the last few years I have felt that the tariff in effect was on a general scale that could justly be described as moderate protection."[56] But how could moderate protection and a stable tariff be continued with a standing offer of reciprocity?[57] Reciprocity with the United States, if ever attained, could not be a stable policy, for it would be renounced at will by the great republic. A budget which contained the offer of reciprocity offered but a hollow guarantee of stability.[58]

If, however, the budget was not acceptable to the Conservatives, neither, of course, was the Forke amendment. As a result, with the exception of A. B. Hudson and A. R. McMaster, only Progressives voted for the amendment.[59] McMaster not only voted with the Progressives, but, in a forceful and cour-

[55]Ibid., pp. 2717-18.
[56]Ibid., p. 2991.
[57]As the Montreal Gazette, May 22, 1923, p. 12, pointed out, they could not.
[58]Can. H. of C. Debates, 1923, III, pp. 2991-3.
[59]Ibid., IV, p. 3082.

ageous speech, denounced the budget as being but a continuation of the National Policy, a policy which was in reality "anti-national" and anti-social.[60] Both Liberals also voted with the Progressives on the main motion.

On this division, indeed, the combination of a solid Progressive group and a solid opposition brought the government's majority down to eight, the vote being one hundred and fourteen to one hundred and six.[61] A policy of dead centre between protection in principle and tariff reduction in practice had brought the extremes together against the middle. The Progressives for once had not allowed their fear of King James to overcome their dislike of King Charles. They had risked defeating the Liberal government. King had forfeited Progressive support by the standpatism of the Fielding budget, and would have to alter course westward if he were to avoid such narrow divisions in the future.

In the debate on the Address in 1923, then, the Progressives had been well handled, had behaved well except for Shaw's aberration, and had definitely put their tariff policy before the country. They had even attracted King's two most independent followers, thus momentarily recouping the loss of Binette and Hammell. On the major debate of the session, however, that on the decennial revision of the Bank Act, a break occurred in the harmony hitherto prevailing. The U.F.A. members, representatives of a province in which the difficulties of a debtor and agrarian frontier, aggravated by post-war deflation and the closing of the American market to agricultural produce, were particularly acute, had been influenced by the teaching of monetary reformers of the United States and Great Britain. This influence gave to the political thought of Alberta another distinguishing trait. It happened that Alberta had attracted J. W. Leedy and William Irvine, and these men, and others, such as C. W. Peterson of the *Farm and Ranch Review*, were stimulated by conditions prevailing in the province to give special attention to matters of credit and money. Leedy made known in Alberta and the West the monetary ideas of Populism.[62]

[60]*Ibid.*, III, p. 3018.
[61]*Ibid.*, IV, p. 3084.
[62]Sharp, *Agrarian Revolt*, 113-14.

Irvine, in the *Nutcracker* and its successors, the *Alberta Non-Partisan* and the *Western Independent*, introduced the theory of under-consumption resulting from a deficiency of purchasing power made current in Great Britain by various writers, of whom Major C. H. Douglas was coming into prominence.

In 1922 these ideas, fused and developed by George Bevington and other monetary reformers, had threatened to capture the U.F.A. Bevington, however, had not been taken into the U.F.A. government, by which he had hoped to have his ideas adopted, and the drive of the monetary reformers on the U.F.A. was repelled by Wood, who was conservative in these matters.[63] The movement was thus turned aside provincially, to resume its course in the great depression a decade later as Social Credit.

These doctrines, however, were carried to Ottawa by the U.F.A. members in response to pressure from home, and found expression in the debate on the Bank Act. Irvine, in a resolution of February 26, with the support of the U.F.A. members and W. C. Good, succeeded in obtaining agreement "to investigate the basis, the function and the control of credit, and the relation of credit to industrial problems." On Fielding's amending motion, it was referred to the Standing Committee on Banking and Commerce.[64]

The Committee began its sittings on March 8, and with its terms of reference widened by the addition of Irvine's resolution, conducted an extensive inquiry. The U.F.A. members made special exertions to bring before it critics of orthodox finance, notably George Bevington, Neal East, another Albertan reformer, Major C. H. Douglas, and Professor Irving Fisher. Bevington expounded his thesis that "the basis of a nation's credit is the number, intelligence and industry of its people, plus the capital equipment and natural resources within its boundaries,[65] and proposed that credit policies be controlled by "an elastic Federal Loan Department with Provincial Government agencies. . . ."[66] East, by pre-arrangement with Bevington, endeavoured to demonstrate the causes and the calamitous

---

[63]*Ibid.*, pp. 166-7.
[64]*Can. H. of C. Debates*, 1923, I, pp. 626 and 651.
[65]*Can. H. of C. Journals*, LX, 1923, Appendix 2, p. 127.
[66]*Ibid.*, p. 128.

consequences of the precipitate deflation of 1920,[67] and how a banking system, developed to serve commerce, was ill equipped to serve industry and agriculture, but operated rather as an agency to build up debt.[68]   Major Douglas and Professor Fisher also set out their heterodox views.   Offsetting these, a number of bankers and economists were heard, Sir Frederick Williams-Taylor, Sir John Aird, Sir Edmund Walker, and Professor Adam Shortt.   It was an inquiry of note, such as parliamentary committees too rarely conduct.   By means of it, the U.F.A. members succeeded in bringing to the notice of parliament and public two concepts, then novel, but since generally accepted: one was that credit could be controlled by banking policy and ought to be controlled by a national agency; the other was, though this was largely developed by the same efforts before the Select Committee on Agricultural Conditions, that the existing Canadian banking system was not fitted to supply the kind of credit the needs of agriculture required.[69]

Having fluttered the dovecotes of the orthodox in committee, the U.F.A. members and their allies carried the war into the House.   There they sought to make certain amendments to the Bank Act in Committee of the Whole.   Alfred Speakman cited his attempt in the Standing Committee, to have the Committee recommend that the Bank Act and the bank charters be renewed for one year only, in order to permit further study, and alluded to requests to the same purpose from the legislature of Alberta, the government of Manitoba, the Canadian Council of Agriculture, and other public bodies.   He moved, seconded by Forke, that renewal be for one year only.[70]   After a spirited debate, carried on by the Progressives against a solid front of Liberals and Conservatives, and interrupted by a running fire of questions and interjections, the amendment was negatived. So were a number of less important Progressive amendments. Then J. S. Woodsworth, referring to the near failure of the Merchants' Bank, moved for the appointment under the Act of a government auditor, empowered to inspect the reports of

[67] *Ibid.*, p. 209.
[68] *Ibid.*, p. 208.
[69] *Ibid.*, Part 1, Appendix 3.
[70] *Can. H. of C. Debates*, 1923, V, pp. 4014-17.

bank auditors and the procedure of banks for protecting their depositors and shareholders.[71]   This too was defeated, as was an amendment of G. G. Coote which would have required auditors to report on the security of loans exceeding five per cent of the paid-up capital of the banks issuing them.[72]   In this fashion, the amendments were despatched with monotonous regularity, as government and opposition supported the Minister of Finance in driving through the bill.   Shaw's attempt to fix the maximum legal rate of interest at seven per cent per annum rallied the Progressives, but it, too, fell, 38 to 64;[73] so also did Coote's motion to fix the rate at eight per cent.   When finally the bill had been dealt with in committee, the Progressives in a series of motions sought to refer it back to the Standing Committee. In five divisions, forty-six Progressives were five times turned back by ninety-five Liberals and Conservatives.[74]   With that the battered and weary Progressives were thrust aside and the Bill passed on to third reading.   The banking system of Canada, so stoutly defended, was secure for another decade against the assaults of the "windy theorists" and "paper money men" from the West.   In August of 1923, in sardonic comment on the safety of conventional banking, the Home Bank was to fail, bringing distress and ruin to thousands of depositors.

This Progressive battle, led and directed by the U.F.A. members, was fought to no avail.   The pre-eminence of the Albertan members and the radical nature of the measures they advocated had the effect, however, of still further differentiating them from their Manitoban colleagues and of causing some uneasiness among these more orthodox Progressives.[75]   The friction in the party marked the beginning of the split which in 1924 produced the "Ginger Group."[76]   Even the conciliatory leadership and personal detachment of Forke could not hope to hold together for long elements essentially incompatible,

[71]*Ibid.*, p. 4087.

[72]*Ibid.*, p. 4091.

[73]*Ibid.*, p. 4119.

[74]*Ibid.*, pp. 4147-62. On other important legislation of this session, such as the Combines Investigation Act, the Progressives voted as advanced Liberals.

[75]See Forke's reassurance, "I think Hon. members may rest assured that nothing very radical or serious is likely to happen in this parliament as regards the Bank Act" (*ibid.*, p. 4044).

[76]*The U.F.A.*, July 2, 1924, pp. 12-13; also Dawson, *Constitutional Issues*, p. 233.

unless the tension of the group in the House and the pressure from constituents were relaxed.

Such was the moral of the session of 1923. None the less, 1924 at first blush seemed to promise better days for the Progressives. The aged Fielding was compelled by ill health to cease to act as Minister of Finance in November 1923, though he was not to resign until 1925. In January 1924, Sir Lomer Gouin resigned as Minister of Justice and withdrew from politics. The advocate of a "stabilized tariff" and the representative of the Montreal interests, the former a genial personification of that art of balance and compromise which is the highest reach of political craft in Canada, the latter neither so reactionary nor so powerful as the West believed, were both removed from the cabinet. The Prime Minister was then, if not from the first, out of leading strings and master of his administration. The way might therefore be open for renewed efforts at co-operation between Liberals and Progressives. Nothing, however, had come of a visit of Premier Dunning of Saskatchewan to Ottawa in the summer of 1923,[77] and nothing overt came of King's calling Crerar there in January 1924.[78] If the Prime Minister were prepared to listen to Progressive counsel in the early part of 1924, as the budget seemed to indicate, by the time of his western trip in the autumn of 1924, he had accepted that of his western Liberal advisers. In his public addresses, he urged on Progressives the need of there being only one liberal party in the country, and asserted that no reason remained for the existence of "Progressivism or any other third party."[79]

The Progressives, for their part, began the year 1924 with a renewed attempt to create a national organization for the next election. A permanent provincial co-ordinating committee was established for Manitoba at a meeting in Winnipeg in January. Its purpose was not only to organize the Progressive campaign in Manitoba, but also to seek the co-operation of other provincial committees "with the aim of completing a national organization."[80] This aim was not to be realized in 1924, and the attempt at organization was confined to Manitoba.

[77]Dafoe Papers, Dafoe to J.A.S., Jan. 28, 1924.
[78]Montreal *Gazette*, June 16, 1924, p. 1.
[79]*Canadian Annual Review*, 1924-5, pp. 206-9.
[80]*The Progressive*, Jan. 17, 1924, p. 1.

The session itself began without incident, as Forke repeated his declaration of Progressive independence. "The Progressive party," he said, "stands where it has always stood since coming into this House. The Progressives are ready to support progressive measures whenever such measures come before the House."[81] There were, unfortunately, degrees of progressiveness. Most of the Progressives found the substantial reductions in the duties on farm implements and other imports for the needs of basic industries in the budget of 1924 advanced enough for one year. So substantial were they that not only was the opposition, as was to be expected, aroused to voice stern criticism; there was also a major defection from the governmental party on the main motion to go into the Committee of Ways and Means. Four Liberal members voted against the budget proposals;[82] one other, Walter G. Mitchell, member for St. Antoine, went to the length of resigning his seat in the Commons in protest against the measure.[83] With the Liberal bolters, to underline how narrow were the limits of tolerance between the solidarity of caucus and members' responsiveness to their constituents, went one protectionist Progressive, William Elliott, member for the industrial constituency of South Waterloo. For the moment, the hope of Manitoban Progressives, that a realignment of parties might be forced on lines of fiscal policy, seemed not impossible.

In this situation, however, the Progressives were to find little cause for rejoicing. J. S. Woodsworth, with intent to win the support of the advanced Progressives,[84] moved an amendment which was substantially that moved by Forke in 1923. It called for the lowering of the tariff on the necessities of life,

[81]*Can. H. of C. Debates*, 1924, I, p. 61.

[82]Montreal *Gazette*, May 17, 1924, p. 1; editorial, "The Vote on the Budget." The *Gazette*, from the opposite extreme, took the line of the *Free Press*, that a realignment of parties was desirable.

[83]*Canadian Annual Review*, 1924-5, pp. 225-8; *Can. H. of C. Debates*, 1924, III, p. 2099; Montreal *Gazette*, May 19, 1924, p. 1, Mitchell's letter of resignation; May 20, 1924, p. 1, King's reply.

[84]So I read his words uttered before moving his amendment; "I do so," he said, "because I believe that in many respects, although some of us advocate theories that seem to be very radical, a very considerable number of the members of this House, especially members on the Progressive side, are quite willing to travel a long way in our direction if they are quite sure we are not advocating anything that is immediately impracticable" (*Can. H. of C. Debates*, 1924, II, p. 1460).

the loss of revenue to be made up by taxes on unearned income, unimproved land values, and a graduated inheritance tax.[85]

Woodsworth's amendment, beyond doubt high-minded in intent, as were all his acts, seemed in effect to have been the inspiration of a sardonic, parliamentary Puck. The hapless Progressives were hoist with their own petard. If they supported the amendment, as principle and profession demanded, they and the Conservatives might defeat the government. If, on the contrary, they voted to defeat it, they would repudiate the substance of their own motion of 1923. The consequence of this dilemma was division, and even confusion, in the group. Forke himself faced the dilemma boldly, setting aside the whole loaf of principle for the half loaf of results. "It had seemed to me," he declared, "that if I voted for the amendment, which in reality would be a vote of want of confidence, that I would have to vote against the budget also. That I think would be a mistake under present circumstances."[86] He therefore dismissed the amendment as "only a gesture,"[87] and added that he was also opposed to the tax on unimproved land values, and to a duplication by the federal government of provincial succession duties.

Forke's refusal to risk a defeat of the government, however, disclosed once more a fundamental weakness of the Manitoban Progressives. They desired the adoption of a certain fiscal policy, and they had some reason to hope that the Liberal government might, as in the budget of 1924, approach a realization of that policy, while they had equal reason to believe a Conservative government would not. As one Albertan Progressive, D. F. Kellner, had complained somewhat ludicrously in the budget debate of 1923, ". . . we are forced into this position of affairs: Should we defeat this government by some measure or another—and no doubt we could do it—what in the name of common sense have we to expect from the Tories?"[88] The Manitoban Progressives could not, on tariff matters at least, regard the two old parties as identical, and, once the

[85]*Ibid.*

[86]The *Grain Growers' Guide*, after analysing the situation, reached the same conclusion, in an editorial, "The Vote on the Budget" (XVII, May 21, 1924, p. 5).

[87]*Can. H. of C. Debates*, 1924, II, p. 1652.

[88]*Ibid.*, 1923, III, p. 2814.

Liberals had made substantial concessions, were bound to support them.

To the doctrinaire Progressives, however, the old parties were identical, and if the pursuit of principle involved the defeat of a government, well and good. In their opinion, the defeat of a government measure need not result in the resignation of the government. G. G. Coote, in one of the periodic reports on the work of the session made by U.F.A. members to their constituents through the pages of *The U.F.A.*, dealt with this point:

Mr. Woodsworth's amendment to the budget, . . . expressed the opinion that the present budget should provide for a reduction of tariff on [the necessities of life]. Some of the Progressives take the view that this amendment is in reality a vote of want of confidence in the Government, and which, if carried, would mean the resignation of the Government, and, as a consequence, no change would be made in the tariff; under these conditions, being anxious to see the budget proposals put through, they feel justified in voting against the amendment. Others state that one of their principles is that no Government should be called on to resign because of an adverse vote on a Government motion, but only in case of a straight motion of no confidence. The matter was dealt with very ably by Mr. Shaw in his budget speech, when he stated in part as follows: "It does not constitute a vote of want of confidence in the Government unless the Government tells us that that is the way they are going to look upon it. But is the Government going to call it a vote of want of confidence because some honorable members feel that their attention should be directed to further reductions in order that the consumers of this country may get further and larger benefits. These mere fictions, this question of a lack of confidence in the Government is some thing that is inherited from a pre-historic past. Why cannot we get rid of these fictions? Why cannot we eliminate them from our procedure, and to that extent at least be modern and up-to-date?" There is probably no single thing which prevents the passage of Progressive measures so much as the obsolete and ancient rules of procedure of the House of Commons, and it is conceivable that it may be necessary to defeat a few Government motions in order to persuade the House of Commons to adopt rules of procedure which would be suitable to a democratic system of Government.[89]

[89]*The U.F.A.*, May 15, 1924, p. 11.

In a fiery speech on the floor of the House, E. J. Garland, the Celtic orator from Bow River, echoed the complaint in terms which foretold the "Ginger Group." "Mr. Speaker," he exclaimed, "I wish to protest against the arbitrary rulings of the whips [that debate be closed]. The day is past when whip rule is satisfactory, at least to those of us who are in a sense independent—independent as far as party politics and political parties are concerned."[90] And he went on with mounting passion to flay the principle of protection and extol the Woodsworth amendment. "There is nothing wrong with the country," he asserted. "What is wrong is that I see my people there digging in year after year in a well-nigh hopeless effort to overcome the handicaps placed upon their industry by the crass stupidity and greed of their fellow men. . . . These men are encouraged to know that even though our efforts are largely nullified by the attitude of opposing interests, they have at least representatives who are pleading their cause without fear of party or press, and who will not be silent while injustice still stands."[91] He denied that the Woodsworth amendment involved any inconsistency with that member's repeated statement that the tariff was not fundamental to the solution of economic problems.[92] That view Garland claimed to share, and in so declaring marked the beginning of the entente between Labour and the U.F.A. from which the Co-operative Commonwealth Federation was to arise. The inconsistency, in his view, lay with those Progressives who said one thing on the hustings and voted for another in parliament. To this philippic, Agnes Macphail's statement of intent to vote for principle and the Woodsworth amendment, was a hurried "amen," uttered on the brink of the division.[93] Fourteen Progressives then voted for the amendment, which was defeated by two hundred and four to sixteen. On the main motion the Progressives as a body supported the government, the Conservatives, three Liberals,

[90]*Can. H. of C. Debates*, 1924, II, p. 2211. This speech was made in defiance of Progressive whips (*The Progressive*, June 12, 1924, p. 1).

[91]*Can. H. of C. Debates*, 1924, II, p. 2214.

[92]A concept of Wm. Irvine's also. "The tariff . . . is not fundamental, and will not constitute an issue in itself" (*Alberta Non-Partisan*, Sept. 16, 1919, p. 5, editorial, "The Liberal Convention").

[93]*Can. H. of C. Debates*, 1924, II, p. 2220.

and Elliott of South Waterloo, a lone Progressive, opposing, in a division of one hundred and sixty-five to fifty-three.[94]

Thus the Woodsworth amendment had brought to the surface again the suspicions, entertained by the U.F.A. members and their Ontario allies, of Liberal influence on the Manitoban Progressives. The Liberal influence they held to be exerted to the end that the Progressives should support, as a group, Liberal measures, of which a majority of the Progressive caucus had approved. Their suspicions were fed, on this occasion, by Crerar's attendance during the vote on the budget, and by the scarcely concealed Liberal sympathies of J. F. Johnston, chief Progressive whip.[95] Other irritations were developing at the same time, such as the difference of opinion on the desirability of voting the expenses of parliamentary delegates to the Wembley Exhibition,[96] one of whom was to be their chief example of crypto-Liberalism, J. F. Johnston himself.

Such irritations aroused a lively sense of the principle of constituency autonomy and of the independence of private members. In consequence, the more doctrinaire of the Albertan Progressives felt they could no longer bear the discipline of caucus.[97] Six of them decided to make a public protest, setting forth the reasons for their opposition to caucus rule. This they did in an open letter to Forke:

Dear Mr. Forke:

With the kindliest feeling towards yourself and after very careful and deliberate consideration, we the undersigned hereby inform you that we do not propose henceforth to attend the caucus of the parliamentary group, of which you are the leader; and in order that there may be no misunderstanding, we herein set forth the reasons which have led to our action and to which we propose to give full publicity.

Our first duty is to our constituents and to the democratic principle of the political movement which they so heroically inaugurated. That

[94]*Ibid.*, pp. 2220-2.

[95]*Western Producer*, May 14, 1925, p. 4.

[96]The final decision to withdraw from the Progressive caucus was not made until the majority had endorsed the sending of the delegation to Wembley (*The Progressive*, July 17, 1924, p. 5, quoting from a statement of Agnes Macphail in the Edmonton *Journal*); see also letter of Ginger Group, 196 below.

[97]The fullest published contemporary account is M. N. Campbell's "The Progressive Split" (*The Progressive*, July 10, 1924, p. 5).

new political movement began among the farmers; it was indeed the political expression of various Farmers' organizations throughout Canada. Negatively it represents a twofold protest; a protest against the economic burdens that have been piled upon the agricultural industry as the result of forty years of class government; and a protest against a party system organized and dominated from the top, and by means of which the financial and commercial interests have retained power for so long. Positively it represents a noble effort to give effect in the political field to that co-operative philosophy which has not only constituted an outstanding characteristic of Farmers' movements, but which is the world's best hope of saving civilization.

There was, we believe, nothing further from the minds of our constituents than the building of another party machine on the model of the old. That this might be made clear the Farmers' organizations, owing to whose activities we find ourselves here, formulated their own political program, did their own political organizing and financing, selected and elected us and commissioned us to co-operate with all parties, groups or individuals, in order to carry our principles into effect. As we see it there are two species of political organization— one the "Political Party" that aspires to power, and in so doing inevitably perpetuates that competitive spirit in matters of legislation and government generally which has brought the world wellnigh to ruin; the other is the democratically organized group which aims to co-operate with other groups to secure justice rather than to compete with them for power. It is as representatives of this latter type that we take our stand, and in doing so not only remain true to our obligations but have regard also to the obligations which we undertood to the Farmers' organization in our constituency. Our task is to represent our constituents by co-operating in Parliament with all parties and groups so as to secure the best possible legislation for Canada as a whole.

In our opinion the principles above outlined to which we adhere have been departed from, and in this connection we desire to draw your attention to a few among many incidents of the past few years. You will undoubtedly recall that as far back as the Saskatoon and Toronto conferences following the 1921 election, and subsequently at the Winnipeg conference, some difference of opinion and viewpoint was apparent as to the purpose, method of action and future of the new political movement then and there represented. The divergence of viewpoint then evident has persisted; indeed has been, we believe, accentuated. Moreover, in our opinion the present Parliamentary organization of the Progressive group tends to perpetuate the type of partyism already described, which we were elected to oppose, and to hamper us in the advocacy of those principles to which we adhere. Some of us have made attempts to secure reorganization of the group on a different basis, but without results.

Bearing in mind the fact that each constituency represented by us is autonomous in the nomination, election, financing and control of its members, it should be evident that it is impossible to secure our support for the organization of a political party organization on the old lines involving majority rule in caucus, whip domination, responsibility for leader's statements and so forth. The effort—perhaps unconscious—to build a solid political party out of our group has been distressing and paralyzing. As an example, you will recall the situation last year when the Bank Act was under consideration in Parliament. After the caucus had agreed, without objection, to support those of its members who were putting up a strenuous fight in committee for what they considered necessary financial reforms, a sudden change of attitude took place and the majority actually hindered the minority from putting up such a fight on the floor of the house as circumstances demanded. As notice had been given to the Government of our intention to oppose with all our strength the granting of bank charters for a ten year period, the minority had to accept a defeat or break with the majority.

You will readily recall similar instances of past differences of opinion struggling against old parties' proprieties and conventions—the question of our immigration policy, this year's budget, and so forth, culminating in the recent action of the majority endorsing a proposal to send a Parliamentary delegation to the British Empire Exhibition at the public expense. The divergence of viewpoint has been so marked, that it would seem in the best interests of the movement that we be left free from constraint to work for the cause, independently of the present Parliamentary organization. Such a course, we believe, would enable us to co-operate more harmoniously and freely with those who remain in the Progressive group and who are in agreement with us on any particular issue.

It is with a full realization of our duty to our constituents, and for the purpose of preserving the virility and independence of the political movement of the organized farmers of Canada that we now feel it necessary to take such action as has been indicated. We desire, however, to make it perfectly clear that we are free to co-operate with all others, and invite and welcome the assistance and support of those of all parties who genuinely desire legislation such as will best promote the interests of Canada as a whole.

[Signed]   M. N. CAMPBELL, Mackenzie,
ROBERT GARDINER, Medicine Hat,
E. J. GARLAND, Bow River,
D. M. KENNEDY, West Edmonton,
AGNES M. C. MACPHAIL, Southwest Grey,
H. E. SPENCER, Battle River.[98]

The dissidents who had so proclaimed their dissidence to the world were promptly dubbed the "Ginger Group," after the Tory members who had criticized the Military Service Act in 1917, and as the Ginger Group they are known to history. To their moderate but explicit statement, Forke replied on June 20 in similar tolerant but uncompromising terms:

While no one can question your right to take the course you propose, the Progressive members regret that you have seen fit to withdraw from the caucus for reasons which they cannot but regard as unsubstantial and inconclusive. When you say that the Progressive group in Parliament has departed from its fundamental principles they must emphatically deny the allegation. Whatever interpretation you place on the attitude or action of your colleagues, it is not true that the group has diverged in any respect from the principles for which it has stood from the first. The principle of constituency autonomy involving methods of organization in the country, does not affect the organization of the group in Parliament and has nowhere been departed from.

The instances which you adduce in support of your contentions resulted from the expression of various sectional viewpoints, but these divergences did not involve a departure from Progressive principles. They were, rather, the honest expression of opinions of men who, like yourselves, are responsible to their constituencies. Moreover, they were mainly differences concerning matters of procedure and other questions which in no sense touch the principles to which we adhere in common. To interpret such instances as a departure from Progressive principles is quite gratuitous and not a little unfair to those with whom you were then associated.

The differences between us would appear to arise in connection with our Parliamentary organization. Three years ago the Pro-

[98]*The U.F.A.*, July 2, 1924, pp. 12-13; letter undated.

gressive members adopted the usual form of Parliamentary organization, with leader, whip and caucus, but they by no means became
servile to it.   The meetings of the caucus have been held in exactly
the same spirit and manner as the meetings of our Local organizations
and conventions at home.   They have possessed the same strength
and the same weakness, neither more or less.

Whip domination, autocratic leadership and majority coercion
would be as distasteful to us as to you, but no endeavour has been
made to establish them, neither has any attempt been made, as you
suggest, to build up a solid political party on the old lines.   Only
time, experience and continued association of the various sections of
the party will produce the ideal Parliamentary organization.   Your
objections to the present form of organization seem to us to be caused
rather by suspicion and personal sensibilities than by anything fundamental.   They arise in every organization where men have full liberty
of expression and will appear in any that might be substituted for the
present caucus.   Unity of purpose and of action and a definite parliamentary organization are essential to any effective action in the
House of Commons to the attainment of the practical reforms which
our constituents look to us to pursue.

We trust that further consideration may lead you to the realization
that co-operation from without the group can never be as effective
for our common purposes as united action within it.

Yours very truly,

[Signed] R. Forke.

on behalf of the Progressive Group.[99]

Though on many matters the two groups agreed, as this exchange of correspondence indicated, the point of difference,
relating to the relationship of the member to his constituents,
was substantial.   By constituency autonomy the dissenting
members meant a close and continuous correspondence between
the representative and his actual supporters organized in an
economic group, while Forke and his followers meant no more
than a like but informal relationship between the representative
and any electors of his constituency who supported him, whether
organized as an economic group or not.   Both sides subscribed
to the same electoral methods of local nomination and of raising
funds by local subscription, but the issue was whether the representative was a representative in the traditional sense, or the

⁹⁹*Ibid.*, p. 13.

delegate of an economic interest. Though the Manitoban Progressives did not follow the political methods of the old parties, the result of their policy, if successful, would have been the creation of a new party of the composite type, broad, flexible, and capable of sustaining a government.

The members of the Ginger Group, for their part, were in principle opponents of the composite party, with its endless compromises and centralized control by the majority in caucus. Party organization, in their view, was no concern of the member of parliament. He was the delegate of his constituency, a student of affairs, a moulder of legislation, a critic of government; his were not the worries of party organization, re-election, or maintaining the administration. As M. N. Campbell was to write in justification of the split: "The basic idea behind it was to preserve the movement in its pure form, and to enable those members to represent their constituents more directly." The Progressive movement "was conceived in political liberty, and dedicated to the ideal that the people must create their own political machinery, and, through it, control their own political destiny. It was not brought forth in the House of Commons, nor in the House of Commons will it die."[100]

In reply to Campbell's idealism John Evans, Progressive M.P. for Saskatoon, replied in language not less idealistic but of a more practical bent: "No group can ever hope to be a force in giving effect to their own principles unless they accept the responsibility of office. To aspire to office is not an evil, but a duty, if you know that what you are standing for is right and just."[101]

It was this uncompromising adherence of the members of the Ginger Group to the basic doctrines of Albertan Progressivism which constituted the fundamental cleavage between them and the Manitoba Progressives.[102] To the Gingerites were soon added G. G. Coote from Alberta, Preston Elliott and W. C. Good from Ontario, and W. J. Ward from Manitoba.[103] Thereafter, members of the Group tended to shun the

[100]Campbell, "The Progressive Split."
[101]The Progressive, July 10, 1924, p. 12.
[102]Grain Growers' Guide, XVII, July 9, 1924, p. 5.
[103]Ibid., XVII, July 23, 1924, p. 5.

name of Progressive. Though the two groups continued to co-operate, as was to be expected, the Ginger Group met separately, in time was admitted to separate representation on committees of the House, and in general developed a distinct character and activity of its own for the rest of the Fourteenth Parliament.

While this difference of opinion had broken the Progressives into two groups, it had by no means operated alone. The split was also a reaction to developments in the House itself. The Progressive group was subject to the constant blandishments of the Liberal party, which were not without effect. These consisted not merely of approaches to the former Progressive leader with a view to his entering the cabinet; it was the fraternity of the corridors, the courtesies of the Liberal whip, the insidious sense of acceptance, which softened the asperity of the original Progressive isolation. The enervating influences were increasingly effective, as the ebbing of the movement in the farmers' associations and the decay of organization in the constituencies made Liberal promises of aid or co-operation in the ever-nearing election more seductive. There was also the influence of former Liberals in the group, impatient to end the breach in the old party and bring the Progressives into firm support of the government.

Of these crypto-Liberals, the chief was J. F. Johnston, member for Last Mountain, who had become Progressive whip in 1922 and so remained until 1925. Johnston's parliamentary career was of some interest in this context. Elected as a Unionist Liberal in 1917, he had attended the Liberal convention of 1919.[104] He was not welcomed there, and continued as one of the independents who became parliamentary Progressives in 1920. In 1921 he was nominated as a Progressive candidate and elected. His selection as chief whip was a acknowledgement of his parliamentary experience and of the weight of Saskatchewan in the Progressive representation, as well as evidence of the ascendancy of Manitoban Progressivism. As whip he at once showed, and continued to show, that badge of Manitoban Progressivism, sympathy with the government, a sympathy he did not attempt to conceal. Such an attitude,

[104]Montreal *Gazette*, Aug. 6, 1919, p. 1.

however defensible in terms of Manitoban Progressivism, could not but seem near treachery to the Albertans. Suspicions of the hard-headed and realistic Johnston, and of the tendency of Manitoban Progressivism to associate itself with the Liberal government of which he was an extreme exponent, were at the bottom of the public breach of June 1924.

The breach, of course, was the final precipitation of the incompatible elements held in suspension in the Progressive political movement. The Manitoban Progressives were insurgents, Liberals by former allegiance for the most part, but Conservatives also, who were in sectional revolt against the caucus rule of the composite parties. They sought, however, only some relaxation of that rule in order to bring about, broadly speaking, a realignment of political forces on the lines of hinterland and metropolitan areas, of primary and secondary producers. The Albertan Progressives were radicals who sought to transform the conditions of politics and the working of the constitution. To them, the old parties contained none to be saved, but were indifferently the tools of the interests, working securely through party, caucus, and cabinet. To them, it increasingly appeared that a mere sectional realignment could not heal the ills of the body politic and economic. The evils of metropolitan domination would work in a free or a protected economy. They increasingly saw the cleavage in society, not as one of sectional alignment, but as one between classes. The cleavage might be closed by a new economic order, in which co-operation would replace competition and inaugurate a commonwealth in which the state would render economic justice to all classes in all sections.[105]

As their thought entered on this course of development, the Albertan Progressives began unconsciously to move towards the ideal of an economy which would be not only state-regulated but|also nationalized. In this, too, they were breaking away from the Manitoban Progressives, who still professed the ideal of the free world market which had prevailed before 1914. At this point, there came to the surface the transitional character of the Progressive movement. It was itself an expression of

[105]In *The Progressive*, June 12, 1924, p. 1, the growing affiliation with Woodsworth and Irvine is noted.

the transition from the era of *laissez-faire* to the era of the managed society. In the movement the Manitoban Progressives were representative of the old order, the Albertan of the new.

The cleavage of 1924, once it had occurred, was to be reduced but never closed. Why it could not be, was, in its superficial aspects, clearly perceived by an observer at the time. "The chief cause of Progressive weakness," A. E. Darby wrote in the *Grain Growers' Guide*, "has been the difference of opinion as to whether the movement should become a political party, or should confine itself to the representation of a single class or economic group." A class appeal would fail in Ontario, and in the West would produce a crop of parliamentary free lances. There should therefore be, Darby declared, a party organization in the legislature and the country. The existing lack of organization, if not remedied, would be disastrous, for the Progressives lacked a programme, a central organization, a properly elected national leader, and the provincial associations were hampered by the principle of constituency autonomy. True it was that "the Progressive Movement [was] in large measure a rebellion against blind partisanship and autocratic party control in Canadian politics," but constituency autonomy was not incompatible with effective political organization. A convention should therefore be called and a national organization brought into being. The result might be the loss of the support of the believers in group government, but this would be more than offset by the gains of a general appeal.[106]

Thereafter, though the Progressives were outwardly reconciled, their weakness was apparent to the world, and King's confidence on his western tour in the autumn of 1924, that there was no longer a place for the Progressives, was no doubt based on a calculation of their approaching dissolution. The general political outlook was, at the same time, dim and uncertain. In the Maritime Provinces, the post-war depression was working itself out in languishing ports and industries and an exodus of sons and daughters from a land which offered neither work nor homes. In the continental West, for the first

[106]A. E. Darby, "Progressive Prospects" (*Grain Growers' Guide*, XVII, Oct. 29, 1924, pp. 8 and 17).

time in its history of discontents came not merely murmurs and loose talk, but bitter public utterances, of the possibility of secession from Confederation.

In 1923 Forke had dismissed these rumours as mere talk and a rural movement, the latter a curious reason for a Progressive to give in belittlement of an issue, even in Montreal.[107] In 1924, however, Colin H. Burnell, president of the U.F.M., declared that the tariff must come down, for by it the West was being bled white. "No wonder," he commented, "one hears increasing talk at farm firesides of breaking away from the East, and while in my opinion it would be a catastrophe if Canada should break in two at the Great Lakes, one cannot help seeing that this sentiment is growing, as a result of economic injustice. Surely the East must begin to realize that people with the spirit of the settlers of these Western plains will not submit to the present burdens forever."[108] In the following year R. A. Hoey devoted his address to the U.F.M. to the same theme. "If confederation," he asked, "can only be maintained on a basis of inequality and injustice, why maintain it?" His remarks were coldly received,[109] and the *Manitoba Free Press* repudiated the proposal emphatically. It went on, however, to point the moral that the two-party system implied the existence of two parties capable of electing representatives in all sections of the country. One national party had failed in 1921 to elect a single representative in six of the nine provinces, while the other old party, though it had elected solid blocs in three provinces, had failed to win a majority in parliament. These failures had been caused by more than a quarter of the constituencies breaking from both old parties, to create "virtually a Western bloc with an Eastern annex." Yet sectional parties were symptoms, not causes, of disunity. The warning, however, had not been recognized, and the malaise had intensified since the sectional revolt of 1921. Dafoe, indeed, was to write

[107]*Canadian Annual Review*, 1923, p. 169.

[108]*Grain Growers' Guide*, XVII, Jan. 16, 1924, p. 7.

[109]*Manitoba Free Press*, Jan. 14, 1925, p. 11, editorial, "The Strains Upon Confederation," a comment on Hoey's speech. The speech was reported in the *Free Press*, Jan. 9, 1925, pp. 1 and 7. It was essentially a plea for a united front in the West, with secession as an alternative to national policies acceptable to all sections.

privately that there was more talk of secession in the country than he cared to admit.[110]

In Saskatchewan the same sectional bitterness found expression in the presidential address of G. F. Edwards to the Saskatchewan Grain Growers' Association in 1925.

We, in the West, [said Edwards] have a right to insist upon equity and fair play, and I should like to point out this fact that sentimental attachments and ties, however strong they may be cannot indefinitely stand the strain of economic injustice. Undoubtedly Canada ought to be able to work out its destiny better as a united country than as one split up in different sections, and I do not believe that the West has any desire to break away from Eastern Canada if we can only have fair play and equality of treatment. It is not those who are pointing out the danger to confederation of the present sectional, short-sighted fiscal policy who are the enemies of Canada, but rather they who are pressing for the continuation of a policy which, if continued, spells "separation."[111]

These utterances, couched though they were in the language of injured patriotism, and, no doubt, calculated to influence the making of the tariff, reflected the smouldering resentment of many in the West who felt that the political revolt of 1921 had yielded few results and whose discontents had not yet been allayed by the Wheat Pools and the modest agricultural prosperity of the late twenties. As such, they were evidence of the strains put upon the hinterlands by the tariff designed primarily in the interests of central Canada and of the burden of discriminative freight rates.[112] They were, however, no more than evidence of discontent. The West, creation of Confederation, was more profoundly committed to Confederation by sentiment and interest than its people had yet realized. The danger, as the *Western Producer* remarked, was from the possibility of eastern sectionalism denying those concessions which would render national policies, shaped by central Canada, tolerable to the West.[113]

[110]Dafoe Papers, Dafoe to Clifford Sifton on Hoey's secession speech, Jan. 22, 1925.

[111]*Grain Growers' Guide*, XVIII, Feb. 4, 1925, p. 11; *Western Producer*, Jan. 20, 1925, p. 3.

[112]J. A. Stevenson, "Strains on Confederation" (*New Republic*, XLI, Jan. 7, 1925, p. 167). The Railway Commission had just set aside the Crow's Nest Pass rates (*Canadian Annual Review*, 1924, pp. 25 and 95-8).

[113]*Western Producer*, Feb. 26, 1925, p. 4.

So grim, it seemed, were the results of three years of Liberal rule and Progressive insurgence. What would come of it all in the next election? The by-elections spoke with oracular obscurity. Of ten in 1923, the Liberals had won four, together with four acclamations, three of which were in ministerial by-elections. The Progressives had held a former Progressive seat. The Conservatives had carried two seats late in the year, one in Nova Scotia, one in New Brunswick.[114] In 1924 the Liberals won four, two in Quebec, none of them an acclamation. The election in St. Antoine, vacated by the resignation of W. G. Mitchell on the budget, was, however, a notable Liberal victory. To these might be added the victory of an independent Liberal, also in Quebec; plainly the Liberal hold on that province had not weakened. The Conservatives, for their part, carried Yale.[115] In the number of victories, and in the victory in St. Antoine, the Liberals had cause for hope. The Conservatives, on the other hand, had regained a foothold in the Maritime Provinces. Nothing, however, had been revealed of the mood of the West, or of the great Conservative revival in Ontario. The Progressive movement was dying out in that province, as the Conservative victory over Drury in 1923 had demonstrated. Both old parties could take comfort from the outlook, and the effect of the division of the Progressives in parliament was to make them decide to fight out the election on traditional lines. In particular, the Liberals had decided, as the budget of 1925 would suggest, not to make too great concessions to the West, lest they deliver the East to Meighen.

The parliamentary session of 1925 was a pre-election session. Little of note in the history of the Progressive movement occurred until the debate on the budget. The budget itself, perhaps as a result of the Liberal defections in 1924, was another "stability," "stand-pat" budget, as Forke described it. It was one the Progressives could not accept, the group as a whole being critical of it.[116] Accordingly, a sub-amendment was drafted for Forke to move, and this was, as anticipated, ruled out of order, the Speaker being sustained over a solid Pro-

[114]*Canadian Annual Review*, 1923, p. 197.

[115]*Ibid.*, 1924-5, p. 237.

[116]C. W. Stewart, M.P., "A Review of the Week in Parliament" (*Western Producer*, May 14, 1925, p. 1).

gressive vote.[117] The Progressives then agreed in caucus to vote against the government on the main motion, though two British Columbian and a few Ontario members had earlier decided to support the government.[118] When, however, the vote on the main motion was taken, J. F. Johnston, chief whip, J. W. Kennedy, chairman of the caucus, T. W. Caldwell and R. H. Halbert, members of the executive, and thirteen other Progressives, voted with the government.[119]

This was something new. The Ginger Group had defied the whip on an amendment, and later had formally withdrawn from caucus. Here, however, was an open defiance of caucus itself on a main motion, and made by men who had no shadow of principle to urge in defence of their action.

Why they did so was a matter of speculation, as it remains. Their own defence, as made by a member of the group, was that, having supported the Forke sub-amendment, they were free to vote as they pleased on the main motion. They had tried, and failed, to have the Progressive policy accepted, and were then driven to a choice between that of the Liberals and of the Conservatives. Little as the Liberals might concede, the Conservatives offered nothing.[120] However this may have been, the general grounds of their action were apparent. The prospects of fighting the coming election without funds and without organization, the disintegration of the Progressive movement in parliament and the country, the impatience of the insurgent Liberals of the group with the doctrinaires, offered a general and sufficient explanation. The Liberals may have improved the occasion with promises of electoral aid in return for support in the next parliament, as the unfriendly Montreal *Gazette* hinted.[121] J. F. Johnston, at any rate, and for one example, was to receive the Liberal nomination and be returned as Liberal member for Long Lake, to become deputy-speaker of the new House and to die a senator. Liberal favours, none the less, were not a necessary or a whole explanation. For the

[117]*Can. H. of C. Debates*, 1925, II, pp. 1586-7.
[118]Stewart, "A Review of the Week in Parliament," p. 1.
[119]*Can. H. of C. Debates*, 1925, III, p. 2740.
[120]*Grain Growers' Guide*, XVIII, May 13, 1925, p. 26.
[121]Montreal *Gazette*, May 6, 1925, p. 1.

Progressive movement was ceasing to be practical politics, and could no longer serve to hold the mere insurgent Liberals.

The immediate result, for the Progressive group, of this bolt of the crypto-Liberals was a stormy two-day caucus. Forke called for a new definition of policy and for a reorganization of the parliamentary group.[122] He may have threatened to resign as leader—it would indeed be implied—if this were not done.[123] In consequence, J. F. Johnston and J. W. Kennedy the latter of whom might have been re-elected to office had he chosen,[124] resigned and withdrew from the group. C. W. Stewart of Humboldt was elected chief whip in Johnston's place and the diminished Progressive representation was restored to such unity as it could command.[125] No redefinition of policy was announced.

From this second disruption recovery was difficult, if not impossible. Since, however, the old parties were now resolved to fight out the election on the old lines and no more advances were made by the Liberals, there was nothing to be done but to put the best possible face on the matter. This Forke did when, at the end of the session, he made a statement in which he declared that the Progressives were once more as firmly united as their principles of organization permitted. "In harmony with the principle of constituency autonomy," he said, "members from each province will work in association with the provincial locals in carrying forward and perfecting the work of organization. . . . The group is thus in a position to present a more united front than at any time since the first division occurred."[126]

On these brave words, indeed, brisk action followed. The U.F.M. had already reappointed the federal political committee of 1924,[127] and it met with the federal members to begin organization in July of 1925.[128] On August 5, the Saskatchewan Progressives met in Regina. When Manitoban representatives

---

[122]*Western Producer*, May 14, 1925, p. 1.
[123]Montreal *Gazette*, May 6, 1925, p. 1.
[124]*Grain Growers' Guide*, XVIII, May 13, 1925, p. 3.
[125]Stewart, "A Review of the Week in Parliament," p. 1.
[126]*Grain Growers' Guide*, XVIII, July 8, 1925, p. 3.
[127]*Ibid.*, XVIII, Jan. 14, 1925, p. 26.
[128]*Ibid.*, XVIII, July 22, 1925, p. 3.

joined them, an inter-provincial committee for Manitoba and Saskatchewan was set up, and the Declaration of Principles issued by the Canadian Council of Agriculture in 1923[129] was adopted as a platform. Though representatives from Alberta attended the conference, they declined to join the inter-provincial committee, but, true to their theory of delegation, remained in provincial isolation. The purpose of the committee was to arrange for speakers and to raise campaign funds. The *Guide* might stoutly assert that "the Progressives cannot afford to abandon their principles of electoral responsibility for election campaign funds and full publicity for the source and amount of such funds. It is an essential of clean politics."[130] The zeal of 1921, of the Saskatchewan Liberty Drive, however, was to be found wanting, and funds were to be lacking.[131] The gathering heard Crerar once more appeal for a broader movement, which would disown the class doctrine of group government, and so have a chance of appealing to the East and of renewing its strength in the West. Such a broadening of the movement, the speaker declared, was necessary to meet the issue of railway rates and the extension of sectional dissension, and also to check the drift of the West into isolation in the country and parliament.[132]

The methods of 1921, and the hope of the Manitoban Progressives that a realignment of parties might yet be accomplished, were revived to little purpose. The great agrarian insurgence was spent. "The Progressive Party," wrote a sympathetic observer in 1925, "has failed."[133] And, as a new party seeking to dominate parliament and shape national policy, it had failed. No realignment of parties had been drawn as a result of the irruption of the farmers into politics in 1921. The futility of political independence under the con-

[129]See 174 above.

[130]*Grain Growers' Guide*, XVIII, Aug. 12, 1925, p. 6, editorial, "Campaign Funds."

[131]*Ibid.*, XVIII, Oct. 14, 1925, p. 5, editorial, "Progressive Dangers": "If the day comes when Progressive candidates have to finance their own campaigns, then there will be mighty little Progressivism in the Progressive Party."

[132]*Ibid.*, Montreal *Gazette*, Sept. 2, 1925, p. 9. The *Gazette* interpreted this as a plea for a Liberal-Progressive coalition, which Crerar denied it was (*ibid.*, Sept. 3, 1925, p. 1).

[133]Dexter, "Will the Prairies Go Solid Again?"

ventions of parliamentary government had been demonstrated. As a national force, the Progressive movement was ended. Broadly true though this conclusion was, by a twist of electoral fate, Progressive voters were yet to return to parliament a sectional group that would for a tense session hold a real balance of power and contribute in the political crisis of 1926 to a decision which would set the currents of Canadian political destiny running in a new course.

The Progressive Movement in the Provinces, 1922-26

T H E federal Progressive party was the major but not the only expression of the political movement of the organized farmers. That movement had won some of its first victories in provincial politics, and in the provinces, as well as in parliament, its fate was to be decided. Indeed, the disintegration of the federal party between 1922 and 1925 was the result, not only of the pressures to which the group had been subjected in the House of Commons, but also of forces working in the provinces.

In Ontario, the U.F.O., weakened by the controversy between the advocates of occupational representation and the advocates of "broadening out," and beset by other troubles, suffered defeat in the election of 1923, and ceased to be a political force in Ontario. The doctrine of occupational representation was accepted and developed by the United Farmers of Alberta, and rigorously adhered to in both federal and provincial politics. In consequence, the U.F.A. governed Alberta from 1921 on, and returned to Ottawa in 1925 a strong phalanx of members. The same devotion to occupational representation did not obtain in Manitoba, and when the United Farmers of Manitoba captured the government in 1922, its representatives were not divided by struggles over procedure or doctrine. The group was left free to begin a cautious evolution towards becoming a provincial agrarian party. By contrast, the provincial Progressive party of Saskatchewan was to have a weak and uncertain existence. It failed to develop character or capture power, and the way was left open for the resumption of the old ties between the provincial and federal Liberals of that province.

These varying fates indicated that in the agricultural provinces the fierce agrarian zeal of 1921 could endure only if it found expression in a political organization based on occupational representation, or in an agrarian party. A traditional party, if sufficiently agrarian, however, could defeat Progressivism, as it did in Saskatchewan. In a province of more complex social structure, such as Ontario, agrarianism was reduced to the futility of an agrarian bloc forever barred from office, unless it could in fact found a "populist" party. This it failed to do in Ontario, and the fate of the Progressive movement there foreshadowed its national doom. Ontario, in 1921 and after, was the key to a national victory of the Progressives, and that key was never grasped. With the disintegration of the political movement of the U.F.O., it is not too much to say, the return of the old parties was assured.

Even if a national triumph was to be denied the Progressives, they might have remained a sectional bloc. To remain such, however, required a measure of central direction, and after the failure of the Winnipeg conference of 1922 to elect a national leader and create a national organization, and the withdrawal of the Canadian Council of Agriculture from support of the political movement, the federal movement was left to the direction of the independent provincial associations. Attempts by Forke to persuade these associations to begin a concerted political organization failed[1]; and thereafter the federal party depended completely upon the activity of the three provincial associations and their organizations in the electoral districts. Inevitably, then, the federal representation of each province followed the course and reflected the character of the provincial political movement. The Progressive movement, like the classic parties, could not divorce federal from provincial politics.

Moreover, after 1921, which was the year of highest membership in the farmers' organizations, there was a great falling-off in the number of paid-up members. High cash incomes down to 1920, growing discontent, and the stimulus of political action, had increased the membership to record heights. Thereafter

[1]See *Grain Growers' Guide*, XVI, Jan. 17, 1923, pp. 7, 17 and 20.

the decline in membership was rapid, from sixty thousand members and sixteen hundred clubs in the U.F.O., for example, to half that number of members and a quarter that number of clubs in 1922.[2]　In the U.F.A. the membership fell from thirty-eight thousand in 1921 to fifteen thousand in 1922.[3]　The membership of the Saskatchewan Grain Growers' Association decreased from twenty-nine thousand in 1920 to twenty-one thousand in 1922.[4]　The membership of the U.F.M. was sixteen thousand in 1920, eleven thousand in 1921, and sixteen thousand in 1922, as it fluctuated with the political action of 1920 and 1922,[5] but by the end of 1923 it had fallen to six thousand.[6] Nor did the membership of the associations increase in succeeding years, as prosperity revived.　The organization of the Wheat Pools, the waning of political interest, and the rise of the new Farmers' Union, weakened the farmers' organizations and diminished their political strength in all the provinces except Alberta, where organization made good the loss of members.

In Ontario, for example, the victory of the U.F.O. had had behind it a well-developed and well-organized farmers' movement, determined to win political representation for the farmer. Its surprising victory in the election of 1919 was to be explained by fortuitous circumstances, resentment aroused by the Military Service Act, the Hearst Government's too professional opposition to farmer candidates, the prohibition issue, and the disintegration of the Liberal party as a result of the formation of the Union Government.　These were not circumstances likely to be repeated in conjunction.　Accordingly, the future of the movement depended upon the adoption of some new line of policy.

The need of a new policy was clearly realized by Premier Drury as he faced the task of governing without an assured majority in the legislature, and was borne in upon him with each fresh session.　His solution of the problem was to broaden the basis of the movement so as to take in all those dissatisfied

[2]*Canadian Annual Review*, 1922, p. 635.
[3]*Ibid.*, p. 828.
[4]*Ibid.*, p. 797.
[5]*Ibid.*, p. 761.
[6]*Ibid.*, 1924-5, p. 399.

with the old parties and their policies. To attempt such a development, however, was, in the eyes of the doctrinaire agrarians led by J. J. Morrison, to recreate that which they had set out to destroy, the two-party system in which the representative became the agent of the party and ceased, it was alleged, to be the genuine representative of his constituents. "We say," declared Morrison, "the responsibility of the government rests in the riding."[7] After much running controversy, Drury precipitated the issue by publishing a letter on July 13, 1922, suggesting the calling of a general convention of the Progressive party of Ontario, with a view to appealing to the urban vote.[8] In a speech at Grand Bend a month later, he defended the proposal: "The Organization [the U.F.O.] was never intended for a political organization, it hoped to work through the old parties, but the people decided it should work separately from the old parties. A party has to be created. . . . My conviction is that group government is impracticable." It was therefore necessary to win the support of other than farm voters and to give them some voice in the shaping of party policy.[9] To this Morrison replied at Delta on the following day. The decision, he said, must not be made by a convention, but left to the organizations in the ridings. "We are not after votes. We are after principles. We don't care whether we control the Government or not. We want enough representatives to look after agricultural interests."[10] Only his suggestion that the provincial government be made over on the model of a county council gave some shadow of responsibility to the stand he took.

Morrison voiced the great agrarian bitterness of the day with respect to rural depopulation, the political neglect of the farmer, the social contumely he experienced, and the accepted dominance of political and social life by the industrial and professional classes. He also spoke for the U.F.O. In convention in December, the organization rejected the proposal to broaden the political movement by resolving "That no change be made

---

[7] *Farmers' Sun*, March 11, 1922, p. 8.
[8] *Ibid.*, Aug. 17, 1922, p. 1.
[9] *Ibid.*, Aug. 19, 1922, pp. 1 and 6.
[10] *Ibid.*

in the form of organization for political purposes, that this convention re-affirms its adherence to the policy of constituency autonomy, that this convention is opposed to the transformation of the Farmers' Movement into a new political party." The resolution was carried by the convention before the popular Drury was heard, and he accepted the decision without comment, contenting himself with pointing out that the rural and suburban population of Ontario was only 41 per cent of the population of the province. "What then," he asked, "should be our course? I believe, while we maintain our organization for ourselves and to ourselves for the purpose of our industry, that when we come to the question of political matters we must seek the support of all those like-minded with us."[11] The U.F.O., however, like the other farm organizations in politics, was in reality too isolated in sentiment, too resentful and suspicious of industry and of labour, to make its own political action the initial impulse of action by other elements.

Nor was this the only obstacle. There was in most urban electoral districts, with the exception of the few dominated by organized labour, no equivalent of the agrarian local organization, nor, given the diversity of urban occupations, was there likely to be. The absence of organized interests in urban seats was a major obstacle to both "broadening out," which could only result in a composite party, and occupational representation which, except in purely agricultural areas, was incompatible with territorial representation.[12] The *Grain Growers' Guide*, in discussing the U.F.O. convention of 1922, seized on this point:

The farmers are in politics as organized bodies; they take political action through their organizations. They do not call individals to their conventions; they call representatives of the unit of the association. Obviously to get the contact that will bring like-mindedness into common action, there must be like organization. How are they to get that organization with say urban like-mindedness if there is no like organization composed of urban members? But given such permanent and continuous urban organization, the way would be open for constituency co-operation between democratic associations for the accomplishing of common purposes. It cannot be done without

[11] *Ibid.*, Dec. 16, 1922, p. 1.
[12] Corry, *Democratic Government and Politics*, 191-5.

urban organization, for there would then be no point of contact between the organization of the farmers and their urban sympathizers.

Mr. Crerar told the recent Progressive conference in Winnipeg that he would like to see a Progressive association in every town, village and hamlet in the country. That is not only the way to get the co-operation of like-mindedness in political matters, it is the one hope of democracy. Men with common economic interests will no doubt find those interests the most enduring bond of association, but where no such interests can be made the bond of association it is better that men should find a bond in ideas than remain in a futile individualism. The associative principle is the most vital idea in modern political philosophy and in the full and proper application of that idea is to be found the solution of the outstanding political problem facing the movement of the organized farmers.[13]

The decision of the U.F.O. not to create a people's party had been taken on the eve of the provincial election of 1923. The election was held in June. The U.F.O. found its candidates engaged in three-cornered contests in 27 constituencies and in more than three-cornered contests in a number of others. It fought an aggressive Conservative party, and a Liberal party which, alarmed by the victory of Morrison in the U.F.O., abandoned its hope of 1919 of absorbing the farmers by not opposing their candidates.[14] Taken on both flanks, the U.F.O. went down to defeat. In place of the forty-three U.F.O. members of 1919, only fifteen were returned in 1923.[15] The resentments of 1919 had faded, the Drury-Morrison controversy had alarmed the village and town voters, and the proposal to broaden out had started a return of voters to their former allegiances. The government's rigid enforcement of prohibition redounded to the advantage of the Conservatives in urban seats. Nor had the government's policy of expenditures on public works recommended itself to the rural voters.[16] After the election came the scandal of the trial and conviction of Hon. Peter Smith, Provincial Treasurer in the Drury Govern-

---

[13]*Grain Growers' Guide*, XVI, Jan. 3, 1923, p. 5, editorial, "Political Organization."
[14]See *Canadian Annual Review*, 1923, p. 531-2, for the episode of the reading in the Ontario Legislature of Senator A. C. Hardy's letter, discussing a linking-up of Liberals and farmers.
[15]*Ibid.*, pp. 577-9.
[16]*Grain Growers' Guide*, XVI, July 4, 1923, p. 5.

ment. This, together with a redistribution of seats diminishing rural representation, made impossible any revival of the political strength of the U.F.O. Ontario had returned to the old party system, and in December 1923, the U.F.O. convention passed a compromise resolution declaring that it would take no further political action as an organization, though it would not oppose the formation of a political party which would further its aspirations.[17] Political action was left to the clubs and individuals; the U.F.O. henceforth devoted itself to educational and co-operative work.

In Alberta, on the other hand, there was no division between advocates of group government and advocates of an independent political party. There was, however, much work of propaganda to be done, and the exploration and clarification of the relations between the political representatives of the U.F.A., their constituents, and the U.F.A. in convention to be attempted. Some years were to elapse before the membership was thoroughly indoctrinated, though given the nature of the task, the work was done with surprising speed and thoroughness. Much also had to be done before the relations of representatives and constituents were satisfactorily defined. Both tasks were greatly advanced, however, by the adoption of an authoritative declaration of principles by the convention of 1922. This read:

Believing that the present unsettled conditions in Canada politically are due in large measure to dissatisfaction with the party system of government, and Believing that present day political institutions fail to measure up to the requirements of present day conditions, in that the present system has failed to develop a sufficiently close connection between the representative and the elector, and that the people desire a greater measure of self-government,

Recognizing the right of all citizens, believing that it is the duty of every citizen to exercise his right of citizenship in the most efficient manner, and in the best interests of social progress, and believing that individual citizenship can only be made efficient and effective through the vehicle of systematically organized groups;

We the United Farmers of Alberta, base our hope of developing a social influence and a progressive force on becoming a stabilized, efficient organization. We therefore place primary emphasis on organization.

[17]*Farmers' Sun*, Dec. 15, 1923, p. 1.

Our organization is continuously in authority, and while through it we formulate declarations of principles, or a so-called platform, these are at all times subject to change by the organization.

We are a group of citizens going into political action as an organization. Our elected representatives are at all times answerable to the organization. Each representative is answerable directly to the organization in the constituency that elected him.

We aim to develop through the study of social and economic problems an intelligent responsible citizenship.

Thus organized citizenship becomes the vehicle not only of intelligent voting, but also of intelligent guidance of elected representatives.

A full recognition of the supremacy of the organization in all things does not nullify the importance of a platform.[18]

The declaration was a clear statement of the objectives and theory of political organization of the U.F.A., and of the responsibility of the elected member to his constituents, which was to remain, with certain amendments, the basis of political action by the U.F.A. until it withdrew from politics.[19] Their clarity of principle, however, did not save the U.F.A. from difficulties in practice. Instead of being merely an agricultural group after the election of 1921, the farmers had found themselves in an absolute majority, and faced with the responsibility of forming a government. As in Ontario, a leader had to be found for a leaderless group. Wood had declined the position.[20] His nominee, H. H. Greenfield, vice-president of the U.F.A. since 1919, was summoned to the premiership. So strong was agrarian sentiment in the group that, in forming the cabinet, it was proposed to make a farmer attorney-general, and the victory of common sense in the appointment of J. E. Brownlee, solicitor of the U.F.A., left no little resentment.[21] On the other hand, Wood's evasion of the responsibility which was properly his provoked bitter criticism from the opposition press.[22]

There was yet a further embarrassment. In the formation of a U.F.A. administration, the U.F.A. majority made un-

[18]U.F.A. Head Office, Calgary, *U.F.A. Annual Report*, 1921, p. 29; report of Provincial Platform Committee, accepted Jan. 21, 1922.

[19]Minutes of Annual Convention of U.F.A., 1939, pp. 23-4.

[20]L. D. Nesbitt, "Notes of an Interview with H. W. Wood."

[21]Statement of Hon. Herbert Greenfield.

[22]*Edmonton Bulletin*, July 30, 1921, p. 7, editorial, "The Anti-Caucusers Meet in Caucus."

necessary, and almost impossible, the application of that principle of group government which would have made the cabinet representative of the economic groups in the legislature and the creature and agent of the House. The farmers had not wished to assume the responsibilities of government. For this there were two reasons, unwillingness to assume the liabilities of the previous administration, and the belief in group government, which required that every group be represented in the cabinet as well as the legislature. In the lack of a legislature so constituted, the U.F.A. had to accept the position of acting "as custodians of the interests of others whom they wish were there themselves to look after their own interests."[23] How much this consideration troubled the leaders may be doubted, in the light of the noncommittal or indifferent attitude of Greenfield and Brownlee towards a resolution to prohibit the government resigning except on an explicit vote of want of confidence.[24] What could be done was done by the inclusion of Vernon Smith, Labour member for East Calgary, as Minister of Labour. This act was a further demonstration, already apparent in the Medicine Hat by-election, of the readiness of the U.F.A. to co-operate with labour, provided it was the co-operation of organized groups, and not fusion into a single political party.

Because of the nature of the situation, the theory of occupational representation could not be fully applied by the U.F.A. within the provincial sphere. Within the federal sphere, however, where agriculture was one among many interests, the theory seemed quite applicable, and there it served as the guiding principle in determining the relationship of the members of parliament to the U.F.A. organization and to their local constituents. It was because of adherence to this principle that the Alberta Progressive representation constituted such a disruptive influence within the federal Progressive movement.

The attention of the U.F.A. was at once drawn to its federal representatives by the negotiations for a Liberal-Progressive alliance in December 1921. At Saskatoon the U.F.A. members had refused to agree to a policy which would lead to fusion,

[23]*Manitoba Free Press*, Aug. 6, 1921, p. 25.

[24]W. L. Morton, "The Western Progressive Movement and Cabinet Domination," *Canadian Journal of Economics and Political Science*, XII, May, 1946, p. 143.

while expressing a readiness to co-operate with any group in carrying progressive legislation.[25] In January 1922, after the negotiations had failed, the U.F.A. convention expressed itself as follows: "Resolved that it is the sentiment of this convention that members of the Progressive Party, although the official opposition,[26] will support all legislation that tends to the benefit of the Canadian people and that this Progressive Party will not affiliate permanently with any other party."[27] This resolution was hereafter regarded a binding instruction on the U.F.A. members at Ottawa.

Attention, however, was called to the relation of member and association in another way, both humiliating and somewhat comic. When the negotiations between Crerar and King had collapsed, King had been forced to fall back on Liberal members, and true to his rigid application of the principle of the sectional and communal composition of the cabinet, had sought a member for Alberta. That province had returned not a single Liberal, else that gentleman, whatever his merits or capacity, would have been whisked into the cabinet. In the absence of a Liberal member-elect upon whom cabinet office could be thrust, King chose Hon. Charles A. Stewart, recently premier of Alberta. Stewart had no seat in his own province, and there was, of course, no lesser Liberal to be persuaded for the good of the party to resign his seat for him. Accordingly, approaches were made to one or more of the U.F.A. representatives. It casts much light on the comparative failure of U.F.A. indoctrination and on the political naïveté of some of the newly elected Progressives, that one, or more, was found ready to resign his seat for a minor government appointment.[28] Only discovery by his colleagues, and prompt instruction in the ways of the world of politics and in the principles of the U.F.A. political movement, averted the disaster. As a result, Stewart had to go far from

[25]See above, chap. v, p. 133.

[26]The decision not to be the opposition had not yet been taken; the assumption that the Progressives would be the opposition and the use of the term "Progressive Party" are good examples of the way the doctrines of the U.F.A. clarified as events developed.

[27]U.F.A. Annual Report, 1921, p. 100, minutes of convention of 1922.

[28]This is based on the account of the late Senator William Harmer, A. L. Sifton's organizer, who conducted this particular negotiation.

Alberta to find a welcoming seat in solid Quebec, and the U.F.A. convention passed the following resolution, the pained tone of which is perceptible:

Whereas certain members-elect for Federal districts in Alberta have been approached by more or less secret methods to resign in order to create a vacancy for the recently appointed Minister of Interior, and

Whereas the position of representative in Parliament is a sacred trust from the electors, and

Whereas all secret and private bargaining with regard to a parliamentary position, is a flagrant violation of trust and a menace to democratic government,

Be it resolved this convention recommends that except for purely personal reasons, no member of parliament resign his seat except with consent of the duly constituted and accredited convention.[29]

Thereafter no U.F.A. member was left in any doubt as to the vigilant scrutiny of his actions which the U.F.A. maintained, and few thereafter wavered in their allegiance.

The developments of the federal session of 1922 and of the Winnipeg conference of November 1922, similarly provoked a statement of policy by the convention. After a recital of the development of group government and of the farmers' political movement, it was resolved:

That this Convention heartily endorse the action of the U.F.A. Federal members in adhering to true democratic principles, by confining their efforts to legislative activities, and we urge them to so continue, and

Be it further resolved, that should any part of the group of farmer legislative representatives decide to organize a Central Committee to exercise any control over the political activities of the electorate, it is the firm belief of this Convention that it would be a violation of the democratic principles on which the U.F.A. political movement is founded for any legislative member of the U.F.A. to endorse or recognize the authority of such a committee, and

Be it further resolved, that we urge our elected members to give their undivided attention to their legislative duties, recognizing at all times that their duties are connected with legislative matters and with the operation of securing just and democratic legislaton and that they should give and secure all co-operation to this end, and

[29] *U.F.A. Annual Report*, 1921, p. 94, minutes of convention of 1922.

Be it further resolved, that we endorse the action of the Winnipeg Conference in creating a Parliamentary Committee composed of a chairman elected by the Conference, and one or more committeemen, elected by and answerable to each Provincial Unit, this committee to function only in a legislative capacity.[30]

Further to clarify its stand, the convention also resolved:

Whereas, the basic principle upon which the U.F.A. organization is built is that of an economic group organization, and

Whereas, action has been taken in both Federal and Provincial politics, and members elected on this principle, and

Whereas, we are now facing a crisis wherein this principle is seriously threatened through the efforts of certain farmers [sic] leaders and others in endeavoring: (1) either to amalgamate or affiliate with the Liberal party, or (2) to form a Progressive political party of "broadening out" from this basis to take in members from any or all other classes;

Be it therefore resolved, that we hereby affirm our adherence to the principle of economic group organization and co-operation between economic groups, and demand that our representatives stand firm in adherence to this principle and that they oppose any steps looking to either amalgamation or affiliation with a political party or to the formation of a new political party by "broadening out."[31]

The U.F.A. thus firmly reiterated the principles of occupational representation. The effect of the resolution was, however, not to shackle the federal members, but to confirm them in their own convictions, and to indicate clearly what their future course must be.

Such was the local background of the revolt of the "Ginger Group" in 1924. This action of the U.F.A. members and their sympathizers was caused by a difference of opinion, not over policy, but over parliamentary organization and procedure.[32] They carried the principle of constituency autonomy to the point of the complete independence of the individual member. Should a U.F.A. member, then, participate in a Progressive caucus, or for that matter, in a U.F.A. group? Was his re-

---

[30]Minutes of Annual Convention of U.F.A., 1923, pp. 26-7.

[31]*Ibid.*, pp. 27-8.

[32]*Grain Growers' Guide*, XVII, July 9, 1924, p. 5, editorial, "The Progressive Division."

sponsibility exclusively to his electors?[33]   The revolt, accordingly, broke up not only the Progressive party but also the U.F.A. group and posed a problem for the U.F.A organization. Henry Wise Wood dealt with the subject of "The U.F.A. Subunits and Their Relationship to the Organization as a Whole," in August 1924:

> Any member nominated and elected in any Federal or Provincial constituency [wrote Wood] is a U.F.A. member only—"independent" of all political parties.   There is nothing in any pronouncement that the U.F.A. has made that would warrant such a member in allying himself as an individual with any political party.   On the other hand, there is nothing to prevent the U.F.A. group of members co-operating with any other group or party in the interests of good legislation.   The identity of the group should at all times be preserved, as all members are elected as U.F.A. and not as party members.

At the same time, the convention of the U.F.A. remained supreme over electoral district associations, to which parliamentary members were responsible, but only as the sole means of preserving the unity of voluntary co-operative effort.[34]

In these terms, Wood, the principal expounder of occupational representation, affirmed the solidarity of the elected representatives of the group against the dissolvent of constituency autonomy.   Presumably, it was his influence which persuaded the U.F.A. members to present to the convention of 1925 a resolution which affirmed the necessity of maintaining their solidarity as a legislative group.[35]   The convention warmly applauded their action and carried the resolution unanimously.[36] Behind this action of the U.F.A. members may have lain some disciplinary pressure.[37]   The resolution did, at any rate, mark the formal end of the Ginger Group.[38]

Thereupon the convention proceeded to define with greater

[33]*Morning Albertan*, Jan. 20, 1925, p. 4, editorial, "The U.F.A. Convention."

[34]*The U.F.A.*, Aug. 15, 1924, pp. 8 and 9; *Morning Albertan*, Jan. 23, 1925, pp. 1 and 10.

[35]*The U.F.A.*, Feb. 2, 1925, p. 3.

[36]*Minutes of Annual Convention of U.F.A.*, 1925, pp. 161-2; D. M. Kennedy, member for Edmonton West, who was absent, was reported in the convention to have concurred; *Morning Albertan*, Jan. 23, 1925, p. 1.

[37]Dexter, "Will the Prairies Go Solid Again?," 75.

[38]*Manitoba Free Press*, Jan. 28, 1925, p. 13.

clearness the principles of political action laid down by the conventions of 1919 and 1920,[39] in the following terms:

1st.   That each elected member who has been nominated by the U.F.A. organization in any constituency, shall be known only as a U.F.A. representative and shall be expected to attach himself to no other legislative group or party, and further, that each U.F.A. member is responsible directly to his own U.F.A. constituency organization and that organization is responsible to the U.F.A. as a whole.

2nd.   That each candidate so elected shall be expected to co-operate as an individual with all other U.F.A. members, thereby forming and organizing a parliamentary group unity; and that this U.F.A. group unit should be expected to co-operate as such, with other parliamentary parties, groups or individual members, when practicable to do so in the interests of desirable legislation.

3rd.   That each constituency shall have the fullest autonomy in nominating and electing a candidate, as outlined in the two above clauses, but this Convention specifically declares that no constituency shall have the right to use the U.F.A. organization in that constituency for the purpose of nominating and electing a candidate on any other understanding than that outlined above, in clauses one and two of this Resolution.   And be it further;

4th.   Resolved, that nothing in the above resolutions shall be so construed as to prevent the U.F.A. parliamentary group from acting with, and inviting into their group councils, individual parliamentary members, especially those elected by other farmers' organizations, similar to the U.F.A., when a majority of the said U.F.A. group decide that it is expedient and advisable to do so.   And be it further,

5th.   Resolved, that when a bona fide farm organization such as the U.F.A., from another Province elects a group of legislative members and these members organize themselves into a legislative group unit representative of that organization, it is the desire of this Convention that our U.F.A. legislative group should co-operate with such a legislative group or groups in the organization of a larger agricultural group containing all such provincial groups, or as many as will so organize.   And be it further;

6th.   Resolved, that the principles and policies, as declared from time to time by U.F.A. Convention, broadly interpreted, shall be the general guiding influence of the U.F.A. members and the U.F.A. legislative group, and that with these principles in mind, they are expected to use their best judgment in dealing, in a practical way,

[39]*The U.F.A.*, Feb. 2, 1925, p. 3.

with all matters of legislation, in the interests of industry as a whole and further that the U.F.A. members and the U.F.A. legislative group shall not be considered as in any way bound by any declaration of principles, or any platform coming from any other source.

7th.   Be it further resolved, that when a special service is required that calls for special training in order to render that service efficiently, the nominations for a constituency need not necessarily be limited to U.F.A. members, nor even to farmers.   The object should be to select a candidate who will be loyal to the U.F.A. and capable of giving efficient service.[40]

This exhaustive statement completed the definition of the relations of the U.F.A. member with his constituents and with the U.F.A. as an organization.   Henceforth the U.F.A. federal members knew beyond doubt that they were the delegates of their constituents, under the supreme authority of the U.F.A. in convention, and that, as delegates, they were expected to act as a body, in isolation, or in co-operation with groups similar in organization and purpose, as the principles of group representation, the policies of the U.F.A., and the wishes of their constituents might indicate.   The U.F.A. was thus forged into a church militant, with doctrine, hierarchy, and apostles, and to this, as well to the debtor and agrarian economy in Alberta, is to be ascribed the singular duration and accomplishment of its representation in parliament.

Not all difficulties, however, were ended immediately by this pronouncement of the convention.   The U.F.A. members at Ottawa were soon after reported to have found it impossible to form a united group among themselves.   The problems of organization were sharpened by the suspicion which the Gingerites, both U.F.A. and others, had entertained of the Manitoban Progressives ever since December 1921.   The anti-Gingerite U.F.A. members, for their part, refused to be bound not to sit in the Progressive caucus, while the Gingerites would not agree that U.F.A. members were free to join, even as individuals. To them the Progressives were, in Agnes Macphail's phrase, "pale shadows of the government."[41]   Not until the U.F.A. federal members reconciled their differences in conference at

[40]*Minutes of Annual Convention of U.F.A.*, 1925, p. 180.
[41]*Manitoba Free Press*, Feb. 24, 1925, p. 13.

Calgary in July 1926 and the stronger anti-Gingerites were eliminated in the following election, was the U.F.A. group to achieve solidarity at Ottawa.[42]

In the meantime the U.F.A. was strengthening its hold upon the Alberta provincial government.   In 1924, Premier Herbert Greenfield lost the confidence of his supporters, and in 1925 resigned.   He was succeeded as premier by Hon. J. E. Brownlee. Under this capable administrator, and aided by better crops, the U.F.A. government began to make headway in its struggle with the provincial debt and the losses on the provincial railway obligations.   In particular, negotiations were completed with the federal government for transfer of control of the natural resources of the province in 1926.   A last-minute obstacle arose when it was found that a condition had been attached to the terms with the purpose of safeguarding the separate schools of Alberta as established by the Alberta Act of 1905.[43]   Such a condition Brownlee refused to accept, and thus the School Question rose for the first time in Alberta politics, to give the provincial government a useful issue in attacking both the federal government and federal party interference in provincial affairs.   "Anyone," declared Brownlee at Gleichen, "who has taken part in public life in this Province, over a period of years sees to what extent the Provincial party is dominated by the Federal.   It exists for the sake of the Federal party.   There is a question that is becoming increasingly important, that is the need of absolute independence of the Provincial Government from the Dominion Government."[44]   With this issue to exploit, and the discipline of the U.F.A. organization to back it, the Brownlee Government was returned to power in an election regarded as a confirmation of the elimination of party politics from the public affairs of Alberta.[45]

While the doctrine of occupational representation was developed by the U.F.O. and U.F.A., and worked itself out to these very different ends in Ontario and Alberta, in Manitoba and Saskatchewan Manitoban Progressivism moved towards its

[42]*Minutes of Annual Convention of U.F.A.*, 1927, pp. 68-9.
[43]*Canadian Annual Review*, 1925-26, pp. 494-6.
[44]*The U.F.A.*, June 10, 1926, p. 1.
[45]*Ibid.*, July 2, 1926, p. 6.

destined end of a reunion of agrarian radicalism with the traditional Liberal party.

In Saskatchewan the reunion was to be swift, because the Liberals held the provincial government, and was to be decisive in its results in federal politics. In Manitoba, however, the process was slower, because there the United Farmers had captured the government and consolidated themselves in power.

After its defeat in 1920, the Norris Government had succeeded in carrying on, however, for two years in what was mistakenly termed an experiment in group government, by means of the support of individual members, now of this group, now of that. In the main, it was kept in office by the votes of the United Farmer members. So uncertain was its life, however, that it escaped defeat on the Smith resolution calling for the election of the executive council by the legislature only by the casting vote of the Speaker, and finally went down to defeat on a vote of censure moved by P. A. Talbot, leader of the anti-school-law group, in March 1922. Thereupon the legislature was dissolved, and the Norris administration, discredited by its weakness and its failure to economize, and reduced by resignations, went to the country.

In 1921, the U.F.M. had decided on taking political action as an organization.[46] The public awaited the event with impatience, not least the business men of Winnipeg, who saw in an agrarian majority the only hope of strong and economical government. There was little hostility to the Norris Government among the farmers except on the score of its heavy expenditures, for which the Provincial Treasurer, Hon. Edward Brown, was held responsible, but the idea had bitten deeply into the rural mind that the lawyers had ruled long enough. The farmers must take over themselves, or at least win representation in the legislature proportionate to their weight as voters. The appointment of G. J. H. Malcolm, a farmer, as Minister of Agriculture in 1920, and of another farmer, John Williams, on his resignation, was a concession to agrarian sentiment too late to have effect. Agrarian sentiment was directed against not only business and the professions, but also against labour. The Winnipeg strike had shocked and angered the farmers as deeply

[46]*Grain Growers' Guide*, XV, Feb. 22, 1922, p. 19.

as it had the urban professional workers and employers. In 1920 only the more radical farmers had taken political action and this had led to some co-operation with labour where electoral conditions called for it. In 1922 these ties were for the most part snapped, and a purely agrarian movement was launched. The U.F.M. district directorate of Dauphin, for example, a district which had returned a Labour member in 1920, ended the alliance on the ground that, while the farmers supported the "legitimate ends" of labour, labour in turn had shown little comprehension of the needs of agriculture. Shorter hours and higher wages had little application to the existing plight of the farmers. The need of the times was to ensure prosperity for the farmer, since in his prosperity all would prosper.[47]

The movement, once launched, had to campaign against the Liberals as well as other opponents, and occasion for hostility was found in Norris's action in allowing his government to seem to be reunited with the federal Liberal party. Advances designed to bring about reunion were made by A. E. Hill, president of the Dominion Liberal Association, and supported by Hon. Edward Brown.[48] The purpose was both to reunite the Unionist and Laurier Liberals of Manitoba, and to strengthen the Liberal party in the West by renewing the federal-provincial party ties in Manitoba broken by the School Act of 1916 and the events of 1917. It was so far successful as to make possible the summoning of a Liberal convention in April 1922, by the federal Liberals with the apparent approval of the provincial leaders. In the convention the federal Liberals were reunited. The impression, however, that the provincial party had rejoined the federal, and the attempt to have a resolution adopted proposing to modify the School Act by allowing instruction in French, told heavily against the provincial government.[49] The United Farmers naturally made the most of these points in the ensuing election. Though Norris declared at Bradwardine that there was no affiliation between his government and the federal Liberals, and that the record of

[47]*Manitoba Free Press*, May 8, 1922, p. 11, quoting *Dauphin Herald*, May 4, 1922.

[48]Dafoe Papers, Dafoe to A. B. Hudson, March 30, 1922; Dafoe to Clifford Sifton, April 10, 1922.

[49]*Manitoba Free Press*, April 28, 1922, p. 15, editorial, "The Manitoban Political Situation."

his government in school legislation made affiliation impossible,[50] the damage had been done. The western Progressive movement had made the separation of federal and provincial politics a cardinal principle, and there was special reason for doing so in Manitoba. "This province," said the *Free Press* editorially, "was debauched and looted over a long period of years for the furtherance of Dominion party interests, and both sister provinces to the West have had practical experience of what it means to have the provincial premier as the leader, for the province, of a Dominion party."[51]

When all other factors were taken into account, however, it was pure agrarianism, lacking, it is true, the indoctrination and discipline of Alberta, which carried the U.F.M. to power in 1922. The platform prepared by the Directorate of the U.F.M. from resolutions submitted by the locals contained little of note in this context, except the first plank which stipulated that the association should be independent of any government, and the second, which required, "in order that all measures coming before the legislature may be considered on their merits, only the refusal of supply or a specific vote of want of confidence [should] necessitate the resignation of a government."[52] Even the organization of a Progressive Committee in Winnipeg among the personnel of the staffs of the United Grain Growers Company and the *Grain Growers' Guide*,[53] and the election of a Progressive candidate in the great distribution centre and seat of the grain trade, so little loved in its own province, did not alter the fact that, as in Ontario, rural animus against urban domination, the rule of lawyers, and city ways was the driving force and principal cause of the farmer's victory in 1922. The candidates of the U.F.M. were returned as the largest group, twenty-eight in a house of fifty-five; with them were seven Liberals, six Conservatives, six Labour and eight Independents.[54]

[50]*Ibid.*, July 8, 1922, p. 1.

[51]*Ibid.*, p. 11; note also the comment of July 2, 1920, on the election of that year: "This Province between 1900 and 1911 financed a Dominion opposition party throughout the whole of western Canada; and this would again have been its fate had the electors listened on Tuesday to the alluring call of Mr. Rogers."

[52]P.A.M., Minutes of Annual Convention of United Farmers of Manitoba, 1922, pp. 2-3 and 8.

[53]*Grain Growers' Guide*, XV, June 7, 1922, p. 14.

[54]*Canadian Annual Review*, 1923, p. 698.

The spontaneity of the movement—or the lack of central direction—was again revealed, as in Ontario and Alberta, by the fact that when the farmers found themselves with a majority in the legislature, they also found themselves without a leader. George Chipman, able editor of the *Grain Growers' Guide*, and a potent moulder of the Progressive movement, had been widely named as the leader of the confidently anticipated farmers' government, but he had failed of election under Winnipeg's tortuous system of proportional representation. Colin H. Burnell, president of the U.F.M., was also among the defeated. A caucus of members-elect met to find a head for the group, and, after canvassing various names, they lighted by a happy inspiration on that of a complete outsider, John Bracken, new president of the Manitoba Agricultural College, a man hitherto as innocent of politics as the most doctrinaire Progressive could desire. It was a choice of leader which the next twenty years proved wise.

It was, none the less, a heavy task the new leader assumed. Not only was the principal industry of the province depressed, and the provincial debt swollen by the extravagance of the Roblin Government and the reforms of the Norris Government; his following was undisciplined and wilful, wedded to the idea of the independency of members and of constituency autonomy. In the first session of the new legislature, several divisions were survived by a plurality of one vote,[55] and only the convenient adoption of the principle urged by the supporters of group government and contained in the U.F.M. Platform, that the government resign only on an explicit vote of want of confidence, gave the administration assurance of survival.[56] This return to the freedom of parliamentary voting before the establishment of the two-party system was carried to extremes in the division in which the Wheat Board bill was defeated; in the vote not only were government supporters and opposition split, but also the cabinet itself.[57]

While Manitoba politics saw a characteristic farmers' victory, there was one element which differentiated the political

[55] *Ibid.*
[56] *Ibid.*, p. 701.
[57] *Ibid.*, p. 699.

circumstances of that province from the contemporary circumstances of Saskatchewan and Alberta.   In both those provinces the provincial Conservative party had disappeared, or practically so, as had the federal Conservative party after 1911. In Manitoba, a province Ontario-born and western-bred, the Conservative party had been salvaged from the disaster of 1915, and had re-established itself as a permanent force in provincial politics.   The provincial by-election in Mountain in 1923 revealed its reviving strength, and pointed to the necessity of a Liberal-Progressive alliance.[58]   Many Progressives who had been Conservatives before 1915 stood in the way of, or at least acted as a drag upon, such an alliance.   Yet it needed only the waning of the farmers' political zeal, as they adjusted themselves to depressed conditions and turned their energies to the creation of the Wheat Pool, and the plight of farmers' representatives left to pay their own election expenses, to make it seem the only hope of saving something of the movement.

Meantime the silent man who had come in from the quiet fields in the loop of the Red River at Fort Garry to the splendid and virginal legislative building, studied it all, listened, and refused to commit himself.   Gradually the course became clear. If there were to be a Liberal-Progressive alliance, it must come slowly.   The approach would have to be made from the federal Liberal side, and the co-operation would involve no affiliation of the provincial administration with the federal Liberal party. There might be a strong Conservative revival in a province markedly conservative by history and temperament, and the U.F.M. stood vigilant, determined, in the words of President Colin Burnell, "to keep political organization under the control of the locals and not under the control of our representatives, . . . [to keep] our representatives in Parliament as legislators and not make them into politicians."[59]   Under these conditions the Bracken Government was cautiously shaped as a straight provincial party, agrarian in basis and sentiment.   It was to carry

[58]Dafoe Papers, Dafoe to Clifford Sifton, Dec. 27, 1923.

[59]*Canadian Annual Review*, 1923, p. 705.   The U.F.M. may be said to have withdrawn from politics, insofar as it was committed to political action, in 1928 (P.A.M., Minutes of Annual Convention of U.F.M., 1928, p. 5).   As in Saskatchewan, the influence of the United Farmers of Canada brought about this decision.

the province again in 1927 and, despite the great depression of 1929, was to see all its contemporaries into their political graves.

Not in Manitoba, then, was to take place, in time to be decisive, a reunion of federal Liberalism with western agrarianism, separated since 1921. The beginning of the reunion was to be made in Saskatchewan. In that province the farmers' movement had failed to create a provincial party capable of capturing the government. The Liberal administration had survived by its concessions to agrarianism on the one hand and, on the other, by severing its connection with the federal Liberal party. The effort to commit the Saskatchewan Grain Growers to provincial political action, which had failed in 1920 and 1921, had been renewed in the convention of 1922. This time it was aided by the farmers' resentment of Premier Martin's support of Motherwell in the federal election of 1921, and by the resultant resignation of J. A. Maharg from the provincial cabinet. Maharg became leader of the independents in the legislature, and he and J. B. Musselman, secretary of the Association, both of whom had hitherto resisted the Grain Growers' entering provincial politics, gave their active support to the movement. In this they were joined by Langley, who had been forced out of the provincial government in September 1921, for interference with the administration of justice in the discharge of a political obligation.[60] The demand for political action by the Association was thus powerfully reinforced. The debate in the convention was stormy, prolonged, and involved. Henry Wise Wood was heard on the merits of group government. Motions were made and withdrawn, amendment clashed with amendment. Finally a motion of R. M. Johnson was adopted: "That the Central Board of this Association create a Committee to assist those Provincial constituencies that wish to take action, and support the declared principles of the Association, to organize themselves for direct Provincial political action."[61] In adopting Johnson's motion, the convention had rejected political action by the Association on the Albertan model. It had also refused to approve the creation of a separate political association, as

---

[60]*Grain Growers' Guide*, XV, Feb. 2, 1922, pp. 3 and 12.
[61]Minutes of Annual Convention of S.G.G.A., 1922, p. 118.

had been done in federal politics. It had merely approved a central committee to assist and co-ordinate local political action, as had been done in Manitoba in 1922.

The decision of the Saskatchewan Grain Growers to aid provincial political action followed the provincial election of 1921 and was too late by a year. Moreover, it was an astute and ruthless foe which was being challenged. Martin's support of Motherwell made his resignation necessary and in April of 1922 he stepped up to the chief justiceship of an enlarged Supreme Court. He was succeeded as premier by Hon. Charles A. Dunning, a Grain Grower and a farmer.[62] Dunning at once announced that he was not "under marching orders to go out and fight the farmers—not at all. The bulk of the Saskatchewan farmers are Liberals. The bulk of the Saskatchewan Grain Growers are Liberals."[63] The agrarian government of Saskatchewan had at last found an agrarian head.

At the same time the independent political movement lost its two powerful recruits when in August of 1922 Maharg became vice-president and Musselman managing director of the Saskatchewan Co-operative Elevators Company. After this loss, the movement for political action decreased in force, and in 1924 the Association rescinded the motion of 1922, and withdrew from provincial politics.[64] The reluctance of Grain Growers who were Liberals to oppose the government, the loss of members, which was attributed to political action, and the rise of the Farmers' Union, a militant organization committed to economic action only, all contributed to the withdrawal. The decline of the Grain Growers and the rise of the Union along with the Wheat Pool brought about in 1926 the union of the two as the United Farmers of Canada (Saskatchewan Section).[65] The union was a victory for the Farmers' Union and its doctrine of economic action, but the united farmers were already under a new pressure to take political action from the Farmers' Political Association, organized in 1924-5 by G. H. Williams.

[62]*Canadian Annual Review*, 1922, p. 790.
[63]*Grain Growers' Guide*, XV, April 12, 1922, p. 6.
[64]Minutes of Annual Convention of S.G.G.A., 1924, pp. 143-5.
[65]*Western Producer*, Feb. 4, 1926, p. 1.

Meantime, the independents of 1921, being disappointed in their hope of support from the Association, had carried on as best they could. In the provincial by-election of Milestone in 1923, they organized the Saskatchewan Provincial Progressive Association to contest not only the by-election but the next provincial election. They lost the by-election, and the organization of their supporters in the district, for both provincial and federal purposes, brought down on them the reproof that they were doing what they charged the old parties with doing, subjecting provincial affairs to federal considerations. The *Grain Growers' Guide* spoke with some severity on this point, and continued:

The principle of separating provincial and federal politics, which the organized farmers have emphasized in the past, has, in this part of Canada at least, an historic background, and should not lightly be abandoned. Apparently the Milestone Progressives felt that the action of the Provincial Government left them no alternative but to pursue a similar course. The broad general principle, however, needs again to be emphasized. These Western Provinces have had sharp conflicts with Ottawa in an endeavour to secure full equality with the other provinces in confederation, and are still suffering in a very considerable degree from discrimination in federal legislation. Too close relationship between federal and provincial parties in the past has been a potent factor in preventing the removal of this discrimination, and undoubtedly the maintenance of such relationships will prove a handicap in the future. It may be difficult to maintain a clear-cut distinction, but the needs of this country will be better served if provincial parties as far as possible adhere to provincial matters and avoid those relationships with federal parties which have proved to be detrimental to the welfare of these western provinces.[66]

The rebuke, with its striking statement of the historical case for the separation of provincial and federal politics, may have been warranted, but *The Progressive*, of which Harris Turner, provincial Progressive leader, was editor, had already argued that the fact that Liberal governments were in power both in Ottawa and Regina invited suspicion and opposition on the part of the Progressive voters of Saskatchewan. Dunning in retort proclaimed his government Liberal while denying that it

[66]*Grain Growers' Guide*, XVI, Nov. 7, 1923, p. 6.

was a "donkey engine" of the federal Liberals. Further, *The Progressives* alleged, no less than four provincial ministers, including J. G. Gardiner, had supported the federal Liberal nominee in the Moose Jaw by-election in April 1923.[67] The Milestone by-election itself had given rise to questionings whether the Dunning Government was as neutral in federal affairs as it professed to be. But disappointment in the West with the federal budget of 1923 and the failure of Dunning's negotiations with King in 1923 and his refusal to go into the federal cabinet in 1924,[68] served to make the neutrality effective, if only conditioned on events.

Events were working, however, for renewal of the old alliance of federal and Saskatchewan Liberalism. The opposition in the provincial legislature continued weak, divided, and not far short of farcical. Some Independents even sat on the government side of the legislative chamber. The provincial election of 1925 was a smashing victory for Dunning; the provincial Progressives made no gains. Only a slight revival of Conservatism forecast the Conservative victory of 1929. Meantime the farmers' political movement in Saskatchewan was passing. Federal Progressive members would therefore find little or no electoral organization ready, and few, if any funds available. Here, in great part, was the cause of the federal split on the budget of 1925.

While the hopes of the Progressives were waning, Prime Minister King still found the Progressive price for co-operation too high,[69] but the defeat of 1925 in the East was to force his hand. In Saskatchewan the possibility of a federal Conservative revival, and the manifest weakness of the Progressive movement, left the way open for the provincial Liberals to return to the federal alliance. Leaving Hon. J. G. Gardiner as premier of a province still unshakably Liberal, Dunning in 1926 could go to Ottawa as Minister of Railways and Canals. In the election of that year he delivered his province to the federal Liberals, and the Liberal party once more rested on the twin

[67]*The Progressive*, Oct. 18, 1923, p. 4.
[68]Dafoe Papers, Dafoe to J.A.S., Jan. 28, 1924.
[69]*Canadian Annual Review*, 1924-5, pp. 207-9, a report of references made by King to Liberal-Progressive relations during his western tour of October, 1924.

pillars of Quebec and Saskatchewan.   The real issue in Saskatchewan since 1921 had been whether low-tariff men could accomplish more as Liberals or as Progressives.   By 1926 the Saskatchewan Liberals seemed vindicated in their support of the federal Liberal party as the chief hope of a downward revision of the tariff.   The way was prepared for the Dunning budget of 1930.

No single cause, it is apparent, explained the success or failure of the farmers' movement in provincial politics. Strength of organization was indispensable to success, but alone was not enough. In Saskatchewan the farmers' organization, though perhaps the strongest of any organization, was prevented, by the Liberal government and its own leaders, from taking decisive action until the time for success had passed.   The organization of the U.F.O., only little less strong, was made of no avail by doctrinal quarrels over political method.   In Manitoba a canny guidance of the political movement gave it a life separate from that of the parent organization.   Only in Alberta did strong organization, good political leadership, and purity of doctrine combine to found the U.F.A. political movement seemingly on a rock. Personalities, such as Wood's, counted for much, but the explanation of these diverse outcomes of the farmers' political movement lay to a great degree in the historical complexes out of which the provincial movements had arisen and in which they had developed.

The Progressive Group in the Constitutional Crisis of 1926

T H E election of 1925 had been called at a time of indecision in the affairs of the country, and the results were to be indecisive. The world was just beginning to move out of the post-war period into the four years of golden hope which preceded the crash of 1929. It seemed that the war was over at last. The post-war depression was beginning to give way to the first swell of the great boom, and even in Canadian agriculture the Wheat Pools and better crops were doing much to offset still depressed prices. The tide was at the turn, but not yet running.

In politics, the Liberal government could not be sure that another session would strengthen it, and the old fear of letting a full term of parliament elapse without going to the country was strong. It might be that the events of the next year would aid the opposition rather than the government. It was the turn of the Liberal party to carry the onus of a record of adminis-tration. However much the difficulties of the post-war years and of the parliamentary situation since 1921 might excuse it, the record was not an imposing one. The position of the party in the country was dubious. In the Maritime Provinces the cry of "Maritime rights" had been raised,[1] and Nova Scotia and New Brunswick, where the United Farmers had failed to organ-ize the discontented, were turning to the Conservatives. Ontario had already reverted to the Conservatives in 1923. British Columbia was as ever divided, the Liberal government of Hon. John Oliver having a bare majority after the election of June

[1]*Canadian Annual Review*, 1924-5, pp. 333-6.

1924.[2] The continental West was still in revolt, though in Saskatchewan federal Liberal prospects were brightening. Only Quebec was sure. The government, therefore, took what cheer it could from three victories in by-elections in Quebec and one in Ontario in 1924, and the victory of the Dunning Government in Saskatchewan in June of 1925, and called a general election for October 29, 1925.

The campaign which followed was without a clear-cut issue.[3] Prime Minister King's election manifesto was a plea for national unity. Speaking at Richmond Hill in North York on September 5, the Prime Minister offered a varied prescription for the restoration of unity among the sections and communities of Canada. The chief ingredients were the improvement of the National Railways, reduction of taxation and the tariff, increased immigration, and reform of the Senate.[4] The plea for unity, the keynote of King's career, was repeated with appropriate local emphasis across the country. It achieved its finest formulation in Montreal on October 19:

We take the position that to keep our country united, to keep Canada happy and contented, we must have regard for all shades and all parts of the country, and any policy that is extreme we must avoid. I say what I said in other provinces, that nothing in the nature of free trade would be possible, for, however it might appeal to some men in the west, it would breed discouragement and discontent in this part of the Dominion, and therefore would make for divisions, instead of harmony. Similarly, I said, speaking in the west, that neither can a policy of higher and higher protection keep this country united. I do not admit for it that it would have the beneficial effect claimed for it, but even supposing it did, if the effect of it was to provoke an extreme movement in the western provinces, sooner or later, those effects would be felt in this part of the Dominion. That is why the Government has sought to find a course that will help to reconcile rather than to exaggerate the differences existing as far as tariff is concerned.[5]

[2]*Ibid.*, p. 444.

[3]W. G. Sharp, "The Canadian Election of 1925" (*American Political Science Review*, XX, Feb., 1926, p. 107).

[4]*Canadian Annual Review*, 1925-6, pp. 22-3.

[5]Montreal *Gazette*, Oct. 20, 1925, p. 9, report of speech by King in Montreal, Oct. 19, 1925.

This was in essence a plea for a party majority drawn from all sections of the country, for a revenue tariff affording incidental protection and for a re-integration of the nation under a Liberal party once more traditional and composite.

While the government's prospects were doubtful, the hopes of the Conservative party were high. It had had the good fortune to be in opposition in a time of trouble. Such trouble the Conservatives could freely ascribe to the errors and blunders of the government while proposing remedies they were not obliged to apply. During these years the policy of the opposition had been simple and consistent. It had been to defend the National Policy and to maintain the principle of protection in the national tariff. The clear-cut stand, taken in 1921, seemed in 1925 about to bear fruit. The party carried Nova Scotia after forty-three years of Liberal rule. New Brunswick was added to Nova Scotia and Ontario. The party was also reviving in Manitoba. It had reappeared in Saskatchewan and Alberta. All over the country, except in Quebec, there was evidence of a revival of Conservatism and of a swing of sentiment towards that party's policy. Quebec remained Liberal still, assured that the Liberal party would adequately safeguard its protectionist interests, although even there, a Nationalist revival had occurred, though ostentatiously not identified with the Conservative party, under the leadership of E. L. Patenaude.[6]

It was therefore with the breath of victory in their nostrils that the Conservatives entered the campaign of 1925. When the country was weary of disunity and sickened of parliamentary manœuvring, the party and the policy of Macdonald might well come as saviour to heal and restore. At Wingham in Ontario Meighen spoke to that effect: "It is the proposal of the Conservative party," he said, "that we pin our faith to a self-reliant and unmistakable protective policy on behalf of the whole country, to put into effect a 'Canada First' policy in every sphere of our agricultural and commercial life, and we propose as well that the entire Dominion shall bear a share of the transport of

[6]Montreal *Gazette*, July 11, 1926, p. 11; speech by E. L. Patenaude describing how the Quebec Conservatives had been separate from the national party, and how they had submerged their differences in response to Meighen's approach.

eastern and western production over the long distances which divide us now."[7]   Railways and the protective tariff would be used to create and consolidate a national fabric—it was the National Policy as Macdonald had shaped it, and as it had since endured.   It was ideally a policy of balanced and reciprocal benefits.   There was, however, no special concession to a Quebec still resentful of 1917.   Once again the appeal of the Conservative chieftain was national, though it would stir most deeply in Ontario.   Was this a formula capable of uniting a a country more diversified, with sectionalism more inflamed, than in 1878, or would it seem but an attempt to have the rest of the country dance to Ontario's piping?

In these circumstances, when no decisive turn for the better had occurred in public affairs, there might well seem to be a great likelihood of the Progressives repeating in large measure their electoral achievement of 1921.[8]   Even when allowance was made for growing resentment in Ontario of the "domination" of the federal government by Quebec, and for the disastrous results of the political collapse of the U.F.O., general conditions in the continental West seemed to point to the election of an agrarian bloc, which under the new distribution, might have numbered forty-five in a House of two hundred and forty-five.   Agriculture was still depressed, debt was heavy, rust ravaged the crops year after year, the price of wheat lagged behind other prices.[9]   The organized farmers' movement had grown more and more radical, notably as the United Farmers of Canada drew off the membership of the Saskatchewan Grain Growers' Association.   The Wheat Pools had just begun to function and were encountering the natural resistance of the private grain trade.   Western Progressives reverted to that blunt sectionalism from which the U.F.O. victory of 1919, and the prospect of a national victory, had shifted them.   In 1925,

[7]Montreal *Gazette*, Sept. 10, 1925, p. 1; report of a speech by Meighen at Wingham, Ont.

[8]Sharp, "The Canadian Election of 1925," 112-13.

[9]S. C. Hudson, "Factors Affecting the Success of Farm Mortgage Loans in Western Canada" (Canada, Department of Agriculture, Publication 733, Ottawa, 1942, p. 14); the differential between the price of wheat and cost of farm purchases was favourable to the farmer from 1914 to 1920, and after 1920, unfavourable.

however, unlike 1919, the sectional clamour was punctuated with comments, despairing, it may be, or calculated, on the possibility of secession.

But neither deepened sectional discontent nor continued depression promised a repetition of the achievement of 1921. The support of the Canadian Council of Agriculture had been withdrawn, the parliamentary group had been rent by public dissension, and only in Manitoba and Alberta did the provincial organizations remain strong. The public and the politicians were aware that the movement was visibly on the wane, and that fact would be reflected in the election returns.

At the same time, the original impulse of the Progressive movement, revolt against the National Policy and the party system, together with its bi-partisan origins, continued to make alliance with the Liberals impossible. Prime Minister King, in his repeated advances to the leaders of the movement, had never shown himself willing to pay the price of coalition, or of publicly avowed legislative co-operation. King was a party man on principle. The last Liberal advance to the Progressives may have been made early in the campaign, but if so, it was offset by the presence of Hon. Herbert Marler, a Liberal bolter on the budget of 1924, in the cabinet, and by the appointment to the cabinet of Hon. Vincent Massey, then best known as the head of Canada's largest farm implement firm.[10] The Progressives were, therefore, committed willy-nilly to fighting the election on their own, which they prepared to do, some, such as the U.F.A., gladly, some by putting a brave face on it.

The Progressives went into the election as groups of independents, scarcely to be termed a party. They made their own national appeal, and sought co-operation from neither Liberals nor Conservatives. Forke issued in Winnipeg on September 17, a frank but uncompromising manifesto:

In Western Canada the Progressive movement represents the almost unanimous popular appreciation of the fact that the measures essential to future development and prosperity will not be carried by either of the old parties. This has been amply proved by experience. In Eastern Canada the primary producers, the professional classes and the consumers generally have been impressed much more widely than

[10]Sharp, "The Canadian Election of 1925," 111.

some suppose with the failure of the two old parties and with the promise of salvation contained in the proposals of the Progressives. The measures desired by the West would be equally efficacious for the removal of the economic disabilities of the primary producers and consumers in the East. The Progressive policy is a national policy and strikes at the fundamental errors in the past administration of public affairs. It is sometimes alleged that the Progressives have failed during the last parliament to bring about those reforms or to induce a clearer understanding of national requirements among the masses of the people owing to the "class" character of the Progressive movement. It is true that the basis of the movement was, and is, agrarian; the Progressive movement finds its greatest strength among those who suffer most from present injustice. But it is also true that it has done much to modify legislation and government policy and to ameliorate the conditions of which complaint is rife. The lack of unanimity, which is found in every Progressive movement and the political inexperience of its representatives have been heavy handicaps. Up to the present the Progressive influence has not succeeded in bringing about that realignment of political forces into "progressive" and "reactionary" which must precede genuine reform and the rebirth of real liberalism in Canada. The opportunity for achieving this realignment has not yet passed. A strong Progressive group in the next parliament, consisting of members fearless and outspoken in advocacy of Progressive principles and careless of the continuance of moribund political parties and of the maintenance in office of particular ministers, would exercise a salutary influence upon Canadian public life, and that is the immediate need of the country. The absorption of the Progressives in the Liberal party, whether in or out of office, and under whatever guise affected would postpone for a generation the attainment of necessary reforms, the reshaping of our national policies and the infusion into Canadian public life of that moral courage and idealism which slavish partisanship has well-nigh destroyed.[11]

There was much whistling in the dark in Forke's manifesto, but it represented a tactical decision, based on the conclusion that the realignment of political forces sought by Manitoban Progressivism was not yet in sight, and that therefore an independent Progressive movement must be kept in being. As such, it was an admirable campaign document, well devised to appeal to both wings of the party.

[11]*Grain Growers' Guide*, XVIII, Sept. 23, 1925, pp. 3 and 4.

While presenting this fighting front, the Progressives campaigned on issues not raised in 1921. The chief of these was the Hudson Bay Railway. That old dream of the West, that wheat might flow out by the Bay as furs had done, had been revived by the pressure of railway rates, and in particular by a new attack on the Crow's Nest Pass rates in 1924. The rise of Vancouver as a wheat port and the renewal of interest in the Bay suggested that the West might at last be freed from the necessity of channelling all imports and exports through Montreal. The secession sentiment created by the freight rates and other burdens the farmers bore also lay behind the agitation for the railway; the promise of the road would relieve in some measure the claustrophobia, the feeling of strangling dependence on the Montreal outlet, which the railway system and the tariff had created in the minds of western Canadians. So much was it desired that, while the Progressives demanded it, King promised it, and Meighen was scarcely less outspoken. The railway to the Bay was in 1925 and 1926 a symbol of the deep frustration of the continental West.

One other noteworthy feature of the campaign of 1925 was confined to Alberta. The Progressives in 1921 had in general not been cordially disposed towards labour; in 1925 those of Manitoba and Saskatchewan were still not inclined to cooperate. In the House, however, the two Labour members, J. S. Woodsworth and William Irvine, had been in close sympathy, and worked closely, as already noted, with the more doctrinaire U.F.A. members. Moreover, in certain Albertan constituencies, both federal and provincial, such as Medicine Hat, Lethbridge, and those of Calgary and Edmonton, the labour vote was of importance. Hence, as the federal and provincial elections approached, the U.F.A. conventions and *The U.F.A.* showed more and more interest in the problem of how the agrarian and labour votes might be combined. Henry Wise Wood, speaking at Jeliff's nomination in the federal seat of Lethbridge, cordially greeted the representatives of labour who were present, and declared it had always been the desire of the U.F.A. to co-operate with labour. But it was to be the co-operation of one organized economic group with another. "Don't," he said, "attempt to mix their policies. It can't be

done successfully, it will only make confusion."[12]   At Calgary
he spoke in the same vein at greater length.[13]   He elaborated
and clarified his remarks in *The U.F.A.* at the same time,
arguing that, "each group represented a separate and distinct
part of a whole industrial system, and, until these parts, along
with all other necessary parts, could begin to be built systematically into a whole, any kind of mixing up between any two
of these distinct parts would cause confusion and delay progress."[14]   However little or much Wood's doctrine may have
been observed in practice, the U.F.A. could claim labour support
in every federal electoral district in which a U.F.A. candidate
was running.   In four districts Labour, or Independent, candidates were supported by the U.F.A.[15]   The co-operation was
another step in the differentiation of the U.F.A. political movement from the Progressive movement.

Elsewhere, the Progressive campaign was fought on the lines
of 1921, except that Forke did not follow Crerar's example and
carry the fight into the East.   He spoke only in Manitoba and
Saskatchewan, and the Progressives, true to character, fought
local soldier's battles, leaving grand strategy and national
campaigns to the leaders of the old parties.   In the ridings
there were few understandings between Liberals and Progressives, except in Ontario, where they served to eliminate a
number of three-cornered fights.[16]   Out of forty-six Ontario
ridings in which Progressive candidates ran, thirty-three saw
three-cornered contests, among Progressives, Conservatives,
and Liberals.   The Liberals elsewhere and especially in Saskatchewan, were trying to make good King's plea that they and
the Progressives should combine against the Conservatives by
agreements not to oppose one another's candidates, but they
met with slight success.   In every province except Manitoba,
where the provincial Liberals had rejoined the federal organization, the provincial government of the day lent its support
to its federal ally.   This renewal of old practices was most

[12]*The U.F.A.*, Oct. 1, 1925, p. 6.

[13]*Ibid.*, pp. 11-12.

[14]*Ibid.*, p. 16, article, "No Fusion with Anybody; Of Course Not."

[15]*Ibid.*, Oct. 17, 1925, p. 3.

[16]*Canadian Annual Review*, 1925-6, p. 30; Montreal *Gazette*, Oct. 26, 1925, p. 12, editorial, "The Progressive-Liberal Compact."

significant in Saskatchewan, where the Dunning Government, secure in its victory of June, and relieved of the spectre of an agrarian opposition by the revival of the Conservative party under J. T. M. Anderson, both as a provincial and a federal organization threw its full weight to the federal Liberals.

A national campaign was fought by King and Meighen across the country, beginning in central Canada, swinging down into the Maritime Provinces, back across the West, to end in central Canada again. The tariff came to be the leading issue, even more than in 1921. Underneath, however, was a bitter personal struggle between the two men, so long and often matched since their college days, for defeat for either might well mean the end of his political career. It had been decided that the post-war era would not be an age of Crerar, but not yet whether it was to be the age of Meighen or of King.[17]

Out of this confused and bitter struggle came a divided verdict. The Conservatives won the election, in the sense that they recovered from the *débâcle* of 1921 and once more had representation from eight of the provinces in Canada, including four members from Quebec. Their representation of one hundred and sixteen in the House of two hundred and forty-five nevertheless was seven short of a majority. Not a single follower of Patenaude had been elected. "Solid" Quebec had denied victory to Meighen.

The Liberals, on the other hand, had suffered a humiliating reverse. They had lost only fifteen seats, their representation declining from one hundred and sixteen out of two hundred and thirty-five to one hundred and two out of two hundred and forty-five, but of the one hundred and two members returned, sixty were from Quebec.[18] Among their defeated candidates were nine cabinet ministers, of whom the Prime Minister was one. The balancing policy of 1921 to 1925 had lost support in the East without gaining adequate compensation in the West.[19] J. E. B. McCready, an old-time Liberal journalist, had expressed eastern resentment in the Charlottetown *Guardian*,

---

[17]D. G. Creighton, *Dominion of the North* (New York, Toronto, 1944), 459.

[18]The other two Quebec seats were won by an Independent Liberal, J. E. A. Dubuc, and the one-time Nationalist leader, Henri Bourassa.

[19]Montreal *Gazette*, Feb. 13, 1926, p. 12, editorial, "The Maritime Provinces."

when he wrote with reference to the budget of 1925: "It is a policy of a government that numbers among its supporters every Bolshevistic, Communistic and Annexationist element in the land."[20] Since Quebec remained true, however, and would so remain while Meighen led the Conservatives, a further bid for western support might yet retrieve the fortunes of the party.

For the Progressives the results were ironical. Gone were the marginal Progressives from British Columbia, the Maritime Provinces, and Ontario. In Ontario only Agnes Macphail and J. W. King survived, the latter by a narrow margin which required a recount to confirm. The Progressive party had become sectional, but even in the West had suffered severely. In Saskatchewan the Liberals had carried fifteen out of twenty-one seats, in Manitoba the Conservatives seven out of seventeen. Even in Alberta, the U.F.A. carried only nine of sixteen seats, though the total was only one short of the ten of 1921. In the result, the sixty-five members of 1921 had declined to twenty-four, and in this number the Albertan Progressives now almost equalled the Manitoban.[21] To such a pass had a harvest-time election, King's promise to lower the tariff and build the Hudson Bay Railway, the diversion of interest among Saskatchewan farmers to economic action and the creation of the Wheat Pool, and the intervention of the Dunning Government,[22] brought the Progressives who in 1921 had seemed to threaten the seats of power in Ottawa.

The group of twenty-four, however, despite its numbers, was in a stronger position than that of the sixty-five of 1921. The scant margin between Conservatives and Liberals gave the Progressives of 1925 a definite balance of power. No administration could exist except at their discretion and on their sufferance. The relative strengthening of the Albertan element made them more than ever inclined to accept this position. With it went a heavy responsibility for what the administration they chose to support might do, and for the continuance or termination of the life of the Fifteenth Parliament.

[20]Quoted in Montreal *Gazette*, May 24, 1926, p. 12.
[21]The *Canadian Annual Review*, 1925-6, pp. 22 and 36-41, is the most convenient source for the above details.
[22]*Grain Growers' Guide*, XIII, Nov. 11, 1925, p. 5, editorial, "The Progressive Defeat."

On the morrow of the election, none the less, the question was not what the Progressives, but what Prime Minister King, would do. The extent of the Conservative recovery, the position of the party as the largest group, the defeat of King himself, all created the natural expectation that the Prime Minister would offer his resignation and advise the Governor-General to call on Meighen to take office. Yet King remained prime minister; and indeed his administration had a perfect legal and constitutional right to meet the House and seek its verdict on the issue. He announced on November 5, 1925, that of three courses open to him, resigning, advising an immediate dissolution, or meeting parliament, he proposed to meet parliament and seek its verdict.[23] What its verdict would be would depend upon the action of the Progressive group. King could quite reasonably expect that group to be prepared to co-operate. Whatever its tactical strength in the House, it had suffered a serious reverse, which clearly would prove to be permanent. Reluctant as the Albertan members might be to support a Liberal administration, which could not fully meet their views on current policy, or on group government, the Manitoba Progressives could have no reason to prefer a Conservative administration as an alternative. Nor could Progressive members, more than any others, be expected to forgo their annual indemnity, which would be forfeited by a dissolution of the House before fifty days of the new session had elapsed. Even temporary support would give King time to strengthen his hold on the West by making concessions which his Quebec followers, faced by the alternative of a Conservative administration, would have to accept. The Progressive dilemma, that the two old parties were not identical, in the eyes of the Manitoba Progressives at least, had been the secret of King's four years of office, and might prove the cornerstone of a second administration, which could appeal to the country at a later date, and in more favourable circumstances.

[23] *Manitoba Free Press*, Nov. 5, 1925, p. 1; that he had the right to meet the House was, of course, vehemently denied by his political opponents; see the Montreal *Gazette*, Nov. 6, 1925, p. 12, editorial, "Whom the Gods Would Destroy," to the effect that King had done what was expected of him, but it was unfortunate he should drag down Liberalism with him, and "unthinkable that the Governor-General would grant him a dissolution on defeat in the House."

Such a calculation, however, could easily overlook the genuine independence and impartiality of the Albertan Progressives. The Albertans were an element which would ensure that Progressive support would be conditional, and that the Progressives could not simply be counted as Liberals in a hurry. The Albertans might, should events so develop, consider themselves, like the Governor-General, above partisan considerations.

Having elected his course,[24] King now set himself to strengthen his hold on the West, and to reach an arrangement with the Progressives. Approaches were made to Premier Dunning which resulted in his coming into the Liberal cabinet in June 1926, as Minister of Railways and Canals. A seat for the Prime Minister was found in Prince Albert; the West having so long refused to come to King, King was at last going to the West.

The Progressives, for their part, were in a conciliatory mood. Their leader, Robert Forke, was aware that the Liberal government could survive only by means of an open arrangement with the Progressives. On November 19, 1925, two weeks after King's announcement of November 5, he acknowledged a letter from J. W. Dafoe, to which he said he was not surprised that an interview Dafoe had had with King had proved unsatisfactory. "The Premier must understand," Forke declared, "that if he expects Progressive support, the Progressives will have to have some say as to what legislation comes before the House." At the same time, western Liberal members would have to cease their attempts to divide the Liberals and Progressives.[25] Forke was also reported as being sure the Albertan members would support an open arrangement with the Liberals; of only one or two of the Saskatchewan Progressives was he doubtful. For his own part, he was content to see the political leadership of the West go to Dunning. As for general policy, he thought it evident that tariff reductions could not be hoped for, but that it would be possible to insist on there being no increase.[26]

[24]*Can. H. of C. Debates*, 1926-7, I, p. 439.

[25]Dafoe Papers, Robert Forke to Dafoe, Nov. 19, 1925.

[26]*Ibid.*, Dafoe to Clifford Sifton, Dec. 5, 1925, report of an interview with Robert Forke.

The moderate, not to say lukewarm, views of the Progressive leader were substantial and sensible, but were to be modified in their application by the U.F.A. delegation. The members of the U.F.A. group met separately before the Progressive caucus was held, and decided that they should sit to the left of the Speaker. Moreover, to assert the independence of the group, it was further decided that "it would be in [their] best interests to obtain a legislative programme from both King and Meighen."[27]   When the Progressive group as a whole was organized, H. E. Spencer, U.F.A. member for Battle River, was elected secretary and whip, while Forke was retained as House leader. The group was organized on the basis of each provincial group being independent, and there was "a distinct understanding that each group retains its identity and that the House organization is only for the purpose of co-ordinating our efforts on questions of legislation."[28]   The Progressives accepted the U.F.A. proposal to obtain the views of the Liberals and Conservatives on a programme of fourteen points, and King and Meighen informed them what they were respectively prepared to carry out in co-operation with the group.[29]   The Progressives were reluctant to assume the balance of power or to make a choice between the parties; in a straw vote taken early in January, the result was 12 to 10 to support the Conservatives. A second vote, taken presumably after King's and Meighen's replies had been received, was 19 to 5 in favour of supporting the Liberals.[30]   The reluctance to make "a choice of evils," and Albertan suspicion of Forke's gentle pressure to commit the group to outright participation in the administration with the Liberals, go far to explain the group's uncertain course. As it was, the support agreed upon was to be support in the House only, and only to the programme of legislation.[31]   No Pro-

[27]Spencer Files, "Minute of U.F.A. members meetings," Jan. 4, 1926.

[28]*The U.F.A.*, Feb. 1, 1926, p. 4, report by Robert Gardiner on the opening of the session; *Grain Growers' Guide*, IX, Jan. 13, 1926, p. 27.

[29]*The U.F.A.*, Feb. 1, 1926, p. 4; *Can. H. of C. Debates*, 1926, I, pp. 213-14; text of Forke's letter to Meighen and Meighen's reply; for King's reply see *Manitoba Free Press*, Feb. 12, 1926, p. 1. See also Appendix D.

[30]*Manitoba Free Press*, July 28, 1926, pp. 1 and 3, report of Forke's speech on accepting the Progressive nomination in Brandon.

[31]See statement by Forke and Spencer, published in *The U.F.A.*, March 11, 1926, p. 4.

gressive member was to enter the cabinet, and there was no assurance given that the group collectively, or its members individually, would support the administration in all its acts or for all purposes.

That this modification was the work of the Albertan delegation there can be no doubt; Forke wrote J. W. Dafoe while the arrangements were being made:

Perhaps you are fairly well informed in regard to what is taking place at Ottawa. The Executive of the Progressive Group have been meeting a Committee of the Government to discuss proposed legislation as proposed in the Speech from the Throne, Old Age Pensions, etc. These meetings have been satisfactory as there seems to be no serious difference of opinion in regard to the main features of the legislation promised. When we come to the more detailed examination of the Bills, there may be some difficulty.

I must say there seems to be a very reasonable spirit in our Group, and that instead of taking a critical position in the House, they will have to defend the legislation that they have had a share in preparing.

I took your advice and stated to the Caucus that I believed our position would be strengthened if we had two of our group in the Cabinet. The Premier seemed to be quite anxious for this. I am not sure that all the members of his Cabinet were of his opinion. After some time, I felt sure that if any of our Group joined the Cabinet, there would be no representation from Alberta. While not exactly hostile to the idea, . . . the inclination on the part of Alberta, was that it would not be advisable at this time, . . . but there was to be open co-operation with the government on a legislative basis.

I have tried to impress upon our Group the fact that we were responsible for keeping the Liberals in power, and that it was not only a case of getting some legislation we thought desirable—but that it was our duty to assume some of the responsibility of the government. I have met the Premier frequently to discuss the situation. He is going West tonight and I understand will see Mr. Dunning. I think I have been able to convince him that Dunning's presence here would not create difficulty with the Progressives.

For himself the post of Minister of Agriculture had been suggested, but that, in the circumstances, was out of the question.[32] The Albertan Progressives had put their stamp upon the agreement, and would be free to vote against the

[32]Dafoe Papers, Forke to Dafoe, Jan. 28, 1926.

administration, should circumstances in their opinion demand it.   The responsibility of keeping the King Government, or any government in power, was and would remain subordinate to their responsibility to their constituents and occupational group. The original division of the Progressives, into proponents of a radical party and those of an economic group, remained embedded in the representation of 1926, and was to affect the development of events greatly.

Yet the rather doctrinaire exercise in group government to which the Progressives were committed was fraught with great danger to the group.   The political tension was extreme, and the situation might develop in unexpected ways, the group be divided and the party destroyed in a new election.   Dafoe, watching the scene from Winnipeg, agreed with Forke that he was wise not to enter the cabinet, since the Progressives were not unanimous in the opinion that he should.   Crerar, too, had been sounded out, but the Progressives themselves were averse to his entering the cabinet.   Dafoe was, however, doubtful how the arrangement made would work out.   Meighen was troubled by dissensions in his party, powerful influences being at work to replace him by R. B. Bennett.   Hence Meighen was fighting, like King, for his political life.

If Meighen can get in and demand a dissolution [wrote Dafoe] he is safe; otherwise he may have very serious trouble on his hands.   One of my reasons for wanting to see a coalition was that if a new deal of this kind were made the Government, in the event of defeat, might reasonably ask the Governor-General for a dissolution; whereas a purely party government, already in minority, would probably be obliged without question to turn over the reins of office to Meighen. It is very obvious that Mr. Meighen is playing for very high stakes; and I shouldn't be surprised if his nerve is beginning to break under the strain.[33]

This analysis, by the shrewdest political observer of his day, who was, as in 1916 and 1917, working behind the political scenes to shape the course of events, touched on the high tension of the situation in which were involved the political careers of two men still young in politics, and, with these careers, the fiscal policy of the country and the future character of the

[33]*Ibid.*, Dafoe to Forke, Feb. 15, 1926.

British Commonwealth. It lay with the Progressives, either as a united group deliberately, or as a divided one by default, to give to King or Meighen the immense advantage on dissolution of going, as leader of the government, to an electorate ripe for a decisive verdict. To the play of these great and subtle forces the practice of group government seemed hardly adequate.

Meighen had already read the lesson of the election, and had attempted to counter King's bid for western and Progressive support by a bid for a following in the province of Quebec. The Hamilton speech, directed to the electors in the Bagot by-election, was an attempt to undo the results of conscription by suggesting that, before Canada engaged in another overseas war, a general election should be held.[34] The proposal exceeded even Laurier's "Parliament must decide" condition, which King had observed in the Chanak affair of 1922. For it there was a dubious precedent, the discussion in the Borden cabinet as to the advisability of a general election in 1914.[35] It was, however, an approach to Quebec which risked support among English-speaking Conservatives, and the indifference with which Quebec received it was matched by the uneasiness it aroused among Meighen's English-speaking followers. Meighen had made his throw and had failed.

With the open but conditional support of the Progressives, then, and faced by a leader of the opposition whose position was only less desperate than its own, the Liberal government was able to meet the House on January 7, 1926. The Prime Minister was absent, wooing the electors on the banks of the Saskatchewan; the front bench was almost solidly French, as all but four of the English-speaking ministers had been defeated. Lapointe at once arose to move a resolution justifying the government in carrying on and pitched to the ear of the Progressives: "That in the opinion of this House, in view of the recent general election, the government was justified in retaining office and in summoning parliament, and the government is entitled to retain office, unless defeated by a vote of this House

[34]A quotation from the text of a report of the speech is printed in Dawson, *Constitutional Issues*, 411-12.

[35]Henry Borden (ed.), *The Memoirs of the Rt. Hon. Robert Laird Borden* (2 vols., Toronto, 1937), I, 462.

equivalent to a vote of want of confidence."[36] Meighen moved
an amendment to a motion for precedence censuring the government for continuing in office.[37] The debate was prolonged and
bitter, but nineteen of the Progressives stood by the government in voting down the Meighen amendment, and the motion
itself carried without a division.[38]

The vote, however, was one hundred and eleven to one
hundred and two when the Address was carried by a division
in which all the Progressives supported the government.[39]
Lapointe then moved the adjournment of the House until
March 15. After a spirited debate, in which H. Stevens moved
the investigation of certain charges against the administration of the Department of Customs and Excise,[40] the motion
to adjourn was carried by a solid Liberal and Progressive
majority.[41] Even so, the opposition had prolonged debate until
March 3.

When the House met on March 15, the situation was greatly
improved. Prime Minister King was back as member for
Prince Albert. Hon. C. A. Dunning, as Minister of Railways
and Canals, was a pledge to the West that the Hudson Bay
Railway would be built. Further evidence of western Liberal
and Progressive influence followed when the budget was brought
down in March, in which a severe cut in the duties on motor
cars was proposed;[42] the reduction had the merit of offering
something to the Progressives while risking only isolated seats
in industrial Canada. The legislative programme as a whole
was such as the Progressives might be expected to support, as
they had participated in drawing it up. It appeared that King
had weathered the crisis.

In the adjourned, as in the first meeting of the House, however, the Conservative charges of misconduct in the Customs
Department had to be faced. Some misconduct there had been,

[36] Can. H. of C. Debates, 1926, I, p. 4.
[37] Ibid., p. 6.
[38] Ibid., pp. 190-1; the five Progressives voting with the Conservatives were
A. T. Boutillier, Vegreville; M. N. Campbell, Mackenzie; A. M. Carmichael, Kindersley; W. R. Fansher, Last Mountain; and W. T. Lucas, Camrose.
[39] Ibid., pp. 629-30.
[40] Ibid., p. 700.
[41] Ibid., pp. 801-2.
[42] Ibid., III, p. 2450.

for the customs tariff, itself a great corruptor of public morals, had been reinforced by that other great corruptor, prohibition, to expose the public, the service, and even the ministers of the Crown, to quite unusual temptations. These had not always been resisted, either under the administration of the Liberals or of the Conservatives. The matter was now one for which the Liberal government was technically responsible. The Select Committee which had been investigating the Stevens charges presented its report on June 18. The opposition moved, on June 22, what was in effect a vote of censure on the government for its administration of the Customs Department, and the Progressive group was faced with an unhappy choice.[43]

The group had undertaken, without compromising its general independence or that of its members, to support the government's declared legislative programme. It had not undertaken to support it on its administrative record, nor could it, as a professedly independent group, afford to support it on a matter so incriminating as the Customs Scandal. The western voters, highly experienced in political corruption and puritanical in consequence, would have dealt shortly with representatives who supported a government with a tarnished record. By June 23, it became apparent that all the Progressives could not be relied upon to support the government. The views of the dissenters were expressed by W. T. Lucas, who with A. T. Boutillier had already on June 15 broken with the Liberals on the question of the transfer of the natural resources of Alberta.[44]

There are those [he said] who think that tonight the fate of the Liberal party is at stake. Mr. Speaker, I am not concerned with the fate of the Liberal party or of the Conservative party, but I am vitally concerned with the fate of the Progressive movement, a movement that many of our people are looking forward to as the one hope of cleaning up our public life and bringing about a better condition of affairs in this fair Canada of ours. . . . When I think of those people back in Alberta from whom I come, who had got almost to the point of despair, feeling they could not trust to the party machine-picked candidates to carry out their pledges and their promises, and who said, "We must pick out men from among ourselves, and we will make sacrifices to pay their campaign expenses so they will not be bound

[43]*Ibid.*, V, pp. 4832-3.
[44]*Ibid.*, IV, p. 3922.

to any political party . . . ," I would certainly be miscreant to my trust if I did not stand up for the principles they sent me to maintain and uphold in parliament.[45]

Lucas declared he had no intention of compromising his principles because of the threat of dissolution and a general election.

It was this hard core of doctrinaire Progressivism, fired by resentment at the handling of the transfer of control of the natural resources of Alberta, which threatened the King Government with defeat,[46] and precipitated King's extraordinary action in advising the Governor-General to dissolve the House before the vote on the resolution of censure was taken. As King himself said on July 23:

> The support given to the Liberal party by the Progressives and other members was not a matter of bargain and barter. . . . It was a matter of honorable co-operation with respect to a known programme of legislation, arrived at in the open, and openly avowed by all the parties concerned. The moment the relations between the parties concerned ceased to have that open and above board character, and it became apparent that, to serve political ends, certain individuals were lending themselves to intrigue, that bargain and barter and party conflict were being substituted for honorable co-operation, that moment I recognized that government in accordance with the high and honorable traditions of Parliament was no longer possible under any leader, and that an appeal from Parliament to the people was in the public interest and inevitable, and I so advised His Excellency the Governor-General.[47]

Such was the reason for the act. The act itself was extraordinary because of the fact that the advice was tendered while the vote on the Stevens amendment was pending, and to that extent was unprecedented and ill advised, in that it looked like an attempt to avoid the censure of the House. That the Prime Minister was entitled otherwise to tender such advice is unquestionable. Whether, in the circumstances, the Governor-General was obliged to accept that advice, was the constitutional issue which altered the political situation at once.

[45]*Ibid.*, V, pp. 4498, 4517. See Lucas's attack on King, reported in Montreal *Gazette*, Aug. 2, 1926, p. 1.

[46]*Can. H. of C. Debates*, 1926, V, p. 4920.

[47]Montreal *Gazette*, July 24, 1926, pp. 1 and 2.

With the constitutional niceties of that situation this narrative is not concerned, but only with the part played by the Progressive group in the staccato action of the political drama which followed. The Governor-General refused a dissolution, and in that, on the whole, the precedents up to 1924 justified him.[48] Meighen, however, when by legal evasion of the law he had formed an administration of acting ministers who did not have to seek re-election, could carry on the administration only with the support of the Progressives. Of this support, the Governor-General sought assurance to the extent of completing the passage of bills then before the House, and to this the Progressives agreed.[49] Such an arrangement, together with the formation of the acting ministry, strongly suggested that Meighen looked not for an administration of any duration, but only for time to complete the business of the session and to prepare to go to the country as the government. Barely had his government been formed, however, when it was deserted by the Progressives whose tolerance had brought it into being. Ten Progressives, Boutillier, Campbell, Coote, Fansher, Gardiner, Garland, Kennedy, Lucas, Macphail, and Spencer, had supported it on the Rinfret amendment to the motion for a parliamentary inquiry into the irregularities in the Customs Department, and, excepting Miss Macphail, on the subsequent vote of want of confidence.[50] On the Robb amendment of July 1 which raised the constitutional issue, fourteen Progressives voted with the Liberals and only three, Boutillier, Fansher, and Lucas, with the government. The motion carried ninety-six to ninety-five, one vote, that of the Progressive, T. W. Bird, being inadvertently cast while paired.[51] Prime Minister Meighen then advised the Governor-General to dissolve parliament.

The Progressives were at once assailed for irresponsible

[48]See E. Forsey, *The Royal Power of Dissolution of Parliament in the British Commonwealth* (Toronto, 1943), for the view that the Governor-General was justified in refusing the advice to dissolve.

[49]Dawson, *Constitutional Issues*, 85-8, quotation from Montreal *Gazette*, July 3, 1926, p. 1, containing the memorandum given to Forke by the Progressive caucus for his guidance.

[50]*Can. H. of C. Debates*, 1926, V, pp. 5155-8 and 5197-8.

[51]*Ibid.*, pp. 5310-11.

conduct in defeating first the King and then the Meighen governments. The charge was denied by the Progressives, on the grounds that the Meighen Government was illegally constituted, and that the refusal of the Governor-General to grant King a dissolution "was unconstitutional and calculated to restore Canada to a purely colonial status."[52] The Progressives, they contended, were an independent group, not committed to supporting either administration in all matters, like party followers. Their sole public obligation was to support the legislative programme of the King Government. They had turned against the King Government, not on its legislative programme, but its administrative record. They were not pledged to support the Meighen Government, but only to assist a ministry they had thought constitutional to complete the work of the session still in hand. It is, of course, generally accepted that it is the function of parliament to sustain the executive and ensure reasonable stability of government, but such a theory of the nature of parliamentary government, the Albertan Progressives at least did not accept; their constitutional doctrine was, in fact, a protest against it. The Progressives, therefore, and the Albertan Progressives in particular, simply did not accept responsibility for maintaining any government in office. Their only concern was to have a legislative programme carried, if not by one administration, then by another.

Were the Progressives throughout the crisis of 1926, it is to be asked, clear-sightedly and deliberately applying the theory of group government to the political circumstances of the Fifteenth Parliament? The picture was by no means so simple. The Progressives, true to the principle of constituency autonomy and legislative independence, were at no time a solid group. Through the events from January to July, three separate groups may be distinguished. One was that of the Manitoban Progressives. The Manitoban Progressives, whose stand was expressed by Forke, undoubtedly wished to support the King Government, and were reconciled to an eventual Liberal-Progressive fusion. Their hopes were destroyed by the Customs Scandal, and thereafter they were flotsam on the parliamentary

[52]Dawson, *Constitutional Issues*, 86-8; *Grain Growers' Guide*, IX, July 15, 1926, p. 1.

waves, drifting with the Liberal party. On June 30, Forke resigned as House leader, giving no public reason for doing so, but was persuaded to continue to act as chairman of the group's House committee for the balance of the session.[53]

The second group was the U.F.A. delegation, whose influence in caucus had led the Progressives to limit their support of the King Government to its legislative programme. The U.F.A. group was in principle completely non-partisan, and was attempting to apply the theory of group government to the rapidly-developing events of the crisis. This theory they had expounded in their reports to *The U.F.A.* In February Robert Gardiner argued that if the claim advanced in Meighen's amendment to Lapointe's resolution at the opening of parliament, that the largest group should be called on to form the government, were accepted, it would interfere with the development of the group government idea by making it impossible for the Governor-General to call on groups ready to co-operate to form a government.[54] E. J. Garland in March expressed similar fears with respect to this Conservative contention, and also to the possibility that the Conservatives might succeed in putting the blame for instability on group government, and so discredit it.[55] Lucas reported in April that what had emerged, from the beginning of the session to that date, was the enmity of both parties to the group system; the Progressives, however, should attempt to maintain the economic group basis of their organization.[56] After the dissolution, *The U.F.A.* editorially, and William Irvine in an article, reviewed the crisis and drew the moral that the use of the power of dissolution to maintain a majority and the party system of which it was a part had been condemned by the events of the session.[57] Wood himself warned that the confusion, caused by the necessity the U.F.A. members had been under of co-operating with groups lacking their own clarity of doctrine and resoluteness of purpose, should not be allowed to encourage a return to "partyism."[58] E. J. Gar-

[53]*Canadian Annual Review*, 1925-6, p. 67.

[54]*The U.F.A.*, Feb. 1, 1926, p. 4.

[55]*Ibid.*, March 11, 1926, pp. 4-5; see also *Can. H. of C. Debates*, 1926, I, p. 189.

[56]*The U.F.A.*, April 15, 1926, pp. 7 and 22.

[57]*Ibid.*, July 15, 1926, p. 3, and Aug. 2, 1926, p. 4.

[58]*The U.F.A.*, Aug. 2, 1926, pp. 1 and 18.

land had also published during the session a thoughtful expo-
sition of the development of the theory and practice of group
government.[59]   In all this there was, to be sure, some modicum
of humbug, but there can be no doubt it was a powerful factor
in guiding the course of the U.F.A. members and Albertan Progressives. As they saw it, since they had not assumed responsibility for sustaining the administration of King or Meighen in
all circumstances, they could not be expected to behave as
though they had.   The one criticism to which they were perhaps
open was that, having failed to modify the conventions of the
House, they should have accepted them in practice until such
time as they were modified.

The third group appeared first in the vote on the resolution
moved by Lapointe on January 8.   Then five members from
Saskatchewan and Alberta availed themselves of the loose ties
of the Progressive caucus to oppose the King Government, and
this they continued to do from time to time.   One was Milton N.
Campbell from Saskatchewan, a former Liberal, but a convert
who believed strongly in the separation of federal and provincial
politics, and in the political purism of the basic Progressive
doctrines.   Two others were A. M. Carmichael and W. R.
Fansher, also from Saskatchewan, both former Conservatives.
The other two, W. T. Lucas and A. T. Boutillier, of whom Lucas
at least was a former Conservative, were U.F.A. members.
They later came out in opposition to the clause safeguarding
separate schools in the agreement for the transfer of natural
resources to Alberta.   This clause had doubtless been inserted
under clerical pressure from Quebec; it is noteworthy that it
was done in January in the absence of Prime Minister King.
It aroused the sustained hostility of the two U.F.A. members
and was used by Premier Brownlee as the reason for rejecting
the proposed terms of transfer and as an issue in the provincial
election of 1926.   Thus the old separate school question played
a minor but significant part in the crisis of 1926.

It is impossible, therefore, to explain in clear-cut terms the
part the Progressives played in precipitating the election of
1926.   The spirit of independence, the theory of group govern-

[59]E. J. Garland, "The Farmers' Group in Politics" (*Canadian Forum*, VI, June'
1926, 270-2).

ment, the school question, perhaps old party ties, all contributed. Three things do seem clear. First, the Progressives as a group acted perfectly honestly. Second, responsibility could not be required of them as a group when they were not able, indeed on principle not willing, to act as a unit. Third, no such group, unless it had been fanatically inspired, could possibly have exercised under the conventions of parliamentary government the balance of power. Either parliamentary government or the group would have been destroyed. Third parties, it would seem, survive in British parliamentary practice only when one major party or the other possesses a clear majority.

The constitutional crisis of 1926, whatever its interest as a constitutional question, cleared the political air like a thunderstorm. The ensuing campaign had many issues, the Customs Scandal, the tariff, the Hudson Bay Railway, but this time, unlike 1925, there was an overriding issue, the question of whether the Governor-General should have refused the Liberal Prime Minister a dissolution. On this issue King seized with the instinct of victory. It was such as to awaken all the atavistic colonial resentments of Grit democracy and French-Canadian nationalism. Lord Byng's offence was that he was an Englishman and a lord, representing an outmoded imperial relationship. Canadians, sensitive on the score of their emerging nationalism, were easily persuaded that they had been treated as a colony might be treated, and the response was instant and decisive. The result of 1926 was the political expression of the new Canadian nationalism, sprung from the war, and since groping for expression. The constitutional crisis of 1926 first gave it a domestic issue of a traditional character on which the electorate could speak with point and emphasis.

Behind this popular sentiment, and operating on the leaders who knew the underlying issues, was a struggle over the character of the Commonwealth, a struggle which involved the issue of a centralized Empire or an independent Canada. That struggle had come to a head in the Commonwealth Conference of 1923.[60] J. W. Dafoe, who had been on the outskirts of the Conference as a press representative, knew what went on within,

[60]R. M. Dawson, *The Development of Dominion Status, 1900-1931* (Toronto, 1937), 272-94.

and perceived the bearing of the issue on Canadian domestic politics. In 1923, and before the Conference, he had written presciently:

Our official Liberal party in Canada is opportunistic; its objective [is] office. It has Liberal elements, but its controlling elements are in reality Conservative. We shall not have reality in Canadian politics until there is a re-alignment—the left wing of the Liberals and the Progressives joining up against a combination of the right wing of the Liberals and the Conservatives. I don't know when the re-alignment will come about. There are influences under the surface making for it; but there are powerful obstacles in the way. The next election will probably result in a strengthened Conservative and a weakened Liberal party, giving the balance of power to the Progressives. If the latter are by that time a disciplined, unified party they may become the dominant half of a new Liberal party, which might—probably would—find itself in opposition. But the Progressives are themselves divided into two camps; they have a left wing devoted to a class-conscious group programme.

One of the difficulties [he continued] in the way of an alignment, which is much to be desired in the interests of the country, is the unsettled state of the question of Imperial relations. This is not realized, but it is the fact. A fusion between the French Conservatives (most of whom call themselves Liberals and are a part of the official Liberal party) with the English Conservatives is made difficult because of the inclination of the latter to wave the flag and pound the big imperial drum, particularly when they are in opposition. The French will never agree to a centralized Empire or to a joint foreign policy really controlled from London for which we will be responsible because of the policy of "consultation" which is really farcical so far as it purports to give us any real measure of control. If this question were cleared up definitely, Quebec would thereafter emerge as the bulwark of a Canadian Conservatism, resting upon economic foundations, tenderness for property rights, opposition to public ownership of utilities, dislike of forward labor policies, and a general attitude in favor of the view that to him that hath shall be given.[61]

The constitutional issue of 1926, therefore, involving as it did a seeming intervention in Canadian domestic politics, appealed to Quebec. It also appealed to Progressives and to those who, having voted Progressive, had returned to the Liberal party.

[61]Dafoe Papers, Dafoe to Alfred E. Zimmern, Feb. 22, 1923.

The Progressives, partly through the leadership of the Manitoban elements under the influence of Clifford Sifton and J. W. Dafoe, and partly out of a sturdy nationalism and a tendency to isolation born of dislike of entanglement in European affairs, had advocated, from the drafting of the Farmers' Platform of 1919, support of the League of Nations, that vehicle of Canadian nationalism, and a re-definition of imperial relations.

So it was that King was enabled to turn from the paths of frustration in which he had walked since 1921, and set his feet on a way which led to a career now become legendary. In the constitutional issue he had found at last an integrating formula which combined the "nationalism" of Quebec with the radicalism of the West, and drew the necessary fringe of seats from the Maritime Provinces, Ontario, and British Columbia. By exploiting this sense of nationalism, which constituted a broad covering for the racial complex of Quebec, the self-assertive radicalism of the West, the dogged independence of the old Grits and Reformers of Ontario and the Maritime Provinces, the covert resentments of the Irish Canadians, the Acadians, and the European Canadians of the West, the Liberal leader, aided by the oncoming boom, was able to turn the minds of his followers from the frustrating conflicts of groups and sections, and lead them forward towards the legislative independence embodied in the Statute of Westminster. King became in 1926, as though by destiny prepared, the authentic exponent of the political nationalism of the Canadian democracy.

Naturally, there were, in the hodge-podge which constitutes any electoral appeal, other inducements to vote Liberal. The Maritime Provinces were promised a commission to investigate the causes of the prolonged stagnation which had prevailed in those provinces. The West was reassured that the Liberal party, if returned to power, would build the Hudson Bay Railway, and relieve it of its long-standing dependence on the central Canadian railways. These, however, were the commonplaces of any general election, and only the lessons of 1925 made the promises so particular and so emphatic. What they signified was that the Liberal party, after long subservience to the financial interests of Montreal, to that "Non-Partisan League of Montreal," in the phrase much loved of J. A. Stevenson, was reverting in fact to its traditional character of the party of minority groups and of the primary producers of the Laurentian hinterlands, as their defender against "British" domination and metropolitan exploitation. The schism of 1917 was being healed, and the Liberal party once more was coming to rest, broad-based and secure, on the rock of Quebec and the plains of Saskatchewan. To the extent that Liberalism again represented the minorities and the primary producers, the Progressive movement had been justified.

To the political nationalism of the Liberals, Meighen had opposed the economic nationalism of his consistent protectionism. That political and economic nationalism should be opposed to one another was one of the main paradoxes of Canadian political life. It was, however, a perfectly explicable paradox. The economic nationalism of the Conservative party was prevented from becoming political nationalism by the "imperialism" of its members, this "imperialism" being the British-Canadian counterpart of the "nationalism" of French Canada, and both the expression of racial sentiment. On the other hand, the political nationalism of the Liberal party, which in the French core of the party was economic also, was prevented from becoming frankly protectionist by the need of retaining political allies in the Maritime Provinces and the continental West. A discerning commentator, J. A. Stevenson, wrote:

The truth is the two historic parties have persisted in maintaining in their avowed principles and programmes a strange inconsistency which is largely responsible for the futile stagnation of our political life. The Conservatives, while favourable to the wider political unit and the promotion of a solidarity of the British nation in the field of foreign relations and other spheres, have sedulously championed the ideal of the narrow economic unit involved in local protectionism. The Liberals, on the other hand, while willing to preach, if not to grasp, the advantages of the wider economic unit offered by free trade, are resolute devotees of the narrow political unit, entailed in local nationalism.[62]

In 1930, when R. B. Bennett had replaced Arthur Meighen, and when depression gripped the land, the story was to be

[62]J. A. Stevenson, "Mr. Meighen's Opportunity" (*Canadian Forum*, V, Dec., 1924, 75-7).

different; then economic and political nationalism were to fuse, and Quebec was to give the Conservative party 25 supporters.

For the Progressive movement, the election of 1926 was the effective end. All the factors making for its dissolution in 1925 were still operative, some more than ever. There was, for example, no electoral organization for the Progressives of Manitoba and Saskatchewan, and no time to improvise one. Of the Progressive movement, John Evans, Progressive member for Saskatoon, was to say in 1931, when analysing before the annual convention of the organized farmers the causes of the failure in Saskatchewan:

> The different organizations in the provinces let go their political organizations. You lost your organizations in the constituencies, and we were left to ourselves. In one or two constituencies—Rosetown— we organized under what is called the Farmer's Political Association. That is what every one should have done and every constituency should have kept going. That was not done. Then the Liberal-Progressives deserted us. They did it for this reason and I want to be quite frank here. They were left to pay their own expenses in 1925. The enemy made them a target in the election of 1926 and over to the Liberal side they went. Why? Because the people in the constituencies had not the interest to keep their organizations going or the interest that would enable them to look after their own business.[63]

Lack of funds and organization led to understandings between Liberals and Progressives in some forty-eight seats across the country;[64] the Progressive party in 1926 had crumbled for want of foundation.

In these difficulties, the Progressives had to face the fact that in Saskatchewan, not only had Dunning gone to the federal cabinet, but the new Premier, J. G. Gardiner, a fighting Liberal of the unsentimental school, was in open alliance with the federal Liberals against the revived Conservatives. Thenceforth there was no pretence that things had changed. The battle lines were drawn as in the good old days of the classic party structures. Only one candidate was nominated as a

[63]Minutes of Annual Convention of U.F.C. (Saskatchewan Section), 1931, p. 309.
[64]This number is calculated from information in the *Parliamentary Companion*, 1927.

Liberal-Progressive. Of the ten surviving Progressive candidates, nine won their nominations on personal grounds or with Conservative support. Only four were to be elected. The lone Liberal-Progressive was also returned. For the rest, sixteen Liberals, and no Conservatives, were elected. In Manitoba, the great Conservative success of 1925, aided by three-cornered contests, and the lack of campaign funds among the Progressives, led to a frank alliance of Liberals and Progressives, an alliance confirmed by Forke's entry into the Liberal cabinet after the election. The independence of the Bracken Government was unaffected, and this, with the strong proportion of continuing Conservative support in the Progressive ranks, prevented a complete merging of Liberals and Progressives in Manitoba. That province returned seven Liberal-Progressives and four Progressives to four Liberals, two Labour members, and no Conservatives. In Alberta the U.F.A., strained though it was by the agricultural depression, loss of membership after 1921, and the great effort of creating the Wheat Pool, remained unshaken and undiminished. It had established a political faith and created an organization which won elections with a mechanical regularity. The provincial Liberal and Conservative parties had been revived, but Brownlee had swept them aside in the provincial election of 1926. In the federal election the U.F.A. phalanx returned to Ottawa eleven in number, to carry on the tradition of legislative independence the Manitoban Progressives had foregone, or were to forgo.

In Ontario, the Progressives, who nominated only ten candidates, with six Liberal-Progressives, were erased except for J. W. King and Agnes Macphail, whose continued presence at Ottawa was a tribute to her personality rather than to the political strength of the farmers' movement.

In the result, King led back to Ottawa one hundred and eighteen Liberals, reinforced by and assured of a majority by the support of eleven Liberal-Progressives. After five years of parliamentary instability, there was once more a parliamentary and national majority in Canada, drawn from every province, section, and community. In opposition sat ninety-one Conservatives, with members from seven of the nine provinces, Manitoba and Saskatchewan being unrepresented. Quebec, however, had not been won by the Hamilton speech, and Meighen's leadership was forfeit. With the Conservatives on the Speaker's left were to sit eleven U.F.A., nine Independent Progressive and three Labour members, the various remnants of the great upheaval of 1921.[65] The disruption of the classic parties, begun by the denial of the sectional demands of the West in 1911, and completed by the election of 1917, was ended. Two composite, national parties, one in power and one in opposition, dominated the House. Government once more rested on the sure foundation of a disciplined party majority. Canadian unity, so severely tried by economic sectionalism and communal hostility, was renewed on the old basis of sectional compromise, the denial of class differences, and the sovereignty of caucus.

[65]All details given are from the *Canadian Annual Review*, 1926-7, pp. 47-53; note, however, that the Liberal-Progressives meant to preserve their identity in accordance with the terms of the resolution passed by the Liberal-Progressive members in Winnipeg on September 22, 1926 (*Can. H. of C. Debates*, 1926-7, I, p. 10).

The Progressive Tradition in Canadian Politics to 1935

T H E Progressive party came to an end with the election of 1926.   The pattern of Canadian politics had resumed its familiar outlines.   The Liberal party was once more a nation-wide and composite party of the classic North American type, and in parliament it was opposed by a party also nation-wide and composite.   None of the independent groups enjoyed, or seemed likely to attain, the status of a third party.

General circumstances were in accord with this return to the familiar in politics.   The political stridencies of the early twenties were mellowed in the golden cadences of the great boom.   Men united in money-making, and the reefs of communal and class animosity were submerged by the tide of prosperity.   Canadians busied themselves with the definition of national status, ignoring the unsolved sectional and social problems the post-war years had posed, and ignoring also the disintegration of the constitutional structure of the federation. As the Minister of Finance announced surplus after surplus, the federal government reduced the war debt and rested in its new-found stability, sharply avoiding the waking of dogs so lately laid asleep.[1]

It is not enough, however, to say that the Progressive revolt, an expression of sectional and agrarian protest primarily, had been smothered by a new surge of nationalism and the revival of prosperity.   The causes of the ending of the farmers' political

[1]*Report of the Royal Commission on Dominion-Provincial Relations*, Book 1 (Ottawa, 1940), 132-3.

movement were at once more particular and more fundamental than the broad pattern of national development reveals.

Among these causes was the passing of the reform movement, itself a powerful undercurrent of Progressivism. It had passed partly because its work had been consummated. Prohibition was the law of the land, and the nation was dubiously viewing its results. In province after province west of the Quebec border civil service reform, and health, labour, child welfare, and other forms of social legislation, had become commonplace. Even Ottawa had been stirred by the breath of reform, as in the instance of the Civil Service Act of 1920, and into the eastern provinces of steady ways the new spirit was penetrating. In all provinces but Quebec, and in the federation itself, the franchise had been extended to women, and politics, though superficially little affected, were never to be quite the same again. In the particular field of Progressive concern, that of electoral reform, the movement had left sharpened Corrupt Practices Acts and a new seriousness. After the experience of Progressivism, the new electorate, especially west of the Ottawa, would be less corruptible than the old. The scandals which had marked the ending of the frontier era, but which might have been perpetuated by use and wont, became fewer, the "machines" less well organized, the voting less predictable.

The reform movement died not only of success. It was also cut short and mutilated by the war of 1914-18. The climax of the movement had come in the midst of the war, with the great Wilsonian reforms in the United States, and, in Canada, the provincial reforms, particularly in the West. Thereafter the zeal and energy which might have carried it further, the sense of mission which fired it, were diverted into the struggle for victory. In the United States, the diversion was caused by the American entry into the war, in Canada by the formation of the Union Government. The war was indeed interpreted by Wilson, himself strongly influenced by Progressivism, as a struggle to advance democracy. The American Progressives had gone on crusade in 1917, and thereafter the League of Nations, in great part the outcome of the North American idealism which both Canadian and American Progressivism embodied, increasingly drew their attention away from domestic reform.   Support of the League, it will be remembered, was the first plank in the New National Policy.

At the same time, the post-war reaction against radicalism of all kinds, in Canada centred on the Winnipeg strike, reduced the support, and hampered the advance of the continuing reformers.   It was a clear indication that public opinion had absorbed about all the reform it could in one political generation, and that the point of saturation had been reached.   Though the farmers' conventions and labour continued to urge new advances, and though the Progressives were in parliament and in power in three provinces, not many reforms reached the statute books after 1921.

The reform movement, however, was much wider than the Progressive movement; the Progressives enjoyed no monopoly of reforming zeal, as the imperfect record of the Union Government and the platform of the Liberal party of 1919 demonstrated.   The Canadian Progressive movement was basically agrarian in character, an expression of the farmers' revolt against the old National Policy and its system of fiscal protection, and against post-war inflation, indebtedness caused by wartime expansion, and the return to the free market in wheat with the termination of the Wheat Board in 1920.   Any political movement which draws strength from transient and remediable causes is, to that extent, subject to the influence of anything which operates to remove those causes.   The post-war depression had liquidated the inflation; bankruptcy, foreclosure, and hard work had diminished, though not removed, the burden of debt.   The post-war unrest had been soothed by the passage of time.   Into the breach caused by the termination of the Wheat Board had stepped the Wheat Pools, the latest application of the doctrine of self-help.

At the same time, the class character of the Progressive movement, arising from transient resentment, failed to develop a sound basis in doctrine.   In so far as such a basis was provided by the preachments of Henry Wise Wood—and that almost exclusively within the U.F.A.—it was by the development of the doctrine of group organization.   The effect of the doctrine would have been to make the lobby public, and to carry it into the open on the floor of the House.[2]   Such an application of the

²Cooling, *Public Policy*, 20.

idea of the farm bloc to Canadian politics failed under the conditions of the parliamentary system. The way to success lay rather in the organization of a conventional lobby, to influence public opinion and the government and parliament as a whole. This very work had been done with great success by such non-political organizations as the Canadian Council of Agriculture, as it was to be done by its successor, the Canadian Federation of Agriculture.

Moreover, the Progressive party of 1921 had been the result of the propaganda for the New National Policy of the Canadian Council of Agriculture among farmers excited by the break-up of parties, post-war discontents and flushed by political successes in the provinces of Ontario and Alberta, and to a smaller degree in Manitoba and even Saskatchewan. What had been devised as a means of exerting pressure on existing parties had become the platform of a new party. Thus the Council found itself fostering a political party its own propaganda had helped to create. Its constituent provincial organizations found themselves in the same position. Soon, however, the Council and the organized farmers of Ontario, Manitoba, and Saskatchewan withdrew from politics, and only the U.F.A. continued direct political action beyond the decade of the twenties. With the exception of that in Alberta, the character of the farmers' movement had been altering. The decline of the Council of Agriculture, the rise of the Farmers' Union in Saskatchewan, and, above all, the rise of the Wheat Pools to take the place of the Wheat Board and to overshadow or absorb the United Grain Growers and the Saskatchewan Co-operative Elevators, all contributed to turn the farmers away from direct political action and back, in part, to lobbying, but more to economic action alone. The change meant a loss of funds, time, energy, zeal, and men for the political movement.

If the Progressive movement suffered from the decline of the reform movement and the changing organization and character of the agrarian movement, it suffered also from its essentially sectional nature. Western grievances were the chief driving force behind Canadian Progressivism. The remedies for these grievances, and the admission of the West to its due place in making national policy, could be accomplished only by federal action. No merely sectional party could procure such action except by gaining, from all the hazards of a general election, and using, with all its apparent risks, the dangerous instrument of the balance of power.   Only a party capable of an iron discipline could have acted as the fulcrum of the national political balance.   The Progressive party from its very nature, however, lacked the necessary discipline.   The party itself was a protest against such discipline.   Moreover, sectional parties, however constituted, can lead only to futility or to secession.   To futility the Progressive party came, except in so far as it induced the Liberal party to accept in part its programme.

That is to say, under the conventions of parliamentary government prevailing in Canada at the time of the Progressive movement, no third party of significant proportions could long endure.   It had either to destroy those conventions or be destroyed by them.   Thus the failure of Irvine's motion to have parliament adopt the convention that the government would resign only on an explicit vote of want of confidence, foreshadowed the extinction of the Progressives.

It was not merely the prevailing conventions with respect to resignation and dissolution which contributed to the failure of the Progressive third party.   Equally, perhaps more, disastrous was the continuance of the system of single-member constituencies.   The possibility of electing only one member for a given constituency, the necessity of voting for only one candidate, meant that the Progressives, in seeking to become a national party, had either to risk being squeezed out in three-cornered contests, or seek electoral understandings with one or other of the old parties.   A new third party is not necessarily, of course, the victim of this process—as a sectional party it will indeed benefit from it—but in North America the doctrinal flexibility of the old parties makes it easily possible for one or other of them to steal enough of the programme of a new party to bring about its collapse.   Thus W. C. Good's failure to persuade parliament to make proportional representation and the alternative vote part of federal electoral law also foreshadowed the doom of the Progressive party.

Of this lack of viability in third parties, no one had a keener appreciation than W. L. Mackenzie King, and his persistent pursuit of the goal of the re-integration of western with eastern

Liberalism in a composite party was by no means the least of the causes of the failure of the Progressives. Hampered as he was by a curious impercipience of the force behind the Progressive movement, and by the counsel of the reactionary and Laurier Liberal wing of the party until 1925, he none the less saw clearly, and pursued with a constant deviousness, the objective of national unity restored by means of a reunited Liberal party. In the desperate circumstances of 1926, he was at once compelled and enabled to make enough concessions to the West to take much of the remaining wind from the sails of the Progressives, and to re-establish the rule of the government majority in parliament.

The Progressive movement, through the operation of these causes, ended as a movement in 1926. It did not, however, vanish without trace, but left behind a continuing tradition in Canadian politics, visibly embodied in the hyphenated Liberal-Progressives, the undiminished and unrepentant U.F.A. group, the Independent Progressives and the Labour group. Here lay the seed, the phoenix ashes, from which were to spring the new parties of the next decade.

The rebirth of Canadian radicalism was an effect of the great depression of the 1930's. In 1926 the Liberals had swallowed the Manitoban Progressives, wholly or in part, except for those who had returned to their original home in the reviving Conservative party. To the digestion of these Progressives the party now addressed itself with adroitness and alacrity. Forke entered the cabinet as Minister of Immigration in 1926. He had done so as a private member, having resigned the leadership of the party, but with the approval of his colleagues from Manitoba.[3] The Liberal-Progressives henceforth attended the Liberal caucus, although, having stipulated that they should maintain their identity, they also met separately. They did not, however, insist on being seated as a separate group, but allowed the Liberal whips to seat them in rows of seats sandwiched from front to rear between rows of Liberal members. The consequent fellowship of neighbourhood, of the whispered aside, of parliamentary jokes and confidences, greatly aided the process of digestion.

[3]*Canadian Annual Review*, 1926-7, pp. 57-8.

The speed and smoothness of this process must not, of course, be exaggerated. The tradition of independence, the suspicions of the voters back home, were still easily aroused. For example, the budget of 1927 was by no means acceptable to the Liberal-Progressives, and when the amendment, moved by G. G. Coote of the U.F.A., struck an authentic Progressive note on tariff matters, J. A. Glen of Marquette warned the government that the Liberal-Progressives must have assurances of future tax reduction.[4] The warning, though rebuffed at the time by Dunning, did not go unheeded, and the partial independence of the Liberal-Progressives of the Liberal whip was a decided factor in the great consideration with which the West was treated during the remainder of the Sixteenth Parliament, a consideration emphasized by the promotion of Dunning to the office of Minister of Finance in 1929. The Manitoban Progressives had not fought wholly in vain, for, if they had failed to force a realignment of the political elements of the country into progressive and reactionary parties, if they had in the end lain down like lambs in the Liberal party with the lions of Montreal and Ontario, they had forced a lessening of emphasis on the protective elements in national policy, and a broader interpretation of that term.

Meantime, the Alberta Progressives existed as an isolated group, sitting on the Speaker's left, meeting in their own caucus, voting for measures on their merits as they saw them. The doctrines of Wood still guided them, the vigilance of the U.F.A. organization marked their every action, and they permeated the life of the House with their capacity for work, the clarity of their doctrine, the single-mindedness of their conviction. Though they neither made nor unmade governments, they raised the quality of debate and enriched the mind of the House, justifying an existence for which the conventions of parliament at last made grudging provision.

As the parliamentary sessions during the great boom rolled on in undistinguished monotony, as Liberal and Liberal-Progressive blended, as time and prosperity softened the asperities of 1921, as the reconciliation of East and West was prepared in the transfer of the natural resources, as sectional and communal

[4]*Can. H. of C. Debates*, 1926-7, I, 551-2.

rancours dissolved in the emollient of the new political nationalism, the U.F.A. group grew more and more conscious of what
they could not but view as a great betrayal brought about by
intellectual blunders and moral softness. Their sense of mission
sharpened, their conviction of rightness hardened. The role of
gadfly to an easy-going, pragmatic House grew wearisome. To
what purpose to be always right, unless rightness bore fruit in
legislation and action? Not forever could they be content with
Wood's large tolerance and his millennial optimism.

As the feeling developed that new avenues of advance must
be explored, a feeling born of isolation and frustration, there
grew up an affinity of loneliness and purpose, already adumbrated in the events of 1924 to 1926, with the small group of
three Labour members, led by the saintly and indomitable
Woodsworth. As the affinity grew, both in the House and
without, the two groups began to explore the possibilities of
systematizing the cordial relations which had existed since 1921
between labour and the U.F.A. The theory of group government did not preclude, but rather called for, such co-operation.
Wood, though advocating the political co-operation of organized
occupational groups had, it is true, been wary of it in practice,
lest it lead to the formation of a political party and the destruction of the original organizations. Wood, however, was
becoming more and more the venerated sage of the U.F.A., and
less and less its practical leader. The younger men, faced with
the realities of political life in Ottawa, could not but think that
perhaps some way might be found by which the political representatives of organized groups could co-operate, and exchange
the ungrateful role of critics for that of moulders of legislation,
to usher in the new Co-operative Commonwealth already proclaimed by Partridge of Sintaluta[5] and from time to time in the
conventions of the U.F.A.

In May 1932, these considerations brought together the
U.F.A. and Labour members in formal meeting to plan co-
operation. "Much consideration," so runs the minute, "was
given to the problem of Dominion organization. A motion was
moved and seconded that a committee be formed to consider
ways and means of carrying out the wishes of the Group as

[5]E. A. Partridge, *A War On Poverty* (Winnipeg, [1925?]), 208.

expressed during the discussion—that is, drafting a tentative plan of organization for future action thereon." The motion was carried, and J. S. Woodsworth and Robert Gardiner were nominated to constitute such a committee with power to add to their numbers.[6] It was the beginning of a new federal party, designed to be both agrarian and labour.

It was not only at Ottawa that such forces were at work. In the provinces in which the Progressive movement had arisen, there still remained elements which were unreconciled to the re-integration of the old parties. The factors which had stimulated that movement, except for resentment of the Military Service Act of 1917, endured and would come to life in a new depression. In Ontario, the U.F.O. remained to keep alive the old bitterness caused by urban and industrial domination. In the industrial cities a labour movement still flickered. The Bracken Government of Manitoba, by now formally separated from the U.F.M. and still bound by the necessity of holding those Conservative votes which in federal politics were cast for Conservative candidates, continued its austere aloofness from ties with any federal party. In Winnipeg, the Independent Labor party throve on the memory of the strike and the political needs of a great transportation, commercial, and industrial centre. The Manitoba labour and agrarian movements, however, remained distinct and even hostile to one another, the farmers remembering the strike, and devoting their political strength to the local problem of redressing the economic preponderance of Winnipeg by shifting the weight of taxation from land to other sources. Thus the co-operation of farmer and labour, barred by the hostility of Winnipeg and rural Manitoba, was rendered difficult and unlikely. In Saskatchewan the breakup of the provincial Progressives after the revival of the Conservative party, and the advent of the Farmers' Union with its gospel of economic action, prepared the way for the rise of an entirely new party, the Farmer-Labor, which appeared in the provincial election of 1925. In Alberta there remained the U.F.A., theoretically committed to co-operation with labour, and indeed practising it in some measure with the Dominion Labor party of Calgary and Edmonton. In these relics of 1921

[6]Olive Zeigler, *J. S. Woodsworth, Social Pioneer* (Toronto, 1934), 184-5.

were the elements of a new progressive party, which might be organized on a doctrinal basis of class interest and group co-operation in a federation of occupational groups, capable of forming a national majority and seizing power at Ottawa. If these sparks of the old Progressive and labour insurgence of 1921 should be fanned by the winds of a new depression, who could say what flame might not be kindled?

So long as the boom continued and the midsummer rains fell timely in the West, so long as Wood, with his long-run optimism and his current scepticism, remained president of the U.F.A., no progress was possible towards effective group co-operation. But in the autumn of 1929 the great depression began, and with it the great drought. In 1930 Canada, seeking blindly some relief from depression, turned at last to the economic nationalism Meighen had advocated so long and so fruit-lessly. The Conservative party, fired by the eloquence of the new leader, R. B. Bennett, proved irresistible. Solid Quebec was broken, Ontario and Manitoba went protectionist as the dairy farmers voted Conservative, and the party which had originated the National Policy slid into power on ways greased by a few cargoes of New Zealand butter. Prime Minister Bennett proceeded at once to "blast his way" into world markets, applying with extraordinary vigour a policy of pro-tection of unprecedented thoroughness and one of currency depreciation which was also protective, policies which were to crucify the West and the Maritime Provinces.[7] In 1931 the old leader of the U.F.A. was bowed off the stage with every mark of veneration and every assurance that his doctrines would continue to guide and inspire the organization he had made his own. The presidency passed to Robert Gardiner, federal U.F.A. member for Medicine Hat since the famous by-election a decade before. This change of leadership signified that the U.F.A. federal members had taken over the organization with the goodwill of the provincial government and U.F.A. members. Spurred by the deepening distress of the West, they carried the U.F.A. into the Co-operative Commonwealth Federation.

The new party of protest, however, sprang not from the U.F.A. alone. In Saskatchewan had occurred developments at

[7]*Rowell-Sirois Report*, I, 151-7.

least as significant for the Federation as the long rule of the U.F.A. in Alberta. In 1921 there had begun at Ituna, in north-eastern Saskatchewan, the organization of the Farmers' Union of Canada. The inspiration of the organizer, N. H. Schwarz, was the success of co-operation among the organized tobacco and orange growers of the United States. Schwarz's purpose was to create an agency to agitate for a wheat pool. Almost simultaneously, a similar group was organized in the same region, at Kelvington, by L. B. McNamee and J. Thompson, former railway workers. These men were inspired by the concept of the "One Big Union."[8] The two groups corresponded and interacted; Ituna took from Kelvington the principle of the "closed door," Kelvington abandoned its concept of one industrial union for Ituna's ideal of a farmers' union.[9] The new organization taught the coming of "the inevitable class struggle," a struggle to be won by organization, so that "they [the organized farmers] may be enabled to fix their own price above cost of production, a price reasonable towards producer and consumer." "Farmers and workers of the world, unite,"[10] was the slogan of the constitution of the first local.

The new organization marked the beginning of the return to economic as opposed to political action by the farmers of Saskatchewan. Its purpose was to promote class, economic action by the farmers of Canada, and in particular to found a wheat pool. It was by its constitution "non-political and non-sectarian." Political influence the Union proposed to achieve "by co-ordination of the franchise to further our interests in legislation." "We farmers as a class," the constitution of the Union affirmed, "have power in numbers, if thoroughly united in common brotherhood, to give sufficient backing to our representatives in parliament."[11] So powerful did the Union become that its inroads on the membership were an important factor in the

[8]The One Big Union was an industrial union movement in the Canadian West; see H. A. Logan, *Trade Unions in Canada* (Toronto, 1948), 329-30.

[9]Verbal account of George Bickerton, of the United Farmers of Canada (Saskatchewan Section), 1945; also in files of S.G.G.A. and U.F.C.(S.S.).

[10]Files of the Saskatchewan Grain Growers Association and the United Farmers of Canada (Saskatchewan Section), "First minute book of Farmers' Union of Canada, Ituna Lodge No. 1."

[11]*Western Producer*, Dec. 11, 1924, p. 3, "Explanation of the Aims of the Union," by William Thrasher, Secretary.

Grain Growers' Association's withdrawal from politics in 1924, the establishment of the Saskatchewan Pool in face of the opposition of the Saskatchewan Co-operative Elevators in the same year, and the fusion of the old Association with the Union in 1926 as the United Farmers of Canada (Saskatchewan Section).[12]

The extraordinary triumph of the new organization, and for economic over political action was, however, accompanied by a parallel development in politics. The waning of the federal Progressive movement, and the weakness of the provincial party, both caused in part by the absence in Saskatchewan of effective local and provincial political organization, gave rise in 1924 to a new political movement. In December of 1924, the farmers of the federal constituency of Last Mountain—the constituency of J. F. Johnston, Progressive whip at Ottawa—organized, under the leadership of G. H. Williams, the Farmers' Political Association.[13] It was at once decided to make the organization provincial in extent, to establish a central board of directors, and to draft a political platform. The purpose was to remedy the great fault revealed by the provincial Progressive movement, the lack of organization, central direction, and co-operation among like-minded groups.

In its objectives, however, the Political Association was much more radical than the Progressives, and inspired by the same spirit as the Farmers' Union. These objectives were: "(1) That normal production must be guaranteed and that the maximum of production must be steadily sought after; (2) That the equitable distribution of the wealth produced must be effected; (3) That no economic group must be allowed to dominate the other economic groups of the social structure." Thus G. H. Williams formulated the objective of the Association, and drove his statement home with a quotation from J. M. Keynes: "The worker no longer believes in the fetish of the national cake."[14]

[12]This rather awkward name was suggested by E. A. Partridge, the fiery old prophet of farmers' organization in the West, and was an inspiration which broke a deadlock over the name of the united organization, just as Rice Sheppard's suggestion, in the early hours of the morning, of "The United Farmers of Alberta, their Motto 'Equity'," broke a similar deadlock in the union of the Grain Growers of Alberta and the Alberta Society of Equity.

[13]*Western Producer*, Dec. 31, 1924, p. 5, letter to editor from G. H. Williams.

[14]*Ibid.*, Feb. 26, 1925, p. 7, letter from G. H. Williams.

The platform, when drafted, not only stated these objectives, but also provided for an elaborate system of nomination of candidates by any six enrolled members of the local political associations through school district primaries, municipal primaries, and conventions of electoral districts.[15]   In essence, this was an attempt to supply that organizational and financial basis without which no political action was possible, made at the time when the Grain Growers' Association had rejected the Alberta union of industrial and political action in 1923[16] and had withdrawn from political action in 1924.[17]   From 1925 on, as the Conservatives revived and the Progressives disintegrated, the Farmers' Political Association and the indefatigable Williams had a losing struggle to wage.   Co-operation with the Independent Labor party of Saskatchewan, however, pointed to an experience more promising than that of the Progressives.[18]   In the election of 1929 they succeeded in nominating three candidates under the name of the Farmer-Labor party but elected none.   This only underlined the necessity of finding some initial help to launch a broader movement, and recourse was had to the obvious source of aid, the United Farmers of Canada (Saskatchewan Section), the economic organization of the Saskatchewan farmers.

Once more a political movement, as in the days of the Nonpartisan League, attempted to capture an economic organization, and once more, as in 1919 in Alberta, depression and drought came to its aid.   In 1929 a resolution to commit the U.F.C. (S.S.) to political action was debated and rejected.[19] In 1930 an attempt to amend the constitution of the association, in order to permit political action, failed to obtain the necessary two-thirds majority, despite the fact that the convention, though dubious about committing the organization to politics, was clearly favourable to political action being taken by the farmers.   A resolution favouring political action by farmers as farmers, however, was carried unanimously, the U.F.C. (S.S.) to assist in initial work of political organization when agreed to by

[15]*Ibid.*, March 5, 1925, p. 12, letter from G. H. Williams.
[16]Minutes of Annual Convention of S.G.G.A., 1923, 83.
[17]*Ibid.*, 1924, p. 143-5.
[18]Coldwell, *Left Turn, Canada!*, 2-3.
[19]*Ibid.*, 225 and 226; Minutes of Annual Convention of U.F.C.(S.S.), 1930, p. 214.

a majority of the local lodges.[20]   It was also resolved that the Board of Directors of the U.F.C. (S.S.) should work in closest co-operation with the organizations of labour.[21]   The association had thus committed itself to the position taken by the Grain Growers in 1922, and, as befitted its more radical character, had also undertaken to co-operate with labour.   It formulated, moreover, a platform, called the New Economic Policy, which was socialist in character.

Deepening depression made it possible in 1931 to complete the advance towards the position of the U.F.A., the immediate goal of Williams and other advocates of political action, although they proposed to advance beyond it.   In the convention of that year, the U.F.C. (S.S.) was committed to political action as an organization by formal constitutional amendment.[22]   The debate on political action was in many ways an inquest into the causes and failure of the Progressive movement, on the one hand, and the success of the U.F.A. on the other.[23]   In the outcome, a resolution was passed, to become operative when accepted by two-thirds of the local lodges.[24]   Subject to such ratification, the resolution authorized the central office of the U.F.C. (S.S.) to call conventions in federal or provincial electoral districts when requested by 15 per cent of the lodges of a district.   The convention might call, by the central office, a conference to act as a co-ordinating agency, this agency to be "at all times ready to co-operate with other organizations with similar aims and objectives."[25]   The last point is of the greatest importance, for in it lay the advance Williams made over Wood, the U.F.C. (S.S.) over the U.F.A.   No longer were the organized farmers in political action merely to profess readiness to co-operate with other organized groups for legislative purposes.   They were to seek such co-operation and organize it for electoral purposes. Williams and the U.F.C. (S.S.) had laid aside that fear which had dominated Wood and the U.F.A., a fear of creating a political party because it might wreck the economic organ-

[20]*Ibid.*, 214, 216, and 269.
[21]*Ibid.*, 269.
[22]Minutes of Annual Convention of U.F.C.(S.S.), 1931, pp. 243-4.
[23]*Ibid.*, address of John Evans, and address by H. E. Spencer, 309 to 376.
[24]*Ibid.*, 364, 383, 384.
[25]*Ibid.*, 410-11.

izations co-operating with it. This was one of the essential steps in the creation of the Co-operative Commonwealth Federation, and it was taken in Saskatchewan.

The convention of 1932, after rescinding, in order to amend and broaden, the resolution of 1931 on political action, set up a Central Directive Board to ensure the co-operation of farmers and labour.[26] This action was followed by the first annual political convention of delegates representing the U.F.C. (S.S.), branches of the Independent Labor party, and provincial constituency organizations, which met in Saskatoon on July 27, 1932. The main features of the discussion, led by G. H. Williams and M. J. Coldwell, were the emphases laid on the "fundamentally socialistic" character of the U.F.C. (S.S.), the determination of all to ensure the co-operation of the farmers and labour, and the demonstrated need of the Central Directive Board. Such a programme, Williams argued, would supply the "loose link" in the Alberta scheme of organization. It was further agreed that the name to be proposed for the new party to be organized at a forthcoming convention at Calgary should be bluntly, "the Socialist Party of Canada."[27]

The subsequent Calgary convention was the climax of developments not only in the U.F.C. (S.S.), but also in the U.F.A., developments begun by the depression and the supersession of Wood by Gardiner in the presidency of that body. A change of tone and emphasis, though not of doctrine, at once appeared in the proceedings of the annual convention and in the columns of *The U.F.A.* What this change signified was that the teachings of Wood and the practice of the U.F.A. were undergoing a rapid and logical application to the events of the depression. From sectional consolidation and the role of critic in parliament, the U.F.A. was turning to co-operation with other groups in a drive for national power, the only way in which a new economic order could be realized then and there. The pace of events was swift. In the convention of 1932, the U.F.A. ceased its preaching of group organization and resolved on co-operation with other organized groups:

[26]Minutes of Annual Convention of U.F.C.(S.S.), 1932.
[27]Files of U.F.C.(S.S.), "Record of the First Annual Political Convention of Delegates Representing the U.F.C., Branches of the I.L.P. and Provincial constituency organizations held in Saskatoon July 27, 1932."

Whereas, the farmers of Western Canada are not adequately represented in the Dominion House and as a result of which we are suffering through discriminatory legislation, and Whereas, a unification of policy by the various farm groups is necessary to ensure a strong vote being polled; Therefore be it resolved, that the Executive of the U.F.A. get in touch with executives of the other farm groups with a view to formulating a policy agreeable to all Western farmers so as to ensure a unified group of farmers in the next Dominion Election.[28]

It was further resolved, "that we pledge our entire support to all efforts toward the creation of a Co-operative Commonwealth."[29]

So instructed, the Executive of the U.F.A., in July 1932, met in Edmonton, and addressed itself to the proclaimed need of the times, "the establishment of a new economic order."[30]

This [said Gardiner] is a task that we as a farmers' group cannot accomplish alone, even if our industry be organized efficiently, not only in Alberta, but from Coast to Coast. We must be prepared to co-operate with other social units who suffer today as a result of the breakdown of the economic system. Many such organizations, as firmly convinced as ourselves of the necessity of social reconstruction, have long been organized. They are now rapidly gaining strength. The conference made a definite offer of effective co-operation with such organizations. Co-operation involves continuous consultation and co-ordination of effort. It involves action not only on a Provincial but on a Dominion-wide scale, for it is only on such a scale that co-operating groups can make a bid for power to bring about the fundamental changes in the economic system upon the necessity of which they are agreed. In order that the whole people of the Dominion may be able to identify the various groups as parts of a great national movement it is desirable that the nation-wide movement should be known under a single national name.[31]

Efficiency of organization was not enough; there must be organized co-operation of groups. Thus was the "loose link" of the Albertan scheme of group government to be made good, and the "group idea" extended from provincial to national politics.

[28]Minutes of Annual Convention of U.F.A., 1932, p. 1.

[29]*Ibid.*, p. 225.

[30]*The U.F.A.*, Aug. 1, 1932, p. 9, address by Robert Gardiner after Edmonton Conference.

[31]*Ibid.*

The Calgary conference followed at once on August 1, so speedily that some of the Saskatchewan delegates, hurrying by car, suffered wreck and sat at what was the natal conference of the Co-operative Commonwealth Federation swathed in bandages. The conference was attended by representatives of the U.F.A., the U.F.C. (S.S.), the Independent Labor party of Manitoba, the Canadian Labor party and the Dominion Labor party of Alberta, the Socialist Party of Canada from British Columbia, the Independent and Co-operative Labor parties of Saskatchewan, and the Brotherhood of Railway Employees.[32] Discussion was rapid, and agreement swift, for all had made up their minds beforehand. Co-operation was agreed to, under the name suggested by J. S. Woodsworth, Co-operative Commonwealth Federation, a name summing up the aspirations of Partridge and Wood and of countless agrarian and labour leaders, and indicating the new purpose of co-operative action. "The new movement," it was pointed out, "is not a political party, it is a federation of groups which in their own sphere retain their autonomy arid identity, but, in support of a common national program, will make common cause from coast to coast."[33]

The common programme was defined in a manifesto setting out the purpose of the Federation:

(1) A Federation of organizations whose purpose is the establishment in Canada of a Co-operative Commonwealth in which the basic principle regulating production, distribution and exchange, will be the supplying of human needs, instead of the making of profits.

(2) The object of the Federation shall be to promote co-operation between the member organizations and to correlate their political activities.

(3) We endorse the general viewpoint and program involved in the socialization of our economic life, as these have already been outlined and accepted by the Labour, Farmer and Socialist groups affiliating.

[32]*The U.F.A.*, Aug. 1, 1932, pp. 7 and 8, says the Canadian Congress of Labor was represented; to be well within the limits of accuracy, the text follows David Lewis and Frank Scott, *Make This* Your *Canada* (Toronto, 1943), 119, in confining union representation to the Brotherhood.

[33]*The U.F.A.*, Dec. 1, 1932, p. 3, editorial, "People Want a Radical Change."

Norman Smith, editor of *The U.F.A.*, commented on the manifesto:

The basis upon which the various units in the Federation will co-operate was set forth in a brief document of six paragraphs [an expansion of number 3 above], drawn up by the joint committee of Farmer and Labour representatives and adopted unanimously after amendment by the Conference. By the acceptance of this plan of co-operation the constituent organizations retain their identity, but agree to collaborate upon a national scale for the purpose of gaining power to undertake the fundamental economic and social reconstruction to which each unit, by the decisions of its own convention, has been committed. Recognition is given to the fact that upon vital matters there is unity of purpose.[34]

In January 1933, the U.F.A. convention formally affiliated with the Federation,[35] as did the other groups represented at the Calgary conference, except the Canadian Brotherhood of Railway Employees. The Federation, thus launched, met in convention at Regina in 1933 to draw up a national platform. The Regina Manifesto was largely the work of the eastern intellectuals of the League for Social Reconstruction, and marked a further stage in the broadening out of the C.C.F. from its original basis in western agrarianism and urban unionism. The election of J. S. Woodsworth as leader, commendable as it was on all counts, quickened the swing away from the sure agrarian foundations laid in the rural constituencies of Saskatchewan and Alberta towards a greater dependence on urban labour and a further increase of the influence of the intellectual socialists.

Such a development, however, was involved in the very character of the C.C.F., that of a national federation of economic groups, such a federation providing the answer to the problem of power which the Albertan idea had faced, and of itself failed to solve. The federation, if it succeeded in winning a national majority, might reform the conventions of parliament so as to make group government in fact possible. At the same time, it could meet the demands of populist localism, for it rested, as an

---

[34]*Ibid.*, Aug. 1, 1932, pp. 7-8, W. N. Smith, "The Co-operative Commonwealth Federation."

[35]Minutes of Annual Convention of the U.F.A., 1933, pp. 19-20.

organization, on a firm popular basis in the C.C.F. clubs, educational, political, and social groups, and on the farmers' co-operatives and the trade unions. In this it perpetuated the popular organization of the locals of the U.F.A., the U.F.C. (S.S.), and the old Grain Growers and also of the lodges of the still older Grange. Like these it had a popular basis the old parties lacked, and seemed incapable of finding.

Yet the fears of Wood were soon realized. The formation of the basic economic organization, if it were ever to be attained, was a slow process dependent on a transformation of society and of politics. The "group idea" left but a fading trace on the new Federation. Its formation was, in fact, a victory for that "broadening out" Wood and Morrison had so strenuously fought. A political organization seeking power must appeal to all possible elements of support, must take ceaseless account of the multifarious diversity of human nature and political society. Wood's concept of the problem of political power, like that of the Marxian and the Socialist, was too systematic to be either organically consistent or politically practical. Hence, in the basic units of the C.C.F. clubs, a common economic interest in the members was not insisted upon, but only assumed. Similarly, it was only assumed that a common interest existed among the co-operating groups. As the existence of such a common interest was relative, varying from time to time, the Federation at once began to take on the characteristics of a political party, the balancing, reconciling, compromising characteristics which made the old parties so indispensable to the working of a far-flung federation and sometimes so inconsistent and undignified. The C.C.F., in spite of its theoretical heritage and the Regina Manifesto, was a composite, not a doctrinaire, party. All this was involved in its quest for power; the price of doctrinal purity, as the U.F.A. had sensed, was abstention from office.

To the same end operated the creation of a central co-ordinating executive in the party leader and the party council. Though the forms of democratic control were rigorously maintained, though the principle of democratic action was sincerely observed, the C.C.F., like the British Labour party, the U.F.A., and the Grain Growers' Associations, at once developed a continuity of leadership and a rigidity of organization the old parties might envy. Democracy, as Wood failed to observe, has its own forms of "autocracy," born of its inherent instability.[36] The party leader, the legislative caucus, the party whip, the party policy, soon became as strongly developed in the C.C.F. as in the other composite parties.

It is to be noted, that these tendencies may have owed their development to the fact that in 1935, in the first federal election fought by the new party, the U.F.A. representation in Alberta, unbroken since 1921, was swept utterly away by the Social Credit movement of William Aberhart. Perhaps nothing could have stood against this tempest. Nevertheless the U.F.A.-C.C.F. members suffered from a fatal handicap. In Saskatchewan, the Progressive movement had failed, and a new insurgence had taken its place. In Alberta, the U.F.A. had logically developed into the C.C.F. The U.F.A. candidates were swept away because they had become "the old gang"; revolutions reverse the barbarous practice of Chronos and devour their own parents. The U.F.A. represented in 1935, not a new insurgence, but the continuation of an historical movement, and in 1935 the Albertan temper was once more revolutionary.

With the advent of Social Credit in Alberta, the history of the Progressive movement in Canada may be brought to an end. The party as such had ceased in 1926; thereafter the rise of the C.C.F. and of Social Credit respectively absorbed and cut off the political movement of the U.F.A. In 1939 that organization itself withdrew from politics, abandoning the field to the C.C.F. and Social Credit. Social Credit was a revolutionary break with the Progressive movement, an inrush into the vacuum created in Alberta, first by the disruption of the old parties wrought by the Progressive movement, and then by the decay of the U.F.A. itself.

Even revolutionary movements have their antecedents, and faults in the historical strata are as much part of the historical process as any other feature. Social Credit was a new departure, but it was also a lawful heir and successor of the U.F.A. and of the Progressive movement. Into pre-1914 Alberta

[36]See H. A. Innis (ed.), *Diary of James Alexander MacPhail* (Toronto, 1940), 142, for a reference to the difficulties of democratic control in the great co-operative organizations.

American Populists had carried soft-money doctrines. Ex-governor Leedy had stumped the province in the cause. George Bevington had carried the torch of monetary reform in 1921 and the doctrines of Social Credit had been introduced into Alberta by William Irvine. The U.F.A. representatives at Ottawa had carried on a long crusade for a more flexible use of credit under state direction, and the events of 1930 to 1935, leading to the founding of the Bank of Canada, were to be their vindication.

They, it is true, were not the founders of the Social Credit movement in Alberta. The fact was quite the reverse. They had, however, sowed the seeds of doctrine, and the U.F.A., destroying the old parties in rural Alberta and then itself decaying, had prepared the way for the rise of some new movement.

Even so, the U.F.A. might have controlled that movement, had not the very depression which had stirred the organization to the new activity from which the C.C.F. emerged, begotten in rural Alberta a mass movement of despair. The great depression and drought of the 1930's are not, in their disastrous effects, easily to be imagined or pictured.[37] When farm prices ceased to possess economic relevance; when organized society could no longer be maintained out of local resources; when once independent men were reduced in their distress to accepting relief from government; when the sun itself was blinded by the driving sand as the nomadic cavalry of drought, the bone-grey tumbling mustard and Russian thistle, charged endlessly across the wind-scoured fields, as endlessly as in the distant and dustless offices of St. James and Bay streets the interest charges mounted: under these afflictions men passed beyond persuasion or appeal. In 1935 the rural electors of Alberta refused to listen to their former leaders. They closed their ears to reason; in their despair, they sought only a promise of salvation.[38] And in this desperation appeared again that curious heightening in Alberta of all the characteristics of the frontier West, the weight of agrarian debt, the cost of organized society in a land of great distances and an extensive economy, the pulls of diverse loyalties and economic watersheds, the claustrophobia of a mid-continental people.

[37]See George Britnell, *The Wheat Economy* (Toronto, 1939).
[38]From a personal account of the campaign of 1935 by Hon. J. E. Brownlee.

The fact of unreasoning and sullen despair may, of course, be exaggerated. Those who fought in both the provincial campaigns of 1921 and 1935 declare that the popular frenzy of the latter was less than that of the former. In 1921 a pitch of crusading fanaticism was fired by the hope of a new social order; in 1935 cynical despair turned to an untried panacea which, at worst, could not make things worse. Had the U.F.A. at the height of its vigour clashed with Social Credit, the outcome might have been different. In 1935, however, the U.F.A. was old in the sense that it had been tried. Its ranks had been infiltrated by the devotees of Social Credit. The leadership was divided on the question of the policy to be adopted in legislating for the reduction of debt. Of two of its leaders, one had been a party to proceedings for divorce, one the defendant in an action charging seduction, and among the rural electorate with adult suffrage, a politician, like Caesar's wife, must not only appear innocent, but be above suspicion.

Nor does undue emphasis on the despairing element in the rise of Social Credit do justice to the demagogic and revivalistic rhetoric of William Aberhart. That propagandist genius compounded out of fundamentalism, enthusiasm, and a gloss of economic literacy, a gospel of evangelistic materialism which carried over the air the promise of secular salvation. He completed that trend of religious materialism which had marked the agrarian movement from the beginning. The U.F.A., lacking Wood, could not match the Prophetic Bible Institute.

The rise of the Social Credit movement and of the Co-operative Commonwealth Federation marked the beginning of a new phase of Canadian political development, a phase of class rather than sectional politics, of urban rather than rural dominance. The period 1910 to 1935 was one of transition in Canada from an agrarian to an industrialized society; with the Progressive movement passed the Canadian, and the North American, agricultural frontier. Social Credit and the C.C.F. were the successors of the Progressive movement rather then continuations of it. The Progressive movement itself had arisen "not from discontents of the moment, but from the necessities of the nation,"[39] and had its own identity in history, when all prece-

[39] *Manitoba Free Press*, April 14, 1924, p. 13, editorial, "Returning to Old Positions."

dents, parallels, and successors have been entered in the account. In its character and its consequences it had its own uniqueness. In what did this consist?

The Progressive movement was a revolt against a concept of the nature of Canadian economic policy and of Canadian political practice. The concept of Canadian economic policy which the Progressives had formed and on which they acted was that of a metropolitan economy designed, by the control of tariffs, railways, and credit, to draw wealth from the hinterlands and the countryside into the commercial and industrial centres of central Canada. The concept of Canadian political practice which the Progressives had formed and on which they acted was that the classic national parties were the instruments used by the commercial, industrial, and financial interests of metropolitan Canada to implement the National Policy of tariff protection and railway construction by dividing the vote of the electorate on "political" issues and by the compromises and majority decisions of the legislative caucus.

To what extent did these concepts correspond to actuality, what success had the Progressive revolt against them, and what are the consequences of its success or failure in Canadian history?

That the national economic policy of the period was mercantilist in its inspiration and metropolitan in its operation may be affirmed without subscribing to the heated conviction that deliberate greed or malice entered into its formulation, or even that it rested on the blind and selfish inertia of its beneficiaries. Arch Dale's cartoons in the *Grain Growers' Guide* of bloated capitalists siphoning off the hard-earned dollars of the western farmer were effective for their purpose and are amusing comments on an epoch in Canadian history, but they belong to the realm of folk-lore rather than to that of historical interpretation. The National Policy was designed to make central Canada into a commercial and industrial empire, based on the development of the hinterlands of the West and North by the construction of railways to serve both East and West. During the Laurier boom, conditions were favourable, and great success was enjoyed in exploiting the virgin lands of the continental West. When those conditions passed, an adjustment of the policy was necessary. The metropolitan East was challenged by the frontier

West it had called into being; the old National Policy was confronted by the New. The adjustment could be either a modification of the policy towards freer international trade, as by an agreement for reciprocity with the United States, or by the metropolitan area assuming, as part of the whole country, the costs of increased benefits to the hinterland areas.

It was to force such an adjustment that the farmers took political action in 1919. Unfortunately, as the controversy over the Wheat Board revealed, they at once fell into confusion about which alternative they would pursue. They strove for results as far apart as a tariff for revenue, and a system of open and organized lobbying in group government, which would have been in practice a scramble for economic benefits distributed by the state. The farmers in the movement represented conflicting interests themselves, and were also responsive to the forces impelling the swift transition from the free economy of pre-war years to the economic nationalism of the 1930's. The seeming unity of purpose of 1919 to 1921 was soon dissolved. In federal politics, the agrarian voters of the West for the most part returned to the Liberal party. In economic matters, the great body of farmers found hope in the new co-operative movement which gave rise to the Wheat Pools. But resentment of the long Liberal domination, and the vision of a stable farm income ensured by government action through a wheat board, remained to drive Conservative voters to support new, anti-Liberal parties, to maintain the U.F.A. in power in Alberta, and to erode the old economic individualism of the farmer with the hope of state action, which would counter the discrimination of the tariff by underpinning the farm economy.

The Progressives, nevertheless, gained certain material benefits for their constituents, especially in the matter of railway rates and communications. The restoration of the Crow's Nest Pass rates, the completion of the Hudson Bay Railway and the proliferation of branch lines in the nineteen-twenties, were their work or owed much to their effort. "With a split representation from the West," wrote the *Free Press* in 1930, "the Crow's Nest Pass rates would never have been restored. The 'National Policy' on this question, favored along St. James Street, would have been imposed upon both parties had there not been a parliamentary contingent from the West free from control in caucus by an eastern majority."[40]   This was spoken in the authentic accents of Progressivism, and it expressed, no doubt, a partial and limited view.   If national politics were a struggle for sectional benefits, however, the Progressives had won a measure of success.

At the same time, the Progressives influenced Liberal fiscal policy to the extent of forcing abstention from increases in the tariff and ultimately of actual reduction.   Their electoral success of 1921 checked a swing towards economic nationalism evident in most countries after the war, even in free-trade Britain, and notably in the United States.   After the disappointments of the Liberal budgets from 1922 to 1929, they seemed at long last to be on the threshold of success in the Dunning budget of 1930.   Indeed, the Conservatives were able to use the cry of western domination with effect in Quebec in 1930.[41]   Otherwise their successes, as in the re-imposition of the Crow's Nest Pass rates on east-bound wheat and flour and in the construction of the Hudson Bay Railway, were in the nature of sectional concessions won from the dominant metropolitan area.   On the whole, the Progressive movement left the metropolitan economy of central Canada unaltered in substance or spirit.

Against the concept they held of Canadian political practice the Progressives revolted with notable results.   Again, of course, they were divided.   There were those who revolted against the composite party because in caucus a sectional group might be consistently outvoted.   These, the Manitoban or Liberal Progressives, sought to force a realignment of parties along the lines of the liberal and conservative elements in the electorate. They wished, not to abolish the practices and conventions of party government, but to use them in the interests of the primary producers, as a party of liberal principle.   The others were the doctrinaire or Albertan Progressives, who rejected party government as such, and proposed to replace it and its accompanying conventions by group government.

[40]*Ibid.*, Aug. 6, 1930, p. 13, editorial, "The Fruits of the Progressive Movement."
[41]*Ibid.*

Both, however, were in revolt against the traditional parties as the instruments of the beneficiaries of the metropolitan economy. Did this concept correspond with actuality? While the Progressive view, undoubtedly, was a caricature of the relations of the national parties and the beneficiaries of the metropolitan economy, the caricature has that grasp of salient features which makes a caricature recognizable. Both parties from 1896 on were the practically indistinguishable proponents of the National Policy, and they acted through the caucus, the party-managed nominating convention, and the distribution of campaign funds.

It was these three focal points of party government at which the Progressives struck. That sovereignty had passed from the legislature to the majority in caucus they recognized, and also that that meant the subordination of the weaker to the more populous sections of the country. Henry Spencer said before the United Farmers of Canada (Saskatchewan Section) in 1931: "Of 240 odd members in the Dominion, the great majority went from Eastern Canada, and so it didn't matter which group was in the majority. The Western vote was so absolutely submerged in the caucuses, that however good a man might be, his vote was lost. That was the reason we took independent action."[42] To restore sovereignty to the legislature, and to make sectional views known, the Progressives refused to be bound by decisions taken in caucus. Nominating conventions they proposed to take away from the parties, and restore to the electorate. Campaign funds filled by private donations, they wished to replace by public subscriptions and a levy on party members.

The revolt against caucus, however, could only have succeeded by reversing the development of parliamentary government. No modern cabinet in the parliamentary system could undertake the vast work of the annual financial and legislative programme without reasonable assurance of the consistent support of its followers. The independence of the legislatures of an earlier day was no longer possible; parliament had become the critic, not the master, of cabinets. The popular control of nomination and provision of campaign expenses depended, moreover upon a zeal for public affairs the electorate failed to

[42]Minutes of Annual Convention of U.F.C.(S.S.), 1931, p. 317.

display for any length of time.   The Progressives put a challenge to democracy only the U.F.A. met successfully.

Did the restoration of the old parties in 1930, then, and the rise of the C.C.F. and Social Credit parties, essentially composite parties like the old, mark a complete defeat of the Progressive revolt against the party system?   To a great extent it did.   Yet the old order of Macdonald and Laurier, when party affiliation was hereditary and party chieftains were almost deified, was not restored.   The two-party system did not return in its former strength.   The rules and conventions of parliament made provision for more than two parties.   The electorate became more independent, indeed, to the point of political indifference.   The authority of the whip became lighter, the bonds of caucus weaker, than in the old days.   These were effects of the Progressive movement, and constituted its mark on Canadian political life.

The mere modification of political conventions and modes was perhaps a slight result of so much effort.   Yet where could the sectional and agrarian revolt have led except to secession or class war, or to an acceptance of the composite party once more, chastened, no doubt, but essentially unchanged?   A free society is an endless compromise between anarchy and authority, union and secession.   To compromise, no doubt, is to corrupt—to corrupt the simplicity of principle, the clarity of policy—but if so, then all politics corrupt and federal politics, the politics of the vast sectional and communal aggregations, especially so. To this conclusion all purists, all doctrinaires, and all Progressives, must ultimately come or abstain from power.   The logical alternative is Robespierre guillotining the guillotiner.

Yet the Progressive insurgence was not merely a sectional protest against a metropolitan economy, it was also an agrarian protest against the growing urban domination of the Canadian economy and of national politics.   As such, it was closely allied to the sectional protest.   As an agrarian protest, the Progressive movement was a response to the industrialization of the economy, and the commercialization and mechanization of agriculture.   In the years of the Progressive movement Canada was undergoing an industrial and urban revolution.   To meet the challenge of the coming order, the old, hard-working farmer with his faith in long hours and sweat was ill-equipped. He had to be made over into a manager, a business man, and a skilled technician. The work was largely done in the farm organizations from which the Progressive party sprang. The professional men, and especially the lawyers, whom the old parties put before the voters to elect were inadequate, not so much to make the legislative adjustments required by the transition from manual to mechanized agriculture, but to express the resentment and discontent the farmer experienced in the throes of the transition, and to speed the work of adjustment. This task the Progressive movement performed, particularly in the two agricultural provinces it captured and held, Manitoba and Alberta. Its very success caused its passing, for the farmer came into business in the co-operatives, into politics in the parties, old or new, to stay. He stayed, not to protest further, but to get on with the job of looking after the interests of the new commercialized and mechanized agriculture. In this aspect the Progressive movement was the expression of the last phase of the transformation of the old semi-subsistence agriculture into the business of farming. With the Progressive revolt, farming ceased to be a way of life and became simply another occupation. Countryman and city dweller no longer inhabited separate social orders; the city had prevailed over the country, but in prevailing had learned, not a little because of the Progressive movement, to respect the countryman. No one after 1921 would have thought of writing Gadsby's "Sons of the Soil," in which the farmers of the great anti-conscription delegation of 1918 had been ridiculed by a slick and too clever journalist.[43]

In a larger view, also, the Progressive movement marked a profound transformation. Behind the sectional protest lay not only resentment of the National Policy and of its agents, the political parties. Behind it lay also resentment of the inequality of the provinces of the continental West in Confederation. They had been created with limitations, imposed "for the purposes of the Dominion." They entered Confederation, not as full partners, as sister provinces, but as subordinate communities, subject to the land, fiscal, and railway policies of the

[43]H. F. Gadsby, "The Sons of the Soil," *Toronto Saturday Night*, June 1, 1918, p. 4.

metropolitan provinces and the special interests of the French Canadian in the French dispersion in the West. They were, in short, colonies under the form of provinces "in a federation denoting equality."[44]   The Progressive party was a full-blown expression of the West's resentment of its colonial status.   As such, it was one phase of the development of the Canadian nation.

As such, also, it had a great measure of success.   Not since the days of the revolt has the West been subjected to the indifference, the neglect, and the fumbling administration which provoked the troubles of 1869, the Rebellion of 1885, and the movement itself.   The swaggering hopes of the boom days, that the West would dominate confederation by holding a balance of power in Ottawa, were happily not realized.   But the increase in cabinet representation from the one lone minister of Laurier's day to the minimal three of the present, was not merely an exercise in abstract justice, but a response to the political weight of the West in the Union Government and to the force of the Progressive movement.   The choice of western leaders by political parties from 1920 on was a similar response to the political power and electoral independence of the West.   At the same time, it is to be observed that just as the Dunning budget denoted the beginning of Progressive success in fiscal matters, so the transfer of the natural resources in 1930, the purposes of the Dominion having been fulfilled, marked the end of the colonial subordination and the achievement of equality of status by the West in Confederation.   This, too, was a response to western pressure embodied in the federal Progressive party and the provincial governments the movement threw up.   The Progressive movement, in short, marked the achievement of political maturity by the West, and the symbols of equality could no longer be withheld.

Yet the resolution of the sectional animosities, of the narrow complacency of the East, and the equally narrow assertiveness of the West, was to be accomplished, not by the bitter exchanges of the 1920's or by enforced concessions.   The work of reconciliation, a work of time, of patience, of manœuvre, the Progressive party advanced by proving that the West, too much tried, would and could resort to independent political action.

[44]Lingard, *Territorial Government in Canada*, 251.

The work might have been completed in that way. It was, however, completed by tragedy. No sooner had the West, through the Progressive movement, begun to win a modification of the National Policy and no sooner had it achieved equality of status in Confederation, than depression drove the country into a defensive economic nationalism. Drought ruined the agrarian economy of the West, and threatened the great co-operatives and the provincial governments with general bankruptcy. The West was saved by federal action, and from the disaster of the thirties came, in East and West, a deeper sense of interdependence than the past had known. The Rowell-Sirois Commission, the great inquest provoked by the disaster, accepted and elaborated the basic thesis of the Progressive movement, that in a federal union of free citizens and equal communities, there must be such equality of economic opportunity and such equality of political status as human ingenuity may contrive and goodwill advance.[45]

[45]See R. McQueen, "Economic Aspects of Federalism" (*Canadian Journal of Economics and Political Science*, I, August, 1935, pp. 352-67), for a sober analysis of the points involved.

Appendix

A.

THE FARMERS' PLATFORM

(From *The Siege of Ottawa*, Winnipeg, 1910)

The following are the resolutions presented to the Government
on December the Sixteenth, 1910,
by the Canadian Council of Agriculture.

THE TARIFF

The tariff demands of the organized farmers of Canada made to
Sir Wilfrid Laurier were in the following words:

This delegation, representative of the agricultural interests of Canada, desire
to approach you upon the question of the bearing of the Canadian customs tariff.

We come, asking no favors at your hands. We bear with us no feeling of
antipathy towards any other line of industrial life. We welcome within the
limits of Canada's broad domain every legitimate form of industrial enterprise,
but in view of the fact that the further progress and development of the agricultural industry is of such vital importance to the general welfare of the state
that all other Canadian industries are so dependent upon its success, that its
constant condition forms the great barometer of trade, we consider its operations
should no longer be hampered by tariff restrictions.

And in view of the favorable approaches already made through President
Taft and the American Government looking towards more friendly trade relations between Canada and the United States this memorial takes form as
follows:

1. That we strongly favor reciprocal Free Trade between Canada and the
United States in all horticultural, agricultural and animal products, spraying
materials, fertilizers, illuminating, fuel and lubricating oils, cement, fish and
lumber.

2. Reciprocal free trade between the two countries in all agricultural
implements, machinery, vehicles and parts of each of these; and, in the event
of a favorable arrangement being reached, it be carried into effect through the
independent action of the respective governments, rather than by the hard and
fast requirements of a treaty.

3. We also favor the principle of the British preferential tariff, and urge an immediate lowering of the duties on all British goods to one-half the rates charged under the general tariff schedule, whatever that may be; and that any trade advantages given the United States in reciprocal trade relations be extended to Great Britain.

4. For such further gradual reduction of the remaining preferential tariff as will ensure the establishment of complete free trade between Canada and the Motherland within ten years.

5. That the farmers of this country are willing to face direct taxation in such form as may be advisable to make up the revenue required under new tariff conditions.

Believing that the greatest misfortune which can befall any country is to have its people huddled together in great centres of population, and that the bearing of the present customs tariff has the tendency to encourage that condition and realizing also that in view of the constant movement of our people away from the farms, the greatest problem which presents itself to Canadian people today is the problem of retaining our people on the soil, we come doubly assured of the justice of our petition.

Trusting this memorial may meet your favorable consideration, and that the substance of its prayer be granted with all reasonable despatch.

On behalf of the Canadian Council of Agriculture.

[Sgd.]   D. W. McCuaig, *President.*
[Sgd.]   E. C. Drury, *Secretary.*

The other resolutions presented to the government were as follows:

Hudson's Bay Railway

Whereas, the necessity of the Hudson's Bay railway as the natural and the most economic outlet for placing the products of the Western prairies on the European market has been emphasized by the Western people for the past generation;

And whereas, the Dominion government has recognized the need and importance of the Hudson's Bay railway and has pledged itself to its immediate construction, and has provided the necessary funds entirely from the sale of Western lands;

And whereas, the chief benefit to be derived from the Hudson's Bay railway will be a reduction in freight rates in Western Canada, due to actual competition, which could be secured only through government ownership and operation of the Hudson's Bay railway;

And whereas, anything short of absolute public ownership and operation of the Hudson's Bay railway will defeat the purpose for which the road was advocated, and without which it would be in the interests of Western Canada that the building of the road should be deferred;

Therefore, be it resolved that it is the opinion of this convention that the Hudson's Bay railway and all terminal facilities connected therewith should be constructed, owned and operated in perpetuity by the Dominion government under an independent commission.

Terminal Elevators

Whereas, we are convinced that terminal elevators as now operated are detrimental to the interests of both the producer and consumer, as proved by recent investigation and testimony of important interested bodies, we therefore request that the Dominion government acquire and operate as a public utility under an independent commission the terminal elevators of Fort William and Port Arthur, and immediately establish similar terminal facilities and conditions at the Pacific Coast, and provide the same at Hudson's Bay when necessary; also such transfer and other elevators necessary to safeguard the quality of export grain.

The Bank Act

Whereas, it is generally believed that the Bank act, forming, as it does, the charter of all Canadian banks for a ten year term, by its present phrasing prevents any amendment involving curtailment of their powers enjoyed by virtue of the provisions of such charter, be it resolved: That this Ottawa convention of delegates desire that the new Bank act be so worded as to permit the act to be amended at any time and in any particular.

Co-operative Legislation

Resolved, that in the opinion of this convention it is desirable that cheap and efficient machinery for the incorporation of co-operative societies should be provided by Federal legislation during the present session of parliament.

Chilled Meat Industry

The government be urgently requested to erect the necessary works and operate a modern and up-to-date method of exporting our meat animals.

We suggest that a system owned and operated by the government as a public utility or a system of co-operation by the producers through the government, in which the government would supply the funds necessary to first instal the system and provide for the gradual repayment of these funds and interest by a charge on the product passing through the system, would give the relief needed, and make Canada one of the most prosperous meat producing countries in the world.

The Railway Case

The organized farmers asked that the Railway act be amended so that the railway companies be compelled to bear a fair share of the responsibility for killing stock, and also:

1. That the principle of fixing the tariffs in accordance with the competition of other roads or the density of traffic or volume of business handled be disallowed.

2. That a true physical valuation be taken of all railways operating in Canada, this valuation to be used as the basis of fixing the rates, and the information to be available to the public.

3. That the Board of Railway Commissioners be given complete jurisdiction in these matters as well as in all other matters of dispute between the railways and the people, and to enable them to do this that the law be more clearly defined.

B.

THE FARMERS' PLATFORM

Drafted by the Canadian Council of Agriculture and endorsed by the Manitoba Grain Growers' Association, Saskatchewan Grain Growers' Association, United Farmers of Alberta and United Farmers of Ontario (December, 1916).

THE CUSTOMS TARIFF

WHEREAS the war has revealed the amazing financial strength of Great Britain, which has enabled her to finance not only her own part in the struggle, but also to assist in financing her Allies to the extent of hundreds of millions of pounds, this enviable position being due to the free trade policy which has enabled her to draw her supplies freely from every quarter of the globe and consequently to undersell her competitors on the world's markets, and because this policy has not only been profitable to Great Britain but has greatly strengthened the bonds of Empire by facilitating trade between the Motherland and her overseas dominions—we believe that the best interests of the Empire and of Canada would be served by reciprocal action on the part of Canada through gradual reductions of the tariff on British imports, having for its object a closer union and a better understanding between Canada and the Motherland and by so doing not only strengthen the hands of Great Britain in the life and death struggle in which she is now engaged, but at the same time bring about a great reduction in the cost of living to our Canadian people;

AND WHEREAS the Protective Tariff has fostered combines, trusts, and "gentlemen's agreements" in almost every line of Canadian industrial enterprise, by means of which the people of Canada—both urban and rural—have been shamefully exploited through the elimination of competition, the ruination of many of our smaller industries and the advancement of prices on practically all manufactured goods to the full extent permitted by the tariff;

AND WHEREAS agriculture—the basic industry upon which the success of all other industries primarily depends—is almost stagnant throughout Canada as shown by the declining rural population in both eastern and western Canada, due largely to the greatly increased cost of agricultural implements and machinery, clothing, boots and shoes, building material and practically everything the farmer has to buy, caused by the Protective Tariff, so that it is becoming impossible for farmers generally to carry on farming operations profitably;

AND WHEREAS the Protective Tariff is the most wasteful and costly method ever designed for raising national revenue, because for every dollar obtained thereby for the public treasury at least three dollars pass into the pockets of the protected interests, thereby building up a privileged class at the expense of the masses, thus making the rich richer and the poor poorer;

AND WHEREAS the Protective tariff has been and is a chief corrupting influence in our national life because the protected interests, in order to maintain their unjust privileges, have contributed lavishly to political and campaign funds, thus encouraging both political parties to look to them for support, thereby lowering the standard of public morality;

THEREFORE BE IT RESOLVED that the Canadian Council of Agriculture, representing the organized farmers of Canada, urges that as a means of bringing about these much needed reforms and at the same time reducing the high cost of living, now proving such a burden on the people of Canada, our tariff laws should be amended as follows:

1. By reducing the customs duty on goods imported from Great Britain to one-half the rates charged under the general tariff and that further gradual, uniform reductions be made in the remaining tariff on British imports that will ensure complete free trade between Great Britain and Canada in five years.
2. That the Reciprocity Agreement of 1911, which still remains on the United States statute books, be accepted by the parliament of Canada.
3. That all food stuff not included in the Reciprocity Agreement be placed on the free list.
4. That agricultural implements, farm machinery, vehicles, fertilizer, coal, lumber, cement, illuminating fuel and lubricating oils be placed on the free list.
5. That the customs tariff on all the necessities of life be materially reduced.
6. That all tariff concessions granted to other countries be immediately extended to Great Britain.

TAXATION FOR REVENUE

As these tariff reductions will very considerably reduce the national revenue derived from that source, the Canadian Council of Agriculture would recommend that in order to provide the necessary additional revenue for carrying on the government of the country and for the prosecution of the war to a successful conclusion, direct taxation be imposed in the following manner:

1. By a direct tax on unimproved land values, including all natural resources.
2. By a sharply graduated personal income tax.
3. By a heavy graduated inheritance tax on large estates.
4. By a graduated income tax on the profits of corporations.

OTHER NECESSARY REFORMS

The Canadian Council of Agriculture desires to endorse also the following policies as in the best interests of the people of Canada:

1. The nationalization of all railway, telegraph and express companies.
2. That no more natural resources be alienated from the Crown but brought into use only under short term leases, in which the interests of the public shall be properly safeguarded, such leases to be granted only by public auction.
3. Direct legislation, including the initiative and referendum and the right of recall.
4. Publicity of political campaign fund contributions and expenditures both before and after elections.
5. The abolition of the patronage system.
6. Full provincial autonomy in liquor legislation, including manufacture, export and import.
7. That the extension of the franchise to women in any province shall automatically admit them to the federal franchise.

C.

THE FARMERS' PLATFORM

(As brought up-to-date, 1921)

Drafted by the Canadian Council of Agriculture, November 29, 1918, and accepted by the member organizations, 1919.

1. A League of Nations as an international organization to give permanence to the world's peace by removing old causes of conflict. [sic]

2. We believe that the further development of the British Empire should be sought along the lines of partnership between nations free and equal, under the present governmental system of British constitutional authority. We are strongly opposed to any attempt to centralize imperial control. Any attempt to set up an independent authority with power to bind the Dominions, whether this authority be termed parliament, council or cabinet, would hamper the growth of responsible and informed democracy in the Dominions.

THE TARIFF

3. Whereas Canada is now confronted with a huge national war debt and other greatly increased financial obligations, which can be most readily and effectively reduced by the development of our natural resources, chief of which is agricultural lands;

And whereas it is desirable that an agricultural career should be made attractive to our returned soldiers and the large anticipated immigration, and owing to the fact that this can best be accomplished by the development of a national policy which will reduce to a minimum the cost of living and the cost of production;

And whereas the war has revealed the amazing financial strength of Great Britain, which has enabled her to finance, not only her own part in the struggle, but also to assist in financing her Allies to the extent of hundreds of millions of pounds, this enviable position being due to the free trade policy which has enabled her to draw her supplies freely from every quarter of the globe and consequently to undersell her competitors on the world's market, and because this policy has not only been profitable to Great Britain, but has greatly strengthened the bonds of Empire by facilitating trade between the Motherland and her overseas Dominions—we believe that the best interests of the Empire and of Canada would be served by reciprocal action on the part of Canada through gradual reductions of the tariff on British imports, having for its objects closer union and a better understanding between Canada and the Motherland and at the same time bring about a great reduction in the cost of living to our Canadian people;

FOSTERS COMBINES

And whereas the Protective Tariff has fostered combines, trusts and "gentlemen's agreements" in almost every line of Canadian industrial enterprise, by means of which the people of Canada—both urban and rural—have been shamefully exploited through the elimination of competition, the ruination of many of our smaller industries and the advancement of prices on practically all manufactured goods to the full extent permitted by the tariff;

And whereas agriculture—the basic industry upon which the success of all our other industries primarily depends—is unduly handicapped throughout Canada as shown by the declining rural population in both Eastern and Western Canada, due largely to the greatly increased cost of agricultural implements and machinery, clothing, boots and shoes, building material and practically everything the farmer has to buy, caused by the Protective Tariff, so that it is becoming impossible for farmers generally, under normal conditions, to carry on farming operations profitably;

And whereas the Protective Tariff is the most wasteful and costly method ever designed for raising national revenue, because for every dollar obtained thereby for the public treasury at least three dollars pass into the pockets of the protected interests thereby building up a privileged class at the expense of the masses, thus making the rich richer and the poor poorer;

And whereas the Protective Tariff has been and is a chief corrupting influence in our national life because the protected interests, in order to maintain their unjust privileges, have contributed lavishly to political and campaign funds, thus encouraging both political parties to look to them for support, thereby lowering the standard of public morality.

Definite Tariff Demands

Therefore be it resolved that the Canadian Council of Agriculture, representing the organized farmers of Canada, urges that, as a means of remedying these evils and bringing about much-needed social and economic reforms, our tariff laws should be amended as follows:

(a) By an immediate and substantial all-round reduction of the customs tariff.

(b) By reducing the customs duty on goods imported from Great Britain to one-half the rates charged under the general tariff, and that further gradual, uniform reductions be made in the remaining tariff on British imports that will ensure complete Free Trade between Great Britain and Canada in five years.

(c) By endeavoring to secure unrestricted reciprocal trade in natural products with the United States along the lines of the Reciprocity Agreement of 1911.*

(d) By placing all foodstuffs on the free list.

(e) That agricultural implements, farm and household machinery, vehicles, fertilizers, coal, lumber, cement, gasoline, illuminating, fuel and lubricating oils be placed on the free list, and that all raw materials and machinery used in their manufacture also be placed on the free list.

(f) That all tariff concessions granted to other countries be immediately extended to Great Britain.

(g) That all corporations engaged in the manufacture of products protected by the customs tariff be obliged to publish annually comprehensive and accurate statements of their earnings.

(h) That every claim for tariff protection by any industry should be heard publicly before a special committee of parliament.

*The Draft of 1919 simply called for the acceptance of the Agreement, which was then still on the American statute books (author's note).

Taxation Proposals

4. As these tariff reductions may very considerably reduce the national revenue from that source, the Canadian Council of Agriculture would recommend that, in order to provide the necessary additional revenue for carrying on the government of the country and for the bearing of the cost of the war, direct taxation be imposed in the following manner:

(a) By a direct tax on unimproved land values, including all natural resources.

(b) By a graduated personal income tax.

(c) By a graduated inheritance tax on large estates.

(d) By a graduated income tax on the profits of corporations.

(e) That in levying and collecting the business profits tax the Dominion Government should insist that it be absolutely upon the basis of the actual cash invested in the business and that no considerations be allowed for what is popularly known as watered stock.

(f) That no more natural resources be alienated from the crown, but brought into use only under short-term leases, in which the interests of the public shall be properly safeguarded, such leases to be granted only by public auction.

The Returned Soldiers

5. With regard to the returned soldier we urge:

(a) That it is the recognized duty of Canada to exercise all due diligence for the future well-being of the returned soldier and his dependents.

(b) That demobilization should take place only after return to Canada.

(c) That first selection for return and demobilization should be made in the order of length of service of those who have definite occupation awaiting them or have other assured means of support, preference being given first to married men and then to the relative need of industries, with care to insure so far as possible the discharge of farmers in time for the opening of spring work upon the land.

(d) That general demobilization should be gradual, aiming at the discharge of men only as it is found possible to secure steady employment.

(e) It is highly desirable that if physically fit discharged men should endeavor to return to their former occupations, all employers should be urged to reinstate such men in their former positions wherever possible.

(f) That vocational training should be provided for those who while in the service have become unfitted for their former occupations.

(g) That provision should be made for insurance at the public expense of unpensioned men who have become undesirable insurance risks while in the service.

(h) The facilities should be provided at the public expense that will enable returned soldiers to settle upon farming land when by training or experience they are qualified to do so.

6. We recognize the very serious problem confronting labor in urban industry resulting from the cessation of war, and we urge that every means, economically feasible and practicable, should be used by federal, provincial and municipal authorities in relieving unemployment in the cities and towns;

and, further, recommend the adoption of the principle of co-operation as the guiding spirit in the future relations between employer and employees—between capital and labor.

LAND SETTLEMENT

7. A land settlement scheme based on a regulating influence in the selling price of land. Owners of idle areas should be obliged to file a selling price on their lands, that price also to be regarded as an assessable value for purposes of taxation.

8. Extension of co-operative agencies in agriculture to cover the whole field of marketing, including arrangements with consumers' societies for the supplying of foodstuffs at the lowest rates and with the minimum of middleman handling.

9. Public ownership and control of railway, water and aerial transportation, telephone, telegraph and express systems, all projects in the development of natural power, and of the coal mining industry.

OTHER DEMOCRATIC REFORMS

10. To bring about a greater measure of democracy in government, we recommend:*

(a) That the new Dominion Election Act shall be based upon the principle of establishing the federal electorate on the provincial franchise.

(b) The discontinuance of the practice of conferring titles upon citizens of Canada.

(c) The reform of the federal senate.

(d) An immediate check upon the growth of government by order-in-council, and increased responsibility of individual members of parliament in all legislation.

(e) The complete abolition of the patronage system.

(f) The publication of contributions and expenditures both before and after election campaigns.

(g) The removal of press censorship upon the restoration of peace and the immediate restoration of the rights of free speech.

(h) The setting forth by daily newspapers and periodical publications, of the facts of their ownership and control.

(i) Proportional representation.

(j) The establishment of measures of direct legislation through the initiative, referendum and recall.

(k) The opening of seats in parliament to women on the same terms as men.

(l) Prohibition of the manufacture, importation and sale of intoxicating liquors as beverages in Canada.**

NOTE.—A plank under Section 10, reading; "A Naturalization Act based upon personal naturalization only," was suggested by the Canadian Council of Agriculture, and was approved by all the provincial associations except the United Farmers of Alberta, which voted to lay this plank "on the table."***

*The first recommendation of the Draft of 1919 was the repeal of the War Time Elections Act, carried out in 1920 (author's note).
**Added to the Draft of 1919 (author's note).
***This "plank" is not in the Draft of 1919, as incorporated by the Minutes of the Canadian Council of Agriculture, November 29, 1918, pp. 31-5 (author's note).

D
(From *Canada House of Commons Debates*, 1926, I, p. 213)

Wednesday, January 6th, 1926.

Dear Mr. Meighen;

At a meeting of the Progressives to-day I was requested to ask you for an outline of your legislative proposals in the event of your being called upon to form a government.

We would particularly appreciate your stand with respect to the following important matters;—

1. The Tariff
2. The Hudson Bay railway
3. The Peace River outlet
4. Mountain differential
5. Statutory freight rates on grain and flour
6. Public ownership of national railways
7. The income tax
8. Rural credits
9. Transfer of natural resources to prairie provinces
10. Trade relations with the United States particularly with regard to livestock
11. A nation(al) coal policy
12. Revaluation of soldier settlers' lands
13. Co-operative marketing
14. Alternative vote.

While sending you this letter we are asking the Prime Minister to give us his proposals in a like manner. We would respectfully request that an answer be given at as early a date as possible, preferably not later than the evening of the seventh inst.*

Yours respectfully,

ROBERT FORKE.

The Right Hon. A. Meighen,
House of Commons, Ottawa.

*The letter to Prime Minister Mackenzie King was identical (author's note).

Bibliographical Essay

I

THE documentation and literature of the Progressive party in Canada is as yet so incomplete and scanty that it seems more useful to offer a bibliographical essay, taking some licence in commenting on the merit or demerit of titles cited, than to prepare a standard bibliography. The writer, moreover, cannot claim to have exhausted the sources which might throw light on the movement; to have attempted to do so would have entailed an examination of a major part of the journalistic and periodical press of Canada for fifteen to twenty-five years. This was not possible in the time which could be given to the task. The researches by which the study was prepared were therefore selective, and the bibliography reflects the fact. Nor is any claim advanced that the selection made was the best possible. With the advantage of wisdom after the event, the writer now thinks that it was not, and where error was incurred, it will be noted in order to increase the usefulness of the essay for future students in the field.

II

State papers were, of course, little used in what was a study of opinion and party politics. The *House of Commons Debates*, were, however, searched from 1910 to 1930. In the debates in the House, particularly in those on the Address in reply to the Speech from the Throne, members often expressed, particularly the Progressive members heady with the intoxication of the movement, the motives and aspirations of their party. Sometimes formal statements of policy were made, or the terms of inter-party understandings laid before the House. On two occasions, in 1926 and 1927, correspondence dealing with such understandings was either tabled or read into the record. The *Debates* accordingly yielded a very authentic reflection of the mind of the Progressives; on the other hand, it was necessary to remember that, by and large, it was the more advanced and more articulate members of the group who spoke. The others were silent backbenchers, who expressed themselves only in division and, it is likely, through the usually brief and by no means allusive utterances of Robert Forke. The *Debates* also revealed the cleavages in the group, both in the speeches of those members who defied the whip, and, of course, in the recorded divisions.

The *Report of the Royal Commission on Dominion-Provincial Relations*, Books I to III (Ottawa, 1940), with its appendices, is, of course, an important source for any student of Canadian history, and is the fruit of a great effort to probe and diagnose those very maladies of the Canadian body politic which produced the Progressive revolt.

Other state papers, such as the *Sessional Papers* and *Journals of the House of Commons*, the *Debates of the Senate*, and the *Statutes of Canada* were referred to only as occasion demanded in the preparation of this study, as were the similar papers of the provinces.

III

Akin to state papers in the documentation of the Progressive movement are the official minutes of the farmers' organizations. They constitute not only a record of decisions taken, of resolutions proposed and adopted, but also afford some insight into the course and temper of debate in the conventions. The minutes of the Canadian Council of Agriculture were held in trust by the United Grain Growers' Company Limited, and through the courtesy and public spirit of the corporation and the Hon. Norman P. Lambert, are now deposited in the Public Archives of Manitoba. The official minutes of the Manitoba Grain Growers' Association and its successor, the United Farmers of Manitoba, are in the Public Archives of Manitoba, together with the general files.

The United Farmers of Canada (Saskatchewan Section) preserves the minutes of the Saskatchewan Grain Growers' Association, as an integral part of its own minutes, at its head office in Saskatoon. Similarly, the official minutes of the United Farmers of Alberta are preserved in the head office of the organization in Calgary. Down to 1923 it was the practice of the U.F.A. to publish the minutes of its conventions, though not, of course, of its directors' meetings, in its *Annual Reports of the U.F.A. Conventions*, but another complete file of these is unknown to the writer. The *Grain Growers' Guide* also published the minutes of the conventions of all three provincial organizations for a number of years. The writer did not look for, and does not know the whereabouts of, the minutes of the United Farmers of Ontario, or of those of the United Farmers' organizations of the other provinces. The desirability of having all these records in one archives, preferably the Public Archives of Canada, is manifest.

IV

Potentially a great volume of private papers and a rich harvest of memoirs may be available for the study of the period of the Progressive movement. The writer, even at this early date, was fortunate in securing access, under the usual conventions, to a surprising number of collections of private papers. Richest of these were the Dafoe Papers, consisting of the correspondence of J. W. Dafoe, editor-in-chief of the *Winnipeg Free Press*, 1901-44, conducted from and received in his editorial office. These papers are catalogued and are deposited in the editorial offices of the *Free Press*. Dafoe was at, or close to, the centre of the main, or Manitoban, Progressive movement, and in addition was an intimately informed and trenchantly spoken, realistic if partisan, commentator on Canadian politics. The papers constitute an indispensable source for the study of the Progressive movement. Linked with them should be the papers of the late Mr. Justice A. B. Hudson, of which Mr. Grant Dexter, who has had access to them, has said: "It will [not] be possible accurately to write the history of those years without access to the Hudson papers" (*Winnipeg Free Press*, Jan. 8, 1947, p. 13). It was through Hudson that the negotiations between the Progressives and progressive Liberals during 1922-5 were largely conducted. Of equal, and in some respects of greater, importance are the Crerar Papers, in the possession of the Hon. T. A. Crerar. These are now being catalogued at Senator Crerar's direction. They constitute a vast mass of material on the farmers' movement, in both its economic and its political aspects. The Wood Papers, if they may be so termed, in the possession of the Alberta Wheat Pool, are a disappointment to the student of the Progressive movement. They consist largely of private business correspondence, receipts, etc., and of clippings from the press relating to Wood and the U.F.A. It is difficult to believe that so important a man as Henry Wise Wood could have left, much less have received, no correspondence of significance, but such is the evidence of the Wood Papers as they exist. Mr. Henry E. Spencer and the family of the late Mr. Rice Sheppard have in their possession various minutes, reports, and memoranda of value, as no doubt have other men of equal eminence in the farmers' movement. In particular, Mr. Spencer's records of the activities of the U.F.A. group at Ottawa, and the late Mr. Sheppard's manuscript autobiography, which throws much light on the development of the U.F.A. in its formative years, merit attention.

In the Public Archives of Canada, the Laurier Papers might be expected to reveal something of the causes of the disruption of parties which opened the way to the entrance of the farmers into politics, but the cream of the papers, on which O. D. Skelton's biography is based, remains in private hands. The papers of the Hon. Charles Murphy, and those of Sir John S. Willison throw much light on the calculations of the practical politicians of the time, and it is to be hoped that they may be supplemented by those of the late Senator Andrew Haydon.

Particularly, of course, is it to be desired that the veterans of the period, all, it is to be thankfully noted, in full health and vigour, may give their memoirs to the public in due course: the Rt. Hon. W. L. Mackenzie King, the Rt. Hon. Arthur Meighen, the Hon. C. A. Dunning, the Hon. Senator T. A. Crerar, the Hon. Senator Norman P. Lambert, and others.

V

A certain body of pamphlet material has survived from the period of the farmers' irruption into politics. This divides into that published by the farmers' organizations themselves, the campaign literature of the old parties, and that inspired by the Canadian Manufacturers' Association. The first consists of fugitive pieces in provincial libraries and archives, the second and third are catalogued in the pamphlet material of the Public Archives of Canada. Of the first, which exist uncatalogued in the Provincial Library of Manitoba and no doubt elsewhere, the following are of importance: G. F. CHIPMAN (ed.), *The Siege of Ottawa* (Winnipeg, 1910); E. A. PARTRIDGE, *A Farmers' Trade Union* (Winnipeg, 1907 ?); *The Farmers' Platform* ((Winnipeg, 1917); *The Farmers' Platform* is in the Public Archives of Canada also as Pamphlet No. 4625; *The New National Policy* (Winnipeg, n.d.), both published by the Canadian Council of Agriculture; *Minutes of Conference of Joint Committee of Commerce and Agriculture* (Winnipeg, 1916); *The Tariff Record of the Liberal Party from 1893 to 1919*, published by the National Liberal Convention Committee (Ottawa, 1919). There is also a group of electioneering leaflets published by the Canadian Council of Agriculture: *Crerar on New National Policy* (Speech to U.F.A., Jan. 1920); *Making Money for the Shareholders* (Winnipeg, 1920); *Canada Compared with Great Britain* (Winnipeg, 1921); *How the Farmer Pays the Bill* (Winnipeg, 1921); *Painted Ships on Painted Ocean* (Winnipeg, 1921); *Railway Burden Means Taxation* (Winnipeg, 1921); J. A. STEVENSON, *Help Old England with Freer Trade* (n.p., n.d.); RUTH PRESTON STEVENSON, *The Tariffs' Toll on Children* (n.p., n.d.). The Council also published pamphlets, after the election and after its severance from the political movement, in carrying on its educational work. Of these two are in the Provincial Library of Manitoba; A. E. DARBY, *Some Observations on Farmers'*

Indebtedness and Rural Credits (Winnipeg, 1924); J. W. WARD, *The Canadian Banking System*, Banking Memorandum No. 2 (Winnipeg, 1924). Of the pamphlets in the Public Archives of Canada the following were found to be pertinent; *The Fielding Reciprocity* (n.p., n.d.), No. 3833; J. CASTELL HOPKINS, *Western Canada and the Empire* (n.p., n.d.), No. 4026; "Clarus Ager," *The Farmer and the Interests* (Toronto, 1916), No. 4410; EDWARD PORRITT, "Canada's National Policy" (*Political Science Quarterly, XXXII*, June, 1917), No. 4486; *Laurier's Manifesto* (n.p., 1917), No. 4623; ALEXANDER SMITH, *General Attitude and Aim of Liberalism* (n.p., 1917), No. 4624; *The National Liberal and Conservative Handbook*, I (n.p., 1921), No. 5077; *Group Government Compared with Responsible Government* (published by Liberal National Committee, 1921), No. 5081; ALEXANDER SMITH, *A Period of New Beginnings for Liberalism* (Ottawa, 1921), No. 5085. By the courtesy of the Liberal party of Manitoba, an opportunity was obtained to read the rare, *The National Liberal Convention; The Story of the Convention and the Report of the Proceedings* (Ottawa, 1919).

The third group of pamphlets was published by the Canadian Industrial Reconstruction Association, 1918-21, and are filed in the Public Archives of Canada: *Agriculture and Industry* (Toronto, 1920); *The Non-Partisan League in North Dakota, The Outlook for Canada* (Toronto, 1920); *Ways to National Prosperity* (Toronto, 1920).

VI

The principal source of information for the study of the Progressive movement was the journalistic and periodical press. In this the farm publications were of special importance. The file of the *Grain Growers' Guide*, 1909-30, was the most ample, reliable and consistent, of such sources; its editorial comment, the work of outstanding journalists, notably G. F. Chipman and W. J. Healy, its reports of events, and its special articles, in themselves contain the history of the farmers' movement during those years, in all its aspects, political as well as economic and educational. The *Farmers' Advocate* and the *Farm and Ranch Review* lack the *Guide's* breadth of interest and consistency of treatment; the former is valuable, however, in that it represents the sceptical conservatism of the old-school farmer, the latter for occasional trenchant editorials or special articles, notably those by C. W. Peterson. These, however, are western publications and their coverage of agrarian events in eastern Canada is neither close nor consistent. For Ontario, this deficiency is supplied by the *Farmers' Sun*, successor to Goldwin Smith's *Weekly Sun*, and the official organ of the U.F.O. The file in the library of the federal Department of

Agriculture was searched from 1919 to 1930, and found of great use, in that the *Sun* reported much that the general press ignored. On the other hand, the cramped and bitter temper of its editorials, expressing a narrow agrarianism, were more representative of the J. J. Morrison wing of the U.F.O. than generally informative. A comparable organ in the West was *The U.F.A.*, official organ of the United Farmers of Alberta. *The U.F.A.* was, as a result of the absorption of the Alberta Non-Partisan League by the political movement of the U.F.A., the successor to a publication of William Irvine's, later Labour M.P. from Calgary East. This was first known as the *Nutcracker*, a lively sheet rather in the *genre* of the famous *Eye-Opener*; it then became the *Alberta Non-Partisan* and organ of the Non-Partisan League of Alberta. When the U.F.A. declined to take it over in 1919, it continued as the *Western Independent* until, after a hiatus, *The U.F.A.* appeared in 1922. The file of Irvine's publication from 1917 to 1920 in the Provincial Library of Alberta is an invaluable guide, and almost the only continuous one, into that political underworld from which the Non-Partisan League and the political movement of the U.F.A. emerged. *The U.F.A.*, though its interests were narrowly restricted to the activities of the U.F.A., within its limits rivals the *Guide* as a source for the study of the farmers' movement. Its devoted editor, Norman Smith, was particularly successful in interpreting to his readers the sometimes oracular utterances of Wood, and his comment illuminates some of the more obscure controversies over the practice and dogma of the U.F.A. The file in the Provincial Library of Alberta was searched from 1922 to 1935 and is, of course, the principal source for the study of the U.F.A. The greatest of the agrarian provinces, Saskatchewan, produced no such record of its early agrarian movement, being served by the *Guide*. In 1923, the provincial Progressive movement, seeking to consolidate itself, undertook the establishment of a Progressive journal. This was *The Progressive*, which lasted only a year, when it was re-organized as the *Western Producer*, a publication which reflected the contemporary swing of interest from political to economic action and which proved itself, in co-operation with the Saskatchewan Wheat Pool, to have the vitality *The Progressive* lacked. The file in the offices of the *Western Producer*, to the best of the writer's information the only file containing the complete series of *The Progressive*, was searched from 1923 to 1930, and found a very valuable source, particularly for information on the Progressive split of 1924, and for the rise of the new farmers' political movement under George H. Williams. For the rest, the writer was unable to find, outside the Maritime Provinces, a file of the *United Farmers' Guide*, organ of the farmers' movement in the eastern provinces, the existence of which was sickly and brief.

VII

The need of searching the farm publications was obvious and imperative. It was, however, impossible to search all the general urban press, much more even to sample the local press, in which, no doubt, much of the history of the origins of the agrarian political movement lies. Accordingly, an attempt was made to select a representative number of journals on the basis of region and political sentiment.

In the files examined, two methods were followed; one, to search consecutively through a given number of years; two, to refer to the numbers issued at the time of some important event in the history of the movement, such as the split of 1924.

On this basis, the following journals were searched: The *Manitoba Free Press*, 1905-30, was a journalistic source comparable with the *Guide*. Not only was it the most powerful paper in the West, consciously speaking for that region; its editor, J. W. Dafoe, was close to the inner councils of the Liberal party down to 1917, and thereafter was mentor of the Manitoban Progressives. In addition, he possessed a knowledge of Canadian politics rivalled by few men. The partisanship of the *Free Press* was blunt and apparent, and hence easily to be discounted. Two other Liberal papers in the West were gone through, the *Regina Leader*, 1911-21, and the *Edmonton Bulletin*, 1911-21; neither added greatly to what the *Free Press* had contributed.

To offset these, the generally Conservative *Calgary Herald* and *Edmonton Journal* were consulted, the *Herald* being searched from 1921 to 1930, as the soundest exponent of western conservatism. Similarly the generally Liberal but independent *Calgary Morning Albertan* was used, and in Saskatchewan, province of fierce personal and political journalistic struggles, the *Saskatoon Daily Star* and the *Moose Jaw Leader-Times*, particularly for the critical year of 1921.

The press of eastern Canada was examined only to the extent of searching two metropolitan dailies, one Liberal and one Conservative, each representative of its brand of partisan journalism: the Toronto *Globe* from 1911 to 1926, the Montreal *Gazette* from 1919 to 1926. The *Globe* has much to offer, both by report and comment, on the disruption of the Liberal party and the political insurgence of the organized farmers of Ontario; the *Gazette* much on the breakdown of Union Government and on the resistance made to the farmers' attacks on the National Policy. A study of the conservatism of the *Gazette* was, of course, necessary to any understanding of what the farmers were in revolt against, but the student is also rewarded by the excellent national coverage the *Gazette* of those years afforded.

VIII

In a class by itself was the *Canadian Annual Review*, 1910-30. This accurate, full, and on the whole unbiased, chronicle of events in Canada is a ready source of information, especially useful for those fields in which the student wishes to make brief excursions in search of facts off the beaten course of his research. The *Review* gives a proportionately full account of the rise of the organized farmers, and rather more during the critical years of 1919 to 1921. In this, it no doubt reflected the concern of its editor, J. Castell Hopkins, with the unity of Canada, and that of Canada with the Empire.

IX

The periodicals searched were: the *Canadian Historical Review*, 1920-48; the *Reports of the Canadian Historical Association*, 1920-47; the *Proceedings of the Canadian Political Science Association*, I-VI, 1913-34; *The Canadian Journal of Economics and Political Science*, 1935-48. On these no comment is necessary. The *Canadian Forum*, 1920-30, was an important source of novel comment and of articles which would not otherwise have found an outlet in Canada during those years. The *Round Table*, 1910-30, was examined for its Canadian articles in each number and for occasional articles on Canada; its anonymity and a curious impercipience and lack of contact rendered it of only sporadic value. *Agricultural History*, the *Annals of the American Academy of Political and Social Science*, the *American Political Science Review*, the *Canadian Nation*, the *Dalhousie Review*, *Maclean's Magazine*, the *New Republic*, the *Nineteenth Century and After*, the *Political Science Quarterly*, and the *Queen's Quarterly*, yielded occasional articles.

X

Only books bearing directly on the subject matter of the study will be noted here.

In memoirs and diaries, the field is singularly barren. The *Memoirs of the Rt. Hon. Robert Laird Borden* (ed. by HENRY BORDEN, 2 vols., Toronto, 1937) is a valuable but guarded source for the election of 1911 and the formation of the Union Government. *The Diary of James Alexander MacPhail* (ed. by H. A. INNIS, Toronto, 1940) has little on the political movement, but illustrates in detail the enormous work of organization which underlay the farmers' movement.

Biographies are more abundant. The *Life and Letters of Sir Wilfrid Laurier* by O. D. SKELTON (2 vols., London, 1922) supplies much by way of letters and comment on the events relevant to the farmers' movement, but is quite blind to the forces which produced the Union Government and the farmers' entrance into politics. J. W. DAFOE's *Laurier: A Study in Canadian Politics* (Toronto, 1922) is a lengthy review of Skelton's biography, and goes far to correct its deficiencies. It displays, in addition, a remarkable grasp of how fundamental were the forces which produced the revolt of 1921. Dafoe's *Clifford Sifton in Relation to his Times* (Toronto, 1931) suffers from an unavoidable restraint and is less penetrating than the *Laurier*; on the other hand, it abounds in points of fact otherwise still inaccessible. *The Memoirs of the Rt. Hon. Sir George Foster* by W. S. WALLACE (Toronto, 1933), though an excellent brief biography, has not a great deal that is relevant to the Progressive movement. *Mackenzie King* by N. McL. ROGERS (Toronto, 1935) is a campaign biography reworked by a gifted academician, but, even so, scantily informative. OLIVE ZEIGLER's, *Woodsworth, Social Pioneer* (Toronto, 1934) is a much superior work of the same type.

The western background of the Progressive movement is to be found in: C. C. Lingard, *Territorial Government in Canada* (Toronto, 1946); W. A. Mackintosh, *Economic Problems of the Prairie Provinces* (Toronto, 1934); A. S. Morton, *History of the Canadian West to 1870-71* (Toronto, n.d.); A. S. Morton and Chester Martin, *History of Prairie Settlement and "Dominion Lands" Policy* (Toronto, 1939); G. F. G. Stanley, *The Birth of Western Canada* (Toronto, 1936); *Canada and Its Provinces*, Vols. XIX and XX (Toronto, 1914). To these should be added H. A. Innis, *History of the Canadian Pacific Railway* (Toronto, 1924), G. P. de T. Glazebrook, *History of Transportation in Canada* (Toronto, 1938), and Robert England, *The Colonization of Western Canada* (London, 1936), because of their special bearing on the development of the West.

The monographic literature of the subject is also limited. *The Crisis of Quebec* by Elizabeth Armstrong (New York, 1937) is an impartial study of the conscription crisis in Quebec which, however, avoids discussion of the wider repercussions of that crisis in the Canadian polity. Hugh Boyd, *New Breaking: An Outline of Co-operation Among the Farmers of Western Canada* (Toronto, 1938) is a graceful and brief account of the farmers' organized economic activity. *The Wheat Economy* by George Britnell (Toronto, 1939) furnishes a scientific but sympathetic analysis of the condition of the wheat economy in the 1920's and 1930's. James, Viscount Bryce, in the section on Canada in his *Modern Democracies* (2 vols., New York, 1921) marks the beginning, with André Siegfried's *Race Question in Canada*, of the realistic study of Canadian politics. S. D. Clark, *The Canadian Manufacturers' Association* (Toronto, 1939) affords an able study of a kind too rare in the literature of the social sciences in Canada. M. J. Coldwell, *"Left Turn, Canada!"* (Toronto, 1945) gives a few details of the origins of the C.C.F. *Public Policy* by Walter F. Cooling (Chicago, n.d.) is an obscure book, significant only because it states Henry Wise Wood's concept of group government with conciseness and force, and was alleged to have been the source of the concept. *Constitutional Issues in Canada, 1900-1931*, compiled by R. M. Dawson (Toronto, 1933) is a useful compendium of contemporary statements of the constitutional issues of the period of this study, clarified by the compiler's own comment. A few of the basic documents of the Progressive movement are included in its pages. *The Masques of Ottawa* by "Domino" (Toronto, 1921) is a series of sketches which, if used cautiously, gives a lively impression of the chief figures at Ottawa during the period of Union Government (I am informed on good authority that "Domino" was the journalist Augustus Bridle). W. T. Easterbrook, *Farm Credit in Canada* (Toronto, 1939) exhausts that difficult subject. M. P. Follett, *The New State* (New York, 1918) is referred to only as an enthusiastic and influential statement of the doctrines of pluralism and guild socialism, which Wood is reported to have read. V. C. Fowke, *Canadian Agricultural Policy: The Historical Setting* (Toronto, 1946) is an excellent study in itself and necessary background reading for the understanding of the Progressive movement. W. C. Good, *Production and Taxation in Canada* (Toronto, 1919) is a well-argued claim for national policies more considerate of the needs of rural life, particularly by shifting the burden of taxation from the tariff to the land by means of the single tax. J. A. Hobson, in *Canada To-Day* (London, 1906), has illuminating comments on the Canadian scene in 1905. William Irvine, in *The Farmers in Politics* (Toronto, 1920) gives a clear and rather persuasive statement of Wood's doctrine of occupational representation, of Irvine's own doctrine that the legislature should be released from control by the cabinet through the power of dissolution, and of the general agrarian claim to representation; a more closely reasoned argument for functional representation is the same author's *Co-operative Government* (Ottawa, 1929). R. L. Jones, in his *History of Agriculture in Ontario, 1613 to 1880* (Toronto, 1946), lays the remoter background of rural unrest in Ontario. O. J. McDiarmid, in *Commercial Policy in the Canadian Economy* (Cambridge, Mass., 1946), puts the Canadian tariff in proper perspective, but curiously fails to suggest the violence of western resentment of the tariff during the period covered by this study. *The Canadian Grain Trade*, by D. A. MacGibbon (Toronto, 1932) is the definitive study of the grain trade in the days of its power. *Essays in Politics* (London, 1909) by Sir Andrew Macphail, yields assurance from a scholar and a gentleman that the farmer's belief, that the tariff discriminated between classes and sections and corrupted politics, was not merely a boorish prejudice. Hopkins Moorhouse, *Deep Furrows* (Toronto, 1918) is a vivid, journalistic history of the rise of the Grain Growers' Associations. John Nelson, *The Canadian Provinces, Their Problems and Policies* (Toronto, 1924) brings together a number of informed and accurate articles from *Maclean's Magazine*. M. Ostrogorski, *Democracy and the Organization of Political Parties*, vol. II (London, 1902) translated by F. Clark, marks the beginning of the study of the imperfections of party government. *A War on Poverty* by E. A. Partridge (Winnipeg [1925?]) is a wild, poetic outburst of western agrarianism from an immigrant from Ontario, which contains a plan for founding a co-operative commonwealth in an independent West. "The Progressive Political Movement, 1921-30," by William Paterson (unpublished M.A. thesis of University of Toronto, 1940) contains some illuminating quotations and some useful analyses of Progressive voting. H. S. Patton, in his *Grain Growers' Co-operation in Western Canada* (Cambridge, Mass., 1928) makes an authoritative study of the subject to the date of publication. C. W. Peterson's *Wake Up, Canada; Reflections on Vital National Issues* (Toronto, 1919) gives pointed expression to the farmers' dissatisfaction with their inadequate representation. Edward Porritt's *Sixty Years of Protection in Canada* (Winnipeg, 1913), a bitter and documented attack on the National Policy, was of great influence on the farmers' movement and is almost in the class of Gustav Myers' *History of Canadian Wealth*, vol. I (Chicago, 1914). Porritt's *Canada's Protective Tariff* (Winnipeg, 1920) re-iterates the theme that both old parties had maintained the tariff for the privileged interests, and brings the analysis down to 1920. *The Race Question in Canada* by A. Siegfried (London, 1907) still constitutes, of course, the frankest treatment of its subject, and, in addition, offers many shrewd comments on Canadian politics. Paul F. Sharp, in *The Agrarian Revolt in Western Canada* (Minneapolis, 1948) approaches the subject from the angle of American influence, and his book is the best and most finished study of the political unrest in the Canadian West from 1911 to 1930. Goldwin Smith's *Canada and the Canadian Question* (Toronto, 1891) plays, at an earlier date, on all those tensions and uncertainties in the Canadian polity which produced the Progressive movement. Melville H. Staples, in *The Challenge of Agriculture* (Toronto, 1920) records the organization of the U.F.O. and the farmers' entrance into politics in Ontario. *The Farmers' Movement in Canada* (Toronto, 1924) by L. A. Wood is full, accurate, and judiciously sympathetic, and is still, despite its early date of publication, not displaced as the general history of its subject. To these must be added S. W. Yates, *The Saskatchewan Wheat Pool* (Saskatoon, n.d.), a careful record of the founding and growth of that institution.

XI

To these directly relevant titles must be added those of four recent political and social studies, which appeared while the manuscript of this study was being prepared, which anticipated many of its findings, and which greatly illuminated the whole field of the study. These are: A. Brady, *Democracy in the Dominions* (Toronto, 1947); S. D. Clark, *Church and Sect in Canada* (Toronto, 1948); J. A. Corry, *Democratic Government and Politics* (Toronto, 1946); R. M. Dawson, *The Government of Canada* (Toronto, 1947).

Index

DATE DUE
